Hiroshima Traces

D1472993

TWENTIETH-CENTURY JAPAN:
THE EMERGENCE OF A WORLD POWER
Irwin Scheiner, Editor

Hiroshima Traces

Time, Space, and the
Dialectics of Memory

Lisa Yoneyama

UNIVERSITY OF CALIFORNIA PRESS
Berkeley   Los Angeles   London

University of California Press
Berkeley and Los Angeles, California

University of California Press, Ltd.
London, England

© 1999 by
The Regents of the University of California

Library of Congress Cataloging-in-Publication Data

Yoneyama, Lisa, 1959–
    Hiroshima traces : time, space, and the dialectics
of memory / Lisa Yoneyama.
        p.   cm. — (Twentieth-century Japan ; v10)
    Includes bibliographical references and index.
    ISBN 0-520-08586-8 (alk. paper)
    ISBN 0-520-08587-6 (alk. paper)
        1. Hiroshima-shi (Japan)—History—
Bombardment, 1945.   I. Title.   II. Series.
    D767.25.H6Y66   1999
    940.54'25—dc21   98-31739
                                                    CIP

Printed in the United States of America
9   8   7   6   5   4   3   2

The paper used in this publication meets the
minimum requirements of American National
Standards for Information Sciences—Permanence
of Paper for Printed Library Materials,
ANSI Z39.48-1984.

Contents

Prologue

Hiroshima Traces is a product of unfolding dialogues. It grows out of, and has undergone numerous transformations as a result of, the conversations and other interactions I have had with many individuals over the years. Intellectual trajectories are full of wonder. They are shaped by unanticipated personal encounters, both within and outside academia, and this book reflects the many pleasurable, unexpected, and sometimes painful turns that I have made during the years in which it has been in progress. I can at long last thank all those who have contributed in many different but equally valuable ways to my research and writing.

The intellectual and philosophical guidance I received from two teachers, Tsurumi Kazuko and Murai Yoshinori at Jōchi University in Tokyo—where I majored in German language studies in the early 1980s and then in international relations as a graduate student—has greatly influenced my outlook on society and culture. In large part, this study remains faithful to the sensitivities these two scholars communicated to me about the necessity of attending to local specificities even when analyzing global political, social, and economic structures.

While I was a graduate student in the Anthropology Department at Stanford University, Harumi Befu, Renato Rosaldo, and Sylvia Yanagisako guided me through the changes that were going on in the field of cultural anthropology during the mid-1980s. They nurtured me, as they did many others, with a rare blend of critical intellectual sophistication and down-to-earth manner. Through them I especially learned that academic engagements can and must go hand in hand with attentiveness to issues of power and to the political milieu within which our works are produced. At Stanford I also received warm encouragement and had many valuable discussions with other teachers and classmates.

In Hiroshima I had the tremendous good fortune of meeting individuals who openly shared their views and sometimes their lifelong observations on questions concerning Hiroshima's history, city planning, issues concerning *hibakusha* (that is, those subjected to the atomic bomb or radiation), local cultures, politics, and other related matters. I especially want to thank Andō Shūji, Akiba Tadatoshi, Ejima Motoko, Ejima Shūsaku, James Foard, Funahashi Yoshie, Hamamura Kyōko, Kasuga Kisuyo, Katō Masaki, Kishimoto Shinzō, Kobayashi Masanori, Maruyama Kōichi, Matsubayashi Shun'ichi, Matsumoto Hiroshi, Murakami Sugako, Nakahara Hideko, Nakahara Shunsuke, O Sŏngdŭk, O Yang-hye, Ohmuta Minoru, Ohtsu Akira, Saeki Toshiko, Satō Izumi, Satoyoshi Kenji, Sŏ Yŏn-si, Soeda Masataka, Tawara Genkichi, Ubuki Akira, Wakabayashi Setsuko, Yakushinji Mariko, Yamada Tadafumi, Yi Chu-ho, Yi Ki-u, Yoshinaka Yasumaro, Yoshino Makoto, and Yoshino Kazuko. They generously assisted me in numerous ways. Many of their views have been incorporated into the book and I have provided specific references whenever possible.

Certain members of two local organizations, Hiroshima o Kataru Kai and Genbaku Higaisha Shōgen no Tsudoi, including Chu Sŏk, Iwamoto Noriko, Hara Hiroshi, Kwak Pok-sun, Kondō Kōshirō, Kuboura Hiroto, Kuwahara Chiyoko, Miyagawa Hiroyuki, Numata Suzuko, and Yamazaki Kanji, deserve special gratitude. First and foremost, they shared memories about their immediate experiences of the atomic destruction. They also generously offered candid accounts of their and others' testimonial activities, the city's and the nation's current politics, and other problems concerning *hibakusha*. They patiently and open-mindedly responded to each and every inquiry I made, as they have done and will no doubt continue to do for the many researchers, journalists, and writers who have visited or will visit Hiroshima in the future. I want especially to thank Toyonaga Keisaburō, whose spiritual robustness and profound optimism about the possibility of building dialogues and networks have greatly encouraged me. Jung Yeong-hae gave me a warm welcome to Hiroshima and while we roomed together shared her perceptive and deeply engaged thoughts and feelings about Hiroshima, as well as about Japanese society in general. Her unique and precious companionship assured me that sisterly and scholarly relationships are more than compatible.

In 1991, when living in Santa Cruz, California, I met a number of scholars at the University of California, Santa Cruz, who offered crucial suggestions and insights on my work in both formal and informal settings. Many of them became valuable teachers, friends, and colleagues. I am especially grateful to David Anthony, Dilip Basu, James Clifford, Christopher Connery, Guillermo Delgado, Norma Klahn, Martia Sturken, and Anna Tsing.

The most significant turning point in this work, and to a great extent in my entire scholarly orientation, came when I took up a position in the Literature Department at the University of California, San Diego, and began teaching cultural studies and Japanese studies. This move forced me to cross the disciplinary boundaries that separate anthropology, literary studies, and cultural studies and radically expanded my views about potential readers and audiences. The department's interdisciplinary, transnational, and historical emphasis also stimulated me to further consider the materiality and historicity of Hiroshima's textual and discursive representations. Chapters 2, 3, and 4 bear significant imprints of this disciplinary reorientation. I especially thank Ann duCille, Rosemary George, Judith Halberstam, George Mariscal, Roddey Reid, Rosaura Sánchez, Shelley Streeby, William Tay, Don Wayne, and Winifred Woodhull for extending their moral and intellectual encouragement. Two individuals deserve particular mention: Lisa Lowe, whose caring mentorship has assisted me so much in responding to the demands of teaching and writing, and Masao Miyoshi, whose venturesome spirit has always inspired me. Eiji Yutani's scrupulous bibliographic attentiveness as a professional historian as well as librarian has facilitated my research in every possible way. Teaching has been a stimulating and learning experience and I would particularly like to acknowledge the thoughtful feedback I received from many graduate and undergraduate students.

Shortly after I began teaching at UCSD, I had an opportunity to spend one year as a postdoctoral fellow in the Program for Cultural Studies at the East-West Center in Honolulu. Members of and visitors to the program added much to my work. Geoffrey M. White, director of the program during the tenure of my fellowship, was especially generous, not only in terms of the institutional support that his program and staff provided but also intellectually and as a trusted friend.

I received many other helpful comments and criticisms at various academic conferences and meetings. I have benefited enormously from the invaluable input of Linda Angst, Andrew Barshay, Jonathan Boyarin, Suzanne Brenner, Alan Christy, Brett deBarry, Norma Field, Charles Hale, Jeff Hanes, Laura Hein, Dorinne Kondo, Smadar Lavie, George Lipsitz, Robert G. Moeller, Mark Norness, Vince Rafael, Naoki Sakai, Irwin Scheiner, Christena Turner, the late Alan Wolfe, and Igarashi Yoshiaki. I am especially thankful to Harry Harootunian, Mellie Ivy, William Kelly, Miriam Silverberg, and anonymous readers, all of whom read and commented carefully on early drafts of the entire book.

In addition, I want to acknowledge the members of the Resident Research Group on "Colonialism and Modernity: The Case of Korea, Japan, and China" at the University of California, Humanities Research Institute (Spring 1995): Yoko Arisaka, Chungmoo Choi, James Fujii, Gail Hershatter, Ted Hutters, Amie Parry, Lisa Rofel, and Shu-mei Shih. They not only provided me with many ideas and insights about the book's composition; they also patiently shared some of the pain of completing this book-length manuscript. The near-final draft of chapters 3 and 4 also benefited from the thoughtful comments of participants at the Paul Getty Institute Seminar on "Memory, History, Narrative: A Comparative Inquiry into the Representation of Crisis," at Warburg Haus in Hamburg, Germany (July 1997).

A trusting relationship with one's editor is indispensable in the long process of completing a book. My gratitude goes to Stanley Holwitz of the University of California Press, whose firmness and patience I most appreciated whenever I faltered. Scott Norton at the Press accommodated many of my requests, including selection of the cover art. My copy editor Alice Falk did more than the usual editing and correcting. She enhanced the clarity of my arguments and especially took great care to ensure that my translations flow naturally while conveying the meaning of the original. Three editors in Japan, Fumio Michikawa of NHK Shuppan and Baba Kimihiko and Kojima Kiyoshi of Iwanami Shoten, need to be thanked as well for their enthusiasm and for constantly reminding me of the scholarly responsibility to reach as broad an audience as possible.

Shima Kuniichi's artwork titled *Trace Hiroshima*, which is exhibited in the Hiroshima City Museum of Contemporary Art, has deeply affected me. Though using a different medium, the artist has dealt with questions similar to the ones I have explored. His work captures a condition of memory in which traces of the past exist in fragments and in palimpsest form. The brutal sutures evident on the frame of the work's wooden box intimate the immensity of the original violence, while reminding the observer that the historical processes before and after that destruction are often neatly covered over by smooth, bright surfaces. When I viewed a video that recorded the entire production process, I was confirmed in my interpretation of the artwork. The artist first builds the wooden box frame with great caution. Not a single nail is used. After long hours of meticulous handcrafting, the box is then abruptly sawed apart into numerous pieces. Then the artist picks up the pieces from the piles of debris and begins to roll them haphazardly over a sheet of paper, one by one, as he traces their trajectories. After this procedure, the fragmented pieces are sutured to re-create the original shape of the box. He then cuts along the traces left on the paper, paints the surface of the paper cutouts, and installs them in random layers onto the restored box. What we see on the artwork's surfaces is therefore not the destruction's immediate wreckage but traces of the remains' movements. Similarly, in this book my task is to remember the conditions and historical trajectories that produced what are now available to us as reminders of destruction. I sincerely appreciate Shima's generosity in sending me the video, and most especially in allowing me to adopt his artwork for the cover of my book.

This book is written from many positions, but especially that of a returnee to two different locations: to Japan as a *kikoku shijo* (returnee Japanese child in 1970) and to the United States as a *kibei* (returnee American in the early 1980s). Although the Chinese ideograph *ki* means to return to the origin or home, to where one properly belongs, the experiences of such returns have resulted in both less and more than contentment and solace. The uneasiness and discomfort accompanying these movements have for me highlighted questions of what it means to belong, of origin and loyalty, and are analogous to the troubling outcomes that frequently result from the travels of the representations of Hiroshima between Japan and the United States. There is no doubt that my particular position has made me sensitive to this transnational aspect of Hiroshima memories. Yet such a position is not unique. Many have written about and from similar positions of in-betweenness. They have acknowledged both the significance and danger involved in such positioning. This study owes much to those who have enabled such problematics to be articulated and explored in scholarly and theoretical terms.

There are certainly ways in which the uncomfortable experience of returning can be alleviated. I thank those who generously offered much personal and emotional support so that my returns to the United States were invariably also sweet and enjoyable: Patti Baba, Lynn Yokoyama Chung, Steve Chung, Danjūrō, Ennosuke, Kyōko Fujitani, Rev. Masami Fujitani, Carey Ida, JoAnn Momono, Lisa Momono, Karen Lee Murakami, Kenny Murakami, Debbie Nakamura, Dennis Nakamura, Alvin Sakoda, Bruce Tsutsui, Kimberly Loke Tsutsui, Verna Uchida, and Arthur Yamashita. I am also thankful for many years of faithful friendship from the following individuals: Cécile Jacquet, Mine Lachaussee, Matsuo Yumiko, Nakajima Yōko, Nakanishi Tomoko, Nakase Emiko, Oba Eri, Ohashi Yukako, Sakurai Keiko, Takahashi Atsuko, and Takino Atsuko.

But my foremost gratitude goes to T. Fujitani. Before and during the ten years that it has taken to write this book, his political and intellectual integrity has been my most dependable source of conviction, encouragement, and constructive criticism. He painstakingly read over, commented on, and edited a seemingly endless number of different drafts of this book. With his patience and inexhaustible sense of humor we were able to appreciate the pleasures of living between two or more languages and cultures.

Finally, I want to express my heartfelt appreciation and to dedicate this book to my parents and to all those who are concerned about Hiroshima. Yoneyama Toshiko, my mother, gave me discipline and strength while my father, Yoneyama Toshinao, always maintained a boundless optimism and affection for life, helping me get through what were often difficult times.

The research and writing of this book would not have been possible without generous institutional and financial support. I received a Post-Doctoral Fellowship in the Program for Cultural Studies, East-West Center, Honolulu (1992–93), a travel grant from the North East Asian Council (March 1995), and a Humanities Research Institute Resident Fellowship, University of California, Irvine (spring 1995). An earlier stage of research, beginning in the summer of 1987 and ending in December 1990, was supported by the following: a Social Science Research Council–MacArthur Foundation Fellowship in International Peace and Security, a Summer Grant from the Center for International Security and Arms Control (CISAC) at Stanford University, and summer research support from the Department of Anthropology, Stanford University. Completion of my Ph.D. dissertation, on which a part of this book is based, was facilitated by a MacArthur Foundation Dissertation Write-Up Fellowship from CISAC.

An earlier version of chapter 1 was published as "Taming the Memoryscape: Hiroshima's Urban Renewal," in *Remapping Memory: The Politics of Timespace,* ed. Jonathan Boyarin (Minneapolis: University of Minnesota Press, 1994). Chapter 5 was originally published as "Memory Matters: Hiroshima's Korean Atom Bomb Memorial and the Politics of Ethnicity," *Public Culture* 7 (Spring 1995): 499–527, and republished with some very minor revisions in *Living with the Bomb: American and Japanese Cultural Conflicts in the Nuclear Age,* ed. Laura Hein and Mark Selden (New York: M. E. Sharpe, 1997). An abridged version of chapters 3 and 4 appeared as "Kioku no benshōhō—Hiroshima," *Shisō,* no. 866 (August 1996): 5–29.

Japanese and Korean names are rendered with surnames first, followed by given names. Korean names and words are written in the modified McCune-Reischauer style except when the individual referred to another spelling, or when there is another conventional romanization, such as "Park Chung Hee." Japanese romanization follows the modified Hepburn style. Long vowels are usually indicated by macrons, but well-known place names such as "Kyoto" are given as they are conventionally written. Translations, unless otherwise indicated, are mine. Pseudonyms are used when I felt it necessary to protect the privacy of individuals.

Introduction

If the past does not bind social consciousness and the future
begins here, the present is the "historical" moment, the
permanent yet shifting point of crisis and the time for choice.
                          Ashis Nandy, *The Intimate Enemy* (1983)

In tracing the development of Japan's architectural modernism from
the 1920s to the 1940s, the historian Inoue Shōichi offers an arrest-
ing story about the possible aesthetic origins of the Hiroshima Peace
Memorial Park. Situated at the heart of the city, close to the site of the
atomic bomb's detonation, the park was built on a vast, open field of
ashes created by the explosion. The park's location was once the city's
busiest downtown commercial and residential district, crowded with
shops, residences, inns, and theaters. Today the commemorative space
accommodates a number of memorials and monuments, museums, and
lecture halls and draws over a million visitors annually. It also provides
a ritual space for the annual 6 August Peace Memorial Ceremony, which
is sponsored by the city of Hiroshima. The design for the Peace Memorial Park was selected following a public competition that took place
in 1949, while Japan was still under Allied Occupation. According to
Inoue, the park's stylistic origin can be traced back to a nearly identical ground plan that had been adopted three years before Japan's surrender as part of a grand imperial vision, the Commemorative Building Project for the Construction of Greater East Asia (*daitōa kensetsu
kinen eizō keikaku*).[1]

Both designs were the creations of the world-renowned architect
Tange Kenzō. For the 1942 competition that took place while Japan
was in the midst of war, Tange proposed a grandiose Shintoist memorial zone to be built on an open plain at the foot of Mount Fuji.

His ground plan envisioned four blocks of buildings that would be laid out within an isosceles triangle. At the center of the triangle's bottom side was the main facility, which would serve metaphorically as an entrance gateway to the commemorative space. Two building blocks, placed symmetrically on each side of the main structure, were to serve as commemorative and exhibit halls, where people could congregate. A central axis extended from the entrance structure in a straight line toward a commemorative monument that would be located at the triangle's tip. The axis served as a "worshipping line,"[2] which was to function, as in similar commemorative spaces built under European fascist regimes, to pull the attention of crowds and their movements toward the central monument. With the collapse of Japan's empire that followed defeat by the Allied Forces and, more important, by anti-imperialist resistance against Japan in Asia and the Pacific,[3] Tange's 1942 plan was forever aborted. Yet the majestic space that he envisioned as monumentalizing the concept of the Greater East Asia Co-Prosperity appears to have been revived in his 1949 postwar design; it was subsequently realized in 1954, albeit at much-reduced scale, with the completion of Hiroshima's Peace Memorial Park.

Nothing epitomizes the Heideggerian irony of Japan's imperial modernity more solemnly than the incorporation of the monumentalized ruins of what is called the Atom Bomb Dome (Genbaku Dōmu) into the park. As in Tange's earlier plan, the central worshipping axis extends from the entrance, through the central cenotaph, to these ruins. This commemorative site is the artificially preserved remains of what used to be the Industry Promotion Hall, a quintessential sign of Japan's early-twentieth-century imperial modernity. Designed by an architect from Czechoslovakia, Jan Letzel, this continental Secession-style building, crowned with a distinctive dome-shaped roof, was completed in 1915. It served as a public space where crafts and commodities from Hiroshima's environs, as well as from different regions throughout the empire, were brought in and displayed. The atomic blast caused extensive damage to the building, leaving only some brick walls and the exposed iron frame of the dome-shaped canopy: hence the name of the ruins, the Atom Bomb Dome.

In the postwar plan, the earlier concept of a sixty-meter Shintoist-style commemorative structure was scaled down and transfigured into the more human-sized, arch-shaped design of the central cenotaph that is now officially named the Hiroshima Peace City Commemorative Monument (Hiroshima Heiwa Toshi Kinen Hi).[4] The symmetrical placement of clusters of structures also, as Inoue observes, remained in large part faithful to the original 1942 vision. Two wings of buildings containing public facilities such as lecture halls and exhibit rooms were placed symmetrically in alignment with the Peace Memorial Resource Museum, the structure that serves as the main entrance to the triangular commemorative area.[5] In this newly recrafted public space, people are to congregate—not to celebrate the modernity, enlightenment, civilization, and dreams promised by the pan-Asian co-prosperity sphere, but rather to remember the inaugural moment of the nuclear age and to imagine the possible self-annihilation of civilization.

Inoue reminds his readers of the striking parallels between what was once hailed as the vision best "representing the sublime objective of establishing the Greater East Asia Co-Prosperity Sphere"[6] and the commemorative icon to prayers for peace and the world's first use of a nuclear weapon. Yet, while Tange's role in designing Hiroshima's Peace Memorial Park is celebrated in tourist pamphlets and other popular accounts, it is fair to say that his earlier commemorative design—and the extraordinary resemblances in the aesthetic forms of the two projects—is hardly known. The structural continuity between the two ritual spaces and, more crucially, the widespread failure to recognize their analogies alert us to the conventional status of Hiroshima memories, both nationally and in global contexts. Whether within mainstream national historiography, which remembers Hiroshima's atomic bombing as victimization experienced by the Japanese collectivity, or in the equally pervasive, more universalistic narrative on the bombing that records it as having been an unprecedented event in the history of humanity, Hiroshima memories have been predicated on the grave obfuscation of the prewar Japanese Empire, its colonial practices, and their consequences.[7]

The unproblematized transition of Hiroshima's central commemorative space from celebrating imperial Japan to honoring the postwar peaceful nation suggests the persistence of prewar social and cultural elements, even at the iconic site that supposedly symbolizes the nation's rebirth and departure from the past. We must begin by determining just what these persistent, albeit forgotten, elements are. Certainly, progressive critics in Japan have observed that the presence of a rising sun flag in the park indicates continuity between the prewar regime and what is often referred to as "A-bomb nationalism" (*hibaku nashonarizumu*). Yet it is not only the fanatical nationalism of imperial Japan that needs to be remembered. More important is the absence of memories of the Japanese Empire in mainstream society,[8] which has resulted in a general tendency to occlude former colonial subjects from the post-1945 national mise-en-scène. When Japan's so-called postwar history began with the collapse of its empire, the universalism in Japanese nationalism ceased to have any sway over its colonizing and colonized subjects. The modernity, progress, and civilization that it represented in the 1920s global milieu came to be possessed exclusively by the West, especially by the United States under its cold war hegemony. Japan came to be imagined as a nation limited to a single ethnos or race, contained within what was internationally acknowledged as its natural sovereign territory. Political exigencies in postimperial Japan rendered the nation's multiethnic, multiracial, and multicultural constituencies invisible and produced a forgetting of Japan's relationship to its former colonies, along with its promises and the agonies it had inflicted upon them. By shedding light on the forces in ongoing cultural politics that seek to contest or maintain such amnesic elisions, this book aims to disentangle the processes that have produced postwar forgetfulness about the nation's recent past. It is an attempt to dislodge memories of Hiroshima's atomic obliteration from their confinement in humanist narratives and national histories, and to reconsider them within the terrain of post–cold war and postcolonial realities.

If we are indeed witnessing a "memory boom of unprecedented proportions," as Andreas Huyssen has observed of the European cultural scene,[9] then it becomes imperative to reflect on why issues have come to be formulated in terms of remembering and forgetting, rather than in other ways. We must also question why and how we remember— for what purpose, for whom, and from which position we remember— even when discussing sites of memory, where to many the significance of remembrance seems obvious. Moreover, the postwar and postcolonial reality within which we remember is one of late modernity, of late capitalist culture, in which a sense of history has tended to dissipate, even as yearnings for the real and the original intensify. What are the implications of recalling the past under such conditions, other than simply intensifying the search for origins and reauthenticating the truthfulness of what has already come down to us secondhand? And what will become of such memories when unearthed? As recovered memories become incorporated and settled into our commonsense knowledge about the past, present, and future, the mystifying and naturalizing effects of remembering itself seem ceaselessly at work.

My study of Hiroshima memories is a reflection on the anamnestic process that has rapidly become a far-reaching, global cultural current of the fin de siècle. Precisely at this historical juncture—when memories throughout Asia, Europe, and other corners of the world appear simultaneously threatening and in danger of obliteration, when different peoples at different locations urgently call for the recovery of heretofore marginalized or silenced experiences—I address the questions that ineluctably accompany attempts to fill the gaps in given historical knowledge. In exploring the cultural meanings and political implications of the practices of remembering, reinscribing, and retelling memories of the past, this book asks how acts of remembering can fill the void of knowledge without reestablishing yet another regime of totality, stability, confidence, and universal truthfulness. How can memories, once recuperated, remain self-critically unsettling?

PHANTASMATIC INNOCENCE

Like the absence of memory concerning the Peace Memorial Park's wartime archetype, during most of the postwar years there has been remarkable indifference about Japan's prewar and wartime legacy of colonialism, military aggression, and other imperial practices. To the world outside Japan, perhaps one of the best-known illustrations of Japan's historical amnesia occurred in 1982. What came to be known as the "textbook controversy" erupted when it was reported that the Ministry of Education, as a part of its routine administrative inspection procedures, was attempting to rewrite textbook descriptions so as to euphemize the history of Japanese expansionism. Specifically, the ministry sought to replace the key term "invasion" (*shinryaku*), which indicates an act of violation and unjust expropriation of sovereign territorial rights, with a vaguer and more neutral expression, "advancement" (*shinshutsu*).[10] In this case, unlike similar instances in the past, government agencies of other Asian nations officially joined in condemning the long-standing historical distortions perpetuated by the Liberal Democratic Party and the Ministry of Education.

Almost two decades earlier, the historian Ienaga Saburō's first lawsuit against the Ministry of Education had brought the inadequacies of postwar national historiography to public attention. In 1965 Ienaga charged that the ministry's censorship of his descriptions of the war in Asia and the Pacific and the Great Nanjing Massacre infringed on his constitutional right to freedom of expression and academic thought. Ienaga's legal battle lasted more than thirty years, as he pursued a number of lawsuits in courts at different levels. The modifications suggested to Ienaga's descriptions of specific historical incidents reveal how those responsible for inspecting textbooks have attempted to obfuscate the immediate agency and involvement of the Japanese government and the Imperial Army in various atrocities.[11]

Still other signs of the widespread inability to confront the specter of Japan as a victimizing nation include conservative politicians' repeated "slips of tongue"—or "phantasmatic statements" (*mōgen*), as the media call them—as well as other public figures' persistent denials and cover-ups of atrocities committed in the name of imperial Japan. In 1986 the newly appointed minister of education, Fujio Masayuki, was dismissed from the Nakasone cabinet for asserting that Korea was partially responsible for its own colonization. The Rape of Nanjing, in particular, has continued to be an event that for most conservative Japanese seems to invite what Alexander and Margarete Mitscherlich, following Sigmund Freud, have termed "the inability to mourn"—a phrase they used to characterize the German collective unwillingness to confront Nazi crimes at a deep psychological level.[12] Ishihara Shintarō, a writer who was elected to office as a member of the conservative Liberal Democratic Party, and Watanabe Shōichi, a professor of German literature, joined others in questioning the credibility of the Chinese government's official figure for those massacred. A decade later, in the spring of 1994, the desire for self-absolution reappeared: newly appointed Justice Minister Nagano Shigeto publicly stated that the Rape of Nanjing was a "fabrication" and was subsequently forced to resign. More recently, the Japanese military's involvement in the sexual enslavement of women from occupied territories—what is known as the "comfort women" issue—has touched off similar denials.

Even when admitting that the war (or, more precisely, defeat in war) did indeed bring disasters and inflict much suffering on people throughout the region, LDP leaders, conservative critics, and officials in the government's ministries have argued from the position that Japan fought the war in defense of the Asia Pacific region against the Western superpowers. According to this view, Japan's military expansion, colonial takeovers, and the Greater East Asian Co-Prosperity project were not schemes to "invade" other territories but instead were intended to liberate the people of Asia from Western domination. The cause, in other words, justified both the ends and the means. According to historian Yoshida Yutaka, whose earlier research includes a detailed and extensively documented reconstruction of the Rape of Nanjing, the most influential works to popularize this understanding of the Asia Pacific

War were essays by the writer Hayashi Fusao, "Daitōa sensō kōtei ron" ("On Affirming the East Asia War"), published in *Chūō Kōron* from 1963 to 1965. Yoshida indicates that Hayashi's argument, which was buoyed by the then-reemerging nationalist pride in economic recovery, reinforced the notion that the war was solely a conflict between Japan and the West and once again obscured the resistance of the people of Asia and the Pacific to Japan's imperialist expansionism.[13] In the conservative historical outlook favored since the end of the war by many, both within and outside the government, the centuries of atrocities resulting from Western imperialism far outweigh Japanese offenses. Thus the Japanese need not feel remorse until the Western powers repent for their original sin.

Yet a significant shift in the formal political arena did appear after the 1993 House of Representatives election, which ushered in the end of the LDP's nearly four-decade-long rule. Immediately after forming his cabinet, newly elected Prime Minister Hosokawa Morihiro defied the dominant LDP position by plainly stating in a press conference that the wars Japan had fought during the first half of the twentieth century were not waged for liberation or self-defense, but were simply self-aggrandizing "wars of invasion" (*shinryaku sensō*).[14] Since then, the Ministry of Education has also reversed its position on history textbooks and has been encouraging descriptions of military atrocities committed in the name of the Japanese Imperial Army, including biological warfare and the military enslavement of women. Moreover, the ministry has resisted neoconservative activists such as historian Fujioka Nobukatsu and others who, in yet another nationalist reaction to changes occurring at the political center, have demanded that descriptions of "comfort women" be eliminated from school textbooks.

As evidenced by the 1995 Diet Resolution commemorating the fiftieth anniversary of the end of the war—in which penitential intent was once again eclipsed by the desire to attribute the cause for the nation's past misdeeds to Western imperialism—these changes have not immediately resulted in any significant compensation for or even apologies to the victims. Yet they reflect the region's shifting condition: nations that formerly were subjected to Japanese domination and that in the subsequent cold war fell under the economic and military aegis of the United States have gained a greater visibility and more independent voice on the international stage. Furthermore, these changes are closely tied to the post–cold war alteration in the U.S.-Japan relationship; Japan's political, military, and economic reliance on the Security Treaty with the United States has come under question and is less absolute. In order to achieve a new stability within the region, it has become imperative that Japanese politicians and bureaucrats carefully settle past wrongs against neighboring countries by laying to rest the memories about them.

At the same time, it is no less true that these transformations in the formal legislative and administrative arena would not have resulted without the counteramnes(t)ic—that is, unforgetful and unforgiving—practices that preceded them by more than a decade. Since the late 1970s, the need to establish a critical awareness about the past has been felt more widely and more urgently; various efforts to counter the hegemony of historical amnesia have increasingly appeared in academic writings, journalism, pedagogical practices, and grassroots peace and antiwar activities. Historians have highlighted the issues left unaddressed by the governmental treaties that technically settled reparations immediately after the war. For the past twenty years, public meetings have been held to disseminate testimonial accounts by the victims of Japanese colonial and military rule. Numerous lawsuits have been filed to challenge governmental as well as corporate neglect concerning individual reparations and full retroactive pay to workers mobilized from the occupied territories.[15] Preparations are currently under way for an international court case intended to clarify the Japanese government's legal responsibilities for compensating those forced into sexual labor. Thus, as this century nears its end, the memories concerning Japan's misdeeds during its first half have been marked by contestation, conversion, and reconsolidation.

As in Germany's *Historikerstreit* (historians' debates) that resurfaced in 1986, the battles over memory taking place in Japan are often seen as symptomatic of a deeper and broader crisis in postwar democracy. Challenges to the regime of forgetfulness also directly criticize various ongoing social injustices and political acts. For example, when the repeated official visits of Nakasone Yasuhiro and other cabinet members to Yasukuni Shrine, where the war dead have been enshrined as gods, became an issue in the early 1980s, the act was on the one hand castigated as yet another indication of a lack of repentance for crimes committed by the Japanese military. On the other hand, the practice was also criticized as a violation of the constitutional principle of the separation of church and state; in fact, the matter has been brought to district courts in several prefectures, and in some cases the politicians' official visits to Yasukuni have been found unconstitutional. Those who have launched such counteramnes(t)ic criticisms have thus tended to understand their positions as inextricably tied to the task of radicalizing Enlightenment ideals and the democratic principles of modern civil society. In this sense, their appeals are reminiscent of Jürgen Habermas's exhortation of intellectuals in Germany to take an active and responsible role in current debates.

Though there are analogies between Germany and Japan, critical differences also separate the two. The disparities do not lie only in the institutional forms that the laws and policies for postwar reparations have taken;[16] more important, memories of past horrors have been addressed intellectually in different ways. In order to explain the divergent understandings and management of the respective crimes committed by the people of the two nations, we must consider how these nations and their victims, as well as their own victimizations, are located in relation to global discourses on humanity, modernity, and the Enlightenment.

The fact that the horrors of Nazism and the Holocaust occurred in the heart of Europe, and the realization that they were not necessarily aberrations but were arguably logical outcomes of European modernity and its foundations, compelled postwar thinkers to depart radically from conventional philosophical formulations that have located virtue, purity, and genuineness at the origin of modern Western civilization. Students of European intellectual history have written extensively on this question, especially through their rereading of critiques developed by scholars at Frankfurt University's Social Studies Institute, including Theodor Adorno, as well as by French poststructuralists such as Paul de Man.[17] It may suffice to note here that this departure from the underlying assumptions of Western metaphysics has produced cultural theories that critically rethink adherence to the notions of totality, the selfsame, fulfillment, future utopianism, and progress. As many have observed, the intellectual agenda in Europe after World War II has revolved around the recognition of and mourning for a loss—a loss of origins and of innocence, which was produced out of the specific historical moment of, and continuous reflection on, European modernity, fascism, and genocide.

In Japan, whose racialized and inauthentic relation to the West stood in sharp contrast to Germany's centrality to the Enlightenment, modernity, and the humanist tradition, concerns about such loss were far less profound. A sense of modern temporality different from that found in postwar Germany has decisively determined how questions regarding Japan's history and tradition have been formulated; Marxists and advocates of other progressive traditions in Japan have almost invariably regarded the nation as lagging in modernity.[18] In comparison to the

West, where normative modernity and the Enlightenment tradition were thought to be located, the absence of autonomous citizens who might form a modern civil society was understood to have obstructed the full-fledged development of modern democratic practices. In postwar progressive discourse, this sense of belatedness has continued to provide the interpretive framework for explaining the history of Japanese barbarism during the first half of the twentieth century. Thus, those involved in counteramnes(t)ic practices frequently emphasize that if the nation is to prevent itself from falling once again into military violence and geopolitical megalomania, the backward elements of prewar Japan—namely, such "feudal vestiges" as the emperorship, patriarchal sexual practices, hierarchical relations, and so on—must be overcome. The universal democratic ideals of modern bourgeois civil society have not yet been realized in Japan. Unlike in Germany, where intellectuals such as Adorno were compelled to place the memories of Nazism and the Holocaust in their ironic and inextricable relation to the liberal European traditions of republicanism, Enlightenment thought, and modernity, progressive intellectuals and activists in postwar Japan have emphasized the gap between such modern democratic ideals and practices and the insufficient maturity of Japan's people and institutions.[19]

The conventional argument in the social sciences has long been that the lag in Japan's modernity and the Enlightenment also resulted in the absence of autonomous and responsible individuals. This formulation is important here because it has served to obfuscate the experiences of ordinary people, who were actively and self-consciously engaged in colonial policies and military efforts. To be sure, as Yoshida Yutaka observes, the claim that political and military leaders alone were responsible for the military disaster—what he calls "*shidōsha sekinin ron*," a widely held grassroots belief in the immediate aftermath of the war—served to challenge "the collective repentance of one hundred million" (*ichioku sōzange*) thesis. The latter, which was officially advocated as early as August 1945 by Prince Higashikuni Naruhiko's cabinet, proclaimed that all of the nation's people were equally responsible for the outcome of the war. Its objective, according to Yoshida, was to deflect accusations against the emperor and the imperial system.[20] Yet *shidōsha sekinin ron* went beyond mere oppositional discourse. As Yamaguchi Yasushi, who has written extensively on the development of postwar political cultures in both Germany and Japan, points out, Marxists and other progressive critics relegated the responsibility of the ordinary people to the ruling elites and thus spared the former from a full investigation into their participation in national projects.[21] The postwar Enlightenment paradigm has to a great extent endorsed blaming the activities of wartime leaders and their supporters alone for prewar and wartime disasters. Indeed, it is precisely because the dominant paradigm has had such overwhelming mystifying power that historians' recent reexaminations of Japanese modernity, colonialism, and nationalism in the first half of the century are so urgently relevant to my study of Hiroshima memories.[22]

Given this intellectual milieu, it is not difficult to understand how memories of the atomic bombings of "Hiroshima and Nagasaki" came to be shaped almost exclusively by the perception that ordinary Japanese people had been the passive victims of historical conditions.[23] Memories of Hiroshima and Nagasaki, together with retellings of the bombings of civilians in practically every major Japanese city and the ground battle fought in Okinawa, as well as more recently revealed horror stories of Japanese colonists who were deserted by the military in northeastern China after Soviet advances—these all contributed decisively to the notion that whereas military leaders, government elites, and perhaps some soldiers were responsible for the disasters, ordinary citizens were only victims of the war and the nation's colonial policies. This is not to say that those assaulted by the U.S.-led Allied air raids and the two atomic attacks were not victims, nor to argue that they were all ethnically or nationally Japanese. Throughout the book I question the nationalization of shared historical experiences, as well as the binarism that unidimensionally identifies such nationalized collectivities as exclusively victims or victimizers.

More important, this phantasm of Japanese civilian innocence came to be enmeshed within the universalist discourse on humanity. The historian Awaya Kentarō has argued that the differences between the handling of the postwar reparations issue in Japan and Germany also stem from judicial treatment immediately after the war; Nazi crimes were strongly condemned during the Nuremberg Trials, but charges of "crimes against humanity" were downplayed in the Tokyo War Crimes Tribunal. That the people of non-Western nations were only marginally included in the category of "humanity" is also demonstrated by the fact that the local B and C class trials investigated the sexual assaults committed against Dutch women, while ignoring the enslavement of Asian and Pacific Islander women.[24] The cold war began to intensify during the Tokyo tribunal, and the interest of the United States and other nations in turning the occupation of Japan to their advantage, vis-à-vis the Soviet

Union, cut short further investigations of a number of individual cases of Japanese crimes. Yet examination of such Japanese crimes was attenuated from the beginning, primarily because those most brutally victimized by Japanese imperial aggression—Asians and Pacific Islanders—were racially and politically marginalized within the hegemonic discourse on humanity in the immediate postwar world.[25] As a result, many serious assaults and colonial crimes were overlooked, including the forced mobilization of people from the occupied territories by the Japanese government and corporations.[26] That several judges on the tribunal court represented nations that had held and were continuing to hold colonies, even as the trial began, greatly affected the course of the tribunal, for the colonialism of both Japan and the Western powers in the region remained unquestioned.

At the same time, the failure to seriously consider that using atomic bombs against civilian populations might be crimes against humanity, despite the unprecedented mass destructive force they had exhibited, generated the widespread belief in Japan and elsewhere that the Tokyo War Crimes Tribunal had resulted in nothing more than "victor's justice."[27] That attacks on Hiroshima and Nagasaki should be treated, unlike the crimes of colonialism, as crimes against humanity was certainly a sentiment shared widely. A number of postwar intellectuals, writers, and critics, both Western and non-Western, perceived the atomic assaults as universal offenses against human civilization and not simply as particular attacks against a people that had been named as the enemy.[28] The notion of using the atomic bombs against populated cities had made even U.S. officials wonder if they might be "outdoing Hitler" in barbarity.[29]

Within this discursive context, the downplaying of crimes against humanity at the Tokyo War Crimes Tribunal created a subtle conflation of Japanese and other Asians, for neither group was granted full membership in the category of "humanity," at least within the West-centric discourse of the tribunal. This historical perception enabled Japanese memories of atomic victimization to fuse with those of the victims of their own aggressions and racism. The idea that the Japanese were as much excluded from the Western-centric discourse of humanity as other victims of Western colonialism shrouded the critical differences, the historical specificities and the asymmetrical positions, that distinguish Japan from its neighboring countries. To put it differently, remembering the atomic destruction of Hiroshima and Nagasaki as events in the history of humanity has significantly contributed to the forgetting of the history of colonialism and racism in the region.

Coming to terms with the past in Japan initially involved weighing the actions of ordinary Japanese against the discourse on Japan's lag in modernity. Moreover, the failure to condemn the acts of colonial and semicolonial domination over the region by Japan and the Western nations as "crimes against humanity" allowed to persist the powerfully seductive "truth" that defined the Greater East Asian Co-Prosperity Sphere as a project to oppose the Western hegemony. That the Japanese were humanity's first named victims of atomic age warfare decisively contributed to this equation of Japan's and the rest of Asia's experience of Western imperialism and racism. The memories of Hiroshima's destruction, secured within the global narrative of the universal history of humanity, has thus sustained, at least in the dominant historical discourse, a national victimology and phantasm of innocence throughout most of the postwar years.

TROPES OF THE NATION, PEACE, AND HUMANITY

Despite Hiroshima's positioning within a global narrative, more often than not the city's name evokes discrepant memories rather than the shared sentiments and understandings of a universal collectivity. For example, in the official histories of nations that achieved independence after liberation from Japan's colonial or military rule, the destruction of Hiroshima and Nagasaki is celebrated as ultimately leading to the collapse of the Japanese Empire. Kurihara Sadako's well-known poem, "When Hiroshima Is Spoken Of," dramatically captures the exasperating way in which "Hiroshima" tends to set loose an endless string of names marking atrocities—Pearl Harbor, the Rape of Nanjing, the Manila inferno, and on and on.[30] More recently, the debates on the Enola Gay exhibit at the Smithsonian National Air and Space Museum reconfirmed that reactions to Hiroshima, as the memory site of the first nuclear catastrophe, almost always produce discourses of nation-states. At various discursive junctures, Hiroshima's atom bomb appears to provoke retaliatory memories of atrocities committed by and against specific national entities.

In postwar Japan, the remembering of Hiroshima has as a rule been associated with the idea that the experience of this catastrophe was a "Japanese" one, whether through self-victimization or as a grave consequence of fanatic nationalism. Yet the nationalization of Hiroshima memories, composed of multiple and often contradictory elements, has been more complex than one might expect. In 1971 the late Sato Eisaku became the first prime minister in office to attend the annual 6 August Peace Memorial Ceremony since it began in 1947 as a "Peace Festival." Appearing as the representative of Japan, the only "atom-bombed nation in the world,"[31] Sato's participation marked the beginnings of the official and statist nationalization of Hiroshima's memory. A much earlier popular mass movement, the nuclear protests of the World Conference against the A- and H-Bombs (Gensuibaku Kinshi Sekai Taikai, or Gensuikin Conference, for short) had paved the way. This nationwide movement erupted in 1954, when a Japanese fishing boat, the Lucky Dragon Five, was exposed to radioactive fallout near the U.S. nuclear test site at Bikini atoll earlier that year. One of the crewmen died of radiation exposure. The tuna that the boat brought back to Yaizu harbor was sent to the Tsukiji central market, where the media reported on its highly contaminated condition. Shortly after this incident, housewives in Tokyo initiated a campaign to ban the A- and H-bombs, a move that in the following year developed formally into the first World Conference against the A- and H-Bombs.[32] In less than three months, this mass campaign succeeded in collecting over a million signatures calling for a ban on nuclear testing, and with it emerged the chain of signification that connected the atomic sites of Hiroshima, Nagasaki, and Bikini. This link, one that was enabled and naturalized by the perception of the three incidents as nuclear attacks that victimized the Japanese nation and people as a whole, served to mobilize a large mass of citizens and all of the major existing political parties.

In the 1960s, when the Japanese central government signed the U.S.-Japan Security Treaty (Nichibei Anzen Hoshō Jōyaku, or Ampo, for short) over the protests of the oppositional parties and a mass movement of citizens, the antinuclear sentiments that had emerged as a national consensus became divided over approving Japan's newly formalized military alliance with the United States. The treaty brought about intense conflicts, protests, and turmoil, for not only did it grant extraterritorial rights for U.S. military exercises on Japanese soil, but it also placed Japan under the protection of the so-called American nuclear umbrella.[33] As he observed the Gensuikin movement's radicalization and splintering in Hiroshima, Oe Kenzaburo saw an opportunity to foster a new and self-critical nationalism by securing the historical experiences of Hiroshima and Nagasaki as parts of Japan's collective memory.[34] As part of a campaign to produce a comprehensive national catalogue on the damage caused by the A- and H-bombs, many antinuclear critics and intellectuals such as Oe criticized the national government for placing economic growth under U.S. military protection above the pursuit of democratic ideals. Certain strands of the Gensuikin movement also continued to object to the treaty itself. Within this context, Sato's official attendance at the 1971 Peace Memorial Ceremony can be understood as an attempt to contain the broad oppositional base that had grown out of the peace and antinuclear activities of the preceding decades. The nationalized remembering of Hiroshima has therefore never been monolithic or without contradictions, even within the apparent homogeneity of Japanese society.[35]

While the memory of Hiroshima, whether in or outside Japan, is often embedded within narratives of national collectivities, Hiroshima always seems to have a universal referentiality. In the city's history, and in other places as well, the temporally fixed sign of "Hiroshima," together with that of "Nagasaki," has among other things stood for humanity's first experience of a nuclear atrocity and for the peace that followed World War II. The instantaneous and massive devastation at this site has also often been construed as an unprecedented experience in human history brought about by scientific progress. Moreover, during the last half century many have visited Hiroshima to seek answers to our "ultimate concerns": the authentic meanings of life, death, bereavement, and human suffering. And poets, priests, revolutionaries, philosophers, and scientists have visited the city to deliver messages of peace. "Hiroshima," a master code for catastrophe in the twentieth century, is apparently all-absorbing as it conflates countless particulars into a single totality in the name of world peace. Moreover, subsequent medical discoveries of the lingering and uncontainable effects of radiation, of their trespasses over geographical borders and temporal limits, have led to a growing sense of alarm that no existing borders—whether national, cultural, or ideological and political—can ensure immunity. The new scientific technology could easily annihilate all of "us." The subject of remembering the bombing of Hiroshima, the instance that simulates a panhuman eschatology, is therefore humanity, the omnipresent and universal subject that transcends all particular locations and differences.

The idea that Hiroshima's disaster ought to be remembered from the transcendent and anonymous position of humanity, and that the remembering of Hiroshima's tragedy should invoke natural and commonly shared human thoughts, sentiments, and moral attitudes not limited by cultural boundaries, might best be described as "nuclear universalism." Through most of the last half century the politics of Hiroshima memories, and the contradictions and slippages it has produced, are at once impelled forward and constrained by this dominant universalist trope of peace and humanity. In this section, I describe three instances in which struggles over Hiroshima memories took the form of conflicts between remembrances from specifically named subjects and from the anonymous, universal position of humanity. The cases not only provide a chronological framing for the present; they also reveal how multiple and intersecting national, transnational, and local forces have worked to solidify the paradigmatic narrative about the bombing that continues to shape the way we access knowledge about the city's past. This analysis will, I hope, help us disentangle the assumptions, stakes, and concerns that have competed in the development of Hiroshima's mnemonic topography. It will also enable us to explore the interplay among several key elements in remembering Hiroshima's catastrophe—namely, the tropes of peace and humanity, the grand narrative of the U.S. cold war world order, and nationalisms of both Japan and the United States.

THE EPIGRAPH DEBATE

One of the earliest public debates concerning the anonymity and universality of the subject of remembering Hiroshima's bombing took place immediately after Japan regained self-government and involved the inscription on the Peace Memorial Park's central cenotaph. The contentious words are engraved on a coffinlike stone memorial that, following Tange's plan, is sheltered beneath the *haniwa*-shaped arch. This is also where a list of all those whose deaths have been linked to the bomb is placed. The epitaph reads: "Please rest in peace (*yasuraka ni nemutte kudasai*), / For we shall not repeat the mistake (*ayamachi wa kurikaeshimasenu kara*)." The equivalent of the second line's subject, "we," does not exist in the Japanese original, and this absence of the grammatical subject, common in Japanese writing, has generated numerous debates about "whose" and "which" mistake the sentence ultimately refers to.

The public controversy began in 1952 when the Indian jurist Radhabinod B. Pal visited the park during the Asian Congress for World Federation (Sekai Renpō Ajia Kaigi), which was being held in Hiroshima. Pal, a forthright critic of Western imperialism, was the only judge at the Tokyo War Crimes Tribunal to have insisted that a ruling on Japan's war crimes should not be made unless the colonial crimes committed by the Western nations were also subjected to interrogation.[36] On his visit to Hiroshima, Pal reportedly expressed his indignation at the words on the cenotaph as follows: If the "mistake" refers to those who are directly responsible for the atom bomb, then their guilt has not yet been expiated. However, if the "mistake" refers to Japanese war crimes, its cause must be attributed not solely to the Japanese but ultimately to the history of the Western colonial powers' invasion of Asia.[37]

Following Pal's criticism, prevailing narratives about Hiroshima's postwar reconstruction have rarely failed to offer the normative interpretation of the central cenotaph's inscription, as prescribed by the city. In fact, there appears to be a nearly obsessive anxiety about the possible resurfacing of the issue; even to this day, the pamphlet for general visitors distributed by the Peace Cultural Center recounts the entire course of the debate at some length. Starting with a description of the epigraph's birth, it provides a narrative of the origin of the universalist position from which the city's atomic bombing should be remembered:

> When the [inscription's] writing was completed, the mayor, unable to repress his joy, brought it into the municipal press conference room. Greatly moved, the reporters greeted [the announcement of the inscription] with loud applause. There was no doubt that the over two hundred thousand victims were *not merely those belonging to any one nation, or any one people, but instead, they were memorialized as laying the foundation for peace for all of humanity.* The understanding [of all in the room] was that those who would pledge antinuclear peace (*hankaku no heiwa*) to these victims ought to be the people of the entire world (*zensekai no hitobito*) [emphasis added].[38]

The description of the joyful moment of the epigraph's birth is quickly followed by a bitter story of unexpected tribulation, the controversy provoked by Judge Pal's visit. However, in the narrative's conclusion, the noble truth ultimately prevails. The controversy ignited by Pal's visit, it is explained, ended when the city administration intervened; it publicized the official interpretation, which followed the bilingual exegesis provided by Saika Tadayoshi, the epigraph's author, who accordingly is quoted: "[The official English translation of the inscription should be] 'Let all the souls here rest in peace; For we shall not repeat the evil.' In short, those who ought not repeat the evil are 'We'; and the epigraph's subject is undoubtedly [each one of] 'us' who prostrates before the cenotaph. Because these are words that all of us human beings (*ningen de aru wareware no minna ga*) need to pledge, [the inscription] is arguably an ultimate expression in which sentiments . . . were sublimated into the level of religiosity."[39] By deploying the universalized "we" as the subject of memorialization, the narrative turns the incident into a historical experience shared by the anonymous collectivity of all of humanity. Nonetheless, judging by the opinions expressed in newspapers during the 1950s, the majority of survivors remained unsupportive of the phrase. They insisted that it did not adequately express survivors' anger toward the bomb's inhumane use.

In 1970 still another controversy over the epigraph was touched off by a group of right-wing intellectuals and politicians. They demanded that the city change the inscription because it was shameful in suggesting that the massacred were apologizing for what had been inflicted upon them. But by this time, it became clear, the majority of citizens actually supported the phrase.[40] Thus in the official remembering of Hiroshima, at least as indicated by the central cenotaph's epigraph and the official interpretation of it, neither the perpetrators nor the victims have been named. The anonymity of the subject of remembering has enabled the dissemination of the notion that atomic annihilation may occur in contexts culturally, politically, and geographically remote from Hiroshima; yet it also problematically obscures the historical relations and differential positions of all those with stakes in remembering Hiroshima.

THE PEACE/BOMB MEMORIAL PARK

Nothing more eloquently illustrates the global workings of the ideology of nuclear universalism than the discursive production of post-bomb Hiroshima. In the years immediately following the end of the war, it was not self-evidently clear that *as* the site of the world's first nuclear destruction, Hiroshima would become a universal symbol of peace. By paying close attention to Hiroshima's transition from the A-bombed city to the so-called mecca of peace, we can see more clearly the necessarily unstable tie between the two signs, "Atom Bomb" and "Peace," in the early postwar years.[41]

The public articulation of the idea that the municipal community ought to play an active role in promoting world peace and culture can be traced back to the 1948 "Peace Memorial City Construction Law" (Heiwa Kinen Toshi Kensetsuhō); the city's post-1970 administrative identity as the "International Peace and Cultural City" was also largely determined by its characterization as the Peace Memorial City in the late 1940s. The concept of "peace administration," or *heiwa gyōsei*, which is used to define the distinctive nature of the city's administrative responsibilities, also derives from this law. Yet the act was notably short on specifics.⁴² Notwithstanding this obscurity, it was believed at the time that the law provided the moral impetus for the city's rebuilding. The idea of reconstructing the city as the central site for world peace was particularly attractive to city planners, who eagerly sought to create special incentives for the central government to provide financial aid. In short, the law provided at once a sublime cause and the means to achieve it, giving a focus to what had thus far been scattered and limited efforts toward recovery.⁴³ The newly instituted law had as its primary agenda the construction of a commemorative space that would properly exhibit Hiroshima's municipal identity, resulting eventually in what we now know as the Peace Memorial Park.

For the lobbyists who exercised influence over the legislation, however, the concept of world peace was carefully severed from the memory of Hiroshima as the site of the first nuclear destruction. For instance, in the authoritative interpretation that he attached to a draft submitted to the Diet, one of the main lobbyists, Teramitsu Tadashi, explained at length that the notion of peace was not linked to the bombs; the term *kinen* (commemoration or memorialization) appearing in the bill was *not* by any means intended to imply "the reminiscent, nostalgic, or in other words negative spirit that the term *kinen* connotes." Instead, it referred to the more "lofty and creative spirit" of constructing a symbol of eternal world peace. Teramitsu continued his convoluted exegesis: although the term may misleadingly evoke "bitter memories" that "the end of World War II was brought about by the atomic bomb attack against Hiroshima," the spirit of the Peace Memorial City Construction Law is "completely divorced from the atomic bomb or 6 August." He concluded, "If one questions why Hiroshima city was chosen to be such a symbolic city, one might provide the historical background of the first atomic bomb attack and the tragedy of 6 August. Although it is certainly a significant instance, that in itself does not mean anything more than that."⁴⁴ Therefore, for him the peace that the city and its commemorative space were to memorialize had no inherent link to the war or to the bomb. The bomb was indeed what justified institutionalization of a special legislative mechanism, as was also true for Nagasaki. Nevertheless, peace in this context signified postwar recovery—what was positive, future-oriented, and not bound by "bitter memories" of the past.

One might suspect that Teramitsu's almost paranoiac downplaying of the bomb was necessary in order to avert intervention by the Occupation authorities. For U.S. policy at that time included the so-called

Press Code, which called for mandatory inspections of and legal restrictions on all publications and public debates about the bomb, regardless of their form.[45] Contrary to such commonsense speculation, however, historians of Hiroshima's postwar reconstruction process have pointed out that the General Headquarters of the Allied Forces—including Douglas MacArthur himself—enthusiastically supported the idea of spatially rearranging Hiroshima so as to turn it into an international showcase for exhibiting the link between the atomic bomb and postwar peace.

For instance, the most influential of the various blueprints for the city's reconstruction sought to transform the vicinity of the epicenter into a commemorative site, as well as to build facilities to accommodate visitors. In particular, they suggested that Hiroshima's planners construct icons and buildings that would commemorate both world peace and the beginning of the atomic age.[46] Unlike Teramitsu and many others, the Occupation authorities and U.S. officials determined that their interests would be furthered by connecting the atomic bomb to the idea of peace and, more important, by displaying that linkage to the world. The commemorative city of Hiroshima was, as it were, designed specifically to demonstrate the interchangeability of "the atomic bomb" and "peace." Remembering a link between the bomb and peace fostered the conviction that without use of the atomic weapon, peace in the Pacific could not have been achieved in a timely manner. This is a historical narrative that stubbornly continues to form our assumptions even today, despite historians' efforts to show that such an argument—more specifically, that use of the bomb was unavoidable if the war was to end without enormous cost in human lives—was fabricated ex post facto.[47]

At the same time, the identification of peace with the bomb also filled an important gap in the doctrine of U.S. nuclear deterrence. It provided a narrative to rationalize the buildup of offensive military force, which, it could then be argued, would effectively contribute to peace and progress. The textual production of Hiroshima as the A-bombed city that revived as a mecca of world peace thus helped disseminate the view that the world's peaceful order was attained and will be maintained not by diplomatic efforts or negotiations, but by sustaining a menacing military force and technological supremacy. Hiroshima's postwar design thus spatially represented the master narrative of the post–World War II order in the Asia Pacific region. The bomb/peace conflation subsequently came to be naturalized, as the cold war narrative for the global order prevailed.

The bomb/peace link is also a metonym for the broader reorganization of postwar relations between the United States and Japan. As the Allied Occupation evolved and the U.S.-Japan Security Treaty subsequently went into effect, the United States' postwar military and economic hegemony over the region came to embrace the nationalist interests of Japanese conservatives.[48] Without the latter's collaboration, the former's global scheme would not have been possible. Moreover, for those in Japan who wished to rebuild the capitalist nation by relying on the prewar power structure, it was essential that the United States provide not only institutional resources but also the powerful intellectual paradigm of modernization theory, a grand narrative that promised the economic growth and prosperity of the free world.[49]

"ANY AND ALL NATIONS PREDICAMENT"

Frictions between what I have been calling "nuclear universalism" and demands to acknowledge historical and structural specificities have emerged in various institutional contexts. Even within the national antinuclear campaign that appeared to have a remarkable consensus as it emerged in 1954, deep fault lines formed; participants were bitterly divided over who should make pledges for peace, and for what causes. A well-known controversy of the early 1960s, often referred to as the "any and all nations predicament" (ikanaru kuni mondai), revolved around such a contradiction.

The any and all nations predicament appeared as a schism within the Japan Council against Atomic and Hydrogen Bombs (Gensuibaku Kinshi Nihon Kyōgikai), the organization that had been at the forefront of the national antinuclear campaign up to 1963. It began as a conflict between those who categorically objected to the use, testing, and possession of nuclear arms by "any and all nations," without regard to the country or political regime involved, and those who insisted on taking particular historical circumstances into account in evaluating the legitimacy of nuclear weaponry. The latter argued that the United States' possession of nuclear weapons differed from possession of such weapons by nations engaged in proletarian revolutions and anticolonial struggles. Because the United States had initiated the nuclear arms race and introduced the threat of nuclear attacks in Asia, Africa, and the Pacific, the subsequent development of nuclear weapons by other nations should be considered a necessary and legitimate defense against U.S. nuclear domination, capitalist expansionism, and the de facto continuation of Western colonial rule. This argument arose in a particular global context: in 1957, the British government had conducted its second nuclear test on Christmas Island in Australia; and in 1960, the French had conducted nuclear tests for the first time in northern Africa.

The dissent within the council materialized as a split between those affiliated with the Socialist Party, on the one hand, and the Communist Party, on the other, during the 1962 Eighth World Conference against the A- and H-Bombs. The division was already forming at the national meeting of the conference held in Tokyo in 1961, when the Local Women's Union (Chiiki Fujin Rengō) and other organizations demanded several revisions to the conference resolution draft. For instance, they proposed that the phrase "the military policy of the *American imperialists and their collaborators*" (emphasis added) be replaced with a less pointed formulation: "the military policy based upon the principle of force."[50] They argued that the language of the draft should be less specific, so that rather than being construed as simply anti-American, the council's antinuclear stance would be seen to apply to countries other than the United States and its allies. The proposal, however, was dismissed.

At the 1962 conference, the conflict resurfaced over the Soviet's 5 August nuclear testing. During the national meeting in Tokyo, the Socialist Party and other affiliated organizations tried to lodge a formal protest against the Soviet Union in the name of the World Conference. When that proposal was voted down, the defeated members declared that they were departing from the Gensuikyō Council's national organization. In the meantime, at the prefectural meeting held in Hiroshima, a proposal was made to remonstrate not only against U.S. nuclear tests but also against testing by the Soviets and their allies. Representatives from China, the Soviet Union, North Korea, and members of the Japan Communist Party displayed their resentment by walking out of the conference.[51] At the meeting one Japanese Communist Party member reportedly proclaimed his willingness to expose himself to nuclear fallout, provided it came from bombs tested by socialist nations.[52]

These disagreements over the proper object of antinuclear protest and the legitimacy of possessing and testing nuclear weapons left an irreparable fissure. In 1965 the former members of Gensuikyō established the Japan National Congress against A- and H-Bombs (Gensuibaku Kinshi Nihon Kokumin Kaigi, or the Gensuikin Congress—not to be confused with the Gensuikin Conference, which had taken place annually from 1955 on).[53] In 1961 those affiliated with the conservative LDP and Democratic Social Party (Minshatō), who had regarded the Gensuikin

Conference as a growing impediment to fulfilling the terms of the controversial U.S.-Japan Security Treaty, had already founded their own antinuclear conference, National Council for Peace and against Nuclear Weapons (Kakuheiki Kinshi Heiwa Kensetsu Kokumin Kaigi, or Kakukin Kaigi). The effects of this controversy are still felt today: the national antinuclear campaign remains split into three organizations, each with a different party affiliation. Yet though their positions on Japan's involvement in the U.S. military alliance in East Asia are opposed, Gensuikin and Kakukin Kaigi have maintained an important commonality: they protest against nuclear weapons regardless of the different contexts within which those weapons are developed or possessed.

The situationalist argument regarding legitimate possession of nuclear force never gained wide support. As the official exegesis of Hiroshima's central cenotaph illustrates, nuclear universalism offered an axiomatic foundation for the antinuclear campaign in the liberal democratic postwar nation-state. In hindsight, especially given what we now know of the uncontainable effects of nuclear explosions, the "any and all nations predicament" may seem absurd. Nonetheless, it exemplifies how the antinuclear campaign as a Japanese national movement lost some of its critical edge when its participants refused to specify the nuclear threats within the particular Asia Pacific context. The Gensuikin Conference did indeed continue to oppose the LDP-led central government insofar as it pressed the latter to maintain the three antinuclear principles—not to produce, possess, or bring in nuclear weapons—which were constantly breached by the base-leasing agreement as stipulated in the U.S.-Japan Security Treaty. Yet its indiscriminate protests against nuclear weaponry also deflected critical attention from the geopolitical specificities of who possessed nuclear weapons, who benefited from the world order that they sustained, and who the accomplices of nuclear domination really were. Moreover, by making the ban on nuclear weapons its paramount concern, the Gensuikin movement as a whole also alienated itself in subsequent decades from student groups and other grassroots peace organizations that tended to regard peace and antinuclear issues as integrally linked to other questions regarding human rights, ecology, and resistance to state violence.[54]

All three examples—the controversy over the cenotaph epigraph, the discursive production of the Peace Memorial City, and the "any and all nations predicament"—reveal how remembering Hiroshima from the transcendent and anonymous position of humanity has embraced and supplemented particular nationalist concerns.[55] Nuclear universalism has served specific interests in a postwar world order in which Japan was incorporated and militarily secured under the so-called U.S. nuclear umbrella,[56] under which the provincial and the partisan masquerade in the guise of the universal. As in the overlooked parallels between Tange's prewar and postwar monumental designs, here the forgotten continuity of the supplementarity of universalism and particularism can be seen in what is transferred between contexts.

Tange's design for the Commemorative Building Project for the Construction of Greater East Asia aimed to celebrate the Japanese nationalist agenda, cloaked under the tropes of peace and humanity. Discourse employing such phrases as "Civilization and Enlightenment" (*bunmei kaika*), "Peace in the East" (*tōyō heiwa*), or "Liberation of Asia" (*ajia no kaihō*) was indeed powerfully seductive within Asia from the late nineteenth century to the period of the Asia Pacific War, precisely because these universal claims had instrumental value vis-à-vis local interests. Though the postwar commemorative space of Hiroshima's Peace Memorial Park had different aims, the structure for achieving them was analogous: the park observed the universal ideals of world peace while embracing the specific concern of defending the free world against the threat of communism. In the newly reformulated master narrative of postwar global relations, the universal values and practices of modernity, progress, freedom, and so on came exclusively under the rubric of the West, especially of the United States. In effect, the dominant mode of remembering Hiroshima resulted in handing over the universal tropes of peace and humanity from Japan's pan-Asian regime of truth to the U.S. cold war commonwealth.

Long lost behind the repeated universal calls for the peace of humanity and beneath nationalized memories of Hiroshima and Nagasaki were, again, the experiences of those who were victimized by the bomb as colonized subjects of the prewar Japanese Empire. In chapter 5 I will discuss the Memorial for the Korean Atom Bomb Victims at some length and explore the ways in which the insistence on universal victimhood has prevented memories of colonialism—and by extension, the call for social justice in current ethnic politics—from infiltrating Japan's mainstream public arena. In 1990 Hiroshima city abruptly made a proposal to relocate the geographically marginalized Korean Memorial into the official territory of the Peace Park, but only after eliminating ethnic and colonial reminders from the memorial. In supporting the city's refusal to include the racially and ethnically marked memorial into the Peace Park, one survivor, a physician and prominent leader of the postwar *hibakusha* movement, expressed his objection as follows: "To categorize people as Japanese or Koreans is a low-level argument."[57] Here, again, the claim that posits a universal category of humanity as the subject of memorialization serves to obstruct condemnations of Japanese nationalism and ethnocentrism. It frustrates cultural practices that attempt to reveal the ways in which culture and society are organized through hierarchies of racial and ethnic differences.

The progressive peace and antiwar discourse, eager to depart from prewar ideology and practices, also contributed to a forgetfulness about those who had liberated themselves from Japanese rule after the war. When Son Chintu, a Korean survivor of Hiroshima, illegally entered Japan from Pusan in 1970 and demanded issuance of a *hibakusha* certificate that would allow him to receive the same medical relief given to survivors residing in Japan (see chapter 3), the incident profoundly disturbed the ethnocentric remembering of Hiroshima, reminding people that prewar Japan was in fact a multiethnic and multiracial empire.[58] Yet even before Son's return to Japan, the conservative faction of the Japanese antinuclear movement had been urgently calling for special relief measures to be established for the forgotten atom bomb survivors residing in Korea. Ironically, it was the conservatives' adherence to prewar imperial practices that bound them to the utopian rhetoric of multiethnic harmony and cooperation.[59] Reported widely in the media, Son's court case mobilized a nationwide citizens' movement; for the first time, the broader peace and antinuclear constituencies began to reflect on the historical conditions and material specificities behind Hiroshima's atomic bombing.

The complicitous relation between Japan and the United States under the cold war global order provided another overarching context for the LDP government's maintenance of a double standard in remembering Hiroshima and Nagasaki. Domestically the conservative party, as Prime Minister Sato's attendance at the Peace Memorial Ceremony demonstrated, succeeded in incorporating local experiences of nuclear victimization into a national victimology.[60] Internationally, however, the Japanese government has never formally charged the United States with using the two atomic bombs illegitimately. One of the numerous incidents attesting to the national government's unwillingness to cast direct blame on the United States occurred during the 1970 World Exposition held in Osaka, an epochal event that demonstrated Japan's postwar progress and its new membership in the international community. During the event, the central government requested the removal from the exhibit of photographic displays depicting atom-bombed Hiroshima and Nagasaki.[61]

As we near the end of the twentieth century, many important changes are taking place within and beyond the grand narrative of peace and humanity. They perhaps appear most noticeably in recent speeches delivered by Mayor Hiraoka Takashi at the annual Peace Memorial Ceremony. He has made increasingly explicit references to the question of historical agency; and the more specifically the speeches refer to imperial Japan's acts of military and colonial aggression against people of Asia and the Pacific, the more strongly they implicate the United States as the agent responsible for destroying the Hiroshima community. Such departures from the dominant tropes of universal peace and humanity appear tied to the interrogation of specific actors in the atrocities of the twentieth century's first half, whether as perpetrators, victims, or accomplices. Moreover, the 1997 speech for the first time openly criticized Japan's protection under the U.S. nuclear umbrella, highlighting more than ever the deep chasm between the municipal government and the central government over the issue of militarism and Japan's relationship to the United States. If the cultural agenda of postwar Germany and Europe have been conditioned by, as Eric Santner compellingly argued, the post-Holocaust and the postmodern, then the politics of memory in late-twentieth-century Japan circulate around different "posts": the post-nuclear, the postcolonial, and the post–cold war.[62] This study examines the remembering and forgetting of Hiroshima memories within such a milieu, in which formerly invisible actors have become visible and multiple, the evident contours of the Enemy have become obscured, and an awareness of the nonbinary and complicitous relations of power has intensified.[63]

ON THE POLITICS OF HISTORICAL MEMORY

In exploring the politics of historical knowledge about Hiroshima, this ethnography deploys the concept of memory as its central device. Indeed, memory has become a primary concern within many disciplines over the past two decades. A number of authors have investigated various dimensions of remembering and forgetting cataclysmic events in diverse local cultures and social contexts. They have attended to such issues as the manifest and repressive mediations of memories, the cleavages of subject positions along which contestations over remembering and forgetting occur, and the hegemonic and contradictory processes of producing, distributing, and consuming knowledge about the past as they take place in institutions and at various material sites.[64] When questions of history are formulated in terms of memory, researchers must examine not only the content of historical knowledge but also the processes whereby that knowledge is accessed. Investigations of memory always focus on how, as much as what, we know about the past.

Therefore, I do not here define "memory" in opposition to "history." Such opposition has taken two quite different forms. On the one hand, in popular writings and in some studies of social history, Memory has often referred to genuine and authentic knowledge about ordinary people's past experiences, in contrast to official History, which is considered to be a product of power, written from the perspectives of cultural elites, colonists, and other members of the ruling classes. Such works have focused on recovering long-suppressed yet persistent popular memories. Commonly the objective has been to foreground anonymous actors and to reveal the ways in which institutionalized History has misrepresented their experiences. On the other hand, Memory has often been associated with myth or fiction and contrasted with History as written by professionals. Thus personal memoirs, autobiographic narratives, and firsthand experiential accounts are treated as a second-class history, written without hard evidence and from myopic, partisan, and subjective points of view; professionally scrutinized History, by contrast, is regarded as further distanced from immediate experiences, and therefore less partial and more synthetic. History tends to stand for rational and scientific knowledge, while Memory is associated with the "subjective," such as nostalgic passion, longing, devotion, or allegiance.[65]

In either case, the imagined opposition between History and Memory seems to rest on and contribute to a false dichotomy. Taken together, the two views reveal not so much that there is a stable distinction between the terms but rather that the production of knowledge about the past, whether in the form of History or Memory, is always enmeshed in the exercise of power and is always accompanied by elements of repression. In this work, memory is understood as deeply embedded in and hopelessly complicitous with history in fashioning an official and authoritative account of the past.[66] That perspective on history, memory, and knowledge also necessitates an interdisciplinary study.

In short, I employ the concept of memory to emphasize that knowing the past cannot be divorced from the contexts within which retrospections on the past occur. Above all, reliance on this concept means that we begin our investigations into the past with an awareness that historical "reality" can only be made available to us through the mediations of given categories of representation and processes of signification. We must therefore suspend the belief that past events and experiences can automatically manifest themselves and their meanings prior to discourse. We need not, however, reject empirical facts, or disavow experiential truths, though detractors have often hastily and sometimes purposefully so misconstrued the objectives of such exercises. Joan W. Scott has warned scholars against unwittingly allowing essentialism to creep back in as they attempt to recuperate hitherto suppressed and minoritized thoughts and practices: "Experience is at once always already an interpretation and is in need of interpretation. What counts as experience is neither self-evident nor straightforward; it is always contested, always therefore political."[67] This often-misappropriated critique of casual uses of "experience" does not promote a transcendent position from which the truthfulness of a version of the past can be verified or repudiated. Nor does Scott overlook how "experiences" decisively shape social practices and cultural meanings. Rather, the critique urges us to question the very processes of mediation whereby certain events or experiences come to appear natural, authoritative, and self-evident, while others remain inauthentic and parochialized. Such introspection enables our exploration of the ways in which power operates in the production of historical knowledge, wielded both in domination and as resistance, and allows us to ask what exactly is at stake in remembering and forgetting past events in certain ways and not in others.[68]

Walter Benjamin's "Theses on the Philosophy of History" and his other related essays on modernity have tremendously influenced the recent rethinking of the project of history. The significance of Benjamin's observations concerning the irreversible transformations that have taken place in modern society, especially changes in the sense of time and the nature of people's relationships to objects, and the implications of his deep ambivalence toward the modernity within which he wrote—these and other topics have been extensively discussed by many, and I will not repeat all their points here.[69] Instead, I wish to foreground Benjamin's criticism of universal historiography and his attempt to radicalize the sense of time embedded in European modernity. For it is on these points that Benjamin's insights become most relevant to my study of Hiroshima memory.

In proposing to "brush history against the grain," Benjamin elucidates the crucial disjuncture between the conventional Marxist and bourgeois historiography that assumes continuity and coherence in the progression of time and the historical accounts that help illuminate possibilities for change:

> Historicism rightly culminates in universal history. . . . Universal history has no theoretical armature. Its method is additive; it musters a mass of data to fill the homogeneous, empty time. Materialistic historiography, on the other hand, is based on a constructive principle. . . . Where thinking suddenly stops in a configuration pregnant with tensions, it gives that configuration a shock, by which it crystallizes into a monad. A historical materialist approaches a historical subject only where he encounters it as a monad. In this structure he recognizes the sign of a Messianic cessation of happening, or, put differently, a revolutionary chance in the fight for the oppressed past. He takes cognizance of it in order to blast a specific era out of the homogeneous course of history.[70]

Whereas the "universal history" loyally recounts the events as they took place, the writing of a "historical materialist" takes into account that which has been omitted from the former's inventory of happenings. It reclaims missed opportunities and unfulfilled promises in history, as well as unrealized events that might have led to a different present. By capturing them as a monad in a dialectics of thinking, as in a moment of revelation, the historical materialist frees "the oppressed past" from a history that is made to appear as if it unfolds through time naturally and automatically.

Such a method of recovering facts and remembering events resists the uniformity and constancy of the empty and homogeneous time that governs universal history. While the universal history endorses the status quo of present knowledge, the historical materialist brings to light the numerous counterpoints—the revolutionary "now-time" (*Jetztzeit*)—to the known course of the past and questions history's inevitability. Elsewhere, Benjamin wrote: "Historical materialism has to abandon the epic element in history. It blasts the epoch out of the reified 'continuity of history.' But it also blasts open the homogeneity of the epoch. It saturates it with *ecrasite*, i.e., the present."[71]

Here the "never again" premise of Hiroshima survivors' testimonial accounts becomes especially relevant, as we will see in later chapters.

For unlike conventional historical narratives, their experiences are remembered with at once an acute sense of irreversibility and an immense regret that compels us to imagine possible alternative courses of
history and to suspect that opportunities to prevent the moment of destruction might have been seized, but were not.[72] It is also important to
note that the testimonies do this historically, not through the mobilization of a priori knowledge beyond material conditions but by strictly
recounting what took place and cannot be reversed.

The counterpoints of history, however, can only be articulated by
"seiz[ing] hold of a memory that flashes up at a moment of danger."
This danger arises as knowledge about the past is constantly assimilated
into a teleological narrative that assumes historical progress. As Benjamin also observed, "'The truth will not run away from us': in the historical outlook of historicism the words of Gottfried Keller mark the
exact point where historical materialism cuts through historicism. For
every image of the past that is not recognized by the present as one of
its own concerns threatens to disappear irretrievably."[73] Rememoration
is a social practice that allows the past to be "recognized by the present as one of its own concerns." At the same time, when past events are
thus made urgently relevant to the present, they in turn question the
commanding power that historical truth is assumed to have over the
present. By interrupting the evolutionary continuity between past and
present, a Benjaminian dialectics of memory allows historical knowledge
to remain critically germane to present struggles for social change.

Susan Buck-Morss's exegesis of Benjamin can help us understand why
his formulation is so crucial to our examination of the politics of remembering and forgetting in Hiroshima. By piecing together Benjamin's
fragmentary writings on *Passagenwerk*, Buck-Morss makes clear exactly what was at stake in his rethinking of conventional historiography.
His purpose, she notes, was "to accomplish a 'Copernican Revolution'
in the writing of history. . . . The goal is to bring into consciousness
those repressed elements of the past (its realized barbarisms and its unrealized dreams) which 'place the present in a critical position.' In the
dialectical image, *the present as the moment of revolutionary possibility* acts as a lodestar for the assembly of historical fragments" (emphasis added).[74]

Jürgen Habermas also adopts this Benjaminian rethinking of historiography in seeing "*a drastic reversal* of horizon of expectation and
space of experience." In his attempt to radicalize the politico-philosophi-
cal tradition of European modernity, working stoically from within,

Habermas argues that Benjamin "twists the radical future-orientedness that is characteristic of modern times in general so far back around the axis of the now-time that it gets transposed into a yet more radical orientation toward the past. The anticipation of what is new in the future is realized only through remembering [*Eingedenken*] a past that has been suppressed."[75] Later, when he intervened in Germany's *Historikerstreit* and criticized the complicity between the neohistoricist use of the past and the growing desire for national absolution, Habermas followed Benjamin in grounding his position on what he identified as the present's "future-oriented responsibility" for the past.[76] This responsibility, when radicalized, necessarily extends to past events with which one may have no ontological relation.

Benjaminian reflections on historical time and memory can be valuable in studies of the experience of modernity outside the West as well. In his analysis of the political and psychological state of mind of those under colonialism, Ashis Nandy also elaborates on the effects of what Habermas calls the "future-orientedness" of remembering. Nandy's description of Mohandas K. Gandhi's politics of memory is strikingly similar to Benjamin's view of history: "Public consciousness was not seen as a causal product of history but as related to history non-causally through memories and anti-memories. If for the West the present was a special case of an unfolding history, for Gandhi as a representative of traditional India history was a special case of an all-embracing permanent present, waiting to be interpreted and reinterpreted." This radical break with historical determinism was crucial in freeing the historical imagination of the colonized from the dictates of the past, with its psychological sedimentation of colonial rule and class constraints. According to Nandy, Gandhi's envisioning of an alternative world and his ability to create a philosophical foundation for the Indian anticolonial struggle were enabled by conceptualizing the past as "a possible means of reaffirming or altering the present."[77]

As will become clear in the following chapters, the challenges to conventional linear temporality attained through the dialectics of remembering have become especially urgent, now that the hegemonic process in the production of Japan's national history is moving beyond amnesia, beyond the mere suppression of past knowledge. The current remembering and partial acknowledging of, for instance, the nation's past military and colonial crimes present a danger analogous to what Adorno once observed in Germany's *Aufarbeitung der Vergangenheit* (coming to terms with the past) in the immediate post-Nazi period.[78] Unlike the unending efforts of *Trauerarbeit* (task of mourning), or the psychiatric process of working through (*Durcharbeitung*), whereby memories of past cataclysmic events or experiences of loss are rearticulated by the rememberers to attain an understanding of their present position vis-à-vis such trauma, the process of "coming to terms with the past," according to Adorno, did "not imply a serious working through of the past, the breaking of its spell through an act of clear consciousness. It suggests, rather, wishing to turn the page and, if possible, wiping it from memory."[79]

This process of remembering, therefore, necessarily entails the forgetting of forgetfulness. In our case, it masks how the nation's military aggression, its destructiveness, and the loss of its brutal imperialist dreams have been deliberately and at times forcibly repressed for almost half a century since the end of the war. The ongoing reformulation of knowledge about the nation's recent past is a process of amnes(t)ic remembering whereby the past is tamed through the reinscription of memories.[80] Precisely because many perceive this danger, the struggles over memory, particularly over the ways in which remembrances take place, have intensified in the local scene of late-twentieth-century Hiroshima.

Adorno's warning finds an urgent echo in Michel Foucault's more recent critique of film and popular memory. In a now well-known interview, Foucault described what he called a reprogramming of popular memory: "There is a battle for and around history going on at this very moment which is extremely interesting. The intention is to reprogram, to stifle what I've called the 'popular memory,' and also to propose and impose on people a framework in which to interpret the present."[81] This foregrounding of the memory question as a central analytical concern also resonates profoundly with Benjamin's future-oriented interrogations of the past. More important, Foucault, like Adorno, warned against the mastery over memory that can occur precisely when people remember what they believe to be new, disruptive, and revolutionary. As in Foucault's work generally, power is envisioned here as operating not by suppression but by endowing popular memories with expression and thereby producing a truthfulness about them. Whenever the past is evoked, Foucault seems to suggest, we need to be vigilant about the ways in which the newly recovered knowledge is encouraged to reemerge within yet another regime of truth and the ways in which it is once again subjugated.

To investigate the constructed nature of historical knowledge is not to disregard political and historical agency. To be sure, for some the concept of memory may connote nothing more than a decentering of the "contestatory, subversive, oppositional" qualities that objectivist historical awareness claims to have.[82] Moreover, it may be feared that celebrating diffusion and diversity in the forms as well as subject positions of those involved in commemorative practices will lead to a debilitating relativism, hampering our pursuit of a concrete political agenda. Similar concerns about the deconstructionist crusade have been voiced, especially by feminist writers and people of color. As Nancy Hartsock puts it, "exactly at the moment when so many of us who have been silenced begin to demand the right to name ourselves, to act as subjects rather than objects of history, . . . just then the concept of subjecthood becomes 'problematic.'"[83] Undoubtedly, making historical facts and past experiences available as inviolable objective realities can be empowering, especially for those in marginalized social positions.[84]

I am sympathetic to such reservations about the radical denial by deconstructionists and postmodernists of the possibility of centered subjecthood. Yet I also believe that we can consider the politics of historical knowledge without entirely disregarding the individual actor's ability to act on structures and to assume historical agency. By formulating the question of historical knowledge in terms of memory, and by illuminating its constructed and mediated nature, we can determine more precisely the conditions of power that shape the ways in which that past is conveyed and ask how such representations interpellate and produce subjects. These exercises also demonstrate that we can conceive of historical agency in terms of the power to renarratize and re-cite past events and experiences. Certainly, narrativity and citationality cannot exist prior to categories of signification and representation. Nevertheless, by juxtaposing and piecing together unexpected stories and forms, memory work can create gaps and slippages within the structural processes that ground an individual's historical positionality. Historical agency envisioned in this manner allows individuals to become subjects of history, of their own conditions.[85] In this sense, to perform an act of remembrance and to possess a means of memorialization become equivalent to demonstrating power and autonomy.

· · ·

In part 1, I examine some of the spatial strategies that have contributed to taming knowledge about the city's past. During the last two decades urban redevelopment and tourism projects have reconfigured the ways in which the discourse on Hiroshima is legitimated and anchored spatially. Capital investment has focused intensively on urban renewal and the promotion of tertiary industries—including tourism, expositions, trade shows, and conventions—while various administrative policies have supported what can be characterized as the postindustrial or late capitalist transformation of the region's infrastructure. This political and economic restructuration also involved a transfiguration of urban space and aesthetics.

Chapter 1, "Taming the Memoryscape," examines the productive and transformative nature of space. The cityspace is an object that reflects and mediates infrastructural conditions—urban development projects can change its landscape.[86] At the same time, the reformulated cityspace may in turn provide a new "container of power,"[87] leading to new knowledge and consciousness, as well as amnesia, about history and society. Increasing forgetfulness and a yearning for what is called "brightness," I hope to show, are intricately intertwined with the manufacturing of spaces that produce subjectivities conducive to the dominant features of the current culture of peace and prosperity. It is precisely this power of space, which can at once illuminate and mystify, which can produce and "hide consequences from us,"[88] that makes urban renewal such a central agendum in contemporary Hiroshima.

The dominant processes of spatial containment define the proper territories for memorializing, prescribing whose experiences should be remembered and when, where, and how they should be invoked. Yet transformations of the memoryscape have not been achieved without provoking conflicts over how to represent the past. Such battles over memories have not simply materialized *as* struggles over actual space; more important, they have developed *out of* and been mediated through space. Chapter 2, "Memories in Ruins," analyzes the preservation campaigns for three structures that avoided complete nuclear destruction and that have been preserved, albeit in varying forms, over the decades. These preservationist efforts reveal the diverse ways in which the "pastness" of the past was perceived. The inconsistent meanings people attributed to conserving the buildings, and the contradictory ways in which they desired to preserve the ever-present past, demonstrate that there are competing attitudes toward remembering, that not all mnemonic sites have endorsed the same sense of pastness, nostalgia, and modernity that underwrite the dominant remembering of Hiroshima's disaster. Attempts at taming the memoryscape, moreover, have paradoxically led to the proliferation of mnemonic sites which interrupt progress toward amnesia in critical ways.

Part 2 analyzes the testimonial practices of Hiroshima's survivors. Often referred to as "witnesses" (*shōgensha*) or "storytellers" (*kataribe*), these custodians of memory have orally presented stories of their immediate experiences and survival to the public. Throughout the book, they appear as crucial guides to the past. To date, many scholars have considered the survivors' narratives from the viewpoint of sociohistorical psychology.[89] But while those studies have usually focused primarily on experiences of the bomb and their psychological effects, my inquiry attends to the diffused and allegorically extended nature of survivors' narrative practices. I concentrate on identifying the quality of knowledge produced through interactions between the storytellers and their audiences, exploring how this knowledge affects the latter's perception of the given order of things.[90]

Chapter 3, "On Testimonial Practices," considers the institutional and discursive contexts within which the survivors' identities as *hibakusha* (literally, "one who was subjected/exposed to the bomb/radiation") were rendered multiple and complex as they began to actively adopt identities as "witnesses" and "storytellers." The chapter contemplates how these categories have encouraged survivors to recollect and narrate their immediate experiences of the atomic atrocity not as an isolated incident in their lives but as inextricably embedded in their entire life stories. Especially from the beginning of the 1980s, many survivors began to situate themselves in multiple ways through the practice of storytelling, even as they have continued to regard their *hibakusha* identity as ultimately foundational.

Survivors often engage in their testimonial practices while accompanying pilgrims to Hiroshima on memorial tours, or *hi-meguri*—the latter generally referring to the excursions of visitors to the city's various memorials, ruins, burials, monuments, and other mnemonic sites. In other cases, volunteers organize and lead outings that are often called "walk rallies" or "peace walks."[91] The specific significance of these spatial tactics as cultural and social critique cannot be fully grasped without considering their relation to urban renewal and tourism. The tourist guides, maps, and pamphlets issued by the city administration often prescribe routes so that visitors might directly empathize with the dreadful experiences of war and nuclear horrors by first visiting the now museumized Atom Bomb Dome and the Peace Park. They are thus invited to appreciate the "preciousness of peace" (*heiwa no tōtosa*) and then encouraged to wander about the streets around the city center, filled with refined museums and expensive fashion boutiques, while entertaining themselves in the culture of peace and prosperity.

The memorial tours and walk rallies do not exist independent of such an official mapping. Nor can they entirely transform the established geography, which is a product of capitalism. Moreover, survivors' testimonial practices throughout the last half century have always had an ambivalent yet inseparable relationship to the development of Hiroshima's tourism and other city planning efforts. By making detours through and around official sites of memories, they manage to inscribe memory sites that are not immediately evident. Thus, mnemonic "de-tours" can be understood as a task of deconstructing tourism's established mapping.

Chapter 4 examines how this tactic of cultural criticism operates not only physically over the cityscape but also discursively and temporally through survivors' storytellings. Their stories include the nonteleological, de-toured courses of their thoughts and lives before and after the bomb. In addition, their testimonial practices illustrate an ongoing contestation between different temporalities within contemporary society—namely, between the linear, progressive temporality of the postwar nation and the alternative temporalities that are negatively dialectical, cyclical, or sometimes even frozen. Chapter 4 discusses in detail the unsettling effects of the frozen time that appears in the storytellers' retellings of the moment of destruction.

Survivors' testimonies are undoubtedly where the past catastrophic moment continues to reemerge, in the selfsame form but with processual differences.[92] The cyclicity of memory, moreover, is enmeshed with conventional calendrical time. In the month of August, for instance, the war and the bomb are remembered at different levels of the society. The national body politic commemorates the end of the war at the official ceremony held on 15 August. Immediately after the municipally administered Peace Memorial Ceremony is held in Hiroshima on the sixth, the city of Nagasaki performs its official ceremony on the ninth. According to the Buddhist calendar, the middle of August is a time when the spirits of the dead make their annual return visits en masse. In Hiroshima, where the overwhelming majority of residents are Buddhist, brightly multicolored lanterns welcoming the dead begin to fill the temples' graveyards as *obon,* the day of the all souls' festival, approaches. But the signs of remembrance do not appear at these places of formal memorialization alone. Flowers, water, and other offerings are also found in riverbeds, at street corners, on tree trunks, and beneath building windows. Every year, myriad mnemonic sites reemerge in this manner and gradually disappear as the month passes, restoring the steady time of the ordinary city.[93]

Furthermore, the deferred effects of radiation, which can erupt at any moment even after many years, have endowed memories of the atomic annihilation with constancy and repetition. A survivor in his sixties who took early retirement in order to become a storyteller described his past forty-some-odd years: "My gums start to bleed; and I wonder if it is due to the bomb. I meet someone I wish to marry; and I wonder if it is all right. We are going to have a child; we wonder if the bomb will have any effect. I begin to get older and worry about cancer; and, again, I wonder about the bomb."[94] A society's collective representations tend to denote, exclude, and domesticate death, but these persistent yet undetectable traces of exposure to radiation disrupt that process. Like a symptom of repressed trauma, the memory of delayed radiation deaths constantly returns to the surface of society.[95]

As individuals who are at once victims and survivors of that moment of mass killing, witnesses and storytellers necessarily possess a double existence. On the one hand, they recount the past as members of the community of the dead, who have been bestowed with the authority of the eyewitness. On the other hand, their very presence in testimonial scenes proves that they are forever severed from the temporality of the deceased. Through their aura as witnesses, these survivors bring the past to full presence in their testimonies; but in the very act of remembrance they simultaneously betray that the past is past, and that it can never be retrieved in its originary form. In chapter 4, "Mnemonic Detours," I argue that it is in this duality of identification and dis-identification of the narrators and their objects, as well as in temporalities of recollection, that the unsettling and transformative quality of the survivors' testimonial practices resides.

Part 3 considers how acts of remembrance have produced ethnic and gendered subjectivities in the postwar years. In chapter 5, "Ethnic and Colonial Memories: The Korean Atom Bomb Memorial," we will observe recent attempts to reprogram memories of Japanese colonialism over Korea, as well as of the postcolonial experiences of those Korean resident aliens (*zainichi kankoku chōsenjin*, henceforth shortened to *zainichi* or *zainichi* Koreans) who have been relegated to ethnically minoritized positions in postwar Japanese society.

By establishing a means for their own remembering, the Korean memorial erected in 1970 has authorized and made visible the ethnic Koreans' presence within Japanese society and history. The memorial constitutes, as James E. Young observed of the Jewish Holocaust monuments, one of those "sites where groups of people gather to create a common past for themselves, places where they tell the constitutive narratives, their 'shared' stories of the past."[96] The Korean Atom Bomb Memorial has been a site where visitors remember the experiences of those who have been interpellated collectively as Koreans. At the same time, the collisions and elisions of the memorial's meanings occur both outside and within the boundaries of nationality, ethnicity, and individuality. The acts of remembrance necessarily entail questions regarding the legitimacy and ownership of memory as well as whether one belongs to the shared past. Who participates in the remembrances, how the event commemorated is construed, and for what objectives—these questions are inherently tied to the issue of communal boundaries and their authenticity. While a number of studies have observed the production of collective identity through commemorative practices, I concentrate on showing how certain forms of remembering have induced "eccentric" and coalitional identities within Hiroshima's politics, both local and translocal.[97]

Chapter 6, "Postwar Peace and the Feminization of Memory," revisits the question of transitions and continuities between the prewar and the postwar, which I discussed earlier in this introduction, to scrutinize its crucially gendered aspect. The transformation of the official characterization of nationhood from a militant empire to a peace-loving democratic nation has often been represented as a change from a country of masculinized prowess to feminized innocence. This shift, moreover, was accentuated by the reconstitution of Japanese womanhood in the postwar regime. At least within the domain of representation, Japanese women as gendered and nationalized subjects, fully enfranchised by postwar reforms, became officially sanctioned and visible political actors and thereby enacted the dramatic metamorphosis of the nation's character. At the same time, the amnes(t)ic remembering of the nation's past has been closely linked to the production of memories of women and mothers as victims of the patriarchal and military regime prior to the war's end, and as postwar victims of U.S. nuclear and military domination. I argue here that through this prevailing mode of remembering the nationalized Japanese women's past—in which the maternal came to be associated with civilian innocence, peace, and victimhood—postwar Japanese womanhood became fully implicated in sustaining the myth of national innocence and victimology before, during, and after the war.

· · ·

Like other ethnographies, this book attempts to mediate between local voices in one social context and engagements in another. Yet many premises of ethnographic writings fail when dealing with questions such as those in this book. Conventionally an ethnographer could borrow his authority from being "there," but without being fully implicated in that local situation. He spoke both as an outsider and an eyewitness to the events described. Moreover, his objectivity was considered to derive from his position as an outsider. Yet the memories and testimonies of Hiroshima, and the state of the postcolonial, postnuclear age that they speak to, forbid virtually anyone from remaining external to this global condition. There is no space for the traditional ethnographer who can presume to be transcendent and impartial.

Nevertheless, the perspective of a different kind of outsider is one that has been consciously pursued in both the research and writing of this book—not because such a position guarantees the *wertfrei* objectivity of traditional ethnographers, but because it is only as an outsider that most of us can approach memories and testimonies of Hiroshima. Too often those who speak of Hiroshima's past assume its inherent and inevitable significance. Yet for many the need to know Hiroshima's past and present is far from self-evident. How can those who see no existential link to this place, its history and people, begin to realize that their lives are inseparably interconnected with what went on and continues to go on there? The awareness of being at once an outsider and insider seems crucial when conveying Hiroshima's politics of memory into another context.

Finally, although the book does not go very far in making explicit comparative analyses, analogies to other locales and historical contexts—such as the innocent phantasm and self-victimology evident at Pearl Harbor's Arizona Memorial, global tourism's trivialization of the history of atrocities in Vietnam, the statist appropriation of Nazi Holocaust memories, and so on—were always on my mind as I described the specificities of Hiroshima. The book may be read as a parable for similar plights of memory and historical knowledge in other locations. One important role of theorization might be to call the attention of readers to analogies that they can draw for themselves regarding different contexts. To be sure, theoretical abstraction and ethnographic undertakings are both plagued by symbolic violence. Attempts to mediate for others inevitably objectify and sometimes even patronize the mediated. Yet such efforts should not be too hastily abandoned. Only through learning the material and historical specificities of others' experiences can we realize how we are interconnected and how we can find rallying points for political alliances. As Trinh T. Minh-ha once put it, reflexivity on "the danger of speaking for the other" does not suffice to transform the relationship between the self and other. Such a limited awareness may only serve once again "as an excuse for [our] complacent ignorance and [our] reluctance to involve [ourselves] in the issue[s]" that urgently need to be addressed in global terms.[98]

PART ONE

Cartographies of Memory

CHAPTER I

Taming the Memoryscape

"Will it make me forget?"
"No, but it will make you not mind remembering."
Logan's Run (1976)

"What film are you playing in?"
"A film about Peace. What else do you expect them to
make in Hiroshima except a picture about Peace?"
Marguerite Duras and Alain Resnais,
Hiroshima Mon Amour (1961)

In 1989 the city of Hiroshima observed two commemorative events. The centennial celebrating the municipal administration's establishment marked the city's official incorporation into the modern regime during the Meiji era (1868–1912).[1] The other event, the quadricentennial of the construction of Hiroshima Castle, commemorated an achievement that was understood to have paved the way for the city's development as an early modern castle town. The city announced that the year indicated a "turning point" (*fushime*), a marker that would inaugurate a new historical era. Numerous corporate and administrative events and projects were planned in order to celebrate this year of special significance.

An automobile company, for example, proposed to erect a spectacular monument. The "Peace Tower," as it was initially named, was to be the world's tallest tower; it would be marveled at as the representation of a new Hiroshima, "a symbol of *akarusa* (brightness and cheerfulness) and local prosperity."[2] The design included "a light of peace" to be placed at about the same level as the bomb's explosion. At ground level, there was to be an entertainment center accommodating a shopping arcade, a festival plaza, and an international youth center. Responding to criticisms that the plan would obliterate the history of the atom bomb, a company executive defended the project: "We certainly do not mean to deny the Atom Bomb Dome. But isn't it about time to pursue not only the misery but also the pleasures of peace (*heiwa no tanoshisa*)?"[3]

Any events or projects that take place within Hiroshima's public space are apparently preordained by history to embrace the ideal of "world peace." Yet the call for peace can be overwhelming. The globally disseminated slogan "No more Hiroshimas" has indeed become invaluable symbolic capital. It has endowed the city with a historical authority that is internationally acknowledged, as is the unassailable moral reason for such a call. But "No more Hiroshimas" invokes the city only as an antithesis. That this "mecca" of peace pilgrimages is simultaneously the site of the world's first atomic destruction has long entrapped city planners in a deep dilemma. Other tourist cities unabashedly commodify their names with familiar phrases like "I love New York" or "I love Kyoto"; why must the identity of this city rest on self-negation? Why must the city refrain from advertising itself with the simple slogan: "I love Hiroshima"?

This chapter explores the spatial politics of taming Hiroshima memories. We will analyze the production of "bright and cheerful peace" (*akarui heiwa*)—as opposed to the "dark" memories of the war and the bomb—through a municipal festival, inner-city and waterfront redevelopment projects, tourism promotion, and other corporate events such as the International Exposition. These examples illuminate the trajectories of memories, the processes through which a landscape of death is being converted into one of opulence, seductiveness, and comfort.

The taming of memory that can be observed in the city's redevelopment projects reveals local mediations and manifestations of transnational as well as national structural forces. The cultural processes we find in Hiroshima's urban renewal, such as the commodification and flattening out of history through tourist appropriations and an accelerated nostalgia for the authentic and the real, cannot be discussed without examining the global condition of advanced capitalism. At the same time, the enactment of a series of municipal planning efforts can be traced back to the national government's advocacy of the "age of localism" (*chihō no jidai*) in the 1970s. The various regional communities' attempts at infrastructural rebuilding, for which they sought guidance and financial aid from the conservative Liberal Democratic Party, often hampered efforts to recuperate local autonomy from metropolitan influences.[4] The corporate and governmental joint production of the municipal festival, examined in detail below, illustrates how the category "citizens" (*shimin*), which in the 1960s had constituted an oppositional subjectivity of autonomous and critically engaged urban and suburban dwellers, has become grossly corporatized, at least within prevailing representations of the city and its history.

The chapter further traces a more recent rearticulation of Hiroshima's local history within the 1980s national milieu that was encapsulated in the phrase "the age of culture" (*bunka no jidai*). Under the aegis of late prime minister Ohira Masayoshi's cabinet, corporate and other institutions with nationalistic tendencies began to marshal the social science discourse of *Nihonjinron* (Japanology) into corporate and academic coproductions of knowledge about "Japaneseness."[5] Scientifically authenticated observations about Japanese culture as unique, timeless, and politically inert were disseminated and treated as if those characteristics were constitutive of the society that had produced one of the world's most affluent economies.[6] The engineering of "bright Hiroshima" is fully imbricated in the cultural forces of the political economy, both transnational and national.

REMAPPING HISTORY

The 1980s' refashioning of national as well as regional images occurred at a time of general consensus that the country had been experiencing what were often labeled postindustrial or post-Fordist global trends. A 1988 proposal by an inquiry commission proffered the vision of Hiroshima as an "International Peace and Cultural City."[7] Originally outlined in 1970, the proposal was restated so that the city might establish a municipal environment that fully anticipated features of the "coming new age," taking into account further advances in internationalization, high technology, high-level information systems, the overall aging of society, and what it called "diversification of individuals' values." The making of Hiroshima into a "*messe* (trade show and market) and convention city," or *messe konbenshon shitī*, was confirmed as the most desirable objective for future development. In order to achieve this goal the city urged the rapid "internationalization" of the city and its people, further technological advancement, and improvements in its ability to dispatch "higher quality" information.[8] These guidelines—Hiroshima's attempt to carve out a new regional identity in the rapidly approaching new century—were the municipal government's response to the central government's promotion of the "age of localism" in the 1970s and the "age of culture" in the 1980s.

The dazzling images of the new age, embellished by "internationalization," "high technology," "high-level information society," or trade
shows and conventions—almost every element of the late capitalist urban desire was included—were exploited in Hiroshima's late-twentieth-
century city planning. These concepts serve as tantalizing and sweeping
images that are both descriptive and prescriptive, providing urban planners with everything from necessary causes, motives, and future goals
to the means with which to achieve what is to come. Yet Hiroshima differs significantly from other Japanese cities in one important respect:
there, urban planners have had to negotiate the signs of peace and late
capitalist prosperity with the memory of the atomic destruction.

Such negotiations are not simple. The Hiroshima prefectural government held a "Sea and Island Exposition" to coincide with the centennial of the municipality, and a city official who was centrally involved
in its production explained to me that he did not necessarily wish to exploit the familiar notion of Hiroshima as a sacred site for peace when
advertising the Expo. He put it bluntly:

> Peace is too often associated with the atomic bomb, and the Expo should
> not offer an uptight (*katai*) image—it must be a festive occasion, a *matsuri*.
> I would rather like people to think about peace at the Peace Memorial
> Park; and at the Expo, people should genuinely enjoy themselves. . . . We
> cannot forever rely on the Atom Bomb Dome or Peace Memorial Park. We
> are aiming to get rid of the gloominess (*kurasa*). It is not desirable to bring
> in any political color; for people are allergic to it.[9]

Thus, even as he identifies the city as the site for peace, he displays
a profound desire to avoid remembering it as the site of atomic annihilation. The statement of this administrator, who has been involved in a
number of city cultural projects, betrays the powerful associations that
connect the bomb, signs of peace, and oppositional politics. It also reveals the strategies by which he and other urban planners have been
and will be attempting to reconcile images of peace and the bomb with
the city's new features. To be sure, the official was not dismissing as insignificant the tourists who visit Hiroshima to at least "think about
peace." Most who have been engaged in city planning do indeed acknowledge that artifacts and monuments of the past, including the
Atom Bomb Dome and Peace Memorial Park, are valuable resources.
But his statement does suggest a spatializing strategy whereby visitors
might be channeled onto different urban topographies that are defined
by dissonant temporalities.

While the strategy outlined by the city administrator was to avoid "political color" by simply suppressing the concept of peace in promotional campaigns, other urban planning and tourism projects have sought to change the texture of the concept of peace itself. The meanings of the new sites that signify a "bright" Hiroshima, for instance, were produced in opposition to the mnemonic sites associated with the atom bomb. According to the city's Office of Tourism, the new Hiroshima Contemporary Museum was deliberately constructed to represent the future, bright and full of potential, not the dark and ghastly past. A contemporary museum of art is also considered to be a prerequisite for any world-class urban metropolis, along with a convention center, subway system, and city university. "If other cities [such as Kyoto or Nara] dwell upon tradition and historical heritage, we will advertise ourselves with everything that is new," explained a city official at the Office of Tourism.[10]

Although some have been troubled by the move to exploit history as a new image for the city, others have apparently succeeded in excavating Hiroshima's past without summoning memories of the war and the atom bomb. A tourist pamphlet demonstrates how memory of the atom bomb has become decentered in recent representations of history. On the second page, headlined "Historical Fugue," are pictures of Hiroshima Castle and several temples. The text reads: "High waves called 'the Trends of the Age' have rolled over Hiroshima, as they have in other places. These historic buildings, still standing, have witnessed history itself, and can tell us its meaning over the ages." While remaining uninformed about the atom bomb's complete destruction of the castle, tourists will "breathe the great passage of time in such historic places."[11]

Of course, some people questioned the forgetfulness that accompanied the manufacturing of romantic nostalgia for the castle. The castle, which had provided the nucleus for Hiroshima's development as a town in early modern Japan, was selected by the Meiji government as the location for its military headquarters during the 1894 Sino-Japanese War. This war is often considered to be the initial act of aggression in modern times that set the stage for Japan's subsequent colonial and military invasion of northeast China. After the war ended in Japan's victory, the castle became an important national site commemorating Emperor Meiji's stay in Hiroshima as commander in chief.[12] For those who problematize the city's militarization during the early twentieth century—the period when Hiroshima flourished as a "military capital" (*gunto*)—the castle symbolizes the unquestionable causal link between the prewar development of the city as a major military center and its subsequent atom bombing. They also point out that military and imperial symbols continue to exist on the castle grounds even today. These include the Hiroshima National Defense Shrine (Gokoku Jinja), where the war dead are enshrined as deities,[13] and other monuments that glorify war criminals and celebrate the war of invasion. For these observers, the castle is an unsettling mnemonic site, testimony to a failure to reconcile memories of colonialism and modernity with the nation's mainstream historiography. Yet for the promoters of tourism, and perhaps for most visitors, the Sino-Japanese War and prewar Japanese militarism belong to a now distant past. For them, these memories have been transformed into recollections remote enough to be summoned with nostalgia and even romance.

The visualization of Hiroshima that is created by particular styles of writing used to represent the city's name can also help decenter atom bomb memories within the official cityscape. The simplified *kanji* (Chinese ideographs) dating from the postwar era that can be employed to write "Hiroshima," and that are most commonly used in Japan today, are the most mundane form; they elicit a rather prosaic image of the city. Whereas this "Hiroshima" posits simply a geographical place, substituting the anachronistic old style of *kanji* suggests an old castle town and the prosperous city of late-nineteenth- and not late-twentieth-century modernity. But there is a third possibility: in tourist and municipal events, the *hiragana* syllabary has increasingly come into use. "Hiroshima" in *hiragana* symbols, with their rounded and soft curves, constructs a new, affable signifier saturated with images of the nurturing hometown, or *furusato*.[14] Because *hiragana* is the most rudimentary form of syllabary one learns in acquiring the language, it may best convey the recently commodified notions of *furusato*—the motherly and domestic space of infantile innocence and nurture.

Yet "Hiroshima" has also often been written with *katakana*, the phonetic symbol system that is used mainly for transliterating foreign words. "Hiroshima" in *katakana* appears most frequently in the discourse of peace and antinuclearism; one of its original uses was to transliterate the English slogan "No more Hiroshimas." This "Hiroshima" stands for abstractions directly related to the specific historical moment of the city's bombing. It encompasses prayers for those killed by the atom bomb, peace oaths, and protests against nuclear war and violence. We should also note that Hara Tamiki, the writer who committed suicide on hearing that President Truman had considered using nuclear weapons during the Korean War, deliberately and strikingly adopted *katakana* in an important part of *Natsu no hana* (*Summer Flowers*), one of the earliest literary representations of Hiroshima's atomic destruction. Hara's narrator/protagonist, who believed that the sights of the immediate aftermath of atomic destruction most closely resembled "surrealist paintings," opted to compose his poem in *katakana*.[15] *Katakana* can thus convey a sense of urgency and shattering disintegration, of something outside the everyday. It also intimates Hiroshima's cosmopolitan qualities. But precisely because it conjures up such powerful visual images of the past, "Hiroshima" in *katakana* effects alienation. As a sign of antiwar and antinuclear ideals, it generates inappropriate images for the city in the "age of localism" because it is too distanced from the mundane local community.

The Motomachi redevelopment project offers a useful example of how the castle's image has been appropriated. The project, initiated by a recently privatized telecommunication company, celebrated both the four-hundred-year-old castle town and the high-tech megalopolis of the twenty-first century. A close look at advertising for the project reveals the ways in which marginalization of atom bomb memories can occur through the self-exoticization of urban space.

Not surprisingly, the young employees of a real estate corporation responsible for promoting the Motomachi redevelopment project explained to me that publicizing the project was difficult because they could conceive of "nothing representative of Hiroshima other than the notion of peace"; moreover, "there haven't been any nice recent images associated with the Motomachi district."[16] In the 1950s and the early 1960s, this stretch of riverbank—an area that the media once notoriously labeled "the atom bomb slum" district—was crowded with the temporary and illegal residences of war survivors, the economically disadvantaged, and people who had been excluded from the city's postwar housing projects.[17] The area's distant past was reexcavated in the hopes of displacing this prevailing image. Street murals, for instance, depicted everyday scenes from the eighteenth-century castle town. To represent Motomachi's more recent history, anecdotes about the introduction of electricity, telephones, and locomotives—romantic signs of the late nineteenth century's "Civilization and Enlightenment Era" (*bunmei kaika*)—proliferated, while there was no acknowledgment of the military uses to which the castle and nearby compounds had been put.

The original plans for a skyscraper (completed as Motomachi Kuredo) were expected to transform the area northwest of the downtown district into a business and entertainment center—"the main stage for an

International Cultural City." The building was to be equipped with multipurpose spaces: hotel accommodations, *messe*/convention halls, plazas for various "cultural activities" and sports, television and radio studios, theaters, shopping arcades, and restaurants. The aim was to remodel the entire landscape stretching from the downtown transportation center to the western riverfront, integrating the castle and existing public facilities such as a museum, gymnasium, and libraries, as well as the new monorail station. The result would be a space of "information, nonstop internationalization, comfort, and amusement."[18]

One of the workers in the promotion office, a man in his early forties who grew up in Motomachi, claimed that the district had been considered a dangerous, lawless place ever since the war. The residents, he explained, were those who had lost practically everything to the bomb. In order to gain some pocket money, he and his friends would collect metal fragments on the riverbed and sell them. They dug for lotus roots and caught frogs in the castle moat. "We brought the frogs to a Chinese restaurant on the way to school. We were paid pretty well." He now thinks that the area has changed a great deal. For one thing, it is safer: "I see young lovers in Motomachi Park even after ten or eleven at night. In the older days, there were no lovers hanging out near the castle, although lovers were always present in the Peace Memorial Park. The Peace Park has been well maintained for a much longer time." The contrast he drew between Motomachi and the city's central ceremonial site appeared to sum up the frustrations and resentments shared by many citizens in the immediate postwar period. Since the economic thrust of postwar reconstruction prioritized the city's ceremonial center, establishing the Peace Memorial Park received far more consideration than rebuilding and maintaining the equally devastated everyday sections of the city. This office worker categorically denied any positive feelings for his natal town: "There is nothing I hope to maintain among the images of old Motomachi. Those who grew up in the area hold only abhorrent and dark (*kurai*) memories."

In the newly recrafted urban imageries, however, even memories of poverty can create moments in which mundane scenes become exotic and exciting. Another worker in the promotion office, a woman in her mid-twenties—bright, gifted, and full of energy—expressed her fascination with making new discoveries from the familiar and explained how she tries to exploit surprising analogies in advertisements. When looked at carefully, she said, scenes of barracks and figures of the homeless on the riverbanks near the railway station "almost remind me of Southeast

Asia, maybe Hong Kong, or could it be Venice?" She also proposed to change the pronunciation of "Motomachi" to make the accent fall on "to"; according to her, this is the way people in Yokohama pronounce their city's downtown area, which is also named Motomachi but written with different characters. The exotic objects possessed by one of Japan's largest port cities—such as historic sites related to port culture, a traditional Chinatown, and even a nearby U.S. military base—apparently suggest the fashionable hybrid of cosmopolitan commodities desired by many in Hiroshima.

During the period of rapid economic growth in the late 1960s, a number of what people remember as "suspicious fires" destroyed the barracks and shacks of squatters. These were gradually replaced by functional and contemporary-looking high-rise apartment buildings. Although that earlier housing project may have been designed to simply hide what was thought to be undesirable,[19] the early 1990s redevelopment project aims at converting the entire signification of the area through displacement and dispersal. It is hoped that Motomachi's new urban spaces will gracefully blend views of high-rise apartments—residue from post–atom bomb economic recovery—into bright and pleasurable scenes of the future. The new project seeks not merely to wipe away stains from the past but to recast the very meanings that memories about that past might convey.

Finally, the illumination project, or the "lighten up" (raito appu) undertaking, was one of the most controversial yet highly effective investments in making Hiroshima "bright and cheerful."[20] The three-year effort, begun in 1989, sought literally as well as figuratively to "light up" several major tourist attractions. These included several popular peace memorials (beginning with the Atom Bomb Dome), buildings and monuments along the riverside near the Peace Park, and downtown streets, parks, and shops. Proponents believed that the neon lights and brightly lit window displays would transform the city into an attractive site for after-hours entertainment, which would in turn provide its citizens with new urban pleasures.

While people in the tourism and commercial industries welcomed the project as a significant effort to improve nightlife in Hiroshima, some have cast doubts on its true purpose. Detractors have argued that the local electric company has pushed the city to raise nighttime electricity consumption in order to justify construction of more nuclear power plants. Others feared the environmental impact of excessive illumination. Some hibakusha interpreted the project as yet another conspiracy to "lighten" atom bomb memories, to trivialize life-and-death experiences that ought to have enormous gravity.

An official in the city's Office of Tourism countered such criticisms, "Just because it is a sacred site, it need not be submerged in darkness. There are ways to illuminate things while presenting them solemnly." When I asked him about resistance from *hibakusha* I had read about, he criticized the mass media for "misconveying" their opinions. "I think media reporters must have exaggerated the responses of people like the interviewed *hibakusha,* when in fact they expressed only a few doubts about the project. I think it all depends on how we do it. If we do it properly, they will be satisfied."[21] Apparently, it was difficult for this official, whose mother was a survivor and who had himself survived the bomb as an infant, to imagine that the very notion of "properness" was being questioned by other survivors.

Numata Suzuko, a *hibakusha* and a retired home economics teacher whose testimonial practices I will examine in some detail in chapter 4, gave me a copy of a newspaper article in which she was interviewed as a survivors' representative. In it she urged that the park be allowed to "rest in peace at least through the night. I feel as if Hiroshima's past is fading away in the glaring lights." The article concluded by quoting the opposing view of a city official: "Precisely because it is a site from which 'the spirit of Hiroshima' (*Hiroshima no kokoro*) is delivered, we must change the present circumstances, which close the place in darkness, repelling people."[22] As she handed me the article, Numata opined, "This is the typical attitude of the city that always says, 'for peace,' 'for peace.'"

When I returned to the Office of Tourism official, he tried to alleviate my fears that the city's tourist administration might be effacing memories of the atom bomb by uncritically subscribing to consumerism: "Promotion of the tourist industry is itself a very act of pursuing peace. Those who visit Hiroshima to seek an experience of peace can be defined as tourists. It is the same as a pilgrimage to a temple (*otera mairi*). The town that exists at a sacred site, a mecca of peace, is the same as one of those towns that develops from nearby famous temples or shrines, that is, *monzenmachi.* So, those who visit such sites can be regarded as tourists."[23] Here Hiroshima's sanctity, its prayer for peace, is transformed into another object of consumption, like any other attractive destination for international tourists.[24] Hiroshima now is placed on the same spectrum as other world cities, such as New York or Kyoto. The difference that distinguishes the site of the world's first nuclear destruction from both the glitter of cosmopolitan urbanity and the eminence of ancient "Oriental" traditions is no longer critical.

The official did not deny the importance of conveying the atom bomb experience to others. "But," he emphasized, "one cannot be thinking about peace or about *hibakusha* twenty-four hours every day." The memory of the war and the atomic bomb must be invoked "properly," at the appropriate place and moment: "One needs *kejime* (to draw lines). Just as in the conservation of cultural treasures, the argument concerning how much one should preserve has no limits. In this respect, the idea of a museum offers a compromise." Nevertheless, past attempts "to build a war museum have not seemed to gain much popularity," he added. According to his ahistorical explanation—reminiscent of popular discourses on *Nihonjinron* that tend to depict various practices and sentiments found in Japanese society as characteristics of "Japaneseness" that have persisted unchanged since time immemorial—the aspiration for brightness, too, is a Japanese cultural trait, a mentality that the people uniformly and naturally share: "I think the Japanese people generally cannot bear to see grotesque things. There is even a plan to relocate all the remains from the atomic bomb, including [those in] the Atomic Bomb Museum. . . . Building a war memorial park would be an alternative. It might be accused of being a bit dismal, though."[25]

The other half of the piece of paper that Numata handed me was a copy of another newspaper report concerning the new waterfront redevelopment project, the Hiroshima River Cruise Project. According to the original plan, cruise boats would leave from the dock southwest of the Peace Memorial Park, proceed north along the park, pass beneath the Aioi Bridge—that is, the bomb's original target—and make a U-turn to their launching point. The plan also included onboard presentations with survivors' atom bomb testimonies. The cruise was designed to complement the "lighten up" project, so that tourists on night cruises could appreciate the illuminated peace memorials, the Atom Bomb Dome, and other buildings alongside the rivers.

The boats were to be named, appropriately, *Suisui* and *Runrun*. *Suisui* is an onomatopoeic word that describes smoothness, particularly in swimming, and is also used to convey effortless activity. *Runrun*, a word associated with the sound of humming, stems from fairly new usages of the term in such expressions as *runrun kibun*, that is, "a *runrun* mood." The word connotes a cheerfulness or lightheartedness. The tourist industry's intended exploitation of the river in such a fashion drew criticism from *hibakusha* and others who felt that their atom bomb experiences were being commodified and trivialized. Another survivor, a retired factory worker and the mother of two daughters, who like Numata has been actively involved in testimonial practices, asked me rhetorically what sorts of stories about the bombing I would expect to hear on boats with names like these. A *shufu*, or housewife, in her thirties who moved to the city sometime ago reminded me that "the rivers in Hiroshima are very special," because, as many others also recalled, "enormous numbers of people have drowned and died there."

FESTIVITY

In May the pleasant days of early summer arrive in Hiroshima. In the fresh breezes and bright sunlight, the people enjoy the verdant cityscape. The mild warm weather continues for a short while, to be followed first by the seemingly interminable rainy season and then by the oppressive heat of midsummer. Early May is also a time of successive national holidays, a period usually referred to as Golden Week. The two national holidays in the first week of May—Constitution Commemoration Day on 3 May and Children's Day on 5 May—are often combined with weekends to make a long holiday, which for many overworked men and women becomes a perfect occasion for short trips and outdoor activities. In recent years, various events, including new exhibitions and traditional folk festivals, have been held throughout the country during this season. In Hiroshima an annual three-day Hiroshima Flower Festival takes place. Since its start in 1977, this festival, which involves not only the municipal community but also the neighboring region, has attracted as many as a million and a half spectators.

On 3 May 1989 I arrived at the Peace Park area shortly before noon. The opening ceremony was just about to begin. Little Cub Scouts, Boy Scouts, and girls in white lace ballet costumes stood along the long pathway from the park entrance to the central memorial. A chorus sang joyful music on the stage, accompanied by a huge orchestra and brass band. The mayor and other executives waited to light a torch on top of a cone-shaped flower tower, ten feet high, to signify that the festival had begun. The transformation of the Peace Memorial Park's entrance area had started earlier. The flower tower appeared in front of the Atom Bomb Museum, and several arcades with colorful signs stood along the Peace Boulevard at regular intervals. A vast "main stage" had been built at the park entrance. The media announced that during the event traffic would be entirely barred from a portion of the Peace Boulevard, which runs on the park's south side. The blocking of this major traffic route through the core of the city suggests both the event's scale and the extent of the municipality's involvement.

As I walked past the stage at the entrance and moved toward the Peace Park's central cenotaph, I saw a few groups of tourists who offered prayers and incense and tried to take pictures with the cenotaph and Atom Bomb Dome in the background. It was not clear to any of them what was about to begin, and they asked, "What is happening?" "How come these people are lined up?" It was difficult for the pilgrims to realize that a festival was about to start because the main stage was too distant to be seen from the cenotaph. The Boy Scouts tried to keep the tourists from standing in front of the cenotaph. When the scouts, with assistance from adults, finally succeeded in creating a small open ceremonial space at the cenotaph, a young woman and man walked up together with a torch in their hands. At exactly noon, everyone present for the opening ceremony, including the young couple and children, paid one minute's silent tribute to the atom bomb victims.

The couple bowed to the cenotaph, turned around, and proceeded down the long passageway, which was lined with children. They brought the flaming torch to the mayor, who waited at the festival's main stage near the park entrance. The mayor, lifted by a crane, marked the festival's opening by lighting a torch at the top of the tower. This rather long and drawn-out ritual performance transferred public attention from the cenotaph at the park's center to the park entrance, separating the two spaces in the process. The dead were enshrined and calmly watched over the living from inside the Peace Park, while the festivities unfolded on the space of the Peace Boulevard.

The parades held on the first and second days highlighted the event. During the three days of the festival, various events took place at small stages and plazas that were set up along the avenue, while marchers paraded over the 1.5-kilometer stretch of the Peace Boulevard, finally arriving at their goal in front of the Peace Park. On these plazas were exhibits and performances: music shows, both Japanese and non-Japanese folk dance performances, tea ceremonies, sake tasting, and bonsai and garden design exhibits. On the side streets, small stands sold foods and soft drinks typically found in neighborhood festivals. The aroma of roast corn dipped in soy sauce filled the air. Booths were everywhere, selling such treats as *okonomi yaki* pancakes, *tako yaki* dumplings, and cotton candy.

The festival offered as many publicity opportunities to corporations with factories and branch offices in Hiroshima as it gave to the city and various tourist-related organizations. The corporations participated in the festival by entering floats, cheerfully embellished with flowers and colorful letters forming company names. To be sure, insofar as it was possible, they resisted crass commercialism and instead highlighted the ways in which they and their products contributed to peace and community welfare. Yet a transportation company entered a giant float displaying professional samba dancers from São Paulo, and one giant sphinx float carried a huge red sign that read, "I feel Coke." A telecommunications company entered a float portraying a wedding ceremony to make the point that technology plays a vital role in creating intimate and significant human relationships. The local salt company's float advertised their product's name, "Kitchen Salt," with the slogan, "We create the richness of human hearts." Various children's sports teams and students from private junior high and high schools marched down the street between the floats, brass bands, and baton twirlers. Other participating organizations included jazz dance clubs, Japanese folk song circles, *taiko* drum troupes, and volunteer welfare associations. In an attempt to lure tourists to their towns and villages, people from neighboring communities joined the procession and exhibited their own "indigenous" festivals. The local association of Korean residents performed an agricultural folk dance.

Perhaps because I was standing near the procession's terminus, the floats and paraders arrived at irregular intervals. The flow of the procession had to be adjusted; some hurried quickly by, while others were made to linger, repeating their performance over and over. Police interrupted the parade to let people cross the street. Restrictions and instructions blaring through megaphones disturbed the supposedly relaxed and festive atmosphere. The constant interference imposed to control both performers and spectators dampened the crowd's excitement. Although most around me apparently enjoyed themselves as they eagerly waited for their families or friends to appear in the procession, a few young people who had come to the festival expecting a more carnivalesque atmosphere expressed some disappointment. Still, the green landscape, the fresh air blowing in from the coasts of the Seto Inland Sea, and the early summer sun over the rivers added immensely to the pleasures of the event.

There were several motives behind the production of this extravaganza. Initiated within the 1970s context of the "age of localism," the Flower Festival was above all understood as an attempt to invent a new culture and tradition for Hiroshima. Thus Higuma Takeyoshi, a professor of economics, interpreted the new festival as part of the birth of a unique local culture, distinct from that of the large metropolitan centers.

> While Hiroshima has always distinguished itself as a model student of state policies, it never provided citizens with comfortable living (*yasuragi no aru kurashi*). Moreover, it experienced the atomic bomb. Now that the city possesses a handmade festival (*matsuri*) filled with hopes, the region for the first time has acquired subjectivity (*shutaisei*). The festival provides the city with an opportunity to become independent from the culture of the center: this is an attempt to gain autonomy. Has this city ever had such a lively experience of creating a new history and culture?[26]

The festival organizers similarly proclaimed that the festival would be an opportunity "to create a setting for Hiroshima that will give birth to culture," or more specifically a "peace culture" (*heiwa bunka*). The vice director of the Junior Chamber of Commerce and Industry argued that Hiroshima needed a *matsuri* in which every individual citizen can participate, a festive occasion that would be appropriate for the International Peace and Cultural City.[27]

The festival also had a less lofty model: the celebration that had been held in Hiroshima to celebrate the victory of the Hiroshima Carps baseball team in the 1975 championship series. Over three hundred thousand people had spontaneously appeared on the streets to honor what was at the time the nation's only local franchise baseball team. About a month before the first Hiroshima Flower Festival, newspapers invoked memories of the ecstatic homecoming parade for the baseball team as evidence of the citizens' strong longing for a harmonious and cheerful communal event. The 1975 event was remembered as a collective experience that had fostered "a new native place consciousness (*kyōdo ishiki*) and communal solidarity."[28] One citizen remarked that Hiroshima's people longed for the "bright and cheerful": "The alienated and dispersed urban people's souls became one for the Carps. When one speaks of Hiroshima, the dark and dismal image (*kurai imēji*) of the atomic bomb haunts. For the first time in the thirty years since the end of the war, the citizens were united by bright and cheerful news (*akarui wadai*)."[29]

Local corporations and retail shops also hoped that the festival would contribute to the community's recovery from the mid-1970s recession.[30] Yet despite the strong corporate initiatives, efforts were made to characterize the event as "contrived and generated by the citizens."[31] The media and the municipal public relations team emphasized the citizens' agency in producing and participating in the gala. A newspaper company, one of the event's main contributors, advertised it as a stage on which "citizens are the main performers" (shimin ga shuyaku). University professors and folklorists likewise stressed the importance of spontaneity and the involvement of every segment of the citizenry.[32] "The new festival is coming," a newspaper article publicizing the Flower Festival noted: "Three days from 3 May, amid the tender spring greenery, the entire area formed by the Peace Boulevard (Hundred Meter Road) and the Peace Park, the symbol of Hiroshima as the atom-bombed city, will turn into a single 'plaza.' Surrounded by flowers, greenery, and music, citizens will together cherish the glory of peace. . . . One of the major goals of the festival is to nurture the 'bud' of a new local community, growing through the intermingling and pleasures of the people."[33]

But even as they cultivated "the bud of a new local community," those involved in the invention of this new festival were forced to confront the dilemma that "peace" could not be divorced from ideas of the war and the atom bomb. To be sure, the Flower Festival's producers attempted to fully invoke peace as the foundation of their community without evoking the "dark" and dismal atom bomb memory. A sugar company president and one of the festival's major contributors told me he had solved the dilemma by conceptually separating two "Hiroshimas," distinguishing the city that had been bombed from the city that has miraculously recovered and is now flourishing economically. He explained, "When one speaks of peace in Hiroshima, it means the atom bomb. Therefore [the image of peace has been] gloomy (kurai). My opinion is that it is okay to keep the Atom Bomb Dome. Hiroshima is indeed a city that once burned to death. But it is a city that also emerged out of that experience—with vitality, that is. To be able to present the city as such, peace as such, and energy as such, is what I have pursued."[34]

Nothing more clearly demonstrates the effort to reconcile the memory of the atomic annihilation with the desire for a new, joyful, and festive occasion for the community than the roundtable meeting that was held shortly before the first festival.[35] In the details of the discussion, which were widely reported to the public by a local newspaper, we can clearly see the process whereby corporate leaders and local intellectuals led the drive to refashion the concept of "peace," along with atom bomb memories, in such a way as to make it compatible with the themes of the new festival. The meeting's participants repeatedly acknowledged that the spirit of the event necessitated "consolation of the souls of those who were victimized by the atomic bomb" (genbaku no irei). Yet at one point the group's statement was quickly rephrased: " 'Peace' here means peace in a bright sense and not with a dark image." It then reemphasized that "the spirit of the festival is peace, and its symbols are flowers and music," not the atom bomb.

Quite understandably, some participants at the meeting table cautioned against further elaboration of the notion of peace. The chair of the executive committee, for instance, argued that even though "the International Peace City's theme cannot be dismissed," the concept did not have to be spelled out in any official slogan "because it is already embedded in Hiroshima's spiritual background." The committee members carefully avoided characterizations that might provoke critical views on the peace issue. They framed the festival as an opportunity "to express what peace means at the citizens' level" (shimin reberu no heiwa towa nani ka). And they highlighted the mundane and the quotidian, dimensions that had been explicitly severed from discussions of peace and antinuclear issues in conventional political discourse. It was thus agreed that the festival would not be "an occasion to think seriously (kataku) about ideologies (ideorogī)." The moderator for the roundtable meeting summarized the members' opinions: "The so-called peace discussion is associated with various complicated issues, but it is hoped that the festival will demonstrate a true happiness, a true peace, and a true festivity. To put it differently, the festival will be an occasion to praise happiness and entrust flowers with the feeling of peace" (emphasis added).

While the festival's images of "flowers and greenery" were to produce "authentic" signs of the urban community's well-being,[36] the stress on "citizens" was meant to underscore that the Flower Festival was a harmonious and convivial communal occasion. More generally, the category has been central to the mobilization of coalitional social movements since the early 1960s: citizens' movements (shimin undō) emerged in self-conscious distinction from existing progressive social movements that had mobilized the masses along the lines of established organizations (for example, labor unions) and their memberships. The term suggests an awareness of being members of a civil society inseparable from but not entirely absorbed by state authority. "Citizens" functioned as the category through which people participated spontaneously and as equals in social protests and critiques of established authority.[37] Yet, when the "Peace in Vietnam! Citizens' Alliance" (Betonamu ni Heiwa o! Shimin Rengō, known as Beheiren) professed that participants in their movements were "ordinary citizens" (futsū no shimin) and refused to acknowledge interpellation by any existing institutional authorities, that identification of "citizens" with universal liberal political subjects also obfuscated the specific, concrete positions from which effective interrogations of the systematic reproduction of inequality and hierarchy had been made.

That one planner at the meeting differentiated the proper subjects of the festival from those at the May Day rally is highly suggestive in this regard. As he put it, "It is quite timely that the festival will take place right after May Day. It will thus also be a joyful occasion for workers (*rōdōsha*), for they will be able to continue their participation [after their rally]." In effect, the concept of "citizens" obscured the category of "workers." The latter, of course, presupposes a particular relationship to the means of production, a position from which class consciousness is enunciated through ideology. Furthermore, "workers" form a category through which people have been mobilized transnationally to address inequality and class conflict. In contrast, "citizens"—mundane, uniform, classless, supposedly liberated from "ideological strife," free from political divisions, and not in the least plagued by such concerns as economic exploitation or oppression—are subjects who celebrate the harmony and innocence of a peace festival.

The new fete not only pacified and harmonized the community of the living; it also domesticated the community's relationship with those killed by the atom bomb. The contrasts that have been drawn between this festival and the 6 August Peace Commemoration Ceremony are revealing. The following typifies how newspapers characterized the event: "A new festival is born in Hiroshima. Thirty-two years after the atomic bombing, a day to celebrate together the glory of peace is born in Hiroshima, the city where heretofore there has only been 6 August, the day of prayer. The new festival is a day to 'praise peace.'"[38] Since its inauguration the Flower Festival has been advertised as an attempt to restore a positive sense of community and harmonious civic relationships—two fundamental elements that were often considered to have been taken from the "original" community by the bomb. The desire for a new communal event, initially expressed by a handful of business leaders, gained strong support from the municipal government. In preparing for the first festival, a high-ranking city official stated, "The 6 August Peace Commemoration Ceremony has taken root. However, a *matsuri* that every citizen can equally enjoy still needs to be invented."[39]

The Flower Festival, in other words, has been defined and redefined not only by what it is, but also by what it is not. The media characterized the two municipal ceremonies as follows: "If the day of prayer, 6 August, is an observation of 'stillness' (*sei*), the new festival celebrates 'activeness' (*dō*)."[40] The sixth of August is a day of mourning and prayer for the dead. It has been characterized as inert and silent. In contrast, the May Flower Festival is seen as a day to joyfully glorify the living. It is dynamic, potent, vigorous, and animated.

To be sure, the day of the atom bombing—"8.6," or *hachi roku*, as it is usually pronounced—has never been "static"; nor have the dead ever been "silent." In the early postwar period Hiroshima's 6 August Peace Commemoration, and other related events held on that day, annually catalyzed the city and transformed it into the site of vociferous protests against the escalating nuclear arms race, as well as against Japan's post–Korean War remilitarization that took place under the aegis of U.S. cold war strategy in East Asia. Right-wing terrorist attacks on the Gensuikin World Conferences also escalated as the Liberal Democratic Party began to denounce the Socialist and Communist Parties, seen as manipulating the conference for their own political interests, and as it subsequently pressured the Hiroshima prefectural government to cut conference subsidies in 1959. Then in 1963, radical leftist students attempted to take over the conference site while demanding a ban on nuclear testing, only to be dispersed by riot police. During the early 1970s the 8.6 scene became even more radicalized as a result of Japan's cooperation with U.S. military aggression in the Vietnam War. Prime Minister Eisaku Sato's attendance at the 1971 Peace Commemoration Ceremony provoked violent protests from youths, primarily because of his support of U.S. military action in Vietnam and Okinawa. Fifty-nine students were arrested. In sharp distinction to Nagasaki, for which the trope of survivors' "prayers" (*inori no Nagasaki*) is often used, partly reflecting the city's large Christian population, "anger" has represented Hiroshima (*ikari no Hiroshima*).[41] The aggrandizing of 8.6 by politicians, the media, activists, and the tens of thousands of visitors from all over the world, as well as the conflicts that have inevitably arisen—these developments have repulsed many *hibakusha* and others who wished to reserve 6 August as the day of serene prayers and memorialization. Yet despite such strains, the spirit of 6 August has not been rendered entirely inauthentic. The day continues to be understood as a profound moment of reflection; for many in the city, including the newly arrived, it reinvigorates their desire for the yet unrealized utopia.

A festive event during which people "respect peace and praise the

pleasures of life"[42] contrasts sharply with an occasion at which community members remember the war and take part in observances for
the dead. In the former, they participate as apolitical "citizens," not as
angry *hibakusha* or as organized union laborers who are peace activists.
In the festival police officers march in brass bands, appearing not as law
enforcers but as moral exemplars for the community. It is also an occasion on which the Cub Scouts and ordinary people, not the riot police,
control the crowds. It is an event for the community and not a ceremony in which thousands of outsiders participate. Though the 6 August
Peace Commemoration Ceremony had originally been designed to serve
as a communal festive event, it turned into an occasion that was more
likely to reveal conflicts in political attitudes and social ideals than to
encourage the willing involvement of all citizens. By definition, a successful communal event is one that generates Durkheimian collective ef-
fervescence and a sense of unity, not discord.

Planners of Hiroshima's peace festival thus sought to produce an occasion that mollified anger and replaced it with "joy." As the young
president of a steel company explained to me, the new event succeeded
in representing the city with the sign of peace, which was clearly differentiated from matters concerning the atomic bomb: "Peace is the face
of Hiroshima. Not the atom bomb, but peace must represent the city.
What is peace? When people get together and have fun, that is what I
call peace. . . . The festival is an incarnation of peace (*heiwa no gu-
genka*), but in this case peace means that which is detached from ideological strife."[43]

The festival thus celebrates the official representation of the late-
twentieth-century Hiroshima—the site not of nuclear devastation but of
peace and prosperity. The parade is a salute to commodities and affluence. As a festival of multinational corporate culture, it also celebrates
diversity in harmony. Different generations, classes, regions, nationalities, organizations of diverse political orientations—all of these are present. Above all, the festival has contributed to taming the concept of
"peace" while decentering atom bomb memories in the city's official historical representation. The associations linking the themes of peace, the
bomb, and political critique, which apparently tormented the city administrator responsible for the prefectural exposition, have been muted.
At least in the discourse of the Flower Festival, peace has become a sign
of innocence and harmlessness. It masks and excludes those questions to
which "people are allergic," including questions of conflict, oppression,

military violence, and corporate exploitation. In the meantime, the memories of atomic obliteration seem to retreat ever further into the long bygone past, becoming the *furusato*'s "once-upon-a-time" story.

. . .

The engineering of a "bright" Hiroshima is complicit with the hegemonic modes of thought, the ways of living, and the paradigm that can arguably be characterized as the culture of the postmodern, of the late modern, or of late capitalism.[44] This prescribed "brightness" is distinctly different, for instance, from that promoted in earlier decades, when the term was used in advocating the new democratic, enlightened era, filled with hopes for postwar recovery and scientific progress.[45] The sentiments encouraged by the discourse of Hiroshima's urban renewal—moderation, comfort, the valorization of cleanliness, and an obsessive desire for brightness, cheerfulness, and lightheartedness—all contribute to the cultural condition that privileges "atmosphere" and images over substance, that constantly transforms knowledge into mass commodities, and that incessantly flattens and trivializes history.[46]

The decentering of memories of the war and the atom bomb that this chapter has considered is, in fact, a local mediation and manifestation of the national and transnational conditions of the present global political economy. The waterfront redevelopment project, which is changing the coastal area from a severely polluted center of heavy industry to a tourist resort space, is part of the shift to post-Fordist flexible capital accumulation as sites of production are moved to areas that can provide less expensive and more manageable labor. This cleanup of the coastal region was made possible in part because the industrial sector could relocate overseas. In the process, industrial wastes were also exported. The sanitized urban space is therefore a product of the nation's wealth and its transnational power, which has enabled the physical displacement of the dirty and unpleasant. And while the shifting of sites of production has reduced the region's pollution, it has in turn accelerated the area's dependence on the tourist economy and its subordination to the industrial metropolis beyond its boundaries.

The effects of the political economy of brightness, moreover, extend to the cultural forces that prescribe perceptions of history and other dimensions of social life. In the period after rapid economic growth, and especially in the late 1980s fervor of the so-called bubble economy, postindustrial reality came to be represented through sanitized and comfortable images. Memories of the era of heavy industrialization and modernization are filled with painful stories of urban alienation, poverty, labor disputes, and industrial pollution. Electricity—"clean" energy—now substitutes for oil and sooty coal. High-tech industry solves environmental problems. And for working women, pleasant office automation replaces backbreaking labor in textile factories. The governing aesthetics enabled by the spatialization of memories will keep aspiring to superficial tidiness and shaping our awareness of history and our understanding of present conditions, ruling our ways of seeing or, more crucially, not seeing the world. By marginalizing and appropriating representations concerning the war and the atom bomb, Hiroshima's urban renewal works to create a state in which all social elements and incidents are naturalized and domesticated. In effect, the remapping of history onto this changed urban space reprocesses knowledge about the past, making that knowledge politically inert and emptying it of critical imagination.

Hiroshima's urban renewal is one facet of the attempt by the city's political and economic power elites to fashion and contain, temporally and spatially, the official territory for memorializations of the war and the atom bomb, while simultaneously redesigning the landscape so that it encourages the uncritical consumption of Japan's power and affluence and accelerates amnesia about the nation's recent past. This is not to deny that the same global conditions found so troubling also might provoke an awareness of problems beyond the scope of local cultural and political imagination. Officially defined as an international city of trade and conventions, Hiroshima cannot escape the intrusion of a multitude of "alien" factors or avoid encounters with the other. My focus here on the problematic consequences of current global culture in no way denies the possibilities of instability and disruptions under these same conditions of late capitalism, or postmodernity.[47]

At least in its official representations, Hiroshima will continue to be transformed into a site of pleasure and urban entertainment. It is becoming a future-oriented megalopolis and an international site of commerce and consumption, still mindful of the four hundred years of its castle town tradition. In the dominant logic of late capitalism, the fabrication of Hiroshima's twenty-first-century cityscape assumes that as the "dark and gloomy" turns into the "bright and cheerful," hardships will be replaced by comforts, disputes by consensus, pain by pleasures, and perhaps even Hiroshima's anger by conviviality. Fully entertained by the multiple dimensions of Hiroshima-ness, we will then be able to enjoy the pleasures of peace without discomfort about the potential for wars or nuclear terror. By endorsing a certain kind of remembering, Hiroshima's urban renewal attempts not to erase but to register differently the memories of the atomic wasteland. Containing them securely on a "proper" terrain, controlling both time and space, it celebrates peace in its weightlessness. In this urban imaginary, peace becomes an icon for the harmlessness and the well-being of postwar Japan. Seldom is it a reminder of death, anger, sorrow, or pain, at least in the official cartography of memory.

This progress, however, this attempt to proceed beyond the past and its firm grip over the present, paradoxically generates mnemonic sites that have the potential to interrupt the accelerating move toward the amnesic way of remembering. The next chapter examines the contestatory memories that have proliferated out of the renewal projects themselves, particularly those sites that have emerged around various demolition proposals seeking to expel physical reminders of the "dark" past.

CHAPTER 2

Memories in Ruins

The concept of progress should be grounded in the
idea of catastrophe. That things "just keep on going" *is*
the catastrophe. Not something that is impending at any
particular time ahead, but something that is always
given. . . . Hell is not something that lies ahead of us,
but this very life, here and now.

> Walter Benjamin, "N: [Re the Theory
> of Knowledge, Theory of Progress]"
> (1989 [1937–40])

A large part of the production of Hiroshima's "bright" new memory-scape involved the clearing away of physical reminders of the war and atomic destruction, and the redefining of memories through spatial and temporal containment. Demolitions, dismantlings, and reconstructions of a number of architectural remains from the bombing have certainly been some of the most effective measures to alter or expel, at least from urban surfaces, sites that might induce painful and disturbing memories. During the late 1980s a number of buildings, walls, and bridges that had survived the atomic explosion of 6 August 1945 to that time were razed, one after another.[1] This massive removal of relics has met resistance from survivors and other citizens, however. Opponents of these renewal projects have formed groups and arranged such events as walk rallies, sketching festivals, and symposiums to raise public concern about the disappearing atomic ruins. Petitions to preserve several buildings have also been submitted to the city. The opposition has in fact led to the proliferation of new sites of memory, while the old have often been consolidated or reinvigorated. The ravages of urban renewal, moreover, have not only erased the debris and relics but actually produced ruins, either as absent presences that are marked by new future-oriented urban structures or as objects preserved in museum culture. This chapter examines the atomic ruins as the sites of memories that have been, or are about to be, disengaged from the present temporality.

I will focus particularly on the preservation discourses concerning the three building structures that became central to the public debates. These structures differed in their degree of damage at the time of the initial destruction, their postbomb condition, and the meaning they came to possess. For each one, the quality of remembering that took place and the nature of allegiance to the past moment varied accordingly. By examining the mnemonic practices centering on these sites, we can see the distinctive senses of time through which individuals understand the categories of past, present, and future and thus their own positions in history.

Two of the debates—involving the proposed relocation of the Nippon Bank Building and a campaign for the permanent preservation of the Atom Bomb Dome—brought into sharp relief a kind of remembering that is propelled by the profound desire to identify the real, driven by a nostalgia for the original and for historical authenticity. In the first case, this longing for the real and the desire to bring back the past ironically intensified just as the building ceased to serve its original function as a bank, thereafter becoming quite literally a ruin. The third example, concerning the Hiroshima Red Cross Hospital, is equally strong in its adherence to the specific past moment, but it illustrates a contrasting (though not necessarily incompatible) quality of remembering. The debates regarding this site focused on whether atomic relics should be retained as functioning parts of the building as the hospital was totally renovated or should be relocated and displayed in a museum showcase.

The clash of opinions over the hospital's renewal plan also displayed two contrasting notions of time: one expeditiously puts the past behind the present observers and proceeds ineluctably forward and the other urges rememberers to pause and contemplate. The former has dominated in Japan, lending support to the postwar spirit of economic recovery and progress. At the same time, the latter—what I would call a contemplative time—has also been powerfully invoked through the recollections, testimonies, and stories that have been produced at such sites as the Dome and the bombed hospital. This chapter reconsiders and complicates observations that I have already made regarding the broader process of the city's spatial restructuring. These sites of memory may appear to be neatly contained; but what has become and what will become of them when and if different stories begin to be told about them, opening up new significations? What will happen when the mnemonic processes begin to exhibit a different sense of time that is distinct from the dominant one? We will see that the politicization of the alternative, contemplative sense of time is increasingly precious and indispensable to our remembering the twentieth century as an epoch of ruins—as an era filled with reminders of catastrophes in which memories demand the cessation of ever-progressive, forward-driven enterprises.

POSTNUCLEAR HYPERREAL

The former Nippon Bank Building is a European neoclassical-style stone structure on the major downtown avenue. It remained almost completely intact after the bombing, despite being merely 400 meters from the hypocenter. The building continued to operate for business during the postwar period. The decision was made to relocate the bank operation by 1992, to dispose of both the lot and the building at the estimated price of approximately 20 billion yen. Citizens who lobbied for the bank's preservation demanded that the city purchase the building and remodel it into a multipurpose public facility serving as a library, a commemorative hall, and a historical museum for literary works related to the bomb. As of 1997, the bank building still stands at its original location, unoccupied and deserted.

"It would be nice if we could have some place where both citizens and visitors could find literature that was written with specific emotions, or under a particular historical condition," a socialist city assembly member offered when I interviewed her regarding the citizens' proposal to restore the abandoned building as a literary museum.[2] Noting that she herself was not a *hibakusha* and thereby distinguishing herself from that collectivity, she continued:

> [To turn this atom-bombed building into] a small theater would also be an interesting idea—a small space where the audiences can have an intimate and heartfelt (*shimijimi [to] shita*) experience, where people can talk about peace in an intimate and heartfelt way. Better to be smaller: the smaller the space, the more sensitive one can be. Even if they may be small in number, I want people to experience something heavy and deep (*zusshiri [to] kuru*). I want to make [the building] into a space where people can cherish their personal encounters with each other. . . . It went through the bombing, survived, and has persistently lived through the postwar years. It is living its history.

Thus it was hoped that when converted to a museum of literature related to the bomb, the space would affect visitors in ways unlike ordinary historical museums. Most museums are secondary spaces to which artifacts from the past have been transported through time and space; this museum would itself be a "living witness," the assemblywoman further added. It would tell people its own history, "how the space was used, what people saw and felt in it, and what kind of condition it was in at the time of the bombing." The literary works that would be displayed and read here are unquestionably artifacts, but they would also be objects forever linked to the spatiotemporal context in which they were produced. In this original space of death and destruction, where the sense of "living-ness" would rule, the authors would not be dead—at least not for awhile.

The longing for an organic presence, for the "intimate and heartfelt" and for "heavy and deep" sentiments, is best appreciated when set against the hegemonic cultural tendencies we observed in the previous chapter. In the ruling aesthetics of "bright" Hiroshima, in the late capitalist milieu that shuns weight and depth, the material rootedness of memories is becoming obsolete. The longing for smallness and microspaces is also antithetical to the ideology of such gatherings as the Flower Festival, in which memories of the past have been refashioned in a grand and yet ephemeral celebration of peace and prosperity. The desire for smallness, weightiness, and profundity no doubt reflects a nostalgic yearning for what is considered passé, a reaction to the prevailing tendencies to circumscribe memories of Hiroshima's atomic annihilation.

Jean Baudrillard may best capture the preservationist campaign around the former bank structure: "When the real is no longer what it used to be, nostalgia assumes its full meaning. There is a proliferation of myths of origin and signs of reality; of second-hand truth, objectivity and authenticity. There is an escalation of the true, of the lived experience; a resurrection of the figurative where the object and substance have disappeared."[3] The preservationist discourse regarding the bank building thus marks a reaction to the accelerating disintegration of historical and cultural authenticity that has occurred in our global cultural condition of late modernity. The campaign for the permanent preservation of the Atom Bomb Dome, the remains of the former Industrial Promotion Hall, appears no less Baudrillardian, for it is yet another reaction to the "hyperrealness" of the world.

Among the few structures that survived the atomic destruction, only the Dome has been preserved without ever having been restored to serve any utilitarian function. Unlike the bank or hospital, both of which were rehabilitated immediately after the bombing and have been used until quite recently, the Dome has always been—and been perceived to be—in a state of ruin. The ravaged brick walls and the remaining dome-shaped iron ceiling do indeed give viewers an intimation of the building's interior space. Yet the structure, damaged almost to the point of collapse, at the same time resists efforts to imagine the mundane activities that

could have taken place within it. Lacking any utility beyond the didactic—that is, to teach people that a horrible thing happened—the Dome
exceeds the economy of the present sense of time and cannot be circulated within it. Unable to be reoccupied, both physically and metaphys-
ically, the Dome has been derailed from the secular course of history.
It has receded into an ahistorical and almost naturalized past. The remoteness of this mnemonic object from commonplace material processes—its inaccessibility, its inhabitability, its out-of-placeness in the everyday urban scene, and its nonfunctionality—confers a certain quality
of sacredness and what Benjamin calls cult value to this icon.[4] Of all
of Hiroshima's memorial sites, this is among the most frequented.

In the introduction we observed the centrality of this ruin in Tange
Kenzo's design for the Memorial Park. The Dome is located on the park's
north-south axis, a line that divides the park almost symmetrically, and
it can be seen in the distance through the U-shaped central cenotaph.
But despite its firm grounding within the ceremonial map, the Dome's
status as an artificially preserved ruin remained unstable until the late
1960s. Between 1966 and 1968, when the city first initiated efforts to
prevent the decaying structure from disintegrating, public opinion was
fiercely divided. During the national fund-raising campaign to preserve
the Dome, survivors were known to be generally less supportive of retaining this painful visual reminder of destroyed buildings, while the city
administration clearly recognized its symbolic capital. Some, perhaps out
of antipathy toward U.S. support for the Peace Memorial Park's construction, also argued that the idea of preserving decaying structures as
ruins originated in the West and that hence it was inappropriate to adopt
such aesthetics in Japanese city planning.[5]

In contrast, during the late 1980s there was remarkable public consensus about maintaining the Dome ruin, in part because in the previous two decades it had acquired a central status among Hiroshima's
mnemonic images. It is also important to note that this was in significant contrast to the fierce debates that arose around the preservation
of other relics, remains, and debris. A national newspaper that strongly
supported the preservation of atomic bomb ruins in general thus felt it
necessary to remind the public that widespread support for the Dome
had not always been unquestioned: "Let us not forget that in the past
even the Dome barely escaped from being demolished."[6]

Work on the permanent preservation of the Dome commenced in the
fall of 1989. The fund-raising campaign for this purpose, which began
in May, reached its target of 100 million yen, one half of the entire ex-

pected cost of renovation, in less than a hundred days. By the beginning of 1990, the total amount donated exceeded 390 million yen. The major *hibakusha* associations, antiwar and antinuclear groups, and labor unions—that is, organizations that have conventionally served as the foundation of peace and antinuclear activities—were instrumental in large-scale fund-raising. Many individuals donated their meager savings, children contributed from their allowances, and some seniors even committed most of their retirement savings. Schoolchildren collected donations in their homerooms and housewives did so among family members and neighbors.

Unlike its reaction during the mid-1960s, the city government's initial response was reluctant, putting it at odds with the enthusiasm of the entire nation, concerned people abroad, and survivors. The conflict that Robert Jay Lifton had observed over twenty years earlier—between the desire, on the one hand, to continue to remember the atomic bomb experiences, remaining faithful and responsible to the dead, and, on the other hand, to suppress the trauma so as to affirm and find pleasure in life, was not at issue here.[7] The city's attitude was mixed, at best, not about whether to retain the ruin but about how. In particular the mayor, along with other city officials and several city assembly members, was hesitant to rely on a mass fund-raising campaign. Such an effort, it was feared, would tend to be dominated by supporters of the opposition parties, communists and socialists, and would most likely be manipulated ideologically. Some argued that this would distort the "pure motives" (*junsui na kimochi*) of donors.[8] Contrary to their worries, however, the public's enthusiasm for the Dome far surpassed that expressed for other memorials or atomic remains. Indeed, the response provided the city with an opportunity, for it could now prove that the Dome, together with the Peace Memorial Park and the Atom Bomb Museum, is the proper and only legitimate receptacle for atom bomb memories.

The Atom Bomb Dome, a museumized object to which a sense of sacredness and transcendence has been attributed, is comfortably situated in a distant ceremonial vista that is visible from the Peace Memorial Park's central cenotaph. It is an officially designated site of memory for the nation's and humanity's collectively shared heritage of catastrophe.[9] The technology available at the end of the twentieth century has allowed this first ruin ever produced by the strategic use of a nuclear weapon to be preserved for perpetuity. Yet the notion of "eternal preservation" can be trusted only if one believes that the present state of things will remain in equilibrium. Are visitors to this site prompted to wonder about

the possibility of future similar destructions? Perhaps. The Dome's image has been the one most often reproduced and disseminated, through
photographs, postcards, models, and news images. Such simulacra, which
blur the distinction between the historical original and its copies, confound the linearity of historical time. The Dome's image may be perceived as preceding some future moment of nuclear catastrophe.

It is equally true that this simulation simply tends to intensify long-
ings for the authentic and the real. The Dome's artificial preservation, its
status as ruins, primarily accentuates the remoteness of the atomic horror of half a century ago. The Dome will then function much like Baudrillard's Disneyland for the postnuclear world: by generating a phantasm of the ever-present real past, it effects an ideological alibi for what
he calls the "reality principle."[10] Assuring visitors of the realness of the
past, the Dome confirms that the atomic destruction actually happened
once upon a time in this original place. At the same time, the Dome's
stark contrast to its background scenery, a magnificently recovered urban
space, assures people of today's peaceful, prosperous, and clean world.
The containment of memories of destruction obscures other contemporary realities: namely, that the nuclear horror may in fact be present
everywhere outside this museumized site, that the world may be thoroughly contaminated by nuclear weapons. Similarly, through its officialization, the Dome creates a focus only on what is perceived to be the
paramount human tragedy, as if mundane and less evident yet equally
perilous acts of violence beyond this site need not be acknowledged.

CONTEMPLATIVE TIME

Whereas the remarkable public consensus over the Dome's preservation may have effectively rendered the ruin the single most important
memory site for the renewed "bright" memoryscape, a flood of painful memories of the devastated building filled the public arena, ensuring
that the process would not be completely smooth. Memories of the atomic
bomb and the war, as well as postwar experiences that transcended generations, appeared widely in the media; many donors included letters
with their donations.

One woman explained that she donated money in order to console
the souls of her close kin, who were victims of the bomb. She expressed
her strong attachment to the Dome, which she said "remains standing
even when its skeleton is exposed." A fifty-seven-year-old man remarked

that donating money became a turning point in his life, the start of a new life as a storyteller (*kataribe*) who might narrate the immediate atom bomb experience to others.[11] A seventy-one-year-old man remembered the day when he found the remains of his father-in-law, who had been working in the Dome at the time of the bombing. He claimed, "now that the city has completely changed its appearance . . . it is only the Dome that can convey to us the apocalyptic situation." A woman, according to her sixty-three-year-old daughter, claimed often during her life that the Dome reminded her of her late husband and son, victims of the bomb, who wished her to "live their years for them as well."[12] A seventy-four-year-old woman whose husband was killed by the bomb while he was working at the Dome recalled her surprise when her son once painted a picture of the Atom Bomb Dome, although he was too young to have remembered his own experience of the bomb. A forty-six-year-old man who had not known that he was a *hibakusha* until ten years previously, when his mother had obtained his health certificate, said, "If the Dome is preserved, my two daughters who are now indifferent to the issues of war may remember some day in the future that their father used to talk about the atom bomb."[13]

The preservation campaign thus ineluctably conjured up memories and sentiments that might otherwise have thoroughly dissipated. Even if the discourses on the Dome and the bank confirmed the postnuclear hyperreal, one must acknowledge that once the ruins in Hiroshima were related to material contexts and narrative practices, they begin to reveal that the "pastness" of the past has been sensed differentially, showing that the meaning of longing for the realness of the past has varied greatly. The ruins and the preservation campaigns, moreover, did not necessarily nor uniformly endorse a single condition of knowledge about the past and present. The preservation campaign for the Hiroshima Red Cross/Atom Bomb Hospital (Hiroshima Sekijūji/Genbaku Byōin) exemplifies a mode of remembering that is not driven solely by the intense desire to secure the real and the authentic. Instead the ruins served the campaign as a site of critical reflections. By intensifying or highlighting a sense of time at odds with the linear temporality of history, the effort to preserve this endangered mnemonic site entered the struggle over the politics of knowledge.

The hospital's main tower and a couple of adjacent buildings had survived the nuclear explosion and also miraculously escaped damage from the fires that immediately engulfed the city. Indeed, it was one of the few architectural structures standing in the open skyline of Hiroshima's charred horizon, though the blast had destroyed practically all internal structures, leaving only the ghostly exterior walls of the building. Still, in the immediate aftermath of the bombing, survivors in search of aid had crowded into this devastated space. They aimed for the tower, a 1920s landmark that the local newspaper had once described as a symbol of "the magnificence of Hiroshima, the military capital."[14]

The hospital was reconstructed shortly after the war, and it soon became commonly known as "the Atom Bomb Hospital" for the special attention that its medical practice and research gave to *hibakusha*'s physical and mental problems. The devoted efforts of one of its doctors, Shigetō Fumio, the "authentic man" of the post-Hiroshima world, have become widely known through Oe Kenzaburo's *Hiroshima Notes*. In the first postblast reconstruction effort, the designers retained an iron window frame, mutilated by the bomb, and a white wall, pierced and scarred by pieces of broken glass. The end-of-the-century plan for further renovation and enlargement, however, required the total demolition of the structure, making it necessary to remove these remains from the site. The hospital's administrators had initially decided that when the old structure was taken down, they would donate a fragment of the ruined wall and the warped window frame to the Peace Memorial Museum. Instead, the preservationist efforts described below ensured that parts of the relics from the atomic destruction would be displayed in a showcase placed at the new hospital entrance.

Not all who witnessed the same timespace of Hiroshima's bombing recollected their memories in the same way as did the proponents of preservation. As the controversy drew the wider attention of the public, a regular column in the local newspaper ran opinions for and against removing the atomic relics. The following letter to the editor was from a reader who identified himself as a sixty-one-year-old man. While the preservationists claimed that their position rested on an allegiance to what had been destroyed, he condemned them as self-indulgent, engaging in a nostalgic infatuation with the past:

> My father, too, was lying beside the entrance hall of the hospital. . . . He died on the night of the ninth. As I close my eyes, I can still remember vividly the scene at the hospital entranceway. Several corpses were floating in the pond; nearby a few naked bodies of female students lay cold. As I stepped into the hallway, I saw an even more appalling picture. There were more people dead than alive. It seems like a miracle that I was able to find my father in such hellish circumstances.
>
> But for me it is sufficient that the horrific scene is kept in my own memories. I do not wish to return to the spot. Moreover, I by no means wish to

explain my father's condition to others. The ghastliness of the atomic bomb has already been recorded (*kiroku*) in various ways. Isn't it better that the aging hospital be drastically renovated so that it can serve those of us who survived? At least from watching TV, the explanation given by the hospital [management executives] sounds reasonable. . . . The Atom Bomb Dome alone is quite sufficient as remains that record the atom bomb experience in Hiroshima city.[15]

This statement encapsulates the temporal ideology that has under-written the instrumental rationality of Japan's postwar recovery and has prevailed in Hiroshima and elsewhere. In it, there is an obsession with the future, with moving forward. The "ghastliness of the atomic bomb" is reduced to an object in need of being "recorded." The Dome, as pro-ponents of urban renewal have argued, suffices as the only official re-ceptacle of memory. Any surplus from the past should be deployed in-strumentally in order to "serve those of us who survived," while those who are no longer here are constantly evaluated according to their con-tribution to the present and future. Such instrumentalization of knowl-edge and objects from the past is justified by the a priori assumption that the unseen future toward which we are compelled to progress is already legitimate.

The testimonial practices of Kuboura Hiroto, a retired national rail-way worker of about the same age as the letter writer, offer a direct challenge to such dominant ideas of instrumentality and progress. Ku-boura lost his left eye to the bomb at the age of nineteen. In his testi-monies he reveals the course of his recovery, from the time he was wounded to the present. He tells of the bitterness and frustration caused by the bomb and his injury. He describes heartless children loudly ridi-culing him as "one-eyed," and he explains how his visual impairment hindered promotions in his railway work. Yet he has managed to main-tain a positive outlook, has raised a family, and for many years contin-ued to pursue a career with the same employer. He credits the words uttered by his father in the bomb's immediate aftermath: faced with Ku-boura's apparent tragedy, on seeing that his son had survived, his father exclaimed, "Good thing it was only one eye!" Ever since, the apho-rism "it's all a matter of perspective" (*mono wa kangae yō*) became his worldly wisdom. It has given Kuboura the versatility and spiritual vi-tality that pervade his testimony.[16] This spirit is also what captivates the troubled souls of many adolescents today when they hear his story.

In the years since his retirement, Kuboura has independently been searching for what he calls "the atom bomb claw marks" (*tsumeato*)— that is, for relics of the bomb. As if to compensate for his lost eye, almost everywhere he goes he takes a hefty camera, impressively equipped with automatic focus, zoom and wide-angle lenses, motorized film advance, and nearly every other imaginable high-tech feature. He mounts his photographs in booklets with detailed explanations inscribed in his own meticulous handwriting. The photos are neatly ordered and pasted in standard notebooks. The handwritten texts include elaborate descriptions of the objects, notes on their exact locations vis-à-vis the bomb's detonation, and his observations concerning the sites today. The texts sometimes allude to the presumed conditions of the objects at the time of the blast. His tenacious search for "clawmarks" might be interpreted as a way of proving the reality of his own life, of demonstrating that he had indeed survived. On this account, the materiality of his existence was repeatedly confirmed through the objects that had also survived, despite having suffered irreparable damage.

Since the effort to preserve ruined parts of the hospital first became widely publicized, Kuboura has been one of its most vocal supporters. When I asked for his opinion on the matter, he stressed the significance of retaining visible sites/sights of memories and quoted from a speech by the late mayor Hamai Shinzō during his 1967 campaign to preserve the Dome. "Things that disappear from sight are bound to disappear from the heart," Hamai had said, and Kuboura elaborated on the statement: "It is meaningful to have [the remains] preserved as they were bombed, in order for others to understand the weapon's destructiveness. The role of the atomic ruins, as witnesses to the bomb, is becoming exceedingly important, especially as human witnesses are aging. . . . To take down the atom bomb ruins means to erase their history." He added, "I feel like I must continue to take pictures of the relics, because I need to protect the human rights of the dead" (*shisha no jinken yūmon o mamoranya*). Like those storytellers I will discuss in the next two chapters, *hibakusha* witnesses such as Kuboura believed that they might become proxies for silenced victims of the bomb by advocating the preservation of ruins. They saw their efforts as a means of restoring an equilibrium between the dead and the living, of bringing the former in the latter's time, of inserting the past into the present.

Another eyewitness account of the bombing, delivered at one of the public meetings organized by the preservationists, also provides a stunning contrast to the letter cited earlier. It, too, is predicated on a linear sense of time, but its focus is uncompromisingly on the past. The narrator, Kataoka Chiyoko, had been a student nurse at the hospital when it was bombed. Softly but clearly, she read a prepared statement in front of the sixty or so people who had gathered together. She was forced to pause frequently, each time waiting for her emotions to subside.

I was in my second year. In those days, we students were all suffering from chronic malnutrition. But the wartime tension kept our minds clear. As I stood facing the window that looked out over the courtyard, a yellow-white illumination, like burning magnesium, suddenly spread all over the window with a roaring sound. It was still as death. I probably stood up immediately. The ceiling had collapsed. The windows were broken. There was no one moving. A patient passed by. . . . We tried to rescue a student nurse who had been hospitalized. She was buried underneath a crushed wooden building. But we were unable to move even a leg. Like the rush of a tide, the wounded survivors rolled into the hospital. Soon, the medicine ran out. . . . With outside help, we cleared the inside of the hospital. . . .

The town of Hiroshima fell to pieces so completely that I could even view the far-off station; and it began to burn. The buried students remained unrescued; Hiroshima continued to blaze brightly. . . .

On the morning of the seventh, we gathered in the courtyard. Only thirteen of us were present among the approximately one hundred and fifty students who had been at the hospital. The wounded people who were packed into the entranceway began to die, one by one. In about a week, everyone was gone. We burned the corpses in the courtyard. We put bones that were still burning inside into envelopes. It continued day after day. . . . At every footstep, bones cracked under our feet. The phosphorus flames continued to burn, as if people were calling to let us know that they had died there.

Defeat in the war was a great shock for us youth. Everything we had received through our education crumbled away. Only empty feelings remained. The ruins before our eyes and the pain of the deep wounds in our hearts—only from there, I believe, may an unyielding will never to repeat war and never to use the atomic bomb grow. . . . I remember when I saw, for the first time since recovering from ten years of illness [caused by exposure to radiation], the white town from the top of Hijiyama. I remembered the town before it had been burned. I also remembered the town that had turned into ashes. And I saw the streets today. I now wish I could have preserved the town of crumbling ruins, fencing it off with a chain. I wished I could have frozen the flames of phosphorus that continued to burn, reminding us that people were dying here. I wish so even to this day. . . .

All wars make people suffer, despite the differences in their gravity. . . . It is not easy to defend peace. The hospital shouldn't be completely renovated, but instead it must be handed down to the generation that did not experience the war. . . . We must make the right decision. For lives are at stake.[17]

In this testimony the narrator's remembrances occur in several time frames. One is the present, the testimonial time in which she is remembering the event after more than forty years. Another time is a decade after the bombing, in which she sees the "white town" of Hiroshima and reminisces about the days before and after its annihilation. The present converges with a more recent past in which the narrator recollects the scene she saw just before the storytelling—a time in which the thoroughly renewed urbanscape of the late-twentieth-century city compelled her to recollect the aftermath of death and destruction.

The narrative proceeds chronologically through the three temporalities, enhancing the remoteness and seeming irretrievability not only of the original moment of loss but even of traces of the loss. In the final instance of recollection, the narrator speaks of wishing that she had preserved "the town of crumbling ruins, fencing it off with a chain" and had "frozen the flames of phosphorus that continued to burn." But because the narrator has already established a stark sense of the progression of time, we are fully aware that the lost reminders of history will forever remain unrecovered and that her wish can never be granted. We are also reminded that because of this loss, the narrator's profound sense of anguish about the friend whom she and others failed to rescue, who was presumably consumed in the flames that swept the city, and her mourning for all the unnamed who huddled for help only to be burned to ashes in the hospital's courtyard can never be resolved.

A number of testimonial accounts of the atomic destruction are filled with similar agony over the loss of reminders of the lost. They include tormenting recollections of the moment when the narrators themselves destroyed what little was left to testify to the bombing. These testimonies describe, for example, the scene of a mother cremating her daughter's body—a corpse found after a long, frantic search.

The novelist Yamaguchi Yūko's unfinished short story "Haha no honō" ("Mother's Flame") is perhaps one of the most powerful illustrations of the anguish of such survivors. Yamaguchi was a frequent contributor to the literary journal *Rivers of Hiroshima*, which I will discuss in chapter 6. She was also centrally involved in publicizing the concerns of the *hibaku nisei*—the children of the survivors. Yuka, the young girl who narrates "Mother's Flame," somehow manages to identify her still-living parents among the corpses in the Red Cross Hospital's courtyard. Both are severely wounded and they soon die. First, someone cremates her father's body, along with twelve other bodies. Yuka memorizes the exact location where it had been put down, "third from the right front," so that she can later collect his bones. The following morning, Yuka sees that her mother has stopped breathing. She obsessively concentrates on a single thought: "I must cremate her; cremate her as soon as possible." With the help of a nurse, Yuka brings her mother's body again out into the courtyard, determined to cremate the body on her own. After a few frustrating attempts, she finally succeeds in lighting the pieces of wood covering her mother's body. Yuka is then abruptly engulfed by the flame.

> That moment, she saw both of her mother's arms extend upward and rend the air. Yuka jumped away and flew from the flame, screaming incomprehensibly.
> "Was it a tremendous mistake to cremate mother?" Suddenly, the thought filled her head. Yet when her burning mother reached out her hands, as if appealing for something, and while the gusty flames chased after her, her feet came to a halt. "I must think. Everything from the beginning, I must think," Yuka murmured, her brow perspiring as she headed back toward her mother's flame.[18]

"Mother's Flame," originally published in *Genbaku to bungaku,* was reprinted in 1992 in an anthology that came out in conjunction with the preservation campaign for the Red Cross Hospital. The anthology's publication, which brought back into circulation this piece and several other survivors' testimonial accounts, again illustrates how in attempting to vanquish dark memories from the cityspace, the dominant political and economic forces ironically stimulated the multiplication and reestablishment of numerous sites of storytelling.[19] Yamaguchi's piece also helps us understand why many individuals in the preservationist campaigns, such as Kataoka and Kuboura, use corporeal analogies in discussing the ruins and remains. For the survivors, the act of relocating the relics into museum showcases signaled that their own belated deaths had finally arrived—their precarious existences of over half a century had effectively and abruptly been brought to an end.

The most distinctive feature of the story is the sudden shift in the narrative's pace in the final scene described above. From its outset—when Yuka and her friend part as they dauntlessly enter the city in search of their families—to the "successful" torching of her mother's body, the protagonist works incessantly to expedite her numerous duties. She is driven to accomplish tasks as quickly as possible, one after another. Once she identifies her mother, she hurriedly locates an empty bed on which to lay her down. Immediately, she takes off to find her father and tumbles over a corpse. She dashes out to fetch water to quench her father's thirst for the last time. As she witnesses her father pass away, she manages to subdue her overwhelming feelings of sadness.

Perhaps the only break in the narrative's rush occurs during the night of the father's cremation. Yuka finds momentary relief in the dark as she overhears a conversation between two men who describe scenes in the city without feeling. Yet even this pause is cut short by the unexpected arrival of a troop of Red Cross nurses from a nearby prefecture, whose presence is captured only through their regimented footsteps, their sanitary aroma, and their "ordinary and brisk voices," which are startlingly out of place. Thus the abrupt slowdown at the end of the story puts the closing moment of contemplation into vivid contrast with what appear to be the almost automatic reactions and swift decisions that have preceded it.

In the context of the preservationist campaign of the late 1980s and early 1990s, Yuka's repentance for her "tremendous mistake" resonates profoundly with Kataoka's call to make "the right decision." They both questioned the conventional inclination to move forward, resisting the habitual and what might be called "precipitous" time. They compelled listeners to pause momentarily, to think, in Yuka's words, "everything from the beginning." Making readers keenly aware that the moment of original loss is already eternally irretrievable, the "mother's flame," like Kataoka's burning phosphorous, calls for vigilance against the imminent threat of final loss, the ultimate forgetting of that which has been lost.

Because they have established the linear progression of time, both Kataoka's and Yamaguchi's testimonies ultimately point to the future. But this future, unlike that of the sixty-one-year-old letter writer, is not envisioned with unquestioned optimism. Their narratives refuse to attribute to the dead any utilitarian value and status in contributing to society's triumphant advance. Instead, the victims in their narratives remain arrested in time. They caution readers to guard against an uncritical optimism about progress, efficiency, and instrumentality. At the same time, such a narrative intimates that the development and use of nuclear bombs were the logical consequence of the impetuous quest for "progress" in the name of science and democracy. Like Benjamin's angel of history, even while these storytellers are carried forward in time, their gaze is directed to the past and its accumulating debris.[20] Yet their nostalgia, produced by the modern perception of history, here becomes critically politicized.

· · ·

The dissipation of the ruins portends the total annihilation of memory, so that in the future even reminders of our own existence might have no sites in which to reside, no traces from which to be remembered.

Those participating in the preservation efforts shared the painful sense of witnessing the very process of such secondary loss. On the one hand, that anxiety intensified their desire to affirm the original historical moment. Such a desire, of course, is itself highly problematic. When the realness of the past is reified, we find it more difficult to appreciate these icons of destruction as products of historical and material processes, thus making it in turn less likely that we will consider crucial questions regarding the production of knowledge (i.e., how the original historical past comes to be known to us).

On the other hand, and perhaps more important, many preservationists also understood that the loss of the ruins meant the ultimate erasure of clues through which one might be invited to think everything from the beginning, to reflect critically on how the present is situated vis-à-vis its history. The ruins in this sense offer a discursive space of remorse and reflection. At these resurrected sites of storytelling, one could begin to ask how the original loss was produced, if in fact the loss was inevitable, and what is at stake in remembering and forgetting the past. As a space of criticism, the ruins, together with other narrative spaces for the dead, question the automatism of historical progress. The fight against demolition was waged precisely over the critical nature of the knowledge produced at the atomic ruins; in some cases its production was contained or dissipated, in other cases successfully maintained or intensified.

In closing part 1, I would like to recall how critical reflection on the past and present is intimately linked to the ways in which the remembering of the dead constitutes politics. The *hibakusha* poet Kurihara Sadako, for instance, saw nothing but gluttony and greed in the promotion of tourism and other related urban renewal projects. In one of the works she sent to a local newspaper bureau, Kurihara likened monetary profit and affluence to the indulgences of a "gourmand" who functioned as an amnesic mega-machine. Overindulgence obliterates the days of agony—including the battle of Okinawa and Hiroshima's 6 August— that she sees as the outcome set by the course of the nation's prewar history. Kurihara ironically appropriates the epigraph inscribed on the Peace Memorial Park's central memorial. In contrast to the original, which pleads, "Please rest in peace / for we shall not repeat the mistake,"[21] her piece instead ends by summoning the souls of the dead:

O deceased
do not rest in peace.
. . . .

You must perturb and awaken
the avaricious living dead
The first evil
may have been a mistake
but the second is a treachery
Faithfulness to the dead
we shall not forget.[22]

Kurihara's reproachful poem seeks to humble the living by reminding us that the means of remembrance we currently have available will
never comfort the dead. It draws a parallel between the insolence of believing that the dead souls can somehow be tamed and society's arrogant sense of material fulfillment in the present. The dead, whose final
consolation is forever deferred, open a void that can never be filled—
an abyss that creates a sense of insufficiency and inadequacy about the
present. The desire to appease the dead rests on self-affirming forgetfulness; conversely, reminders of the restless dead, unable ever to be fully
conciliated, prevent such self-contentment. Part 2 further explores the
spatial and temporal politics of memories by examining the testimonial
practices of Hiroshima's survivors. In its two chapters, we will consider
how, as in Kurihara's poem, the narratives of and for the dead have become central to struggles over the politics of knowledge, over the ways
in which we remember the past.

PART TWO

Storytellers

CHAPTER 3

On Testimonial Practices

Read dialectically, narratives indicate that language and
discourse do affect human life in determining ways, ways
that are themselves shaped by social history. Giving rise
to questions concerning language itself, the sovereignty
of our identity, and the laws that govern our behavior, they
reveal the heterogeneous systems that resist the formation
of a unitary base of truth.

> Ramón Saldívar, *Chicano Narrative* (1990)

Former [Holocaust] victims speak of where they are going,
but not in order to unify it with where they have come from.
It would be more honest and accurate, when confronting
their testimony, if we were to pluralize identity and address
the question of multiple identities.

> Lawrence L. Langer,
> *Holocaust Testimonies* (1991)

Narrating one's own experiences of surviving the atomic bomb, whether
in speech, in writing, or in pictorial forms, is inextricably tied to the
constitution of a narrator's subjecthood. During the early postwar years,
the conventional discursive settings that urged people to tell their stories subjected them to the truth paradigms within which they spoke and
produced the narrators of nuclear victimization as *hibakusha;* literally,
"those subjected to the bomb and/or radiation." The identity of a *hibakusha* as a one-dimensional speaking subject was constituted by pri-
oritizing the speaker's ontological relationship to the bomb over his or
her numerous other social relationships and positions. In contrast, the
"testimonial practices" (*shōgen katsudō*) of the 1980s provided these
survivors of Hiroshima with the means with which to intervene in the
institutional processes that had usually interpellated them singularly as
hibakusha.

Chapters 3 and 4 consider the public testimonial practices through which survivors orally represent their memories of the immediate experiences of the day of mass slaughter and their subsequent lives. Through examining their self-conscious explorations to produce a distinctive style of narrativizing from the early 1980s and analyzing how survivors construe their own acts, the two chapters contemplate the nature of knowledge produced through their storytellings.

One does not automatically become a witness (shōgensha) or a storyteller (kataribe) simply by telling personal memories to public audiences. Such self-definition is accompanied by an attempt to critically intervene in given cultural and social contexts. Genbaku Higaisha Shōgen no Tsudoi (the Atom Bomb Victims' Assembly for Witnessing) and Hiroshima o Kataru Kai (the Hiroshima Narrating/Relating Society), the two prominent Hiroshima survivors' associations discussed in this chapter, were both founded between 1983 and 1984. When the survivors assigned themselves the responsibility of conveying their personal memories of Hiroshima's atomic obliteration to the general public, they did so out of a sense of urgency and with a great deal of self-awareness about the act of telling the past. In the process, many of these storytellers have come to question the given discursive arrangements that have structured first-person accounts of the atomic disaster. As we will see, the conventional narratives of Hiroshima and Nagasaki have often established the survivors as speaking subjects, while at the same time subjecting them to the regimes of truth production in national and legal-bureaucratic procedures, in medical and psychiatric investigations, and in the then-powerful oppositional discursive paradigm of the peace and antinuclear movement. One of my tasks here is thus to cast light on the politics of naming: to investigate how the uses of such terms as hibakusha, survivor, or witness/storyteller constitute a contestatory site of interpellations and self-references. The awareness of becoming a witness/storyteller was necessarily linked to the decolonization of the language with which to speak of oneself.

While chapter 3 examines the institutional contexts for testimonial practices and the discursive shifts that began to be recognized especially in the 1980s, chapter 4 considers the implications of the survivors' narrative practices for the overall conditions of knowledge in contemporary society. The quality of knowledge produced in the hibakusha's testimonial engagements is to a great extent determined by the survivors' presence as what, in Jacques Derrida's formulation, might be termed a "trace."[1] By closely following the thoughts and practices of several survivors, chapter 4 delineates the critical dialectics of memory in their narratives that traverse both time and space. In particular, I attend to the tension between the desire for full recuperation—restoration of and identification with the lost collectivity—and the solemn awareness that such a possibility must be eternally deferred. Together the two chapters making up part 2 seek to identify the quality of knowledge that the *hibakusha*'s rememberings and testimonial practices produce textually and transtextually. I begin here by considering some general questions concerning survivors' testimonies, focusing especially on what it means for survivors to convey their memories to public audiences not through written texts or visual images, but primarily in oral form.

SPEAKING THE UNSPEAKABLE

It is fair to say that survivors' testimonial practices have been, in general, received with a great deal of suspicion and ambivalence. Some have interpreted survivors' loquaciousness cynically, and not infrequently I heard unkind remarks concerning the storytellers. It was said, for example, that those who escort tens or even hundreds of visitors on bus trips, who offer guided tours through the Peace Memorial Park while presenting memories of "that day," are little more than tourist guides who sell their stories in exchange for pocket change. Many who have dared to publicly expose their painful memories and display their physical scars and wounds speak of being the targets of such accusations. Moreover, although Hiroshima and Nagasaki testimonies were once deployed as a critical moral component of oppositional politics against Labor Democratic Party–backed attempts to accelerate Japanese remilitarization and to reinstitute patriotic education, in recent years leftists have charged that by narrating their self-victimization, the survivors only help perpetuate the government's suppression of memories about Japan's aggression toward other parts of Asia and the Pacific, before and during the war.

Survivors themselves have been divided. For survivors in the early postwar years, public displays were one of the few means available to inform others of the bombs' harmful effects on human bodies. Yet some survivors have despised those who would thus expose their experiences, believing that the mass media's sensationalized treatment of the survivors' stories trivializes even the experience of nuclear devastation by turning them into commodities. Such critics see publicly representing memories of the bomb as betraying the past moment of deaths and suffering that they alone have witnessed.

Therefore, the survivors' reluctance to speak is often regarded as authentication of the experience. Children of survivors frequently claim that their parents completely suppressed stories of the bomb. A newspaper corporation worker, for instance, remembered that his father, whose entire family—including his first wife and all their children—was killed by the bomb, never uttered a word about the experience during his lifetime. But toward the end of his life, the father began to visit the Peace Memorial Park to offer prayers. The son speculated that his father might have begun to realize that his life was beginning anew after the birth of his first grandchild.[2] The story epitomizes another commonly held idea, that survivors' very ability to talk about the bomb indicates the degree to which they have recovered, psychologically and materially. Similarly, the city official whom I discussed in chapter 1 related that his father, who witnessed the aftermath of the bombing as he was managing the removal of corpses in the city, never once mentioned the bomb. If he had asked, the official said, his father might have spoken about it, but no information had ever been volunteered. Those who really suffered cannot talk about it, he often remarked in my conversations with him, for if you knew the real experience of the nuclear annihilation, you would not even wish to recall it. For the official, the truth of the violence lay in the simple repression of traumatic memories.

Although it is tempting to attribute the survivors' silence to a natural human propensity, such a hasty deduction would not adequately explain why, despite such a strongly perceived threat to their authenticity, a number of survivors did begin to talk about their experiences at some point in their lives. Rather than looking to some universal psychological explanation, we need to examine the specific cultural, social, and political forces that condition survivors' conflicting attitudes toward the public sphere. Still-prevailing social prejudices toward *hibakusha* are at least partly to blame for the refusal of many to disclose their identities as survivors, even to this day. Ignorance and lack of data contributed to the suspicion that the survivors' exposure to radiation might lead to hereditary physical problems, including infertility, or that it would affect work productivity. Many even thought that such effects were contagious.[3] Of those who published their eyewitness accounts of the bombing during the immediate postwar years, many later became totally silent because they faced the harsh reality of discrimination against survivors when they sought employment or marriage partners. Discrimination also explains why many survivors only began to publicly testify to their bombing experience after passing the stages of their lives at which such sanctions might apply, waiting until retirement or the marriage of their youngest child.

Moreover, when claims about the incommunicability of the experience shift from the individual level of coping with remembering and forgetting to universal generalizations regarding the authenticity of memory and the essential meaning of survival, they begin to repress and control heterogeneous voices and contestatory forms of memory. For instance, as we saw in chapter 1, urban redevelopers, who are among the local power elites, tend to be skeptical about survivors whose protests of urban renewal projects and tourism plans appear in the media. They also fear that survivors' storytellings have harmed the city's image by continuing to promote one-dimensional and politicized images of the city's past and present. These survivors, they suspect, keep on speaking to the public about their past not so much because they genuinely believe that their storytellings can somehow deter the further use of nuclear weapons but because they wish to further partisan political interests. These redevelopers believe that those who "really know the bomb" would not be able to talk about it so openly.

Given the intertwining of such elements, it would be hard to overstate the difficulty that many survivors have in "talking about" their experiences. On many occasions, I was reminded by survivors and nonsurvivors alike that even after nearly half a century no more than a small scattering of the over 370,000 survivors who witnessed the Hiroshima and Nagasaki nuclear atrocities have openly voiced their survival memories.[4] In that context, and contrary to the already noted skepticism about the survivors' talkativeness, those who find significance in remembering the Hiroshima atrocity have seen the breaking of silence as an extremely courageous act.

Most storytellers are acutely aware of the aspersions against them. They are also cognizant that whenever they try to present their experiences in public, they risk their authenticity as survivors. At the same time, survivors themselves are constantly disheartened by the incommunicability of their experiences. Invariably they are disappointed by both visual and written representations of nuclear holocausts, including films and novels such as *The Day After* and *Black Rain*, paintings and photographs, or even documentary films of Hiroshima and Nagasaki. They find the illustrations much too diluted. The horrors depicted in the media, they claim, are nothing like their actual experiences; it is perhaps impossible for those who did not live through it to really know what it was like. Nor are their own attempts to re-present their atom bomb experiences through speeches more successful. They often describe their feelings with the word *munashisa,* or a sense of hollowness and pointlessness. At every utterance, storytellers are confronted with their language's inability to reconstruct the past as they believe they really experienced it. They face the failure of every means of representation they use when trying to accurately convey their experiences. In response to this "empty and blank feeling," to the deep pessimism about communicating what happened to them, many survivors disregard their "assumed audiences," believing that in so doing they can preclude their representations from falling into the abyss of arbitrary interpretations. For those to whom writing is a familiar everyday practice, the crisis of representation is often circumvented by a process of bracketing, severing communication from remembering.

Several methods are thought to be able to prevent arbitrary appropriations of meaning. It is not uncommon for survivors to write about their recollections, even as they feel reluctant and often apprehensive about speaking. "I would have wished to talk to someone [about the bomb]," Takenouchi Taeko wrote to the editors of the local newspaper readers' column, "but I never had enough courage. Putting down words would only reveal one-ten-hundredth of what I saw on that day."[5] Yet she decided to break forty-five years of silence and write about her brother. Twelve years old at the time of the bombing, he was then living in a student dormitory in order to attend a junior high school in the city; he has never been located. Although Takenouchi had not been able to articulate her memories of the time when she and her father, searching for the brother, roamed around the still-burning city in ruins, one day she felt compelled to record her recollections in writing. Still, the retired schoolteacher does not feel bold enough to become a storyteller, to present her memories in spoken words. And those who try to speak may stop. I learned of one such man through a medical caseworker's report.[6] Once, after testifying at a political meeting for peace activists, he was left with "empty and blank feelings": the audience appeared to be envisioning "something completely different" even as they listened to his testimony. Ever since then, he has preferred writing to speaking in presenting his experience. His story effectively captures the feelings of many survivors who obstinately keep silent, but who also explore other means of representation that they believe will allow the wholeness of their experiences to be retained.

Pictorialization of memories is also sometimes thought to split the process of remembering from assuming an audience. Between 1974 and 1975, the Hiroshima branch of the Japan Broadcasting Corporation collected over 2,000 drawings from those who witnessed the bombing. Many of those who sent in the drawings were ordinary citizens who had never painted anything substantial or tried to share their bomb experiences. Each drawing captured a particular site of memory, such as the red flares of city fires, a raft filled with the wounded, a blue white flame burning on a hand, or a burned mother trying to breast-feed her dead child. Often there were explanations scribbled on the drawings, which tended to be brief and to describe only the particular scene.

Beneath this pervasive reluctance to present memories in spoken language lies a feeling that many survivors seem to share: that to retain the authenticity of the original experience they must preclude the arbitrary interpretations of willful audiences. The gap between their own memories and those in the minds of listeners leads these survivors to trust the written medium, while refusing to speak about the bomb. From the survivor's point of view, writing limits the process of memorialization to the relation between the individual and her or his own past moment, to the dialogue between those who remember and the remembered event. By contrast, the survivors who engage in oral testimonial practices as witnesses or storytellers may be thought of as those who have come to terms with audience intervention in the process of remembrance. By casting themselves in narrative performances before haphazard and skeptical audiences, storytellers make the communicative performance itself a higher priority than the authenticity of original meanings. Hiroshima's storytellers are perhaps most acutely aware of a reality in which, as Derrida has said of total nuclear war, to most of us the catastrophe "is for the time being a fable, that is, something one can only talk about."[7]

In this light, the storytellers' insistence on the criticalness of conveying the moment "as it really was" (*arinomama ni*), or the emphasis on "facts" (*jijitsu*), should not be read too literally. To be sure, a vast number of examples indicate how elements in the ideology of modern historical representation sustain the survivors' understanding of their own acts of testifying. They emphasize, for instance, the need to present, as witnesses, the "facts of victimization" (*higai no jijitsu*) or the "actual conditions of the atom bombing" (*hibaku no jissō*). The accumulation and dissemination of this objective knowledge, many trust, will inform future generations of the imminent threat of nuclear disaster and help prevent an even greater catastrophe from occurring. The question of the ideology of realist representation and the Enlightenment idea of knowledge inherent in Hiroshima's testimonial discourse will be discussed further in the next chapter. What here needs to be emphasized in discussing the *hibakusha*'s testimonial practices is that the claims for mimesis are in constant tension with a keen awareness about the incommunicability of the past.

Whether they choose to write or to speak, the survivors must confront the fact that their witnessing of Hiroshima's obliteration can never be reconstructed or conveyed in its original form. Indeed, that the storytellers have survived that moment of destruction to speak about it in the present tense, as if it were happening now, paradoxically underwrites an absence: the atomic obliteration is no longer present in its immediacy and fullness at the storytelling scene. When the survivors admit that "putting [the memory] into words would turn it into a lie," they are acknowledging that their storytellings in effect refer to the absence of the original. Furthermore, that the stories prompt references to "something completely different" in the minds of the audience also speaks to their allegorical nature. The meanings of the survivors' texts can never be agreed on; rather, they constitute an infinite chain of signification. For the survivors as authors and narrators, it is a truism that the language with which they reconstitute the remembered event does not guarantee shared referents among audiences. They understand all too well that in the narrative process signifiers cannot be self-evident. In other words, survivors' testimonial practices posit an ever-deferred nonidentity among meanings, representations, and the original historical moment.

NAMING THE TESTIMONIAL SUBJECTS

Narratives concerning the atomic bombings of Hiroshima and Nagasaki are not nearly as suppressed or marginalized as those in oppositional politics often lead us to believe. The enormity of the ghastly destruction of course makes easy recollection impossible, as even the most experienced storytellers claim. Continuing prejudice and discrimination against *hibakusha*, moreover, discourage survivors from publicizing their witnessed accounts. Yet despite such intense suppression at the emotional level and the stark reality of the survivors' socioeconomic peripheralization, settings that encourage narrating about the nuclear disaster have always existed and continue to multiply.

With regard to the transformation of confessional practices concerning sexuality in nineteenth century bourgeois society, Michel Foucault observed that "the agency of domination does not reside in the one who speaks (for it is he who is constrained), but in the one who listens and says nothing; not in the one who knows and answers, but in the one who questions and is not supposed to know. And this discourse of truth finally takes effect, not in the one who receives it, but in the one from whom it is wrested."[8] The speaking subject is thus always doubly constituted as both the agent of speech and as one who is subjected to a discursive paradigm that encourages rather than suppresses utterance. In examining the testimonial practices on the nuclear apocalypse, we must likewise be attentive to their duality: precisely at the moment when memories are recollected and told, and when the act of telling reinforces the narrator's position of power, such utterances are authorized and encouraged by existing discursive and institutional apparatuses.

Primary examples of how this dual process affects the *hibakusha* can be found in the application procedures for their health certificates, their *hibakusha kenkō techō*. Since 1957, through the Law Concerning Medical Care for Victims of the Atomic Bombs (Genshi Bakudan Hibakusha no Iryō nado ni Kansuru Hōritsu), the Japanese government has provided special medical compensation for the survivors of Hiroshima and Nagasaki. In June the city of Hiroshima started to offer *hibakusha* health certificates; by the end of that year over 70,000 certified survivors were considered eligible for the free medical care given to those exhibiting illnesses that the Ministry of Welfare recognizes as resulting directly or indirectly from the bomb's effects. In 1968, an additional Law Concerning Special Measures for the Victims of the Atomic Bombs (Genshibakudan Hibakusha ni taisuru Tokubetsu Sochi ni Kansuru Hōritsu) legislated supplemental medical and social welfare benefits. Together, these two laws, referred to as the "two atom bomb laws" (*genbaku nihō*), have constituted the governmental remedies available for survivors.[9] In order to obtain the certificate, a survivor needs to provide documentation proving his or her presence at a specific location within the city between 6 and 20 August. If such documentation is unavailable, one must offer either a firsthand account or the testimony of another that can prove that the applicant was present in the city at the time of the bombing. Defined as "a type of certificate that verifies that the said individual is a survivor of the atomic bomb,"[10] it legally authorizes the individuals' atomic bomb experiences.

This institutionalized medico-legal procedure determined to a great extent the style of narrativization that atom bomb memories later took.

Because it measured damage by calculating spatial and temporal proximity to the location and the moment of explosion, classifying individual survivors accordingly, survivors' accounts also tended to be saturated with exact figures and scientific terms. References to precise and
detailed data on the number of casualties, the temperature of heat rays,
the strength of the atomic blast, and the height of the bomb's explosion helped fashion survivors' accounts, translating the catastrophe into
measurable and calculable damages. The city's spatial configuration also
came to be narrativized through images of concentric circles radiating
from the hypocenter, a spatial cognition that I will discuss at greater
length in the following chapter. Damages are calculated not against the
numerous variable circumstances in which individuals found themselves
at the time of the bombing. Instead, they are assessed by the single standard of distance from the hypocenter.

The medical and legal discourse inserted into the survivors' accounts
an external authority that dissected and inspected their encounters with
the bomb. At the same time, it subjected their narratives to the scrutiny
of bureaucratic procedures. This medico-legalization of the atom bomb
experiences thus turned an individual survivor's testimony into a fragmentary account in need of identification and verification by an external institutional authority. Whether conscious of it or not, the survivors became alienated from their pasts, as whatever evidence they
supplied for their own experiences was surpassed by externalized and
objectified criteria. In psychoanalytic interpretation—as in Foucault's
treatment of sexual confession—the externalization of authority became
even more thorough as clinical experts were trusted to discern and label the psychological trauma that remained unnoticed by the individual
survivors themselves.

Reactions to this process of alienation have taken two forms. One,
which stemmed from the desire to restore wholeness and aura to the
original moment of destruction, I will discuss in detail in the next chapter. The other, which emerged out of collective efforts to reestablish the
integrity and autonomy of individual survivors, is especially notable
within the context of the discursive transfigurations of the 1980s on
which we are focusing here.

The "life history survey" (seikatsushi chōsa) project, which actually
began in the 1970s, was especially significant in this regard. Advocated
initially by the sociologist Ishida Tadashi, this project was premised on
the notion that the specific life experience of a particular individual can

never be fully reproduced.[11] Nor can it be interchanged with the experience of another individual. The project also was aimed at nurturing the survivors' abilities to relativize their own situations by helping them understand how the hardship and struggles they experienced as *hibakusha* were caused partly by external social and political conditions. As a Marxist humanist literary convention, not unlike that of an earlier life history composition movement (the *seikatsu tsuzuri kata undō*), this procedure had the objective of establishing the individual survivor as an autonomous and self-conscious political subject, who could rationally grasp and then act on the environment. Also, it was hoped that by narrating their accounts of "the atom bomb experiences" the narrators/survivors would constitute themselves as subjects and objects of the knowledge that they produced. The survivors' audiences—which might include counselors, journalists, researchers, and the public at large— were no longer considered authoritative interpreters. Instead they were reduced to the status of listeners, primarily receptive yet also interactively eliciting information, who might aid the survivors in coming to self-consciousness.[12]

But the narrating of an entire life course, whether in writing or in speech, contains another contradictory process. On the one hand, it constitutes the survivors as politically aware *hibakusha,* subjects bestowed with the power to possess and control their experiences. On the other hand, it inevitably leads to the awareness that what has been referred to as "the atom bomb experiences" (*hibaku taiken*) can be grasped in a meaningful way only if they are construed vis-à-vis each individual survivor's "personal life history" (*jinbunshi*)—a life history that obviously extended both prior to and after the bomb. I will return later to the question of how these autobiographical efforts are related to other changes of the 1980s; suffice it to note here that once grasped in its processual historicity, a life story resists inscription into a totalized experience that can be remembered singularly from the unified subject position of the *hibakusha.*

At the same time that the medico-legal discursive processes interpellated them as *hibakusha,* these individuals came to possess an awareness of themselves as autonomous, integrated political subjects; and they in turn constituted themselves as effective actors in the postwar social and political arena. As subjects marked with a common desire and political will, these *hibakusha,* thus constituted, were able to organize themselves into a consistent collectivity; this primarily took the form of interest groups, including the Japan Confederation Hibakusha Organizations (Nihon Gensuibaku Higaisha Dantai Kyōgikai, or Nihon Hidankyō), which was founded in 1956. Some members of Hidankyō also sought legislative measures to grant governmental compensation and formal recognition of the state's responsibility for the nuclear destruction. Though often falling far short of survivors' demands, these administrative and legislative relief measures would not have materialized had it not been for the identity politics pursued in concert by uniformly identified political subjects. The testimonial subjects, therefore, were at once empowered by, and subjected to, the regime of truths within which they spoke.

Postwar antinuclear discourse should also be mentioned in this regard. During the early stage of development of the World Conference against the A- and H-Bombs (Gensuibaku Kinshi Sekai Taikai, or the Gensuikin Conference), testimonial narratives of the Hiroshima atrocity were primarily delivered to the public as formal accounts at official political gatherings. By conveying the atrociousness and horror of the new destructive weapon, the survivors' authoritative accounts were instrumental in promoting the antinuclear campaign. At mass rallies and world conferences, survivors have appeared on stage to testify, warning against further nuclear threats. While the medico-legal discourse authorized the truthfulness of their accounts, antinuclear movements constituted the survivors as autonomous and coherent political subjects whose desire and will were yet again absorbed into a unitary political agenda: in this case, the total abolition of all nuclear weapons. The growth of these social movements opened a discursive channel through which survivors might speak, even as they were being produced exclusively as *hibakusha*.

In antinuclear campaigns, survivors' testimonial accounts have tended to be conflated with the specific political end of preventing future nuclear devastation.[13] Through their involvement in oppositional politics, the survivors' subjectivities—their ideas concerning the reasons for existence and suffering, the objectives of life and death, the meanings of survival, and the purpose of their narrative practices—also came to be contained by their identity as *hibakusha*. Their self-fulfillment and worldly satisfactions, it was understood, derived exclusively from the realization of world peace and the total ban on nuclear weaponry. We should remember (as the introduction made clear) that the development of antinuclear discourse, of which the survivors' testimonies are a crucial component, has been intertwined with the unfolding of postwar discourses on Japanese nationhood.

The survivors' subsequent narrative practices from the late 1970s and early 1980s contested the notion of the *hibakusha*'s subjecthood as it had thus far been universally and uniformly constructed in political, medicolegal, and national discourses. As we will see, members of such associations as Kataru Kai and Tsudoi did not understand their identification as *hibakusha* to be either exhaustive or uniform. Rather, they have resisted representations that constantly try to confine individual subjectivities to the single category of *hibakusha*—all remembering, thinking, feeling, and acting consistently, without contradictions.

Narrating one's memories of the bomb is by no means the practice of autonomous individuals who can transcend the conditions of power. The act of telling and thereby becoming the subject of speech has always been enmeshed in the powerful discursive configurations of medicolegal institutions, postwar national narratives, social movements, and other oppositional politics (such as antinuclear campaigns). It is certainly critical to keep this warning in mind when observing the survivors' testimonial practices, along with the accompanying process of their subjectification and individuation as narrators, that developed after the late 1970s. But even more important is acknowledging that this Foucaultian process of subjectification is never accomplished within a singular nexus of power. Rather, the subjects are almost always constituted by multiple, contradictory, and discrepant social, economic, and cultural relations. The establishment of the "witness" or "storyteller" category did not decenter the dominant *hibakusha* identity altogether. However, the epistemological break that became increasingly evident during the 1980s helped sustain the gaps and slippages between what constituted the narrators/survivors as *hibakusha,* on the one hand, and other intersecting and competing structural forces that have been equally crucial in constituting the multiple dimensions of subjecthood, on the other.

SURVIVORS, *HIBAKUSHA, SHŌGENSHA:* MULTIPLE SUBJECTIVITIES

Local researchers and critics have observed that the period around 1980 marked a significant transformation in how Hiroshima and Nagasaki survivors engaged with the public sphere. They note in particular the situation in 1982—the escalating nuclear crisis and a growing sense of the imminence of destruction—that drove "both those taciturn survivors and the apathetic generations that did not experience wars to gradually speak out."[14] The sheer number of publications pertaining to the survivors' firsthand atom bomb experiences also soared in 1982.[15] These included survivors' memoirs and monographs on their life stories, as well as journals and magazines that featured survivors' recollections. Even those survivors who had until then been most determined in their silence over the past decades began to share their memories with the public, in one way or another, around that time.

I do not mean to single out a limited number of specific events at a particular time that resulted in drastic changes in survivors' attitudes and self-awareness. Nor am I suggesting that the forms and contents of orally narrativized memories in the 1980s and later had no features similar to earlier oral accounts. But undeniably a number of noteworthy factors came together in the 1980s to have a decisive impact upon the survivors' relationship to the general society. Indeed, we will see that the shift they caused was not merely a quantitative one but, much more important, an epistemic or paradigmatic transition. These transformative events and activities were yet another aspect of the overarching changes in local mediations of the nation and capital that we have already observed in chapter 1, involving the rearticulation of Hiroshima's regional identity and urban memoryscape.

In order to grasp the social milieu of the early 1980s, we must note several events that occurred in the international political arena. In May 1978, the Special Session on Disarmament (SSDI) opened at the United Nations General Assembly in New York; for the first time, members explicitly acknowledged the United Nations' commitment to global disarmament and to the search for concrete measures to end the nuclear arms race. Over three hundred delegates from Japan, including Korean resident alien survivors, attended and brought with them over 18 million signatures of those demanding a total ban on nuclear weapons. The meeting concluded in June by adopting a resolution that the United Nations reorganize the Geneva Committee on Disarmament (renamed the "Conference" after 1984) in order to facilitate the participation of non-nuclear nations in decision making and observe the annual "UN Disarmament Week" on the anniversary of the organization's founding on 24 October. This occasion provided an international stage on which survivors could openly speak as *hibakusha* about the devastation of Hiroshima and Nagasaki that they had witnessed. Pope John Paul II's visit to Hiroshima in 1981 also enhanced the international visibility of *hibakusha*. In his forthright antiwar, antinuclear message, presented in nine different languages, John Paul II generalized the meaning of the atom bomb experience within the context of Christian humanism: "War is the work of man. War is destruction of human life. War is death. Nowhere do these truths impose themselves upon us more forcefully than in this city of Hiroshima, at this Peace Memorial."[16]

In 1982, in part encouraged by the SSDI and in part anticipating the second United Nation's Special Session on Disarmament (SSDII), which was to be held in June, various special reports related to peace and antinuclear issues began to appear in both visual and print media.[17] In January some three hundred literary celebrities, including Oe Kenzaburo, Oda Makoto, and Ibuse Masuji, issued a manifesto in Tokyo, demanding that the Japanese government follow the three antinuclear principles: not to produce, possess, or bring in nuclear weapons. Responding to this movement in the nation's cultural center, Hiroshima literati such as Kurihara Sadako, schoolteachers, and amateur writers belonging to local literary circles also delivered their own antinuclear statement in the following month.[18]

This internationally and nationally heightened awareness about the threat of nuclear disaster culminated locally in a mass antinuclear rally that mobilized over 200,000 participants. The '82 Hiroshima Action for Peace (82 nen Heiwa no tame no Hiroshima kōdō), held on 21 March, was initiated by the Hiroshima Prefectural Labor Conference (Hiroshima-ken Rōdō Kaigi), the main organizational body of the Gensuikin movement. It was also much inspired by the antinuclear uproar in Europe of the previous year that had included a mass rally of 300,000 people in what was then West Germany, a 200,000-person antinuclear protest in London, and many other demonstrations and political gatherings. As in the earlier antinuclear actions, the primary organizer of the 21 March Hiroshima rally was again the union-based peace organization. Yet the rally succeeded in mobilizing unconventional participants, such as nonunionized workers and schoolteachers, retired salarymen, housewives, and high school and college students. Some had faithfully attended mass rallies as a form of political protest since the violent marches of the 1960s, and others had never before taken part in any form of collective public demonstration. The 21 March Hiroshima rally recruited into the public sphere a normally anonymous sector of society, the so-called grass roots.

Urgent domestic issues also lay behind the 1982 movement's far-reaching involvement in peace, antinuclear, and antiwar issues. Conservative politicians and high-ranking bureaucrats had become unabashedly vocal in pursuing their antidemocratic and nationalistic agenda. The legalization of the custom of naming eras by emperors' reigns (*gengō hōseika*), which some understood as a reversion to the emperor-centered nationalism of the prewar and wartime years, passed the Diet in 1979. In 1981 Edwin O. Reischauer, the former ambassador to Japan, publicly revealed that an oral agreement between the U.S. officials and LDP-led government at the time of the 1960 signing of the U.S.-Japan Treaty allowed U.S. naval vessels carrying nuclear warheads to make port calls, in disregard of Japan's antinuclear principle. Concerns about threats to the separation of church and state also intensified in the late 1970s with the growing frequency of official visits of LDP Diet members to Yasukuni Shrine, where the war dead have been enshrined in Shinto form. By the time that Prime Minister Nakasone Yasuhiro and his cabinet members went in 1985, his advisory commission had determined that such official visits to Yasukuni were constitutional. Furthermore, the LDP cabinet members' and the Ministry of Education's censorship of school textbooks also escalated as the state continued its intervention in the production of historical truths. The well-publicized 1982 "textbook controversy" epitomized the historical revisionism contrived by the conservative elite. The shift in the survivors' relationship to society's remembering and forgetting of the nation's past was in part generated by their reaction to such overall changes in the domestic political milieu.

The increasing emphasis on nationalist values in formal educational settings fostered an unmistakable sense of urgency among liberal and progressive educators. Many *hibakusha* also felt that their memories of wartime violence were being overshadowed by the increasing celebration of national power. As a result, a growing number of schools and local municipal communities arranged "peace study" tours to Hiroshima. The number of school excursions to Hiroshima, during which survivors guide students on memorial tours and offer their testimonies, reached a peak in the mid-1980s. While there had been a number of union-based avenues for making contact with Hiroshima's survivors in the past, a more formal channel was established in 1982 when a former junior high school teacher took early retirement to devote himself to helping schools in the Tokyo metropolitan area organize graduation trips to Hiroshima.

Through their regular visits to Hiroshima, these schools gradually established intimate relations with individual survivors.[19]

In examining the shift in survivors' self-perceptions and attitudes, a consideration of changes in the life cycle of *hibakusha* is equally crucial. As the average age of the entire *hibakusha* population reached into the sixties during this period, the lifestyles of the majority of them also changed: they entered into different life stages. Their everyday lives were no longer taken up by corporate work, homemaking, and child rearing but began to be shaped by retirement from work, by their children's financial independence, and sometimes by becoming grandparents. For many survivors, release from organizationally assigned roles was experienced as a loss of purpose in life; but it was sometimes an opportunity to reevaluate the lives they had led up to that point. The task of grandparenting also forced many survivors to imagine far into the futures of successive generations, bringing a sense of new responsibilities. At the same time, some began to feel closer to the past moment as their families, colleagues, and former classmates—with whom they had survived the disaster and had shared postwar hardships—began to die in greater numbers. Reaching what was called "cancer age" (*gan nenrei*),[20] many survivors inevitably entered the new life stage with anxieties about sudden and imminent death. This renewed sensitivity toward death, as discussed further in chapter 4, also pushed some survivors to a greater sense of responsibility to remember and memorialize the victims of the original destruction.

Thus, during the 1980s survivors' self-perceptions and identity as *hibakusha* became both more firm and more diverse. On the one hand, the transnationally shared awareness about the threat of total nuclear war certainly contributed to the increasing visibility and legitimation of survivors speaking as *hibakusha*. The numerous antinuclear rallies and peace conferences held throughout the world multiplied the opportunities for the survivors to appear as witnesses of the world's first nuclear attack. On the other hand, *hibakusha* became increasingly aware that even those who had once shared that intense memory do not lead identical lives. Moreover, diversification of the ways by which outsiders might connect with survivors also allowed different dimensions of the *hibakusha*'s lives to be heard. The schoolteachers who planned trips to Hiroshima sought to meet *hibakusha*, not only because they had survived the bomb and spoke out against the A- and H-bombs but also because the teachers hoped to introduce students to individuals with alternative

views about the nation's peace and prosperity, who worked against social stereotypes and prejudices. The significance of the survivors' identity as "witnesses" or "storytellers" should be understood within these
various contexts.

In a 1989 newspaper interview, Kikkawa Ikimi spoke of her late husband, who had been known through the U.S. media as "the first atom
bomb [victim]" (*genbaku ichigō*): "He was willfully (*katteni*) labeled by
others as 'the first atom bomb [victim]' and he continued to bear the
atom bomb throughout his life. I believe he wanted others to know the
man who was not 'the first atom bomb [victim].'"[21] Kikkawa Kiyoshi,
portrayed as a souvenir store owner in Robert Jay Lifton's work, was
one of the founders of an organization that reflected and represented the
specific problems faced by *hibakusha*. Ikimi, also a survivor, recalled that
in the course of editing Kiyoshi's autobiographical manuscript in the
early 1980s, a publisher had completely omitted the portion that described the half of his life prior to the bomb. Ikimi's comments about
her husband's frustrations at the time are especially revealing of the
ways in which the dominant, mass media discourse, like the other institutional processes already mentioned, has both encouraged and con-
stricted survivors' personal narratives.

At about the same time that Kikkawa Kiyoshi's negotiations with the
publisher were taking place, two associations were established in Hiroshima: Kataru Kai and Tsudoi. Although different in many respects, both
shared a sense of urgency to diversify the ways in which survivors might
talk and be heard. This urgency was felt especially acutely by those who
took up storytelling relatively late in their lives. Rather than encouraging survivors to speak of uniformly shared experiences and desires and
discouraging any mention of the multiple dimensions of subjecthood,
the discursive fields shaped by these two associations enabled their members to rearticulate the multiple constituents of their lives and existences.
In other words, their identification as "witnesses" (*shōgensha*) or "storytellers" (*kataribe*) allowed the narrators to articulate and situate their
own subject positions within shifting interactions and overlapping social relations. This process, however, entailed a new understanding about
what, for whom, and why they testify. The founding philosophy and activities of Kataru Kai and Tsudoi reveal how the two associations sought
to intervene in the conventional environments in which the survivors'
narrativizations have taken place.

In the case of Kataru Kai, particularly notable is the refusal of the association to include in its name such common phrases as "*hibakusha*"

or "*hibaku taiken*" (experiences of subjection to the bomb). References to what exactly is being testified or narrated about are kept deliberately ambiguous, while stress is clearly placed on the act of telling—that is, on "narrating" (*kataru*). The alteration in emphasis from "the bomb" or "*hibakusha*" to the act of testifying itself indicates a critical transition in the ways in which survivors have defined and construed their testimonial activities. Kataru Kai's founding philosophy explicitly states that its primary objective is for its members to convey their experiences orally to successive generations. Its four-line inaugural statement can be found on the opening page of a small leaflet introducing its membership (short synopses of individual members' witnessed accounts follow): "This collection of testimonies stands as a proof of our determination to engage in testimonial practices [*shōgen katsudō*], a responsibility of those who survived [*ikinokotta mono*]."[22]

To be sure, the object or the content of its members' storytelling can be inferred from the purposeful use of *katakana* syllabary in writing the word "Hiroshima" in the association's name. As we observed in chapter 1, Hiroshima in *katakana* crystallizes the antinuclear and antiwar values and peace ideals that have evolved out of the city's atomic disaster. Yet the inaugural statement also makes clear that Kataru Kai avoids denoting the ultimate end toward which the stories should be told. The statement underscores the members' conviction that their primary concerns are commitment to and ongoing engagement in testimonial activities—the belief that the act of retelling memories is more central to their present lives than their physical exposure to the bomb. The latter does not automatically render ultimate significance to one's existence. Moreover, because telling *is* an act, "relating" and "witnessing" become nothing less than proof of existence after survival.

The inaugural statement suggests still another important point regarding the politics of naming. In it testimonial engagement is stated as "a responsibility of those who survived." The self-perception of being "one who survived" the historical moment is not simply prior to self-identification as a *hibakusha*; more crucially, to be "one who survived" is to be part of a collective identity that has been imposed on a group of people, even though survival itself can never be shared communally.[23] To be "one who survived" invokes another possibility: one could have been a part of, but was in fact decisively severed from, the collectivity of the dead. The term "victim" (*higaisha*), in contrast, obscures this demarcation between the dead and the living. It is this tension inherent in the collectively occupied yet incommensurable position of being the "one who survived" that determines the nature of the narrative practices and the memory processes that I discuss further in chapter 4.

Likewise, Tsudoi's full name, the Atom Bomb Victims' Assembly for Witnessing (Genbaku Higaisha Shōgen no Tsudoi), highlights who the narrators are but does not indicate the specific content of their testimonies, although certainly that content might be to some extent inferred. More important, as can be seen in its more common name, Assembly of Witnessing (Shōgen no Tsudoi), is the emphasis placed on the situation in which narrating takes place. We should also note that use of such words as *tsudoi* (assembly) or *kataru* (narrate) indicates the members' acute awareness of the presence of communities of listeners. As we will see in the next chapter, it also suggests their willingness to engage in dialogic interactions, which might result in undermining the authority that normally derives from their position within the testimonial hierarchy as narrators.[24]

If anything, however, Tsudoi was perhaps more concerned than Kataru Kai to convey the specificities of the disaster that took place in 1945. Tsudoi was founded in 1984 in affiliation with a medical and social counseling organization. Many of Tsudoi's members joined the group after participating in a one-day commemorative gathering in which they spoke to a public audience of their survival memories. This occasion had been and continues to be held annually by the counseling organization. Open to virtually anyone, the gathering has provided those who visit Hiroshima for the various 6 August ceremonies and conferences with an opportunity to meet the survivors of Hiroshima and to listen to firsthand accounts of that historic moment. The participants are divided into small groups of from ten to fifteen people, who are gathered around one witness. For many visitors, it is their first experience of meeting a *hibakusha;* for some survivors, the first experience of narrating their recollections of that day. Because of Tsudoi's close association with the counseling organization, a therapeutic meaning has been attributed to testifying, although the survivors may be less conscious of this dimension than the caseworkers. The act of telling is believed to function as a crucial means by which survivors can "work out" their suppressed memories as they expose and confront their traumas.

The medical and social workers frequently observe that many survivors live with a powerful blend of strong emotions, including remorse, loneliness, fear, sorrow, guilt, and resentment. Some blame themselves for the loss of their children and other family members, while others continue to feel responsible for the deaths of their classmates, students, and subordinates.[25] Still others remain tormented over the memory of the brief moment in which they believe they put their own survival over that of others. Moreover, many live in constant apprehension of the lingering threat of radiation and of further complications. Because of the delayed effects of radiation, many women who married into conventional patriarchal families especially suffered, for they were not able to fulfill the usual duties of daughters-in-law, such as providing labor, bearing sons, and managing households. Many survivors questioned whether they should even be glad to have survived, given that *hibakusha* suffered financial burdens; discrimination in employment, in marriage, and in other situations; and innumerable other hardships following the bombing. For survivors confronting these everyday problems, the counselors have determined that testimonial activities can be therapeutic. Through recollection in the form of storytelling, they hope, survivors will be able to piece together and find meaningful order in their discrepant thoughts and sentiments.

To be sure, as we have already seen, the nationwide campaign against the nuclear arms race and the reparations movement for *hibakusha* had earlier offered similar storytelling opportunities. The former, especially, was regarded as providing occasions on which survivors might feel fulfilled about their lives and the very fact of survival. A transcendent meaning was often ascribed to *hibakusha* testimonies, which were received by eager crowds as authentic messages from the past, delivering lessons that would save the future of humanity. The well-publicized phrase one survivor exclaimed after having testified in public at the first World Conference against A- and H-Bombs, "I am glad to have survived" (*ikite ite yokatta*), is often construed as indicating that *hibakusha* can find ultimate meaningfulness in their survival only if they realize that their testimonies can help ban nuclear weaponry. And indeed, the survivors' involvement in the nationwide antinuclear campaigns did offer even the most deprived of them a sense of purpose in life after the bomb, and a language with which to articulate their recollections.[26]

Yet the medical and social caseworkers were among the first to directly observe the survivors' disillusionment with the ways in which their witnessed accounts were appropriated by existing institutions. Caseworkers encountered survivors who, afraid of being identified and labeled, obstinately refused to apply for *hibakusha* certificates and receive their benefits. Intimate and frequent contact led, as a matter of course, to many caseworkers becoming acutely aware of inconsistencies in survivors' witnessing of the bomb, in their remembering or not remembering the destructive moment, and in their subsequent lives. They also recognized that the heterogeneous qualities of the survivors' past and present socioeconomic statuses, family situations, political orientations, and subsequent broad life experiences precluded uniform identification of all survivors as simply *hibakusha*.

A closer examination of how Kataru Kai members themselves articulated the significance of their testimonial engagements and their organization further suggests what was at stake as they challenged conventional representations of *hibakusha*. Kataru Kai's 1983 founding was initially prompted when several survivors, who had known each other through the activities of a local literary circle, met with a group of high school students from Osaka who were on a school excursion. A 1984 TV documentary, *Kizuna* (*A Bond*), closely traced the relationships between the survivors and the students that developed over a year. It won the grand prize in the 1985 "Age of Localism Visual Contest," and director Kawara Hirokazu later published a book in which he reflected on making the documentary. He noted that when the group's members decided upon their association's name, "they purposefully avoided the word '*hibaku*' (being exposed to the bomb). In order to narrate their diverse conditions of life (*ikizama*) and to broadly address present nuclear situations, and so forth, the ideographs for '*hibaku*' were too delimiting."[27] Members concurred that narrating the experience of "that day" alone was insufficient. To speak of Hiroshima required more than simply telling what had occurred at the moment of destruction and how they had survived it. Rather, to echo Kawara's emphasis on a particularly significant word used by the members, it was necessary to narrate their *ikizama*—to speak of their struggles, transformations, and lives over the course of the past approximately forty years, as they pursued the meanings of survival. The members thus "relate Hiroshima" in the double sense of the term: through memory work they relate, as they narrate, the moment of destruction to the other dimensions of life that are equally constitutive of them as social beings.

Avoiding the term "atomic bomb" serves to acknowledge that a *hibakusha* is in reality more than just an individual who was once "subjected to the bomb." Kataru Kai thus outwardly proclaims the obvious diversity of its membership. Active members include poets, owners of small shops, retired factory workers, an ex-convict, a retired city council member, university faculty and other schoolteachers, retired factory workers, and homemakers. Individual affiliations with formal political associations also vary: some members support the conservative Liberal Democratic Party, others belong to what used to be called the Japan Socialist Party, while still others insist on disengaging themselves altogether from parliamentary democracy. Some are loyal union members on the left, while others are candidly antagonistic to any kind of progressive movement. The Korean nationals who belong are affiliated with two different political regimes, the People's Republic of Korea and the Republic of Korea. The members' ages at the time of the bombing also vary, from nine years old to late thirties. In other words, it was understood that the ways in which the historical moment takes on significance differ according to individual members' diverse positionings within overlapping and sometimes competing nexuses of structural relations.

Funahashi Yoshie, a historian of European thought, has noticed the same shift—that is, from narrating the historical event of Hiroshima's annihilation to the survivors' lives thereafter—in personal historical writing, or *jibunshi*.[28] Funahashi has been observing *hibakusha*'s testimonial practices through long involvement in survivors' grassroots writing groups, including the award-winning *hibakusha* mothers' association, Yamashita Kai. The preface to a published anthology, *Ikiru: "Hibakusha" no Jibunshi (To Live: "Hibakusha"'s Personal Histories)*, lends credence to her argument.

> In *hibakusha*'s personal histories, we wrote not only about "that day" but also how we have lived through [it]. . . . What in our lives until then was destroyed by the atomic bomb, how our lives were disfigured, and how we have confronted the bomb in our lives thereafter. We wrote about our own appearances and our feelings as we stood motionless on the streets of vast, charred, and open fields, and *how these came to acquire meanings in our irreplaceable and irreducible lives thereafter* [emphasis added].[29]

It might be argued that the notion of *ikizama* and expressions like "our irreplaceable and irreducible lives" before and after the bomb stem from a reaction to the condition I described earlier—namely, the fragmentation, externalization, and alienation of survivors' personal experiences. These terms do indeed reflect the desire to recover experience in its entirety and fullness. Given the modern and postmodern conditions in which knowledge has become alienated from being and is instead relentlessly turned into transportable, reproducible, exchangeable objects, these narrative practices must be understood, at least in part, as an attempt by the storytellers to regain the original and irreproducible aura of their experiences. This longing for totality and singularity has emerged simultaneously with an aspiration to recover the originary moment and the lost collectivity. And that originary moment is often sought in one's imaginary tie to the dead. The next chapter discusses at some length how such developments affect survivors' narrative practices.

To understand the notion of *ikizama,* as well as the multiplicity of subjectivities that the term permits to be articulated in survivors' narratives, it is perhaps crucial to grasp that the term does not refer solely to the range of lifestyles displayed by discrete individuals. Nor is the word used simply to highlight the plural stages of lifeways as conceived of in the conventions of Bildungsroman and other biographical narratives. Again, Funahashi's remarks may serve as a guide to grasping the concept's critical dimension. She points out that *ikizama* has a specific connotation for the generation of people who were accustomed to wartime use of the related term *shini-zama,* which can be translated "manner of dying." Furthermore, commonly used expressions today—such as "*ano zama wa nanda?*" or "what kind of a pathetic state is that?"— demonstrate that the suffix *-zama* tends to be associated with the abject, the pitiable.[30] Similarly, Miyagawa Hiroyuki, a former high school principal who has been involved in a number of citizens' relief efforts for overseas *hibakusha,* stresses the value of precisely the negative and abject images that the term elicits. Miyagawa points out that *ikizama* symbolically summarizes the multiply subordinated positions to which the survivors were often confined and the struggles and challenges that many have confronted, not only at the time of the original atrocity but also during later adversities. Its virtue, Miyagawa emphasizes, lies precisely in its ability to illuminate the structural relations of power—what he refers to as the "sociohistorical" dimensions—that have constituted survivors' lives and subjectivities.[31]

The intellectual shift in survivors' testimonial practices during the 1980s is more easily understood once we realize its affinities with moves made in recent autobiographical manifestos striving to decolonize the language through which subjects are constituted. Especially relevant are challenges that have been made within Euro-American literary and cultural conventions. The departures of the Hiroshima narratives observed here resonate strongly with feminist and postcolonial reassessments of biographic writings. Julia Watson and Sidonie Smith, for instance, argue that recent autobiographical practices of women in minoritized and/or colonized positions challenge and decenter the Western autobiographical conventions that have long presupposed and reproduced the auton-

omous, integrated, and transcendent subject. More generally, the shift
in survivors' narrative practices toward the articulation of multiple subjectivities is closely related to recent developments in Euro-American
feminist theory. Women in primarily minoritized or colonized positions
have criticized mainstream liberal feminism for privileging a singular
and uniform gender identity. In both their analysis and political actions,
they refuse to posit a universal category of womanhood, arguing that
concepts such as "subjecthood" and "identity" are sites of differentiation and displacement that are constituted by heterogeneous and often
contradictory relations of power and structural interpellations. Priori-
tizing the single category of "woman" neglects other relations, such as
race/ethnicity, sexuality, or generation, that are in equally urgent need of
being addressed and redressed.[32] Kataru Kai's explicit acknowledgment
of its members' "diversity" must be understood as part of such global
reformulations of identity and subjecthood.

· · ·

Kikkawa Kiyoshi's disillusionment at being cast as the "first atom bomb
victim," Kataru Kai's founding philosophy, and the hibakusha's autobiographical practices all indicate a profound desire by the narrators of
Hiroshima's catastrophic moment to recuperate the irregularity, incon-
sistency, circularity, and heterogeneity of personal time. Survivors' testimonial practices restore, diverge from, and yet eternally intersect with
the fixed and uniform temporality—6 August 1945—of the established
discursive order of official history.

Unquestionably, the central employment of survivors' narratives evolves
around recollections of that day, and the trauma and victimization brought
about by the atom bomb. Yet the signification process varies according
to the positions of the survivors at different times, and in different contexts. On the one hand, to have "survived" the atom bombing profoundly affected one's life thereafter. The survivors therefore eternally
and uncompromisingly speak as "hibakusha." The existing discursive
arrangements also contribute to making this subjectivity most central.
On the other hand, to speak as "witnesses" or "storytellers" allows the
survivors to narrate the diverse ways in which memories of the catastrophic moment have acquired meanings within the multiple temporalities through which they have been constituted.

The testimonial practices of Toyonaga Keisaburō, a former high
school vice principal who has been instrumental in mobilizing citizen's
efforts to support atom bomb victims now residing in Korea, illustrate

another important dimension of how individuals identify themselves as *hibakusha*. Toyonaga recalls his experience of the bomb at the age of nine. However, his narrative underscores that he had no particular idea about being a *hibakusha* until he encountered a survivor in Korea by chance; he then decided to apply for the *hibakusha* certificate. He believes that his certificate was "bestowed upon him" by Korean survivors. Thus in Toyonaga's narrative, his present subject position as a Japanese survivor is linked to Japan's former colonial subjects, and his social activism—stemming from the experience of being confronted by a stark gap in the conditions that circumscribe the two subjectivities—now impel his remembrances of that day. The memories that Toyonaga recuperated as he began to see the urgency of present crises in turn established his identity as a *hibakusha*, but one that is specifically marked with the privilege of a Japanese resident.

There is yet another important consequence of excluding or deemphasizing signs denoting the single, originary historical event—as Kataru Kai does in its name. Such a move obscures questions regarding the legitimacy of speakers and the authenticity of narrative content. Whether intentionally or not, this obfuscation allows the association's membership to extend beyond those who might congregate around the concerns limited solely to *hibakusha*, or to the immediate witnesses of Hiroshima's atom bombing. It opens up the possibility of inviting listeners to participate in the narrative practices of so-called witnesses or storytellers. Kataru Kai's approval of the inclusion of survivors' children as members is particularly suggestive in this regard. Katō Yōsuke, participating in the group as a survivor's son, does not, of course, have an immediate experience of the bomb. His narrative is not composed of witnessed accounts of that day or the physical problems that the children of some survivors (*hibaku nisei*) suffer as a direct result of the bomb. Rather, it consists of observations about how the experience of massive destruction and death, and the total destruction of the community, have affected his mother's and other family members' postbomb lives. In keeping with Kataru Kai's investment in "the *succession* of storytelling" (*katari tsugu koto*), Katō's testimonial engagements do more than ensure that the next generation is able to talk about the past moment. They also force us to radically rethink the very meaning of "testimony" and its implications for effective cultural critique, a point to which I will return in the next chapter.

While self-identification as "witness" involves the articulation of multiple positionalities that cannot be subsumed under the single category of *hibakusha*, there is another overlapping yet distinct "hibakusha" subjectivity that is represented when the term is written using the *katakana* phonetic system. When written with Chinese ideographs, two characters with different meanings can be used to represent the syllable *baku*, making it possible to indicate the distinct historical circumstances under which *hibakusha* were produced: by subjection to the bomb and by exposure to radiation. But when written with *katakana* phonemes, the term can interpellate individuals doubly, according to the two meanings contained in the sound. "Hibakusha" in *katakana* highlights the commonality of nuclear catastrophes across space and time. It occupies a transnational location that cannot be contained within the singularity of "Japan, the only atom-bombed country." Furthermore, while marking the historical specificity of the two atom bombings, it also represents the location from which an apocalyptic scenario of our postnuclear age, the catastrophic moment, can be narrated: any time and any place. The freeing of stories about atom bomb victimization from a single, specific point, set in the past, has special significance in the politics of contemporary knowledge.

CHAPTER 4

Mnemonic Detours

What science has "established," memoration can modify.
Memoration can make the incomplete (happiness) into
something complete, and the complete (suffering) into
something incomplete. That is theology; but in memoration
we discover the experience (*Erfahrung*) that forbids us to
conceive of history as thoroughly a-theological, even
though we barely dare not attempt to write it according
to literally theological concepts.

> Walter Benjamin, "N: [Re the Theory of Knowledge,
> Theory of Progress]" (1989 [1937–40])

This space protects the weapons of the weak against the
reality of the established order. It also hides them from
the social categories which "make history" because they
dominate it. And whereas historiography recounts in the
past tense the strategies of instituted powers, these
"fabulous" stories offer their audience a repertory of
tactics for future use.

> Michel de Certeau,
> *The Practice of Everyday Life* (1984)

For our very first encounter on 20 March 1989, Numata Suzuko, whose
testimonial practices I discuss in this chapter, designated a meeting place
inside the Peace Memorial Park: a particular parasol tree. I immediately understood why; from the visual and print media, I knew well
that the tree had served her as a kind of totem. A parasol tree had
been growing in the courtyard of the building where Numata worked
at the time of the bombing but it had died in the nuclear blast—or so
it was thought. Yet it miraculously revived several years after the war.
Though scarred and painfully disfigured, it thrives today with its new
growth of leaves and branches. A branch was taken from this original
tree and transplanted in the Peace Park, there to be memorialized as
"the atom-bombed parasol tree" (*hibaku shita aogiri*). In her testimo-

nies, Numata frequently projected her mutilated body and spirit, as well as her rebirth, onto the story of the tree's life history.

At the tree, Numata briefly introduced herself and then proceeded to explain how learning of the tree's resilience and tenacity had saved her life. We then started walking toward the nearby building where most of our conversation would take place. However, rather than head straight toward the main streets, she first guided me through and around the Peace Memorial Park. We briefly walked through the meandering narrow streets to a graveyard behind a small temple. Numata pointed to the tombstones on which the dates of deaths prior to August 1945 were engraved. Many of them were fractured, worn, and discolored; the graves bore clear marks of the atomic blast. Even the dead had not been able to escape the destruction. She then drew my attention to relatively newer gravestones. A number of these were inscribed with the names of family members, which is not unusual for individuals with extended households. But Numata's point lay elsewhere. She noted the narrow range of the dates on the stones: the summer after the nuclear destruction, the next year after that, and so on—almost all of the dates seemed to fall within a few years following 6 August 1945. Numata guided me out of the graveyard and into the bright daylight, onto the main downtown thoroughfares where it became impossible to see the graves that were still only a few meters away.

Numata's short guided tour alerts us to the necessity of being attentive to space when considering *hibakusha*'s testimonial practices. Spatial metaphors of the city have powerfully conditioned both the memories of Hiroshima's atomic obliteration and the rememberers' subjectivities as witnesses. Almost without exception, the survivors' accounts include the distance they were located from the hypocenter, precisely given in meters or kilometers, at the instant of the bomb's explosion. The witnesses' memories are mediated by the visual image of a city map on which the by now familiar concentric circles, radiating outward and measuring distance from the hypocenter, have been superimposed. Since the witnesses' utterances were encouraged within such a spatial paradigm during the postwar years, references to precise "distances from the hypocenter" (*bakushinchi kara no kyori*) determined to a great extent the narrators' identities as *hibakusha*.

At the same time, the image of concentric circles radiating outward over a map of the city replicates the vision of the pilots who dropped the bomb and inspected its aftermath. The power of the bombsight to objectify, determine, and name everything that survived beneath it was such that hardly anyone has been able to narrate postnuclear Hiroshima from outside this perspective. This gaze from above, a transcendental sight, was forever inscribed on the landscape and came to condition any subsequent attempt to represent the incident. It has also subsumed survivors' diverse experiences and subjectivities under the universal and anonymous identity of *hibakusha*. The testimonies concerning Hiroshima's nuclear disaster have always been shaped by and against this dominant spatial representation. As was mentioned in the previous chapter, this spatial re-cognition of the city has also been one of the crucial components of both medico-legal and antinuclear discourses on Hiroshima's atomic bombing.

In this chapter, I will track the sites of memory that emerge out of a variety of spatial tactics *hibakusha* and others deploy in order to construct their narratives about the past. To be sure, the space of storytellings that emerges out of such geographic traffickings does not exist beyond the hegemonic spatial representations of late-twentieth-century Hiroshima, nor are they capable of taking over the dominant memory-scape. Yet it is also possible that linking sites that ostensibly have no historical relevance to one another may elicit knowledge that has not otherwise been manifest. The physical and discursive movements guided by these storytellers traverse not only urban surfaces but also the geopolitical boundaries of the nation-state—and in this sense the storytellers' tactics operate through what might best be understood as "mnemonic detours."

The sites of storytellings that proliferate through these mnemonic detours generate memories of Hiroshima that are hardly reconcilable with its official historical self-portraiture. The latter is grounded on memories of the hometown's collective victimization and the image of a peace-loving, cosmopolitan metropolis that has miraculously recovered. Even those sites and stories that previously had been related exclusively to the nuclear disaster begin to enunciate various social relations and meanings that are not necessarily confined to the discourse of the city's, and by extension the nation's, victimization, or to the dominant narrative of postwar prosperity. The spaces enunciated in the survivors' performances may be processual and transient, appearing only briefly at moments of remembrance. Moreover, they are conditioned by the structure of the official memoryscape and at times may even unwittingly underscore its dominance. Yet because the survivors represent the authoritative embodiment of the original catastrophic moment, they ensure that the interjected sites will continue to disrupt Hiroshima's urban scenery, even in its renewed state. In what follows, we will consider the specific ways in which some survivors' testimonial practices and spatial tactics help destabilize, and often even challenge, hegemonic ways of knowing about the past and present.

NARRATIVE MARGINS AND CRITICAL KNOWLEDGE

Narrators' testimonial practices often have the effect, whether intended or not, of unsettling the world that listeners accept as self-evident. The narratives and activities of Numata Suzuko—one of the founding members of Kataru Kai, who already has been introduced as an opponent of recent renewal efforts—perhaps illustrate this best. Numata's narrative practices generate what might be called critical knowledge: that is, knowledge that works to denaturalize the taken-for-granted realities of society and culture.

Numata Suzuko was twenty-two when she lost her left leg to the bomb. Because the bomb almost completely destroyed all hospitals and medical equipment, as well as killing medical crews, her wounded ankle was left untreated for three days, resulting in suppuration. She was accommodated at what was left of a ruined hospital, where her leg was amputated without anesthesia. Even after the war's end she remained bedridden, and by the time she was finally released from the hospital she had undergone four operations. Today, she lives with her younger sister, Fusako, who is also a survivor.[1] Although her injuries from the explosion were relatively minor, Fusako developed breast cancer at the age of thirty-nine. She had two operations and continues to suffer from various side effects of cobalt therapy.

In March 1989, shortly after my arrival in Hiroshima, I made an appointment with Numata Suzuko over the telephone. I had learned from others that although some elderly survivors find it improper for strangers to arrange meetings except through letters, Numata welcomes anyone who makes the effort to talk with her. The following day, we met at exactly the appointed time outside the former Peace Memorial Building in the Peace Memorial Park.

I only learned a few months later that the place she would bring me to is a multipurpose space used for conferences, small meetings, accommodations, and consultations for various hibakusha-related matters. As we walked into it, she greeted an elderly man who was working at a desk on the first floor and invited him to join us in the upstairs meeting room. His role was to facilitate the application procedures for survivors wishing to obtain *hibakusha* certificates. He immediately appeared with a large quantity of materials to remedy my possible lack of basic knowledge about Hiroshima's atom bomb. These included leaflets that explained atom bomb damages in general, literature with statistical data concerning the survivors, and a map of the city on which the familiar concentric circles radiating out from the hypocenter had been superimposed. After the man left the room, Numata provided me with a few additional photocopies: printed and handwritten materials that transcribed excerpts from her testimonies, and again, a map with the concentric circles. She then told me her story, a story that began on the morning of "that day," 6 August 1945.

The following transcription translates her narrative almost in its entirety. Later we will examine how the structuration of her stories constitutes a politics of knowledge, both within the text and in relation to other texts she has produced.

On that morning, I went to work at the Hiroshima Telegraph and Communication Services Department, which was located 1,000 meters away from the hypocenter. Three members of my family worked at the same place. My father worked on the fourth floor, my younger sister on the third floor, and I worked in an office built on the roof of the building. My older brother was working at the Hiroshima Main Post Office, which was located 1,500 meters away from the hypocenter. My mother stayed at home. . . .

I was engaged then. My fiancé was conscripted and sent to the front five months after we became publicly engaged. Our wedding was arranged for the fall of 1945. By the time he left for war, I had met him only three times. I hadn't had a chance to even hold his hand. It was the older days, you see. Just as many other young women of those days, I too was yearning for marriage and I was determined to become a good wife. My heart was fluttering. In those wartime days, marriage was indeed something cheerful, something we could look forward to.

So, on that day too, not having even the slightest idea that Hiroshima was chosen as an atomic bomb target, I went off cheerfully to work. I was especially excited then because I had just received a postcard from my fiancé, noting that he would come back to Hiroshima sometime in August. So my heart was fluttering even more, as I thought, "Oh, I can see him again." But at that hour, the plane was in fact already up to here [pointing to the Enola Gay's navigation map and its position at 7:31 A.M., 6 August]. But nothing was revealed to me (*nanimo shirasarete inakatta*).

[At the workplace,] since the three other workers were not around, I cleaned the office by myself. Although I usually put away the cleaning stuff on the rooftop, somehow on that morning, I decided to use the fourth-floor bathroom. So I walked down the stairs with a bucket in my hand, looking at my colleagues outside the building. I stood in the hallway in front of the bathroom, and suddenly, I clearly saw in front of my eyes a flash of brightly colored light, like a magnesium explosion. And the next second I was completely unconscious.

When I became conscious, I was in a dark room, crushed underneath something extremely heavy. My body was apparently blown away by the blast because I had been standing in the hallway. I heard some people yelling and running down the hallway. I was shouting half unconsciously, "Please help me," and a rescuer found me underneath [the collapsed building] and hurriedly pulled me out. My left ankle was already almost entirely cut off. . . . We escaped to the courtyard. There is a fire ahead of us; the surrounding trees, too, are burning. When I looked back at the building, the inside was red and flames were leaping out from many windows like billowing curtains. If there had been a second's delay in my rescue, I would have vanished groaning and in agony, with tears of enmity (onnen). . . .

The doctors amputated my leg without anesthesia. When I was told that my leg must be cut off from my thigh, I cried and resisted, saying, "My fiancé is coming back. I can't get married." But then someone told me, "It is not only you that's suffering. If you cut off your leg, you will be able to live." So I decided. . . .

Later in August, I was told that my fiancé was killed in the war. He was already dead in July. All the while I was feeling thrilled about his returning to Hiroshima, he had in fact already passed away. I knew nothing about it.

Thus, I was made to live (ikasareta) among thousands of those who fell victim to the bomb. After forty-some-odd years of this agonizing life, I came to believe that what I must do is embrace the voiceless voices of the dead—so that they do not have to feel they died in vain—and also to convey my own experience to youths like you who do not know the reality of the atomic bomb. Through telling stories (hanashi te iru uchi ni), I gradually begin to understand the sentiments of the dead and begin to see (mie te kuru). Had it been me before I ever told the stories (hanashita koto no nai watashi datta ra), even when someone might have said to me, "This is so, that is not so," I would have simply dismissed them, saying, "Ah, is that so." What is important is to become able to see with eyes wide open and to know (shiru to iu koto) so as not to repeat the tragedy ever again. We must become aware that even if we are having a fun time now, no one knows what may happen the next minute. . . .

It is great that you came to see me. Let's cherish this encounter. To come to meet people like this is really a form of actual practice (jissen). This, too, must be some kind of en (karma). I hope you will learn a lot [from Hiroshima] and you, too, will someday become a storyteller.

Numata worked as a home economics teacher for twenty-eight years. She recalls that in those days she almost never told others of her memories of the bombing.[2] She would tell her students, for example, that she lost her leg in an automobile accident. In 1979 she retired in order to assist her younger sister in caring for their bedridden mother. At the nursing home where her mother stayed for nearly five years until her death, Numata met a number of senior survivors who were ill, poor, and isolated. Their sufferings, she later recalled, were forgotten in what she called the "ravine" (*tanima*) of the nation's affluence and economic prosperity. This encounter with senior survivors was certainly one of the profound moments of awakening in her life.

Yet it was not until she became involved in a documentary film project on Hiroshima's atomic bombing that she decided to become a witness/storyteller. This film, *Ningen o kaese* (*Give Me Back Humanity*), the title of which was taken from Toge Sankichi's often-recited poem, was based on footage originally shot in April 1946 by American military crews as they surveyed the atom bomb's effects. The film, which captured the physical destruction caused by the bomb, also included visual examples of wounded survivors. Over 85,000 feet of film was brought back to the United States, classified, and stored in the National Archives in Washington, D.C., together with another documentary that had been made by a Japanese private film corporation immediately after the bombing and was subsequently confiscated by U.S. officials.[3] In 1980, several Japanese filmmakers who discovered that the film could be copied for 3,000 yen per ten feet started a campaign to "purchase back" the film from the United States. Their fund-raising campaign, called the "ten feet movement," met with great success. Contributions amounted to over 100 million yen, and four separate documentaries were eventually produced from the original footage.[4]

Numata told her biographers of her violent reencounter with the past through the film footage.[5] Since it depicted persons, rights to privacy were involved; the campaign organizers therefore contacted the survivors who appeared, or their families, in order to obtain their approval to release the relevant scenes. Numata recalls her shock when Nagai Hideaki, who spearheaded the campaign, somehow discovered where she lived and one day appeared at the front door, abruptly asking permission to disclose to the public that she was a survivor of the bomb. When she later previewed the film, she spotted the image of herself displaying her amputation to the American film crew. The violence of this representation ruptured the superficial calm of her everyday consciousness. The encounter with her own filmic image, she recalls, put her in a state of emotional disarray: the cathartic moment of remembering left her feeling appalled at the gap between the objectified self-image projected on the screen and her long-standing denial and silence. Another *hibakusha* who had already been active in testimonial

activities approached Numata, hoping to convince her of the preciousness of her witnessing as one who had survived the historic moment of
a human-made catastrophe. Convinced, Numata then began to tell her
stories about the bomb to the public.

In Numata's narrative, phrases such as "I knew nothing about [the
bombing]," "Nothing was revealed to me," or "not having the slightest idea" appear repeatedly. Although the contents of the story she tells
vary to some degree depending upon the type and size of the audience,
they generally work by juxtaposing two types of knowledge: for example, she was unaware that the Enola Gay was approaching precisely at
the moment when she blithely appeared in her office; or, she endured
the pain of amputation in order to save her life without knowing that
her awaited fiancé had already been killed a month earlier, and so on.
By coupling the two disjoined temporalities, and by incorporating multiple discursive levels, Numata's narrative puts into relief both the immediate presence of the world she experienced and the reality that "was
not revealed" to her.

One of the central morals of her story concerns the importance of
"knowing." On the one hand, there is a knowledge that Numata at
times calls "*chishiki*," which she describes as made up of "surface facts"
(*omote no jijitsu*). While *chishiki* is usually rendered into English as
"knowledge," her usage of the term suggests instead "information," or
instrumental knowledge, which equips individuals with enough information to achieve particular objectives. On the other hand, she refers
to "hidden knowledge" (*ura no jijitsu*)—what I would call, following
Foucault, subjugated knowledge.[6] This unrevealed or peripheralized
knowledge about the world is indispensable in establishing and sustaining the centrality of instrumental knowledge. At the same time,
subjugated knowledge has the power to unsettle the surface facts precisely because it has been marginalized.

Numata's warnings about the fallibility of knowledge are most clearly
heard in her portrayals of the ways in which, within the contexts of
nationalism and colonialism, she came to understand herself as a *hibakusha*. Having established herself as a witness/storyteller, Numata
also became a traveler on crutches. She made trips to various sites of
violence—not only of war, genocide, and nuclear disaster but also of
poverty, discrimination, and oppression. Trips that were initially arranged for her to tell stories about Hiroshima's disaster gradually turned
into broader encounters and opportunities to listen. Numata recalls that

this all began at a meeting in Tokyo with a survivor of the Rape of Nanjing. As she traveled, she met an ever-wider range of people: Filipina women factory workers, residents of Pingdingshan in northeastern China where the Japanese army had massacred nearly 3,000 villagers, survivors of U.S. napalm bombing hospitalized in Vietnam, members of a women's antinuclear group in Belau, survivors of Hiroshima and Nagasaki now residing in the Republic of Korea, and so on.

One travel narrative that she incorporates into her storytelling recalls her encounter with Malaysian representations of the atomic bomb. At that moment, she realized how differently the atomic bomb is perceived by those who stand on "the other side of the history." In Malaysian official history, the atomic bomb attack on Hiroshima and Nagasaki is celebrated as a sign of liberation from the war, torture, and massacres that were brought on by the Japanese invasion. At small gatherings of Kataru Kai and a few other groups, she often spoke of a trip to Yi Long Long village in Negeri Sembilan, Malaysia. There the Eleventh Regiment of the Japanese Imperial Army's Fifth Division, formerly headquartered in Hiroshima, is known to have massacred over 1,400 Chinese residents:[7]

> there was a sign on the street [in Hiroshima] with the name of the Eleventh Regiment. . . . As young female students we would walk—back and forth, back and forth—right in front of the gate [where the troops were stationed], trying to become friendly [with the soldiers]. In those days, [the soldiers were] objects of our romantic admiration (akogare no mato). And we paraded with lanterns in our hands, celebrating, "Nanjing surrendered!" "Singapore surrendered!" Did we ever imagine that such horrible things [as massacres and tortures] were happening behind those scenes?[8]

Again, we find two unreconciled temporalities juxtaposed. On the one hand, Numata remembered herself as a "military girl" (gunkoku shōjo), innocently participating in exultant celebration of the enemy's surrender; on the other hand, the troops she so adored were slaughtering ordinary Chinese citizens. Her story about survivors now residing in the Republic of Korea is also told through such contrasts. It brings into relief at once the overseas hibakusha's deplorable conditions, conditions due in large part to Japan's colonial and postwar/postcolonial policies, and Numata's focus on the immediacy of her own victimization. In other words, as she accumulates and processes newly obtained knowledge about the past through fresh encounters and new travels, her memory work reconstitutes her "experiences."

The mass media and some progressive educators have praised Numata as one of the few *hibakusha* courageous enough to have broken out of the mold of infatuation with victimhood to talk about Japan's history of invasion and colonialism. In the climate of the 1980s, which I described in chapter 3, individuals such as Numata who were willing to publicly reflect on historical responsibility were readily welcomed: Numata fulfilled the desire to demonstrate the Japanese conscience. However, this new interpellation carried with it the danger that testimonial practices would once again be subjected to the existing discourses of mainstream history; the narrator might again be contained by a position from which she could speak only the nation's newfound Truth.

The media and the educators expected witnesses/storytellers like Numata to edify their audiences, through firsthand accounts, about the history of atrocities committed by the Japanese. They anticipated that storytellers would fill the silences in official history by making manifest knowledge that had previously been censored or deleted. Yet those eager for progress and enlightenment have oversimplified the nature of the knowledge produced in *hibakusha* testimonial practices. Witnesses like Numata do not necessarily consider the history of Japan's military and colonial aggression to be self-evident knowledge. Nor do they tell this alternative history in the belief that the meaning of this knowledge is preestablished within the nation's existing historical narrative. Their narratives do not simply fill the gaps in the official history or satisfy others' desire to know. Instead, they refer to what is everywhere and always present: the haunting absence of knowledge, the inevitability of memory's deficiency.

This narrative margin, the segment of history that is not recalled by the narrator as manifest knowledge, marks a void in the wholeness of established, official knowledge about society.[9] At the same time, this deficiency is indispensable to establishing and defining what constitutes the center, or the mainstream. By intimating the presence of an absence, the *hibakusha*'s narrative practices suggest that manifest knowledge, about both the past and present, is predicated on what has been subjugated. It is this narrative margin in three senses of the term—the peripheral, the void, the surplus—that is essential to the economy of testimonial engagement. The unimagined proximity of the Enola Gay, the unknown death of the fiancé, the bloodshed of over one million Chinese as set against the Japanese nation's euphoria, the continuing agony of South Korean survivors during postwar Japan's rapid economic growth, the jubilation of liberated Malaysians over use of the new weapon of mass destruction—these emplotments in Numata's narrative point toward realities beyond what is imaginable. By suggesting to her audiences something exterior to the world of self-evidence, her narrative makes them suspect that knowledge can never be complete.

A public lecture that Numata delivered on the interplay between what she sees as instrumental knowledge and a critical way of knowing reveals her own perspective on this issue. Numata began by describing how the difficulties of living with "a disabled body" (shōgai no mi) and "a bombed body" (hibaku shita mi) had long confirmed her belief that she was simply a victim, a legitimate object of sympathy. She recounted how she had gradually come to realize "how dreadful it can be to remain indifferent and ignorant, [when one imagines] what might result from such attitudes." She continued: "After having been made to live for forty-four years [after the bombing], I finally became an individual who can think [critically]. . . . I had always thought I was knowledgeable at the level of instrumental knowledge (chishiki) about various issues—issues concerning the disabled, the Korean minority, or the so-called discriminated against communities. . . . [But through telling stories] I became convinced that somewhere there are always hidden facts."[10] Numata's reflections on the doubleness of knowledge, which emerge dialectically from within her autobiographical narratives about the past, extend further to become commentaries on the contemporary conditions within which her own narratives are constructed:

> During the war, I was turned into a person who could not listen [to other stories]. I only believed in unidirectional truth (ippōteki na koto). . . . And now, as I live in the present, I am once again becoming yet another human being who cannot see. This very process is the most frightening. . . . I believe that what enables me to rise up like this is my desire to pursue the unseen. I feel that I have been transforming myself in such a way [since I became a storyteller]. . . . In this information society age, facts appear to be conveyed. But I am afraid that this is only a sham (misekake).[11]

To be self-aware as perpetrator as well as victim does not reaffirm the historical causal linkages often seen as justifying the United States' use of the atom bombs. Indeed, Numata's point can be applied to yet another side of the same history: namely, the ways in which United States policy makers and citizens welcomed the bomb. The "enemy's" casualties and deaths were similarly erased and forgotten during the United States' more recent wars (e.g., with Vietnam and Iraq).

It is important to note that Numata does not use the idea of "surface" to mean a "false" image that distorts "real" conditions. The "surface knowledge" she refers to in her narrative—about victories in war, for example—is no less real than the "hidden knowledge" of such matters as the war of invasion. Both participated in the constitution of the nation's momentary communal dreaming. Her positions as victim and victimizer, moreover, are two immediate dimensions of her past and present existence that are equally engraved onto her body. To this extent, the critique of knowledge in Numata's narrative should be distinguished from the conventional Enlightenment practice of critiquing ideology. Hidden knowledge is not assumed to be any more complete or more authentic than surface knowledge, and even when exposed, "the unseen" does not represent any final truth. The instant it is revealed, it forms yet another layer of surface knowledge that may well conceal other subjugated knowledge. Furthermore, the self-reflexive narrator, as the above quote suggests, can situate herself within this infinite negative dialectical process.

One might argue that Numata's testimonial practice promotes the indefinite deferral of ultimate referential truth, the endless task of deconstruction. The open-ended and dynamic nature of her narrative practice certainly helps deter containment and appropriation within either the powerful national narrative or late capitalism's hegemonic cultural restructuring. But one a priori truth does in fact exist for this narrator/author: namely, that whenever and wherever knowledge is manifest, there is always already another knowledge that is hidden and that these two knowledges are never in equilibrium. Indeed, her understanding of their configuration by asymmetries of power is precisely what prevents her from degenerating into an abyss of relativism and the ambiguities of a simple and uncritical pluralism.

FABULOUS MEMORIES: THE TEMPORALITY
OF THE "NEVER AGAIN"

The mnemonic detour, as understood in this discussion of the politics of memory, is not limited to physical movements over the cityspace. It also concerns discursive happenings in *hibakusha* testimonies. Like Numata's narrative, composed of stories from discrepant geographical locations, the following illustrates such testimonial practices. In order to meet the witness and hear this narrative, however, the ethnographer also was required to undertake a small detour.

One July evening, as was usual after formal meetings, I sat with several members of Kataru Kai and joined in their conversations. Just then we happened to see a brief feature about a survivor on a TV news show. Typically, broadcasts of specials on the atom bomb increase as 8.6 approaches every year. Yet the portrayal of this survivor caught the group's attention. The following is a paraphrase of the news report:

> Matsuda Go, a survivor in Kure city whose days are numbered because of terminal lung cancer, devotes the remaining days of his life to telling his life stories to schoolchildren. He has been cultivating warm and heartfelt ties with these youngsters. Since Kure city provides a base for the Self-Defense Forces, one of the themes of his stories concerns Japan's present military situations. "There isn't much time left," he said in the interview, "so it must be told now. . . . My anger—anger toward prewar education and toward that day—keeps me going." He does not wish his audiences, most of whom are from primary to high school students, to learn only about the atom bomb. Rather, he wants them to think about the conditions of war more generally. He himself learned to kill in the name of the country. Wars could make people willing to abandon their own children. And it is too late to realize this after the war. His extremely soft and hoarse voice almost sounded as if it were being strained out of his slender body, word by word. He concluded, "I try to convince myself that I will remain strong, that I will stay healthy and retain the energy to tell stories, until the very day of my death." For Matsuda, to live means nothing but "to carry on the storytelling" (kataritsugu koto).[12]

After the program ended, a deep silence engulfed us; Numata was first to break it. Agreeing with Matsuda's statement in the TV interview we had just heard, she underscored a point that she too has repeatedly made—namely, that the survivors should not limit their storytelling to their experience of the atom bomb but should tell other stories of the war as well. Other members concurred, saying that stories of the atomic bomb alone only served to foster a sense of pity and did not help create an active desire to "do something for peace." Another survivor sympathized with Matsuda's comment that time was running short for the survivors. Our discussion that evening ended with the unanimous suggestion that I should meet Matsuda as soon as possible during my stay in Hiroshima. I little realized at the time that Matsuda had earlier been criticized by other survivors, though not by these members of Kataru Kai, for being "too radically political."

A week later, I was on a train bound for Kure, a city located only a few miles away from Hiroshima, to meet Matsuda. During its modernization period, beginning around the turn of the century, Kure had

developed around its military harbor and munitions industries. Hiroshima had been a "military capital" in a symbolic sense, prospering
through diversification and accommodating a wide range of modern facilities in finance, industry, and education (such as banks, museums, uni-
versities, factories, a harbor, entertainment facilities, and so on), but Kure
had developed around a single resource, the Imperial Navy. During the
war, unlike Hiroshima before the atom bomb attack, Kure was among
the many Japanese cities that had suffered massive damages from conventional air raids. In the postwar period of rapid growth of heavy industry, Kure prospered through its shipping industry, like many other
coastal cities along the Seto Inland Sea, while offering a naval base for
Japan's Self-Defense Forces.

As I rode on the train I thought about a statement that an antinuclear activist in a grassroots organization had once made at a public
gathering. He had said that a spatial "division of labor" exists between
Hiroshima and its neighboring cities, Kure and Iwakuni: while Hiroshima sells peace, Kure stations the Self-Defense Forces and Iwakuni accommodates the U.S. military. The name of this activist's organization,
Peace Link (pīsu rinku), was aimed precisely at connecting the three
geographical sites in a spatial imaginary in order to foster critical perspectives on Hiroshima's sanctification of peace, thus dismantling mystifying ideas about the region's present conditions. Members of Peace
Link have criticized Hiroshima's peace-related administrative policies
(often referred to as heiwa gyōsei), on the grounds that while the city
ostensibly promotes world peace and antinuclear ideals, it also masks
the hazards that threaten the environment of the surrounding regions.
They warn, for instance, of the dangers posed by the continuing military buildup, the numerous accidents involving the U.S. nuclear submarines stationed nearby, and the area's increasing dependence on nuclear power. The train ride to Kure took only a few minutes. Though
suspicious of too facile a notion of false consciousness, I found myself
deeply convinced that such a spatial division of labor does indeed mystify the nation's present remilitarized conditions and landscape. The proximity of the two cities confirmed how easily one could forget the realities outside the self-contained space of peace-full Hiroshima.

From the bus that I had boarded after reaching Kure, I could see
Matsuda standing alone at the stop closest to his home. As I stepped
down to the street, Matsuda greeted me. I bowed to him. From the
news segment I knew of his terminal lung cancer, and I wondered about
his condition. His wiry physique bespoke not so much a physical as a

spiritual strength. He walked very slowly and spoke softly. As we approached his house, a junior high school student, apparently a neighbor, passed by and cheerfully greeted him. Matsuda smiled and waved to her. I was led to a modest wooden house where his wife awaited. Vegetables grew on a small strip of ground near the house's entrance. He closed the windows and turned on the air conditioner so that the smell of organic fertilizer would not bother me.

I immediately discovered that, like Numata, Matsuda was most adamant that his testimonies have a critical effect on his audiences; he carefully crafted them with his relationship to audiences in mind. This self-consciousness about how narratives affect audiences further attests to the fact that testimonies are understood to be more than self-contained acts. Whether viewed as cultural critiques or memorial services, *hibakusha* testimonies are always conceived as practices that are enabled by the storytellers' interactions with their audiences. In Matsuda's case, his narratorial intention was to create audiences who, to borrow his own words, can begin to "see Japan with different eyes" (*chigatta me de Nihon o miru*).

Most survivors recall that when they first began storytelling they were unexpectedly surprised by the enormous intensity and fascination of their listeners. Many, in fact, attribute their desire to become *shō-gensha* and then to continue the practice to this original experience. But it is also true that many *hibakusha* have expressed a sense of futility about narrating to student audiences. Observers of survivors' testimonial engagements have noted how immensely disappointed storytellers are when, after forcing themselves to recall the unbearable, they receive only bland responses, such as "Thank you for the stories. I wish to cherish this peaceful time."[13] This kind of audience reaction to the survivors' storytelling is also often reflected in the anonymous comments left by visitors at the Peace Memorial Museum: for example, "I feel terribly sorry for what happened. And I feel grateful that I was born in this peaceful age."

Individual propensities aside, such reactions may be related to the flood of simulations to which audiences have already been exposed. Many *hibakusha* believe that teachers present students with too much material in the classroom before their actual visits to Hiroshima. Often students have already been bombarded with information, including detailed scientific data about nuclear explosions, numbers of casualties, crucial dates, and so on. In some cases students' comments have been prepared even before they actually hear the *hibakusha*'s testimonies. Moreover, most visitors to Hiroshima have been preexposed to many versions of stereotypical stories that the mass media provide year after year, constantly converting survivors' testimonies into commodities. Saturated with such simulations and a deluge of objectified information, many of us feel that we have enough knowledge about the atomic bomb, even prior to our visit to the site. As a result, we, like many of these students, often conclude our visit to Hiroshima by reaffirming what we already know.

While many survivors and observers of survivors' testimonial engagements have noted these problems, Matsuda believes that the potential of survivors' testimonies to transform listeners ultimately resides in each storyteller's philosophy and his or her relationship to those listeners. Thus Matsuda vehemently objected to the news report that introduced him as a "kataribe" (storyteller), quoting from a dictionary to assure me of just how distinctly antithetical his narrative practice was to that of the traditional kataribe. According to the formal definition, the term kataribe refers to professional troupes that recited legends and mythical histories in the preliterate era. The traditional storytellers, as Matsuda and other hibakusha emphasized, were forced to learn these stories by rote, regardless of their individual will. Moreover, their narrative knowledge about the past, unlike the survivors' testimonies, was neither scrutinized for its facticity nor actively remembered as their own experiences. Rather, the knowledge was simply handed down from generation to generation to serve the establishment—or, more precisely, the imperial court. Furthermore, Matsuda refused to be associated with another meaning of kataribe, which refers to entertainers who used to make a living by telling tragic, "tearjerker" (onamida chōdai) stories, as he put it, to gain sympathy. His disavowal of this label succinctly evidences the self-conscious, self-responsible, and antiauthoritarian political subjectivity that permeates his testimony.

Matsuda consciously deploys several tactics to preclude the possibility that his testimonies would merely endorse the present state of knowledge. For instance, Matsuda's firsthand accounts of the Hiroshima atom bomb make up no more than one-fifth of the entire narrative. What remains are supplements to this main story; but it is these subplots that Matsuda regards as crucial in determining the effects and nature of his testimonial practices. As he explained to me on the day of our interview,[14] his first supplementary stories concern atrocities committed by the Japanese Imperial Army during the war, and the nation's present militarized condition. To emphasize the latter point, Matsuda reinforces his storytelling with several photographs of missiles and submarines he has taken at Kure harbor. These enlarged photos serve as further witness to Japan's current full-fledged remilitarization. Another material resource that he adds to his testimony is a copy of a 1947 booklet published by the Ministry of Education, titled *The Story of the New Constitution* (*Atarashii kenpō no hanashi*). It explains in plain language the virtues of Japan's postwar constitution and the renunciation of the use of military force to resolve international conflicts.[15] In the early postwar years, the booklet was assigned as a textbook for use in every junior high school in order to educate students about the new constitution's underlying principles, including basic human rights, equality between the sexes, democracy, the new role of the imperial household, and, above all, the permanent abdication of war. After the booklet ceased to be used officially in classrooms, a branch of the Japan Teachers' Union reprinted it and began to use it as supplementary material for their peace pedagogy.

His narrative, Matsuda noted, contrasts this early postwar governmental stance on the new constitutional ideals with the reality of Kure's military harbor. According to his audience, he might also comment on the institutional linkage between national tax revenues and the procurement of weaponry from the mega-military-industrial complex. He underscores that such preparations for war have consistently benefited and will continue to bring profits to industry and to politicians who represent corporate interests. By reminding young audiences of the gap between constitutional principles and reality, Matsuda interrogates the failures of the government's own institutional memory. Matsuda stressed that he seeks to relentlessly de-romanticize and de-heroize militarism and military achievements through his stories. He often reads aloud an article of the constitution in which the Self-Defense Forces are described as defending the "country" (*kuni*), but not the "people of the nation" (*kokumin*). He emphasizes that "the people" do not ultimately benefit from the military: "The article states that the Self-Defense Forces will defend the country, but nowhere does it say it will defend the people. In order to defend the country, the first and largest obstacle is its own people. Think about Okinawa." Historians and local witnesses have shown that the ground battle of Okinawa produced over 200,000 casualties as a result not only of U.S. attacks but also of Japanese Imperial Forces who exploited the islanders as shields. Recent research and grassroots interviews have revealed that under the mission privileging military and national security, Okinawan civilians were forced to demonstrate their loyalty to the country by killing themselves and members of their families and communities.[16]

To complement his narratives, Matsuda deploys photographs of the Rape of Nanjing committed by the Japanese Imperial Army. The enlarged black-and-white reproductions he showed me are included among the various visual materials that the Hiroshima Peace Institute has compiled and made available for classroom use. Matsuda pointed to a picture in which a Japanese soldier holding a Japanese sword stands next to a young Chinese woman. Her belly is torn, presumably after having been brutally raped. "He stands next to her and is able to smile. But he doesn't look like a person who can commit murder, does he? He is still just a little boy." Matsuda quickly links the scene captured by the photograph with his own memories by returning to accounts of Hiroshima. The temporal context of war remains the same, but the location is different: "One is numbed by seeing so many people killed. It didn't feel odd at all to burn layer after layer of corpses [after the atomic bombing]. . . . Even mothers could kill their children. That is what war is about. . . . I, too, learned to kill like this. It was natural to kill. The schools taught me how to kill. Girls learned to also, with bamboo spears." Such a recounting of the past would be immediately linked to his audience's own time, as Matsuda would add, "This soldier [in the photo of the Rape of Nanjing] could be your own grandfather." His testimony would then conclude with a warning for the present day: we support the military "without realizing it." Matsuda makes sure to remind his audience, "You are all taught in such a way that you do not have a critical view of reality . . . in just the way I was taught during wartime."

His supplementary stories would end here. Matsuda tells of his own experience in Hiroshima, on 6 August 1945, only with and only after these detours through space and time—from Nanjing, via Okinawa, to the harbor of Kure, and through the 1930s, extending into the immediate postwar period, and up to the contemporary moment. A transcription of Matsuda's customary testimony informs us that he was seventeen years old at the time of the bombing. He then worked at a prefectural government office located about 800 meters away from the hypocenter:

> A person was stripped of skin; walking without noticing that pieces of clothing that had remained around his hip had caught on fire; groaning grotesquely and hands dangling. A body completely blackened from soot

collecting on the blood that covered the surface of skinless human flesh; enormously huge eyeballs; and eyeballs drooping out—the figures of children are even more pitiful. Hands and legs squirming underneath collapsed buildings, but not even a thought given to rescuing them.

Heard someone, apparently an old woman, whose body was so utterly disfigured that it was impossible to distinguish her sex, saying, "Damn it! Americans . . . Get back at them, please." . . . The voice reminds me of the fact that I am still alive and I feel spurred on to somehow rise up for the emperor, yet the next second I am thinking, it's all over. Yet there is a firm conviction that the Divine Wind will bluster without fail, that Japan is a divine country, that there is the emperor, and that we will never lose, even if stripped of skin or with lives taken. . . .

Everywhere in the city I saw corpses; some ten people were dead, their heads in a water tank; their legs were half burned, some bones were exposed and smelled horrible. A baby girl grinned at me, sucking on the skinless breast of a woman who appeared to have been alive until a few minutes earlier. . . . We were taught to believe in the Imperial Rescript on Education, with loyalty to the emperor and love for the country (*chūkun aikoku*), and in selfless devotion to the nation (*messhi hōkō*). We were also made to believe in the slogan, "we will not desire anything until we win"; and many were killed even without having been provided with sufficient food. In the eyes of these individuals, the names of those responsible for the war have not yet been disclosed.[17]

The detours in Matsuda's narrative might be understood as producing stories of universal victimhood. They could appear to flatten out historical specificities and political relations: all wars are bad, war victimizes everyone equally, and there are no victors in the age of nuclear warfare.[18] Matsuda's story also suggests that everyone may indeed be complicitous in the conduct of wars. Indeed, it is the sense of shared victimhood that allows the audience to identify with the storyteller, thus generating an important moment of sympathy. As we will see below, the audience becomes capable of sharing resentment toward those who caused that fatal moment only by empathizing with the storyteller's agony as a *hibakusha* and by mourning his approaching death. Yet, at the same time, the narrative's deliberate naming of every responsible actor at every scene of violence—for example, Japanese soldiers in Nanjing and Okinawa, the Ministry of Education, the Self-Defense Forces, the military industry, Americans who used the bomb, the emperor for whom many were killed, and lastly the storyteller himself, who had not been able to give "even a thought" to rescuing victimized children—relentlessly reminds the audience of critical differences within the community of universal victimhood.

That Matsuda's narrative detours through time and space can strongly affect his listeners is clear from letters and comments from people in various audiences. The commentaries, though in somewhat inchoate language, offer a critique of knowledge and power gained from shock and amazement at Matsuda's testimony.

> I had learned about Hiroshima's tragedy throughout elementary and secondary school. So I thought I knew some things. But I keenly felt that what I had known and learned were only superficial. What impressed me most [in Matsuda's story] was that we have been increasing our military strength, although unwittingly.
>
> (A female high school student.)

> There is a magazine I read every day. It is a kind of magazine that is made up of illustrations and opinions sent in by readers. One-third of the illustrations are filled with "battles" and "blood." It is not that the editors prefer them, but they only seem to receive those kinds of letters. The majority of the letters also have comments like "the fighting is cool," or "the person who coughed up the blood was beautiful." In other cartoon magazines, about 90 percent of them have "battles" as their themes, as if to say that not fighting is outdated. Although I too used to feel up until now that these things are "cool," teacher Matsuda's story made me think, if I were in that situation, I would never think it was "cool." Maybe I was able to enjoy them because they seemed too unreal.
>
> (A third-grade elementary school girl.)

> Mr. Matsuda's story began to make me feel uneasy, for I came to realize that we are going through things that are similar to [what went on] in prewar Japan.
>
> (A male high school student.)

> Until now, whenever I heard stories, saw movies, or read books about war, I only thought "how pitiful" or "I don't like it." But today, I felt that these feelings won't do any good. Until now, I thought, "wars are to be blamed"; but now, I feel we are lending our hands in making our situation close to one in which making wars is inevitable.
>
> (A third-grade elementary school girl.)

> Listening to your story about Hiroshima as you actually witnessed it, I thought peace is nothing more than a fancy word. Mr. Matsuda said, please think about what "peace" is. I thought, but could not come up with words. . . . Whenever listening to war stories, I used to feel they were "pitiful" or "horrible"; but after having heard Mr. Matsuda's story, I now realize that those words can never fully express wars. The story about the Self-Defense Forces made me feel for the first time that the country we live in is dirty. I felt that we must change this dirty country created by the adults into a cleaner one, little by little.
>
> (A third-grade elementary school girl.)

I went home . . . and I asked my parents, as you told us, "If today my arms
or legs were amputated; and if I asked you, why didn't you do something
to prevent the war? What would you do?" Then both my mother and father became silent. "You cannot respond, can you?" I asked them. Then
they said, "You're right." So I told them exactly as you told us. Then my
mother said, that person seems to have grasped the world. I don't think I
will ever forget those words.

(A sixth-grade elementary school girl.)[19]

These reactions suggest an important general observation that can
be made about the communicative dynamics between *hibakusha* witnesses and their audiences—namely, that many listeners are in fact
moved by Matsuda's authoritative presence as a witness, by the compelling understanding that, as I will later discuss at greater length, the
storyteller is one who has survived an actual, real historical event. More
important for our purpose here, they demonstrate that Matsuda's young
audiences do indeed often begin to "see Japan with different eyes," as
was intended by the narrator. They show that Matsuda's testimonial
practices have produced a community of listeners who have at least
begun to feel skeptical about the familiarity of the accepted world. It
is also evident that audiences often sense the instability of language.
Their comments make explicit that they in fact perceive the limitations
of the storyteller's ability to represent atrocities in Hiroshima and elsewhere. At the same time, it is possible to see that they begin to question the transparency of accustomed signs, such as peace, "self-defense,"
and war.

What distinguishes Matsuda's testimony from others who might
induce tears but not critical reflection on the status quo may be his
"anger," the profound resentment that saturates his stories. When I in-
quired about what had initially prompted him to become a storyteller,
a question that I asked whenever interviewing *hibakusha* witnesses, he
described a particular incident. In 1971 skeletal remains of over six
hundred individuals were excavated in Ninoshima, a small island off
Hiroshima's south shore, where hundreds of the wounded had been accommodated in the immediate aftermath of the bombing. Many died and
the corpses were either buried or cremated there. On hearing the news,
Matsuda visited the site to pray for the unearthed dead and took some
photographs of the bones that had been exhumed after some twenty-
six years. Shortly thereafter, members of the Hiroshima Peace Institute
asked him to present his photographs to some schoolchildren. He recalled for me his feelings at the time:

[When I saw those bones] my own experience overlapped with [those of the dead]. I felt anger rising inside of me. Shedding tears was not enough. Instead, I felt genuine anger—anger against the prewar education I had received, anger against my own ignorance, and anger against the present system. But today, no one seems to be angry. I want people to be angry. What are we engaged in storytelling for? Isn't there a place where we should direct our anger? To simply give up, thinking that it could not be helped, is not the right attitude. But today everybody's anger has somehow completely disappeared.

His "anger" toward the establishment, toward the decision makers, and toward his gullible, uncritical self is what prevents audiences from being able to aestheticize Matsuda's testimony. This anger distinguishes his narratives from the conventional storytellers' "sob stories," which might well move audiences to cathartic tears but which rarely lead to any further thoughts or sentiments. Once such audiences have left the enchanted scene of storytelling, they tend not to reflect on their own conditions. In this sense, the traditional sob stories reentrench the status quo. Matsuda's anger forbids listeners from immersing themselves in feelings of pity or sorrow for victims, for his audiences are constantly confronted with the vengeful rancor of those victims—from Nanjing, Kure, Hiroshima, and elsewhere—against their perpetrators. While liberal and humanist antiwar discourse sustains the idea that what happened to others might happen to oneself, that all wars are bad, and that we are all equally potential victims, Matsuda's testimony unmistakably distinguishes the structural positions occupied by the perpetrators from those of the victims, even as it is enabled by the shared horizon of the two. Matsuda's anger furnishes his historical knowledge with a sharp critical edge.

Furthermore, while the conventional form of Hiroshima narratives does not question the linear course of history, thereby reinforcing a sense of fatalism about what happened, Matsuda's narrative challenges the very notion of inevitability. Other witnesses commonly open their testimonies by recalling an innocent morning in August that was suddenly engulfed in the utterly unexpected catastrophe, and then proceed to describe hellish scenes of survival and later adversities. In contrast, Matsuda's narrative reminds his audiences that his approaching death is not a matter of course. It was caused, or could have been prevented, by the decisions of people in power. To put it differently, his narrative shows young listeners that power produces knowledge, action, and historical consequences.

Detractors may claim that the students' comments are in fact predictable, showing compliance to authority—whether that of the storytellers or of the classroom teachers. In the elementary school system particularly—where a single teacher is responsible for evaluating a child, not only in school subjects but also in overall personal behavior—students may indeed be savvy enough to detect what is considered to be desirable, and they eagerly seek to meet the expectations of their teachers. Some educators judge that the survivors' stories have instrumental value for disciplining youths. Furthermore, it can be argued that even if these momentary critical reflections are indeed genuine, their immediate social effects cannot be measured; nor can we expect them to be sustained until the young people mature into full-fledged political subjects. At the same time, and even given that such an outcome is certainly not inevitable, it is equally possible that the storyteller's indignation, inscribed in listeners' memories, may reemerge at some later point in their lives. Like haunting dreams, the storyteller's anger may be translated into future questionings of the mundane and the familiar, albeit in ways that may not seem remotely to concern the issues originally problematized by the storyteller.

As we have seen, Matsuda's narratives were deliberately fashioned to induce young audiences to begin to think critically about their knowledge of the nation's past and its supposedly "peaceful" present, as well as about the general questions of war, life, and death. Yet why is it so important to be critical? Isn't any message about Hiroshima's nuclear disaster already critical? Moreover, according to the domestic values of our bourgeois society, children should remain happy and innocent. "Parental discretion" ought to protect young people from being emotionally disturbed by shocking stories of violence and bloodshed. To my question, Matsuda responded plainly that critical thinking was necessary "so that children will not have to go through what I experienced."

Matsuda's testimonial practice is thus propelled by a desire for deterrence, to prevent what once happened from recurring. And this is perhaps the basis of any kind of "never again" discourse, a warning for the future that is extracted from a lesson about the past. But retelling the past, no matter how accurately the horrors may be reproduced, does not in itself guarantee against recurrence. To be effectual, the witness's testimony must be heard as resonating across time: the audience must be able to imagine the story about the past as a possible future event. The "never again" aphorism is therefore predicated on a dialectics of memory—a constant movement between memory constituted by the authenticity that derives from the witness's capacity to tell what actually happened and memory cast into the future. While the former establishes the story's historical truthfulness, it is the latter process that transforms what is remembered in testimony into that which should be anticipated.

Matsuda's testimony also involves a different yet related dialectics of memory. It compels audiences to envision the possibility that the suffering and agony of an enormous number of war victims—including the storyteller's belated but now imminent death—might have been averted, that they were never inevitable. Like Benjamin's materialist historiography discussed in the introduction, Matsuda's testimony, even while recollecting the events as they actually occurred, emplots alternative courses of history. While the call "never again" gains its force by seeing the past as a possible future, this memory work makes it possible to imagine multiple possibilities in the past. By interrupting the linear sequence of conventional historical narratives, Matsuda's remembrance generates a space in which counterfactual histories can be told.

To understand that space and fully grasp the fictive nature of the knowledge generated by Matsuda's storytelling, the writings of Michel de Certeau are particularly suggestive. In the passage quoted as an epigraph to this chapter, de Certeau asserts that spaces telling popular tales and fables create a space that protects "the weapons of the weak." The fictional popular legends of magic and heroes do indeed allow one to imagine alternative "hands" in the game one has been dealt. But more important, the "'fabulous' stories" told in such spaces make available to their audience imaginative means with which they may intervene in the future course of history. As powerful prophecies that are at the same time scrupulously empirical, the survivors' testimonies produce knowledge that is splendidly mesmerizing, spectacularly extraordinary, and filled with precious wisdom "for future use," in a way that reminds us of fables.

NARRATIVES OF AND FOR THE DEAD

In a statement quoted earlier, Numata Suzuko explained that her commitment to testimonial practices stemmed from a "desire to pursue the unseen." But such a pursuit is not necessarily the only reason why *hibakusha* witnesses begin and continue to tell their stories. As we have seen, Numata has also said that as a survivor who was "made to live among thousands of those who fell victim to the bomb," she feels a need to "embrace the voiceless voices of the dead—so that they do not have to feel they died in vain." Testimonial practices are thus believed to serve the mystical task of recuperating the presence of the deceased, even as they work to spark a critical rethinking of what seems self-evident.

Many storytellers are sole survivors of wartime collectivities—for example, of families, classrooms, neighborhoods, or workplaces. Yamazaki Kanji, for instance, lost all seven members of his household when he was seventeen, including his fifty-four-year-old single mother and an aunt and her five young children, who had relocated from Nagoya—ironically, to escape air raids.[20] Yamazaki is also one of the few survivors of his neighborhood of Tenjinmachi Kita-gumi; located less than 300 meters southwest of the hypocenter, it was thoroughly obliterated by the bomb. This downtown community on the banks of the Motoyasu River had once been crowded with small shops, inns, houses, cafés, and movie theaters. The space of the annihilated community now takes up the Peace Memorial Park's southern end. Yamazaki's own research confirmed that among the estimated total of over three hundred Tenjinmachi residents who are known to have been killed by the bomb, there are about thirty whose names are still missing from the 148,177 recorded on the Name List of the Atom Bomb Dead (*genbaku shibotsusha meibo*).[21] While the city's official registry has been recording the names of victims as they are reported and confirmed, these individuals have not been listed because no one survived who witnessed their deaths or who could testify to having seen them when they were living. About ten of them are believed to have been sojourners at inns; their traces can perhaps never be recovered.

After taking early retirement from a successful career in a large corporation involved in heavy industry, Yamazaki joined Kataru Kai. He says that his current job as a water bill collector for the city is demanding but good for maintaining his health. A man of inexhaustible exuberance and energy, Yamazaki has for some years been organizing, among other things, an annual memorial service for his former neighborhood community. On 6 August, at the Memorial for the Tenjinmachi Kita-gumi Community, Yamazaki puts up panels of photos filled with the faces of about two hundred former residents. The small circle-shaped memorial was built in 1973 in the approximate location of the former town.

In his narrative Yamazaki recalls how he managed to escape from underneath the collapsed school building where he had worked as a substitute lecturer. He walked through a city raging in flames, dragging his severely injured leg. He returned to his home only to discover that everything had disappeared. Occasionally rescuers would glance at him but quickly moved on. Deserted, Yamazaki survived for three nights and three days, alone and immobile on a street filled with death and stillness.

His narrative, however, does not dwell exclusively on scenes of devastation. Perhaps even more significantly, it describes the early modern Hiroshima of several centuries before that had developed as a prosperous castle town, and the city since the turn of the century—how it came to be equipped with the material signs of modernity, railroads, motion pictures, the cultural products of returning emigrants (such as the "Café Brazil"), men in military uniforms, and the like. Tenjinmachi was at the heart of all these changes. Yamazaki reminisces that the streets always bustled with commercial and other downtown activities. "In the olden days, Hiroshima's riverbanks were not raised as high as they are today. People who commuted on the ferryboats could access the streets more easily." Peddlers and barterers commuted to Tenjinmachi on ferryboats; ferryman would wait, chatting and drinking until high tide. Graceful geishas and other entertainers who performed in local inns walked along the streets. Soldiers used to visit the town to spend recreational time at cafés and movie theaters. Yamazaki and his friends caught fish and small crabs along the river and when the tide was low, the riverbank became transformed into an open field that was perfect for playing baseball—"riverbed baseball," as he and his friends used to call it. Yamazaki's narrative, however, does not fail to add that the river that was a "source of life" metamorphosed into a space of death, where he and others "pushed away piles of corpses to drink the water." Yamazaki's narrative, rich in stories about lively everyday scenes of community on the river, attempts to recuperate in their full plenitude the time and space that were thoroughly and instantaneously exterminated.

For Yamazaki, therefore, the space that is now the Peace Memorial Park is a vast graveyard, a site of memorial prayer. He refers to his testimonial practice as an act of *irei*, that is, memorialization or, more strictly, "consoling dead souls." He also calls it a form of *kuyō*, a Buddhist term for a memorial service, which literally means to provide for and nurture the dead. He memorializes not simply his own family but all those affiliated with the neighborhood, and in fact all of the livelihoods that had unfolded in this space. He also considers his narrative to be a means of recovering and reclaiming the existence of the enormous number of people whose deaths no one can fully confirm, and whose remains will forever be missing. The subject of his narrative, therefore, is at once the narrator himself, an irreducible individual who possesses the singular experience of survival, and the many collectivities, both of the dead and the living, of all those who experienced the moment of destruction.

Similarly, the grammatical subject in Saeki Toshiko's testimony oscillates between one that recollects memories of her own survival and one that re-members the collective experience formerly shared with those who did not survive. Anyone in Hiroshima who has even the slightest interest in the history of the bomb and its consequences easily recognizes Saeki by her distinct silver-gray hair, her dark-colored outfit, and her regular appearances at the Memorial Mound.

The Memorial Mound accommodates the remains of tens of thousands of victims, including both those who have been identified but are as yet unclaimed and those who have not been identified. While the anonymity of the latter is conducive to collective remembering, the former remind visitors of the moment's unprecedented brutality. One is struck not so much by death in and of itself but by the totality of destruction that deprived the dead of anyone who might offer proper tributes and remembrances. The Memorial Mound fosters the urgent sense that memorial services for the victims must be held, while the belatedness of such acts only reinforces the feeling that no form of memorialization could ever suffice. Because of this quality of the site, and in part because of the need to maintain the separation of church and state, the city conducts its formal religious memorial service here, with various denominations participating, and not at the central cenotaph where the name registry of all identified victims is kept.

Saeki visits the Memorial Mound almost daily to sweep its interior and surroundings. There, this custodian of memory remembers and nurtures the dead. In one storytelling scene, Saeki began by reminding the audience that memories of the day of the bombing persist into the present: "For us, yesterday was 'that day.' Today is yet another 'that day.'"[22] She then briefly described how Hiroshima's postwar reconstruction had been obstructed on a number of occasions by the exhumation of bones at construction sites, emphasizing that the streets we walk form a palimpsest with the layers of debris from the destruction lying just below.

Since Saeki entered the city immediately after the explosion to search for her mother and sister, she encountered the city in total chaos and devastation. As she wandered through the charred streets, someone abruptly grabbed her leg from beneath the rubble, pleading to be rescued. But noticing Saeki in tears, the person let go. "This was truly a great relief—I can escape freely." No longer did she desire to search for her sister; she could barely save herself. Her older brother, who had initially escaped to safety, went back into the city to find their mother. He returned with something bundled in wrapping cloth. To Saeki's disbelief the wrapping cloth contained not some broken bones but a solid skull. Her brother embraced the skull and howled in tears, pledging to return with the rest of the body. He gradually lost his sanity. Wrapping himself in layers of white sheets, like a bandaged mummy, he would claim that he was experimenting, that uranium had turned him into a giant, and that once he succeeded with his experiments he would save all the wounded. Her brother's remarks about the effects of radiation, Saeki adds, were not entirely wrong.

Insofar as the scenes of 6 August are concerned, Saeki's testimonial contrasts strikingly with Numata's. While Numata's testimony centers upon her own pain, the torturous amputation without anesthesia, and her struggles thereafter to come to terms with her radically transformed state, Saeki's speaks of the miscellany of sights she witnessed at different locations. Typically, her testimonies are filled with references to one apocalyptic sight after another—people's demonic appearances, their screams and groans, the river overflowing with floating corpses, smashed abdomens, unrescued infants, disfigured bodies, charred corpses, blistered faces swollen like balloons, sagging and bloody skin, naked burned bodies, people stripped of their clothes, piles of festering horse carcasses, drooping eyeballs, and more. They recount, as in an inventory, the random fragments of objects destroyed. Like the mother's skull that appeared out of her brother's bundle, or his thoroughly bandaged figure, each of these powerful images encapsulates the cataclysmic event. They are still images, encouraging an arrested consciousness dislodged from an endless dialectics. They remain frozen, divorced from the wholeness and stability of everyday contexts. These fragmentary images challenge audiences, inscribing in their minds not so much the meanings of the devastation as its simple and awful extraordinariness.

By subjecting the event and its sights, bodies, and voices—the objects of recounting—to her gaze, the witness establishes her testimonial authority. Yet at the same time, Saeki's authenticity derives from her identification with what the narrative objectifies—that is, from the audience's understanding that the narrator was also a part of the catastrophic scene. When she testifies, the subject and object of representation are constantly conflated, and it is this convergence that produces the narrator's authoritative presence as a survivor. From that position Saeki challenges her listeners at this space reserved for the dead: "If the dead could utter words, I am certain that they would beg of you, 'Please grasp something in your very own language.'" Saeki's narrative comprises a number of sentences of this type, in which Saeki speaks in the first-person voice for the third person. In her narrative, utterances constantly shift between materialized voices *of* the dead and memorial testimonies *for* them.

As the desire to identify testimonial practice with memorialization has accelerated, so has the acute sense that memories of the nuclear devastation have become increasingly obsolete and irrelevant. Protests against the engineering of "bright" cityspaces, as we saw in chapter 1, are most illustrative in this regard. These resistances emerged as a normative discourse arguing that we ought not to forget the incinerated and the drowned, including those who to this day remain unexhumed beneath the city's streets. Those who survived now protest in proxy for the dead.

The aspiration to speak for the dead has also been intensified by what is often described as the "withering of Hiroshima" (*Hiroshima no fūka*). The phrase is often used in reference to the lessening of commitment and will to protest against war and the nuclear buildup. It also suggests that this "mecca of peace" has lost much of its former status within peace and antinuclear discourse in postwar Japan. In the past, three premises have sustained the historical originality and charismatic character of Hiroshima, and to a lesser extent Nagasaki: the atomic disasters of the two cities were historically unprecedented events that were brought about by the new scientific technology, nuclear fission; the new weapons produced a type of destruction unprecedented in its instantaneousness and its long-term effects; and finally, it has been, and should forever be, unrepeatable. And yet representations of nuclear catastrophe have been produced and reproduced during the past decades in various media forms, including film, photography, print, paintings, and so on. Print and electronic media have annually planned "8.6 specials." Visitors' emotional reactions to Hiroshima have been reported in great detail in television news programs and documentaries. *Hibakusha* storytellers, as noted earlier, have also observed that classroom lessons and peace education prior to visiting Hiroshima have produced a numbing effect on young students. The withering of Hiroshima marks the disintegration of the city's charisma, its reduction to yet another banality. The mystical move toward identification with the dead is inextricably linked to the attempt to recover experiential authenticity and originality against the hegemonic tendencies of the late capitalist information society.

Tawara Genkichi's activities are relevant to this resistance. The former journalist—who once participated in a project to produce a white paper on the A- and H-bomb disasters and who currently represents the Pika Resource Center (Pika Shiryō Kenkyūjo) under his new pseudonym, Seseragi Ryō—has committed himself to scrupulously identifying and correcting every existing error in descriptions of Hiroshima's and Nagasaki's atom bombings. Erroneous illustrations and representations usually result from citations and re-citations. He thus instructs younger volunteer researchers who participate in his projects to refer directly to the primary sources, the originals. The amount of materials and historical sources Tawara has collected in order to expose all the lies about the atomic bombs is purported to be immense. For him, erroneous representations are tantamount to desecrating the dead. Yet those who are being misrepresented have been dispossessed of the power to expose the errors; someone must voice their objections in their stead.

The pseudonym "Genkichi" supposedly derives from a phrase Tawara fashioned to characterize himself, "*genbaku kichigai*," the closest translation of which would be "atom bomb nut."[23] He travels throughout the city searching for data on the atom bomb, and he appears at ceremonies that are performed at various memorials. At bookstores he does not purchase books but skims through them, searching for lines that refer to the bomb. Few people, except for those whom he trusts as friends and working partners, know where or how he lives. Correspondence usually reaches him through his post office box. Some say he has a family, others say he lives by himself. Uncovering each mistake, every error, can be strenuous work. When exhausted, Tawara says, he visits the graves of the bomb victims and drinks till dawn. As he converses with the dead, he feels that his energy for the seemingly endless battle against distortion and misinformation is gradually replenished. Moreover, Tawara's research tenacity can make important contributions to critical public discourse, as will be seen when in chapter 5 I discuss his crucial, if unintentional, input into the controversy concerning relocation of the memorial dedicated to Korean atomic bomb victims.

Numata Suzuko's narrative practices, described earlier, are also indicative of how survivors have reacted to the hegemonic cultural trend of the late twentieth century. Arguably, her decision to become a storyteller was initiated by her reaction to the fragmented objectification of her experience in the documentary film. She can be seen as attempting to regain the "aura"—that which is original and irreproducible—of a storyteller. Her storytelling is a mode of resistance to the condition of modernity under which knowledge has become alienated from the individual's being and is constantly converted into shards of exchangeable information and manageable objects.[24] Through her authoritative presence, she hopes to restore a sense of materiality and substance to knowledge and thereby to the relationships between narrators and narratees—to the narrative scenes that are situated in a world where the aesthetics of ephemerality and depthlessness rule, where the superficiality of infinitely reproducible images dominates.

The desire to speak in proxy for the dead suggests that there is a tendency to regard the dead as the ultimate source of authenticity. Those who claim to speak for the dead also claim the ability to do so without error; to talk about the past incorrectly is to betray one's loyalty to the community of victims. Conversely, the capacity to accurately represent the past authenticates one as a legitimate member of that community and thus bestows authority and power on the narrator. In other words, the battle against the loss of charisma, caused by an excess of copies, is waged by attempting to be one with the dead, to reestablish unity with the truly authentic and original.

Nevertheless, the testimonial practices of survivors like Yamazaki and Saeki disavow mystical identifications with the community of the dead. The very presence of survivors who narrate in the present itself already attests to the absence of the past: the event narrated is indeed "past" and no longer exists. When narrators speak of how they witnessed the deaths of their closest family members, how they trod on corpses, or how they rejected hands that called for help, they foreclose the possibility of sentimentalizing and aestheticizing any such nostalgic unity. Rather, their stories make listeners conscious of the reality that those who survived and speak for the dead are not identical with the dead.

Oral narrative practices underscore the distance between living and dead even more painfully than written testimonials because the narrator and the narratee occupy the same time and space. As we have seen, the very task of speaking as proxy for the dead already marks the lat-

ter's silence. The survivors' narrative practice, as a trace, reminds us of
the absence of what is presented, certifying that the dead and the surviving will never again share the same temporality. Knowledge produced by such narratives *for* the dead therefore necessarily defers and
disidentifies. Furthermore, acknowledgment of this absence is precisely
what generates a sense of mourning for the lost, while recognition of
the limits of representation, of the fact that the past can never be recovered in its fullness and originality, is what allows the audience to
glimpse the immensity and gravity of the catastrophic experience. The
ceaseless process of disidentification generates the critical nature of the
survivors' narrative practices.

Yet to acknowledge the nature of the *hibakusha*'s testimonial practices, particularly as acts of memorialization and prayer, we must also
grasp that this critical process of disidentification occurs *even as* it is believed that a mystical oneness with the dead is achieved, though only
momentarily. The survivors' testimonial practices, like a shamanistic ritual that summons dead souls, resurrect the deceased and endow them
with voices. They intimate to the audience that no one will die a death
devoid of significance—that no living beings, even those who meet seemingly "absurd" and cruel deaths, will perish without leaving traces from
which the meanings of their existences can be retraced. For many survivors, their testimonial practices are attempts to represent the disappearing voices and sentiments of the dead, to convey the final feelings
and thoughts of those who were silenced by the instantaneous mass
killing. They do so by identifying with the dead, translating the latter's
utterances into languages that are intelligible for those who listen. In
this instance in which the narratives *for* the dead transfigure into those
of the dead, the critical process of disidentification does indeed come
to a halt. At that moment, when the negative dialectics is arrested, the
deaths can be addressed as nothing else but deaths. No further process of signification is possible; there can be no appropriation and co-
optation of memories of the dead by existing dominant discourses.

•   •   •

Social and cultural systems have constantly reconstructed the dead as
their Others, as that which is suppressed yet essential for existence. The
dead have been left behind in the linear course of time; having aided
in the nation's development, social and political progress, revolution,
or the awakening of humankind, they are remembered only as those

who have "passed away." In the often-heard cliché—"the precious sacrifice of those victimized by the atomic bombings have laid a firm foundation for Japan's postwar peace and prosperity," or words to that effect—the atom bomb dead are endowed with teleological meaning. They are understood to have contributed to the uninterrupted history of national progress. In the mystical moment of identification between the narrators and the dead who are narrated, by contrast, the dead are emancipated from the endless chain of signification and recalled without being given any meaning, except as such. In this respect, the type of knowledge produced by the memorializing quality of the *hibakusha*'s testimonial practices can be characterized as utopian, redemptive knowledge, analogous to that which emerges out of what Walter Benjamin called "dialectics at a standstill."[25]

Benjamin regarded dialectics at a standstill, on the one hand, as being inseparable from one's uncritical aspiration for and identification with that which is believed to have the capacity to fully recuperate and represent one's life, sentiments, desire, and existence. This mystifying aspiration leads to the various dangers unique to modernity: fascism, wars between nation-states, and commodity fetishism. On the other hand, Benjamin also saw it as a necessary moment for politicizing historical knowledge and generating critical reflection on the ideology of enlightenment and progress. Fredric Jameson has articulated this duality within the context of Marxist literary analysis: "a Marxist negative hermeneutic, a Marxist practice of ideological analysis proper, must in the practical work of reading and interpretation be exercised *simultaneously* with a Marxist positive hermeneutic, or a decipherment of the Utopian impulses of these same still ideological cultural texts."[26] Jameson's formulation about the necessary ambivalence in critical intellectual practices is especially useful in understanding the effects of the *hibakusha*'s storytellings that we have been observing. The survivors' testimonial practices accomplish the double operation of simultaneously enabling an unremitting affirmation of one's existence and generating viable critiques about the ways in which the world is known to us. Listeners' reactions to the storytellers are very revealing in this regard.

Kizuna, the television documentary described in chapter 3, closely followed the exchanges between the members of Kataru Kai and a group of teenage students. It traced the course of the students' daily activities from their return to high school after their first visit to Hiroshima to their reunion with the survivors a year later. Director Kawara Hirokazu has pointed out in his reflections on the documentary that their school is notorious for teenage violence and dropouts. Many of the students live under difficult economic conditions, in part because of troubled relations with their families. Many support themselves financially by working after school or when school is not in session. Some also face daily discrimination such as police harassment and negative stereotyping because of their ethnic backgrounds or because they are members of so-called discriminated-against communities (*hisabetsu buraku*). These students are keenly aware of the social injustices committed against them and feel deprived, frustrated, and hopeless. The documentary highlights the curious metamorphosis that several students experienced as a result of their encounter with the *hibakusha*. Those who had been known for their "problematic behavior," for committing violence and cutting classes, began to take initiative in school activities. They became engrossed, among other things, in planning a second Hiroshima trip. These students also became actively involved in students' affairs, negotiating with teachers to improve the overall educational environment; they succeeded, for instance, in helping to institute special measures for self-supporting students.

In his documentary Kawara asked these students why they felt so attracted to Hiroshima's survivors. One male student responded:

> I feel like I am in a similar situation. [People always say,] "It's a dumb school," "Only dumb kids go to that school." It seems like those *hibakusha* must be having a hard time from discrimination. . . . When I listen to those kinds of stories, I feel that I really understand them well—at least every once in a while. Because we share the same situation we can learn [from them] when we go [to Hiroshima], you see. About how they have struggled, or how they were discriminated against—things like that. People normally won't praise you for those things. . . . It also makes me feel that I should try harder.[27]

The student's identification with the survivors derives from his feeling as if the latter were "similar" or in the "same situation," when in fact *hibakusha* occupy positions that have been constituted by radically different historical and cultural conditions. The testimonial event at which narratees are moved to tears as they listen to narrators and feel compelled to protest against war and nuclear weapons is analogous to what Naoki Sakai has described as a "ritual of sharing a pathos in synchronicity."[28] As testimonies *for* the dead turn into narratives *of* the dead, the event further allows a "community of sympathy" to emerge between the narrators and the narratees, and thus the perception of a unity between the living and the dead develops. The danger of such sympathy, or what Sakai rereads as the synchronicity of pathos, is the tendency to generate the (mis)perception that the dead and listeners always share the same horizons beyond time and space—for example, a common nation, experiences of injustice, and so on—while occluding heterogeneity and actual contradictions.[29]

Yet we must remember that listeners are also constantly compelled to critique their own recognition of unity and identification, whether with the narrator or with the narrated dead. I have already shown how testimonial scenes ceaselessly forbid any complete identification between survivors and the deceased, between the spoken and the unspeakable, between memories and events. The survivors' desire to accurately convey the past is likewise in constant tension with their profound awareness of its incommunicability, the recognition that their immediate experiences can never be conveyed to others as they really happened. Moreover, the narrators' various positionalities and their multivocal subjectivities also obscure the object of empathy and identification. The survivors' testimonial practices indeed foster the communal sense that narrators and narratees, the narrators and the narrated dead, and presumably the remembered victims and those who listen to their voices share sentiments and experiences. Nevertheless, the critical nature of the testimonial practices simultaneously generates a sobering warning that this sensation of identification, fullness, and unity can only take place in fleeting and fragmentary instances, in what we might call moments of sympathy. As the high school student filmed by Kawara remarked, listeners can feel that they have understood the catastrophic destruction and agony told by narrators—but only "every once in a while."

The "standstill" in the negative dialectics of survivors' narratives allows the dead to be referred to in their fullness. It promises listeners that no matter how death comes, no one vanishes without leaving any traces; and it will always be possible for someone to recuperate the sufferings of one's life in singular and authentic form. It is this sense of plenitude and wholeness that endows their testimonies with a quality of a utopian fulfillment and salvation. At the same time, the survivors' narratives reveal that the promise of totality can only be fulfilled in quickly passing moments. A profound tension exists within the *hibakusha*'s testimony as memorialization—a tension between the hope that such an ultimate redemption might in fact be possible and the knowledge that the temporal and spatial recuperation of the past in the present can never be accomplished.

But the promise is what matters. Without provisional trust in the possibility of utopian moments of sympathy, any attempt at a dialogue would be vain and meaningless. To be sure, the identification generated by the *hibakusha*'s testimonies does not necessarily work to maintain collective unity and consistency in the fashion of, say, "all the oppressed," or "all victims." Rather, the fleeting and fragmentary moments of sympathy for the dead produce coalitional social and cultural practices. They provide opportunities to link the diverse relations—of subordination, absurdity, complicity, alienation, and so on—that constitute the heterogeneous and contradictory structural elements of one's positionality.

PART THREE

Memory
and Positionality

CHAPTER 5

Ethnic and Colonial Memories

The Korean Atom Bomb Memorial

People are shown not what they were, but what they must
remember having been. Since memory is actually a very
important factor in struggle . . . if one controls people's
memory, one controls their dynamism. And one also controls
their experience, their knowledge of previous struggles.

> Michel Foucault,
> "Film and Popular Memory" (1989)

To articulate the past historically does not mean to recognize
it "the way it really was." . . . It means to seize hold of a
memory as it flashes up at a moment of danger.

> Walter Benjamin, "Theses on the Philosophy
> of History" (1969 [1950])

In performing acts of remembrance—erecting memorials, testifying,
holding public commemorations, or writing autobiographical histories,
for instance—one seeks to reterritorialize the existing cartography of
memory. Such acts authorize the past, marking it with a signature distinct from that of others. To possess and present one's own memories
is inextricably tied to questions of power and autonomy. Inscribing a
unique way of remembering—whether collective or individual—onto
a society's history ensures that that presence will be visible and that
voice heard in the production of discourses on the past.

The erection in 1970 of a memorial dedicated to the Korean colonial subjects who were killed by the atom bomb achieved precisely such
effects for Koreans in Japan. It inscribed their presence onto Hiroshima's and Japan's history and society. The memorial restored the
sovereignty of those dead who had been deprived of independent national status under Japan's colonial rule, and who consequently were

doubly victimized as a result of the U.S. nuclear attack. Records indicate that among the 350,000 to 400,000 in Hiroshima assaulted by the atom bomb or exposed to lethal postexplosion radiation, at least 45,000 were Korean. Of the one million former colonial subjects who returned to Korea after liberation, approximately 30,000 were survivors of Hiroshima and Nagasaki. Among those survivors at least half are known to live in the Republic of Korea.[1]

Following the devastation caused by Japan's colonial takeover of Korea in 1910, large numbers of Koreans began to migrate to Hiroshima. By the end of the war at least two million Koreans were living in mainland Japan. Because Hiroshima had grown into a modern, industrial city of the colonial metropolis, many from North and Southeast Asia migrated to Hiroshima to seek opportunities for employment and education. Moreover, under the National Manpower Mobilization Act (as extended to Koreans between 1939 and 1945) the Japanese government brought approximately 700,000 Koreans to Japan for forced labor in coal mines, in munitions factories, and at various other dangerous construction sites.[2] Because many Koreans worked in the factories located near Hiroshima, the city's Korean population also increased toward the end of the war. Yet these facts about the relationship between Korea and Hiroshima have not been widely known. The Korean victims and their specific sufferings have been virtually absent from past official representations of Hiroshima's atomic atrocity, which portray the devastation in ways that encourage memories of a universal human experience. In the overarching narratives of the Peace Memorial Museum, those who suffered the nuclear attack have tended to be cast simply as undifferentiated "victim" of a moment unprecedented in human history. Until 1990, the speeches of political elites at the annual municipal Peace Memorial Ceremony on 6 August never referred to the 20,000 to 30,000 (and perhaps even more) Korean atom bomb dead, who comprised between 10 and 20 percent of those killed immediately in the Hiroshima bombing.

The vagueness of estimates of the Korean dead—ranging from 5,000 to 50,000—is evidence that the bomb's impact on the racially and ethnically minoritized population has been considerably neglected. Officially assigned school textbooks lack information about Japanese colonialism generally and Korean laborers in particular; middle and high school teachers in Hiroshima wishing to rectify the situation have had to publish their own supplementary handbooks. Therefore, among the numerous commemorative sites of the Hiroshima nuclear obliteration, the memorial for the Korean atom bomb victims stands as one of the very few visible reminders of the tribulations and suffering of those minorities interpellated as Koreans. And over the last two decades, the Korean memorial has provided an important space of discursive interventions for Japan's former colonial subjects. It has contested and denationalized the ways in which Hiroshima memories are articulated; in particular, it has challenged the remembering of Hiroshima's atrocity exclusively as victimization of the "Japanese."

This memorial's physical location has also been crucial in determining its quality and meanings: it is starkly isolated from the official commemorative site, the Hiroshima Peace Memorial Park. As one can easily imagine, segregation of the ethnic memorial site from the city's central commemorative space has often been regarded as symptomatic of the subaltern status of Korean resident aliens in Japan—*zainichi Kankoku Chōsenjin* (*zainichi* Koreans, or simply *zainichi*)—who are invariably subjected to legal and administrative practices that are commonly summarized as "discrimination, assimilation, and expatriation." The Immigration Control and Refugee Act and the Alien Registration Act, the two laws that presently define the legal status of approximately 700,000 *zainichi*, unquestionably show their derivation from a colonial policy that treated Korean people and other colonial subjects as second-class citizens. The legal practices that continue to subordinate *zainichi* Koreans include the requirement that all, including permanent residents, carry an alien registration card at all times; the extraordinarily extensive discretionary power of the Ministry of Justice vis-à-vis *zainichi*, which makes them vulnerable to deportation; the strictly selective naturalization process that employs very arbitrary standards; and informal administrative pressures to assimilate that Korean and other aliens experience when they are compelled to adopt Japanese-like family names.[3] The memorial therefore has done more than provide a ritual space for the annual memorial ceremonies for Korean victims. By allowing rearticulations of past and present knowledges about colonial experiences, the memorial and the discourse on its location have also constituted a critical locus for the ethnic politics of Korean resident aliens in Hiroshima and elsewhere.

This chapter explores the controversy that erupted in 1990 over the city's proposal to relocate the Korean memorial to within the Peace Park proper. In examining in detail the discourses that emerged during this dispute, I focus here on the attempts to contain and domesticate these as yet unreconciled discourses on the nation's past and on the resistance to such domestication. The argument over the memorial's location necessarily raised the question of how the Japanese government should face its responsibilities for colonialism and the war of invasion.

Furthermore, in analyzing how the Korean memorial has become central to the local politics of Korean ethnicity, I attend to the process whereby the memorial and its location constitute a double discourse. The memory practices revolving around the memorial separate the remembered and those who are remembering the event from the rest of Japanese society and identify them as ethnically minoritized by Japan's social and legal arrangements. Yet at the same time these narratives and practices of memorialization constitute contradictory elements in the production of subjectivities, thereby making distinctions within the group as well as within each individual. On the one hand, the Korean memorial and its discursive processes differentiate nationally and ethnically those who claim ownership to the memories specific to this icon and those who feel a sense of belonging to the mnemonic community built around the history shared specifically as Koreans. On the other hand, the narratives and practices of memorialization inevitably shape diverse *zainichi* consciousness about history, ethnicity, and nationality— in other words, about those elements that cannot be entirely subsumed by the totality of collective identity or by what are imagined to be shared communal experiences.[4]

In exploring the diverse and conflicting narratives produced by Korean resident aliens and others involved in the public dispute, the chapter disentangles elements within the web of memories that often collapse diverse referents into the single totality of a "Koreanness." It pays attention to how they are differently positioned through the matrices of nationality (i.e., being North or South Korean), generation, region, gender, sexuality, and class (although I cannot discuss them all), while at the same time underscoring the strategic indispensability of organizing and mobilizing individuals primarily by race/ethnicity.[5] In examining the 1990 relocation controversy, I ask how the Korean memorial managed to remain a site where contestatory representations of Japan's colonial history could be enunciated, thereby providing those concerned about the local community's future with the possibility of forging new alliances, questions, and visions that might exceed the boundaries of ethnicity and nationality.

CONTENTIOUS MEMORIAL

The memorial for the Korean atomic bomb victims stands northwest of the Peace Memorial Park, across the river that demarcates the park's western boundary. Because of its siting, those who visit the park tend to miss it altogether, unless they deliberately seek it out. It is set at the foot of a bridge, at a narrow fourway intersection. A statue of a mythic turtle supporting a fifty-foot-high granite column stands there.

The turtle rests on a terracelike platform and is fenced with small columns connected by metal bars. To the side of the memorial are some rose of Sharon trees, symbols of the Republic of Korea. Offerings of colorful cranes and children's original artworks forming the Chinese characters for "peace" are placed neatly at the fence. Every piece of artwork or cluster of cranes is labeled with the young artist's individual and school name. A white pebbled area surrounds the platform and separates the memorial from dark granite tiling the ritual floor. Among the pebbles are stones on which schoolchildren have scribbled their names, ages, and classes. Some even have slogans or handwritten phrases, such as "antidiscrimination" (*hansabetsu*), "peace and human rights," or "toward a society without war" (*senso no nai shakai o*). Visits by student pilgrims make many of the memorials in the Peace Park—such as the Atom Bomb Dome, the Statue for the Atom-Bombed Children (which commemorates Sasaki Sadako, who died as a teenager from radiation late-effect leukemia), or the memorial for mobilized students— more than mere stone monuments. The plenitude of offerings at the memorial site indicates that the Korean memorial is among the most frequently visited memorials, despite its physical isolation.

On the front of the memorial is an engraving made up of Chinese characters that reads *Kankokujin genbaku giseisha irei hi,* or "memorial for *Kankokujin* (South Korean and/or Korean) atom bomb victims." Next to it is a second line, also with Chinese characters but in a different style of calligraphy: "In memory of Prince Yi U and the other 20,000 or more souls." Below them is a horizontal line engraved in English, "THE MONUMENT IN MEMORY OF THE KOREAN VICTIMS OF ABOMB" [*sic*]. The names of the fifty-seven Koreans and three Japanese who were involved in its construction are listed on the memorial's right side.

The memorial has provoked a number of interpretive contestations over the past two decades. One issue has been whether this monument memorializes all souls of the Korean atom bomb dead, or only those survivors affiliated with the Republic of Korea. The term *Kankokujin,* at least in contemporary Japanese usage, generally refers to nationals of the Republic of Korea; another term for Koreans, *Chōsenjin,* is used either to specifically denote nationals of the Democratic People's Republic of Korea or to indicate the larger ethnic group. The schism in the homeland, brought about by the history of Japanese colonialism, U.S. cold war hegemony, and the Korean War, led to a corresponding chasm in memorializing the atom bomb dead. Members of Zainippon Chōsenjin Sōrengō (the General Federation of Korean Residents in Japan, known as Chongryun, and commonly referred to in Japanese as Sōren), an organization that provides various administrative services for those affiliated with North Korea, claim to have been excluded from the commemoration at the existing memorial; since 1975 they have been requesting that the city allow construction of their own memorial.[6] But Zainippon Taikan Minkoku Kyoryūmindan (the Association for Korean Residents in Japan, known as Mindan) officially holds the view that the memorial stands for both North and South Koreans, on the grounds that Hanguk, or Kankoku in Japanese, was the official name of Korea before Japanese occupation.[7] For example, the representative of the Hiroshima Prefectural Headquarters of the Special Committee for the Atomic Bomb Victims affirmed Mindan's position that "the memorial stands for the Great Korean People, with no distinction between south and north."[8] The "ownership" of the memorial is thus made to appear self-evident.

Another interpretive crisis stemmed from the erasure of a portion of the memorial's engravings giving a brief history of Korea. About two of the nineteen lines originally inscribed in Korean on the back of the memorial column are now painted black. This conspicuous obliteration created an absence that viewers of the memorial have attempted to fill with their own historical narratives. When the inscription was erased in 1974, newspapers widely reported the explanation of Chang T'ae-hŭi, the head of the memorial's construction committee: he had eliminated the section referring to the ancient history of Korea in response to complaints from the Korean government that the description was too "disgraceful" and inappropriate for foreign eyes. He also feared that the sentences were so obscure that they might be "misinterpreted" as referring to Japan's colonial aggression against Korea, when in fact, he believed, they described ancient Chinese rule over the Korean peninsula.

Notwithstanding this authoritative exegesis, there is no consensus about the particular historical period and actors referred to in the erased passage. Some have argued that it described the cruelty of Japanese colonial rule and that the Japanese pressured the Koreans into eliminating a description that they considered unbearably embarrassing. A leftist *zainichi* youth group saw the deletion as proof of that interpretation. Moreover, its members suspected that the order to eliminate the inscription had in fact come from the Park Chung Hee administration, which had previously suppressed protests against the Japanese government's treatment of Koreans in Japan and discouraged attempts to uncover Japan's colonial past. Some storytellers have explained to schoolchildren that the lines probably described the exploitation of Koreans by the Japanese and that the Japanese ordered the Koreans to erase them because they considered the description to be historically inaccurate.[9] During my first visit to the memorial, a Japanese college student, born and raised in Hiroshima, provided a slightly different explanation: the section had been covered over, according to her, because it contained an expression that criticized the Japanese emperor. Regardless of the actual content of the sentences in question, these varying interpretations were highly revealing of mainstream Japanese society's historical consciousness and awareness about the mistreatment of minorities: they seemed to agree that the Japanese had committed an injustice against Koreans.

As Chang suspected, the concealed sentences were indeed ambiguous. They gave no specific dates or names and were composed in the simple past tense, as if they told of a legendary time. They followed a description of how the Korean nation (*minzoku*) never "robbed or harmed" other nations; although it enjoyed a period in which it was "more advanced and prosperous than others," invasions of the more powerful surrounding nations also often threatened the people's welfare. "For instance," the eliminated sentences read, "there were stories in which families of royalty and high-ranking officials were sent as hostages; there were also sorrowful stories in which a number of lovely maidens were offered as tribute; and there were stories of dethronement, in which our royal king was forced to kneel before the enemy king."[10] The erasure ends here and the ensuing narrative describes the atom bombing: "Throughout the five thousand years of the nation's history, however, there had never been anything comparable to the grief and anguish that those twenty thousand souls who are here enshrined have undergone."

Chang's worst fears were in fact realized, though in a wholly unexpected way. The misfortunes endured by Korean royalty and incarcerated young women, as described in the lines, dangerously resemble the by now familiar stories of adversity and ill-fate suffered not only by Prince Yi U himself but also by the "comfort women" forced into sexual slavery. The irony is that in the very act of concealing the source of ambiguity, the founder of the memorial inspired the reading he had hoped to prevent—that is, that the narrative denoted Japanese assaults on Korea.

The final interpretive crisis involving the Korean memorial has concerned its location. As many observers, including those in the media, have noted, the memorial stands outside the administrative boundaries of the Peace Park. To be sure, the Korean memorial is not the only one beyond the official territory. But the majority of the other frequently visited memorials that are not contained within the Peace Park itself are located just outside the eastern and southern peripheries and are spatially integrated into the park's overall scheme by extended greenery and paths. In contrast, the park's northwest end is much further removed from the central commemorative sites. Moreover, visitors to the area where the central cenotaph for the atom bomb victims, the Peace Memorial Museum, the Atom Bomb Dome, and other memorials are clustered rarely approach the Peace Memorial Park from its western boundary. Its relative lack of traffic is in part because of the layout of public transportation routes and also perhaps because the park's western periphery is adjacent to a more or less residential neighborhood, while the three other sides are contiguous to the downtown entertainment area and to other public facilities.

An open letter addressed to the municipal government in 1986— coauthored by Sō Tokai, a first-generation *zainichi* poet and activist, and his Japanese collaborator—expressed great perplexity and resentment about the situation:

> On August 6, after the Peace Commemoration Ceremony at the Hiroshima Peace Park[,] . . . we made a pilgrimage to the memorial for the Korean victims. But how could this be? The memorial stood not in the wide open space of the Peace Park, but outside, that is, across the river at the western foot of the Honkawa Bridge. Frankly, we could not restrain our astonishment and anger. Discrimination even against the dead? Discrimination even among the victims of the atomic bomb? . . . We demand that Hiroshima city fulfill its own responsibility (*mizukara no sekinin ni oite*) to swiftly relocate the present memorial, or to construct a new memorial inside the park.[11]

Since that letter was written, voices questioning the memorial's marginal status have become much louder. In response to growing public criticism, the city has to the present day consistently offered three reasons for denying requests to relocate the memorial.

First, the city has insisted that it must observe the regulation it established in 1967, prohibiting the construction of any more memorials inside the official zone of the Peace Memorial Park.[12] Second, the city has argued that if the memorial were to be relocated inside the Peace Park, it would bring political controversy with it, apparently assuming the impossibility of creating a "unified memorial" so that those affiliated with the Democratic People's Republic of Korea, as well as with the Republic of Korea, could pay their respects without conflict. The city administrators maintain that the Peace Park is a sacred site where prayers for all of humanity are offered and which should not be desecrated with political dissent. Third, the mayor and the city administrators in general contend that the central cenotaph in the Peace Park enshrines all souls lost to the bomb, without regard to nationality or race; therefore there is no need to have a separate memorial dedicated solely to the Korean atom bomb victims.[13]

At least for those who have problematized the Korean memorial's present location, its treatment is usually understood to be an index of ongoing discrimination against *zainichi* Koreans and a sign of their continuing alienation. The physical location of the Korean memorial, therefore, paradigmatically crystallizes official history's suppression of Korean ethnicity through the marginalization of their memories. Visitors to the Korean memorial pass through the park proper and sense its periphery as they approach the border greenery. They then walk across the bridge to finally arrive at this small, cramped corner lot. The memorial's physical isolation reinforces the pilgrims' sense of the very reason for their visit. For them, the memorial confirms and condemns *zainichi* Koreans' exclusion from Japan's national memory.

MONUMENT TO HOMELAND

Despite the ever-growing public discontent, however, some *zainichi* Koreans have not regarded the present location of the memorial as a sign of discrimination. One such person was Chang T'ae-hŭi, a key representative of the committee that had both initiated and executed the memorial's construction; he is a first-generation Korean and retired president of a small business. In interviews by the media and activists he has repeatedly asserted that although he wishes to see the memorial placed within the Peace Park, as promised by the former mayor, he does not believe that its present location is in any way "discriminatory" or a "disgrace." As he has done on numerous other occasions, during my interview with him Chang reiterated the significance he saw in the memorial's present location:

> [The location where the memorial stands today] was the site where the Korean prince [Yi U] was found at the time of the bombing. The river was already filled with dead corpses floating like rafts. There they found one body glittering with accessories. "This must be someone important," people thought, and they pulled the body out of the river.[14]

A nephew of the Yi dynasty's king, Prince Yi U became a victim of the bomb while serving as a lieutenant-colonel in the Japanese Imperial Army. Without pausing, Chang went on to describe how Korean royalty have been perceived.

> Unlike the Japanese imperial family, the former Korean royal families are not cared for. The Korean kings and their families are regarded as national traitors. They actively created a pro-Japanese camp. During the colonial era, the Japanese [in Korea] occupied every position of leadership. They controlled everything from financial unions, farmland registration, and the rice mills [one of which Chang's father owned] to forced mobilization (kyōsei chōyō). In our prefecture, they built munitions factories designated by the navy under the slogan of "Korea-mainland unification" (naisen ittai). When we were preparing for the construction of the memorial, many wanted us to use the word "kankoku," as [the character kan] had been used in nikkan heigō (Korea-Japan annexation).

What prompted this founder of the memorial to choose Prince Yi U to represent the Korean victims of the bomb, when in fact he is among those who are "regarded as national traitors"? Chang's narrative suggests that Yi U and Korean royalty as a group are considered to be victims of Japan's colonial policy, just as much as any other Koreans, including zainichi and Korean victims of the atom bomb. Perhaps Chang was projecting onto Yi U's tribulations his own personal history: he himself at one time was accused of collaborating with Japan's war effort and colonial rule. The choice of Yi U might have been part of his personal effort to restore the good name of the many Koreans who had cooperated with Japan and who have long been scorned as collaborators. And as the memorial redeems the Yi family and other subjects who presumably shared a similar destiny, it simultaneously, at least in Chang's interpretation, resurrects the essential ideograph (han, or kan in Japanese) in the name of their sovereign country—the name that was forcibly wrested from them during Japan's colonial rule.

The nation's name, language, history, and prince, though tarnished, mark the memorial's referent and distinguish the dead enshrined there from other atom bomb victims. The roses of Sharon offer yet another intimation of the homeland. The granite stones and pebbles are also native products of Korea that were processed there and then shipped to Hiroshima. These material objects from the soil of the home country are said to console the souls of those who are thought to have died while yearning for their homeland. Moreover, the memorial, embellished as it is with Korean national symbols, signifies the victories of Koreans who survived Japanese colonialism, the war, and even the atom bomb. The memorial honors the national culture and the existing political regime; it also celebrates timeless and unwavering ties with Korea. For instance, the Republic of Korea's national flag is engraved on the left side of the memorial. Below the flag are the names and titles of two individuals: I Hyo-sang, chair of the national congress of the Republic of Korea at the time of the memorial's construction, who provided the calligraphy for the main inscription; and Han Kap-su, a Seoul University professor who authored the memorial's history of the Korean victims. Describing this icon of Korean national and anticolonial pride, one of the construction committee members wrote, "Like a [magnificent] stork among a [common] flock of chickens, this solemn memorial, which is reminiscent of a king's tomb that crystallizes the pure spirits of Silla, is absolutely [peerless] among the numerous monument stones in the Peace Park."[15]

In this sense, unlike Hiroshima's other memorials, which register defeat in the war, the monument provides witness to the victory of the martyrs of independence. It stands for the triumph over Japanese aggressions and also signifies the fulfillment of emancipation from colonial injustices. While registering the emotions of grief, atonement, and consolation, the Korean memorial simultaneously serves as a nationalist icon, embodying the pride and glory of the Republic of Korea.[16] It is likely that Chang's way of remembering the Hiroshima atrocity is predominant among first- and perhaps some second-generation *zainichi* Koreans. But it is certainly not the only way the remembrance takes place, even for those who are supposed to have shared a similar generational history.

Sō Tokai, mentioned above as coauthor of a letter criticizing the memorial's location, does not subscribe to the narrative of great Korean national glories. Born in 1919, Sō considers himself one of the oldest

among those who can lay claim to being *zainichi*. He is a poet who
has earned his living primarily as a construction worker and day la-
borer. Today he receives welfare payments from the government. Virtually homeless, he lives in the corner of a common room in a university
students' dormitory. He is also widely known as the first individual to
have protested against discriminatory legal restrictions on resident Koreans by publicly setting fire to his alien registration card. On 1 September 1990, Sō delivered a lecture as part of a study session commemorating the sixty-seventh anniversary of the Korean massacres that
followed the Kantō earthquake of 1923. While the main theme of his
talk concerned postwar compensation for Korean victims of the Asia
Pacific War, in response to a question he also expressed his opinions on
the Korean memorial issue.

Underlying Sō's narrative regarding the Korean memorial, radically
different from that of Chang and most other *issei* (first-generation *zainichi*), is an obstinate refusal of any communal boundaries regarding
what is assumed to be the shared experience of Korean victimization.
Sō began by criticizing the Gensuikin Conference: "During the seven-
ties, when the Gensuikin movement gained popularity, in the cries that
called attention to the cruelty of the atomic bomb, I did not even once
hear the claim that there are survivors in Korea." He continued, "When
Mindan began to build the memorial and when people asked the city
for its permission, did any of those organizations that claim to fight for
human rights . . . express any sort of [supportive] attitude? I believe
members of those organizations regarded [the issue of the Korean atom
bomb victims] as irrelevant to their own problems." His criticism of the
mainstream Japanese peace organizations' treatment of the Korean atom
bomb victims extends to the general problem of postwar reparations,
as he pointed to the unjust policy under which former colonial subjects
who fought as Japanese imperial subjects during the war have not received monetary reparations equal to those given Japanese nationals. He
concluded, "In Japan, the object of rescue is always limited to the [eth-
nic] Japanese. And people don't think it's odd."[17]

While he criticizes the ethnocentrism in Japan's national war memory, Sō at the same time distances himself from those *zainichi* Koreans
who employ such words as *dōhō* (fellow country people) or *sokoku*
(homeland) in order to reinforce a sense of pan-Korean solidarity. For
him, such a tie is illusory and dangerous not only because it may create another boundary for the "community of sympathy" but also be-

cause it obscures the hierarchies within such an imagined community. From his point of view, moreover, it is hypocritical for Koreans in Japan to identify with Koreans in Korea, as if they share the same subjective world. As a way of demonstrating his own notion of being a *zainichi* Korean in Japan, he refuses to pronounce the Chinese characters of his name according to their Korean reading, "Song Tu-hoe," insisting instead on the Japanese pronunciation. He also considers it natural that Koreans in Japan speak Japanese as their first language. He defiantly remarked during the lecture, "I once told a *zainichi* activist who always summons camaraderie with the Koreans back in the homeland that they shouldn't dare say that Koreans in Japan and Koreans in Korea share the same horizon. We were making money in Japan when Korea was suffering during the [1950] Korean War. Our roads were separated a long time ago."

Sō's refusal of the nationalist narrative also led him to form a critical outlook on the Korean memorial—a view that contrasts sharply with Chang's: "But that memorial itself is in fact quite nonsensical (*nansensu*). Why is a specific individual's name inscribed? . . . Moreover, why does only the prince receive special treatment when tens of thousands of Koreans also died? . . . What does the memorial exist for? That there is only an inscription for the Republic of Korea's national flag [when in fact there are people belonging to two separate nations] should also be a matter of controversy."

In concluding his populist narrative, Sō cautioned that if the Korean memorial were moved into the park proper, the municipal government might co-opt ethnic minority issues: "The fact that the memorial for the Korean atomic bomb victims stands across the river is very suggestive. It expresses the reality of *zainichi*. The fact that it is located across the river from the Peace Park is in itself very significant. It's important. Isn't it quite natural that the memorial should stand across the river precisely because the *zainichi* exist across the river?"

A *partial* fulfillment of demands might lead to the further occlusion of yet unresolved questions. Sō's narrative, undoubtedly voiced by very few *issei* and high-ranking members of Mindan, situates the memorial within the context of the *zainichi*'s current location within Japanese society: that is, in the midst of their ongoing endeavors to build their futures in a society that casts them as others who should be assimilated. Sō's position, which relentlessly denies yearning for the homeland and advocates a radical politics of difference, resonates curiously with the recent strategies of ethnic politics pursued by many second- and third-generation youth, a point to which we will later return.

EXCESS OF MEMORY

Shortly before the forty-fifth anniversary of the city's atom bombing, the Hiroshima city government, despite its decade-long refusal to consider any requests for the memorial's relocation, suddenly shifted its position. Unilaterally disregarding the prohibitive 1967 regulation, the city announced that relocation would be welcomed, provided that the North and South Koreans could agree on a unified memorial. The spring of 1990 was indeed a time when different political constituencies—the South Korean government, the Liberal Democratic Party and the Japanese government, Sōren, Mindan, and the municipal government—focused (with a variety of motives) on the Korea-Japan relationship. Several incidents staged in the national political arena during the earlier half of the year, including the May visit of the Republic of Korea's president, Roh Tae Woo, finally brought representatives of mainstream institutions to discuss the long-deferred question of the Korean memorial.

For instance, in April 1990 the minister of foreign affairs, in response to questioning by a Socialist Party Diet member, expressed the central government's intention to pressure the city of Hiroshima to relocate the Korean memorial. The Korean consul general at Shimonoseki then visited Hiroshima toward the end of the month and requested that the city government transfer the present Korean memorial into the Peace Park proper by 6 August. Reportedly, the consul general proposed that given the reality of the division between North and South, it would be appropriate to pursue a "two-step" process of first relocating the existing memorial and then entering into negotiations for a unified memorial. The mayor of Hiroshima's only reaction to the proposal was to reiterate the long-standing official position—namely, that the present memorial's relocation was contingent on the complete agreement of those affiliated with both the Republic of Korea and the People's Republic of Korea.

At the national level, the discursive field concerning the Korea-Japan issue shifted significantly with President Roh's visit to Japan in May 1990. The media covered the president's activities in great detail, treating them as top news stories throughout his three-day-long stay. Letters from Japanese expressing apologies for past deeds, as well as hopes that relationships would improve, filled the readers' columns of national newspapers. At the same time, threats by right-wing terrorists who opposed President Roh's visit were also reported at length. Finally, despite the usual vagueness of his words and the lack of agency in his sentences, Emperor Akihito's expression of "painful regrets" (tsūseki) about Japanese colonial rule marked the climax of the presidential event in the public's eyes. With the new emperor's official "apology," the government and the media attempted to proclaim an end to the painful relationship between the two countries. Ironically, however, the louder the official blare, the deeper public skepticism grew; for people wondered why it had taken nearly half a century just to utter such a simple phrase. Thus, far from satisfactorily resolving the lingering problems between the two countries, President Roh's visit, if anything, helped bring Korean issues to the awareness of many Japanese nationals who might otherwise have given them little thought.[18]

At the local level, Hiroshima city administrators and other economic and political elites discovered their own interests in relocating the memorial. As the 1980s drew to a close, the city's two most pressing matters involved hosting the 1994 Asian Games, an athletic competition involving "all of Asia," and preparing for the fiftieth commemoration of the city's atom bombing, which was to be held in 1995. To the dismay of city officials, however, visitors from the very Asian countries with which the city had been promoting "international friendship" became increasingly vocal in denouncing the peripheral state of the Korean memorial just as these preparations began in earnest. "Discrimination persists even after death?" With news captions such as this, the local media incessantly reported on tourists' outrage toward the city and the Japanese people for their irresponsibility regarding the memorial. As revelations of the suppression of memories of Japanese aggression continued, it appeared most likely that the city would experience even more embarrassing moments at such international events.

The 1990 proposal to relocate the Korean memorial was symptomatic of the broader national agenda, namely, to officially acknowledge the memories of Japan's aggression. Yet, much as Theodor Adorno had observed of Germany's mnemonic milieu in the 1950s (discussed in the introduction), this process of "coming to terms with the past" inevitably meant forgetting in the form of remembering.[19] To secure international markets and to maintain political stability in the Asian and Pacific region, the government has had to incorporate memories of Japan's colonial and military atrocities into the officially recognized national history—but in a manner that would not threaten the present order of knowledge. That the Hiroshima city administration agreed to permit the Korean memorial's relocation must be understood in this context of process of amnesic remembering, which required that the memorial be converted into an innocuous object.

Once permission was officially given, an advisory committee was appointed by the mayor's office, informally dubbed the "eight-person committee" (then the "seven-person committee" after a member resigned). It consisted of local celebrities, including well-known Japanese journalists and academics, and was headed by an internationally acclaimed doctor who was a longtime supporter of *hibakusha*. After many debates and complications, the committee submitted the following concrete proposals to the city.[20] First, the main inscription on the front of the memorial, the committee suggested, should be changed to *genbaku giseisha ireihi* (memorial for the atom bomb victims), eliminating the term Hanguk, or Kankoku (Republic of Korea), as well as Prince Yi U's name. The revision was needed to ensure that the memorial would represent both North and South Korea. Second, four Chinese characters, *man'go yuban*, which would in Japanese be read *banko ryūhō*, should be placed above the main inscription. Taken from classical Korean literature, according to the committee's official explanation, this idiom means that "the precious death of the people will remain as a fragrant stream forever in people's hearts." And finally, two small Hangul letters, *ch'udo*, reading "tribute to the dead," should be added across the top of the inscription.[21]

Despite strong support from high-ranking members of Mindan and Sōren, the attempt to move the memorial into the park by 6 August 1990 ultimately failed because of strong protests from *zainichi* Koreans, Japanese nationals, and other non-Koreans. Fierce objections were specifically directed against the proposed alterations of the present inscription, which were seen as unilaterally dictating the appropriate way in which to remember the Korean experience of the atomic attack. Chang, for instance, who had initially made great personal sacrifices to build the memorial, felt that such changes would be a tremendous insult to those who had directly contributed to the memorial. One Japanese housewife questioned the status of the committee, charging that it in fact was merely rubberstamping the administrators' decision. She argued that advisory committees often helped the city's administrative branch minimize the intervention of the city assembly, by pretending to provide a citizens' consensus. A third-generation *zainichi* Korean grocery store owner, O Sŏng-dŏk, whose ethnic politics I will describe later, expressed his disappointment that the head of Mindan agreed to the alteration of the inscription, adding that he also felt sympathetic to senior members of the organization who were forced into accepting the city's offer because they felt the need to maintain a cordial relationship with the city. Toyonaga Keisaburō, whose activities as a storyteller and in relief efforts for *hibakusha* in South Korea I discussed in chapter 3, was then a high school vice principal and was considered to be the key liaison between Mindan and the committee; he resigned from the committee over this issue. He gave his reasons forthrightly: "In relocating the memorial, [the city] must take into consideration the opinions of various individuals, including those *hibakusha* in Korea. Moreover, if we respect the ideas of those who actually built the memorial, the Japanese people cannot dare to change the content of the inscription. . . . I cannot do justice to the Korean people if I stay on this committee any longer."[22]

To proponents of the move, it may have appeared that the opportunity to relocate was spoiled solely because of the controversy over altering the present inscription. Those in Mindan and Sōren who tentatively agreed to the alteration were certainly hopeful that unifying and relocating the memorial would be a change for the better. Some argued that the move into the park would enhance the general visibility of ethnic Koreans in Japanese society. Others saw it as an opportunity to eliminate Prince Yi U's name—a name that for many in Korea evokes unpleasant memories. Though not without some reservations, many also expressed their desire to see the dream of the "unified homeland" fulfilled, if only in the memorialization of those who had fallen victim to the bomb. However, the plan ultimately failed because of the city officials' insistence that the site could and should remain free of "ideological conflicts." This stand was hardly to the city's advantage. Given the imminence of the fiftieth annual commemoration of the atom bombing and the certainty of international criticism should the memorial remain outside the park, what compelled city officials and others to obstinately refuse to relocate the memorial *without* the controversial alterations?

The present memorial is involved in at least two processes of signification. On the one hand, as we have seen, the memorial has served many as a site of discursive intervention. It has been a location where knowledge about the consequences of Japanese colonial rule over Korea is enunciated by evoking memories of the adversities that Korean atom bomb victims have encountered. At one public symposium organized by several citizens groups in Hiroshima, an invited speaker, Ch'oe Sŏng-won, extolled the memorial for bringing the public's attention to the adversities faced by survivors living in Korea. Because the public does not understand the delayed effects of radiation, these survivors have faced great difficulties obtaining financial and medical support. "In that sense, I am pleased that the memorial exists," said this *nisei* entrepreneur who had at one time served as a member of the memorial's construction committee, "For the memorial not only consoles the souls of the victims; it also helps urge people to think about the very fact that there were this many Korean survivors [and] why Korean victims—who amount to at least 100,000 and perhaps more survivors and 20,000 dead—have been ignored ever since the war's end. I think it is an obvious outcome of discriminatory policy against us Koreans."[23]

On the other hand, the memorial has also always been "a tribute to the dead," a moral and affective site. As a shrine where dead souls are memorialized, as a public grave for those who have never been properly mourned as individuals, it has always called up sentiments that are not restricted to ethnic Koreans alone. While he spoke as a member of the Korean collectivity, Ch'oe's narrative on the Korean memorial also assumed his universal position as a *hibakusha*. His recounting of 6 August has remarkable commonalities with other stories of survival, while the different experiences that might have accrued from his subaltern ethnic status are hardly evident. "I myself am a *hibakusha* as well," the *nisei* Korean man emphasized as he began:

> At the time of the bombing, I was a sixteen-year-old in middle school. My fourteen-year-old younger sister was bombed while engaged as one of the mobilized students who, as all of you must know very well, were demolishing buildings [in order to prevent the spread of fire in the event of air raids]. I discovered her on the shore of the river [near our home] and carried her body on a board. I brought her next to our father who was lying down because of injuries, where she breathed her last.
>
> I buried her thereabouts, and even to this day, I still cannot recall where exactly that was. I am sure that anybody who experienced the atomic bombing must have gone through similar experiences.
>
> That day, in the apocalyptic condition, no one could afford to think about where to bury a body, or where to build a tomb. After many years have passed, I say to myself, "where did I bury my sister, I must look for her," yet things have changed so much [that I realize it is impossible to identify the original burial site].
>
> I therefore firmly believe that the present memorial serves as an enormous mausoleum (*kyodai na haka*) for the over 20,000 [Korean] people who were burned to death in that atomic bombing of Hiroshima, on that day. I have looked at the memorial with such an understanding to this day.

In my case, I lost one younger sister. And my grandmother, father, mother, and my younger brother are all *hibakusha*. I will continue to feel the pain as a survivor just as you all will.

The loss of one or more close family members, the chaos and turmoil in the bombing's aftermath, and the nagging memories of not having being able to pay adequate respects to the deceased—these are the all-too-familiar memories and sentiments of most Hiroshima survivors. Given the immense destruction, some may even feel that Ch'oe was among the fortunate few: after all, he was able to find his sister in the turmoil. Many survivors, Korean or Japanese, might envy Ch'oe for at least being able to provide his sister with care in her last moments and, more important, witness her death. In this regard, the Korean memorial, like a number of other memorials in Hiroshima, pays tribute to all who were indiscriminately killed by the bomb. After all, it could be argued that the United States attacked and massacred those present in Hiroshima on that day as a homogeneous collectivity, regardless of their military or civilian status, age, class, sex, or nationality. Besides, can there be any difference in the value of individual human lives, in the sentiments of the bereaved, in their deepest desires to offer proper homage to the deceased?

Such a universalist understanding, however, often serves to obscure important cleavages, incommensurabilities that are both politically and culturally constituted and that therefore need to be addressed precisely in those terms.[24] There are indeed important differences between Japanese and Korean atom bomb victims: the second-generation Korean survivors almost invariably recall the mistreatment of their parents by Japanese soldiers and civilians at relief stations, even as they remember the horrific experience of survival itself.[25] Moreover, the journalist Nakajima Tatsumi, who has written extensively on Korean survivors' issues, has argued that in contrast to other survivors in Japan, Korean atom bomb survivors have suffered in multiple ways. In particular, those who returned to Korea endured what he calls "triple afflictions." First, according to Nakajima, as a result of immigration and forced mobilization, the population of Koreans tended to be concentrated in the city proper, and hence they were close to the bomb's hypocenter. Second, unlike many Japanese survivors who sought shelter outside the city with family members and friends, most Korean survivors had no choice but to remain in the city and thus suffered greater exposure to radiation. And finally, those Koreans who returned to Korea have not been able to receive medical care comparable to that of survivors in Japan.[26]

Ch'oe challenged the city and committee's 1990 relocation plan by arguing that in order for the memorial to "urge people to think about the very fact that there were this many Korean survivors," the referents of memory—that is, who is being memorialized—must be obvious. Moreover, the ethnic curators of the memories of the dead—*zainichi* Koreans—are not the only ones who should be made aware of the nationality of the enshrined. The communicative dynamics of this memorial must extend to the broader Japanese society and reach out as far as the Korean peninsula. The memories it involves must constantly spill over the boundaries of ethnic memory. Ch'oe concluded that the newly proposed inscription would make it "impossible to know the nation and the people, as well as the reason, for which this memorial stands." The existing memorial marks just that kind of difference, a distinctly "Korean" kind of memory. The Korean memorial speaks specifically to the Korean nation's victimization by Japanese colonialism and the war of expansion. It embodies memories that have been collectively reconstituted and distinguished from those of the perpetrators. The memorial therefore stands for the irreconcilable chasm between the colonizers and the colonized, for the disparity of memories that even the sincerest sentiments for the dead cannot easily conflate.

As a monument, the present icon not only mourns the victims; it also, for the reasons described earlier, celebrates the Korean nation's independence and its emancipation from Japanese colonial rule. Moreover, its messages delegitimate the Japanese government's policies toward Koreans in the past and present. By defacing these memories, the city and committee would have made the relocated memorial commensurate with other icons in the Peace Memorial Park. It would have converted the magnificent, the monumental, and the accusatory to a banal, universalizing "tribute to the dead." What the city and committee would have canceled was any excess of memory in Japan's official remembering of Hiroshima's atomic annihilation that might have revealed the nationalism and racism underlying the trope of humanity.

THE ABSENT MAJORITY

During the past twenty years, Chang's favorable perceptions of the memorial's location and his refusal to construe it as a sign of discrimination have anchored popular knowledge about the memorial's meanings. While providing the Japanese public with an authoritative account of the memorial's history and condition, the views of the head of the construction committee have shaped the mainstream Japanese perspective on ethnic Korean issues in a more general way.

Chang's opinions have been cited whenever the mnemonic crisis has reemerged and the memorial's present location has needed justification. This was certainly true during the relocation controversy just discussed. When several individuals who had petitioned for the memorial's relocation, including myself, confronted a high-ranking city official at a negotiation table in the summer of 1990, the official asserted without so much as raising an eyebrow that he did not in the least suspect any Japanese racial or ethnic discrimination against the *zainichi* Koreans, precisely because the location was known to have been selected by members of the Korean community themselves. In another instance, I heard a Japanese storyteller at the Korean memorial during a tour of memorials (*himeguri*) explain to a group of junior high school students that the location had been chosen by the Korean survivors because it was believed to have unique cultural and historical meaning within the Korean community. Her narration concluded, "So this is by no means a sign of discrimination as is suspected by some people. We must all become friends and work together to create a peaceful world." Claims for the distinctly bound collective history and memory thus allowed a facile embrace of ethnic difference under the liberal rhetoric of multicultural harmony.

In this section we will examine the discursive conditions that allowed the city to maintain its control of the situation and justify its actions. For instance, whenever Chang told the story of how the memorial's site was chosen, connecting the location and the memory of Prince Yi U's adversities, he consistently added that the mayor in office at the time of the memorial's construction gave his word that the memorial would be transferred into the Peace Park itself in the not-too-distant future. However, the existence of that oral pledge is hardly acknowledged in the media's subsequent treatment of the memorial. The print media in particular have so produced and distributed the dominant knowledge concerning the memorial's history that the municipal government's legislative as well as administrative responsibilities—or, put differently, the "Japanese" responsibilities—have been obscured. The obfuscation of agency in these narratives, the absence of a named subject who bore responsibility, in turn fostered the widespread belief among the mostly Japanese public that the outcome of the relocation debate depended entirely on choices made by the Korean community itself and its willingness or unwillingness to cooperate with the city authorities.

The remarkably consistent ways in which the 1990 controversy was depicted and conveyed through print journalism shaped the public's understanding of the situation—who the main actors were, what forces were responsible for causing the conflicts, what the clues were for problem resolution, and how these actors were expected to behave. These narrative mechanisms immediately produced evaluative judgments, thereby constituting the dominant readerly position on the matter. The coverage served to reproduce the mainstream Japanese point of view on the history of Japanese colonialism and its relationship to the ethnic Koreans living in Japan.

On 19 May, the day after an official announced the city's intention to reconsider the transferring of the memorial into the park, a newspaper article began: "When the memorial was built, there was probably no 'discriminatory' intent with respect to the construction site." It continued,

> But as time passed, Japanese began to discuss "the fact that it stands outside the park" and furthermore, the desire to relocate the memorial into the park became stronger among the North and South Koreans. But the city maintained its obstinate attitude. . . . Although the memorial is to be relocated by this 6 August, the problem lies in last-minute negotiations prior to that date. The city holds as the condition for the relocation [that the memorial should be] "one which can enshrine every victim's soul." It cannot be denied that the present memorial inscription is too political. . . . From now on, the city must pursue the role of mediator between Mindan and Sōren. Is it possible to create a setting for communication between these two organizations that have never sat at the same table officially?[27]

As we have seen, the city authorities argued that although the 1967 regulations could still not be dismissed altogether, a "solution from a humanitarian standpoint" was needed to resolve the Korean memorial issue. Subsequent news articles reported on the city's decision to convene an informal gathering of concerned citizens to provide advice on the relocation issue. The controversial recommendations of the "eight-person committee"—all Japanese nationals and celebrities who were acclaimed in Hiroshima as scholars, journalists, and activists who had been involved in some way in survivors' issues—have already been discussed; here, we will focus on how the deliberations were reported.

On 19 June newspapers noted that in their second meeting the committee members had discussed the necessity of transferring the existing memorial, but had agreed that part of its inscription would have to be altered to make it acceptable to North Korean residents, in addition to others.[28] When the committee agreed to delete the entire engraving on the present memorial prior to relocation and began considering alternatives, the committee head was quoted: "We wish to be as cautious as possible, because it will be enormously regrettable if we by any chance do damage to this rare opportunity. We therefore wish to refrain from publicly disclosing the actual proposals for the new inscription."[29] Those outside the immediate negotiations were therefore effectively kept in the dark about the substance of the committee's debates over the proposals.

A few days later, the local newspaper rather abruptly reported the response of ethnic organizations (*minzoku dantai*) to the committee's proposal. The recommendations presented to Mindan and Sōren apparently included the following plans: to completely omit the present inscription, contingent upon Mindan's agreement, and to create a new inscription that would contain the phrase *Chōsen hantō* (Korean peninsula). The article concentrated on detailed coverage of a turbulent meeting held at the Mindan Prefectural Headquarters on 26 June, when the organization's members had decided, under considerable pressure from its leadership, to accept the committee's proposal—above all to eliminate the present engraving—despite numerous objections to using the term *chōsen*. The report suggested that there were still "some complaints among Korean youth and those who had been involved in the actual construction of the present memorial," but Sōren was said to be in basic agreement with the committee's recommendations. It concluded, "Therefore, in order to realize the memorial's construction (*konryū*) by 6 August, the major hurdle concerns how to reconcile the positions of the two [Mindan and Sōren] with respect to the memorial inscription. The eight-person committee's handling of this issue should be carefully observed."[30]

The media coverage consistently downplayed the city administration's presence as a responsible political subject by focusing instead on other actors in the narrative scenes. Leaders of Mindan and Sōren, members of ethnic organizations, and the committee members, though the latter were cast merely as moderators, were placed in the public arena as the only visible agents capable of resolving the problem. Thus it most likely appeared to readers that those primarily responsible for resolving the issue were neither the city authorities nor Japanese citizens in general. Effacing the agency of the city administration and municipal assembly simultaneously produced the collectivity of ethnic Koreans as a conspicuous and autonomous political subject and made the Japanese representatives virtually invisible. Thus ethnic Koreans were made to appear responsible for solving the problem: the Korean memorial issue became a "Korean" problem and not a Japanese one. By voiding the "Japanese" positionality, this process helped readers obliterate historical specificities—for which they, as individuals identified by that name, might have been accountable.

Furthermore, the discursive structure supplied by the print media made the ethnic Koreans' reality only partially visible to readers. It is important to recognize that the visibility of zainichi Korean in the public arena was disproportionately high in coverage of the relocation "problem"; when more mundane social matters are related, ethnic differences are rarely mentioned. The media, for instance, are silent about the fact that many "Japanese" individuals who are integral to the society—including the owners of major corporations, entertainers, and professional athletes—are actually of Korean descent. The one-dimensional and unbalanced coverage of zainichi Koreans' reality serves to reproduce dominant ideas about the minoritized: in particular, it lends credence to the commonly held assumption that the presence of ethnic minorities always creates social tensions and disturbances.

I am not suggesting that there should have been no coverage of the diverse and often conflicting ideas about the memorial within ethnic organizations such as Mindan. When Mindan held a meeting to discuss the proposal to eliminate the present inscription, some members, according to O Sŏng-dŭk, argued that the engravings should be altered in their entirety. Some believed that the description of forced mobilization and the colonial experience was "too shameful" and that it would not be appropriate on the memorial. Others agreed with the city's claim that reinscribing the country's name Hanguk, as on the present memorial, would make it appear as though the north/south division were being recognized and that the term might become inappropriate if unification were achieved and the nation's name changed. Such internal debates should certainly have been reported and publicly discussed; to do otherwise would have precluded even the possibility that mainstream Japanese and others not belonging to Korean organizations might share in and negotiate these issues affecting the local community. Yet they needed to be handled with much greater care, in order to avoid what indeed happened: responsibility was once again shifted from the city government and the Japanese representatives to the ethnic Koreans, thereby obfuscating the very issues being debated.

Newspaper accounts of the relocation controversy further diverted the public's attention from issues of responsibility and obligations by focusing on technical matters. On the one hand, the media simply reiterated the city's position. For instance, they never challenged the requirement that the new memorial be a unified one. And when the committee head described the situation as a "rare opportunity" to relocate the memorial, reporters never questioned who had earlier limited such opportunities. On the other hand, the newspapers continued to report in great detail on how to raise funds, where to build the memorial, and which words would be appropriate for the new inscription. Rather than investigating how and why the issue had remained unresolved until it became a major international controversy—and the role that was and should be played by the city and by mainstream Japanese—the media concentrated simply on how the relocation should be accomplished and consistently stressed that "the major hurdle" was whether the Koreans could agree on the new inscription.

Finally, the media reports uncritically promoted the city's insistence on a "solution from a humanitarian standpoint," casting the administration less as a responsible agent with a proposal for resolving the dilemma than as a benevolent neutral party that had offered Koreans a "rare opportunity" by daring to reconsider the 1967 regulation. In this scenario, the ethnic Koreans were expected to graciously accept the city's "humanitarian" offer: those who criticized or protested the city's irresponsible stance were deemed to be improperly ungrateful. That the memorial still remains outside the park, on this account, simply reflects the Koreans' own incompetence; at best, it is the result of disturbances created by a small number of discontented radicals.

The media representation of the relocation controversies thus fostered a negative image of *zainichi* Koreans. It not only promoted a sense of the ethnic issue's insignificance but also portrayed the so-called minority as incapable of solving its own problems and as responsible for inflicting those problems on others while unjustly blaming the innocent and conciliatory majority. One *zainichi nisei* woman pointed out that the city's passive and irresponsible attitude reinforced the public's negative stereotype of "threatening Koreans" by creating the impression that "the Koreans are complaining and demanding again."[31]

Immediately after the city first announced its intention to allow the memorial's transfer to the park, a day before President Roh's May visit, the "thousand paper crane wreaths" that had been offered at the Korean memorial were set on fire, presumably (but not necessarily) by Japanese right-wingers who objected to the memorial's inclusion in the

Peace Park. The media treated the arson incident, the third of its kind since the construction of the memorial, as an assault against ethnic Koreans. Though various newspapers deplored the vandalism, most offered no explanation of why such racial onslaughts continued. One exception was a column in a national newspaper that quoted the poet Kim Si-jon, a resident of a Korean community in Osaka. Kim succinctly gave voice to the belief shared at that time by many who were concerned about the relocation issue, as he observed that ultimately it was the city's decades-long neglect of the question that had produced the prevailing sense among the Japanese that Korean issues are "insignificant": "By leaving the memorial outside the park, the Hiroshima city authorities allowed the notion of 'the lowly likes of Koreans' (*chōsenjin gotoki*) to grow among the Japanese. If the incident were merely a prank, it raises questions with regard to the city administration, as well as Japanese consciousness. We should recognize the city administration's shame rather than accuse the arsonists."[32]

MEMORY MATTERS: "MINZOKU"

The 1990 blueprint for the Korean memorial's relocation was part of yet another attempt to contain and domesticate some of the many memories that threaten to disrupt the seemingly self-evident knowledge in contemporary Japan about the nation's past. But the resistance to the plan also demonstrates how struggles over endangered memories are crucial to engaging in a politics of difference. Those Koreans and their non-Korean supporters who objected to altering the memorial's inscription did so precisely because they saw that the city's and the committee's intervention in their acts of remembering threatened to erase the elements that differentiate ethnic Koreans from other residents in the local community.

For some *nisei* and many *sansei* Korean resident aliens, the memorial issue took on a further significance that could not be contained by the monumentalized narrative of the South Korean nation. In objecting to the memorial's alteration, they resisted what they perceived as the political containment of ethnic memory—as control over the very manner in which they were supposed to remember the past as ethnic subjects (*minzoku toshite*). The younger generation of Koreans in Hiroshima regarded the relocation issue as one of a number of questions relevant to their ongoing civil rights struggles that the city needed to address in its administrative policies. O Sŏng-dŭk, the *sansei* grocer who is a member of several ethnic organizations, understood the memorial issue as follows: "Those who belong to our generation do not have an awareness of being Korean citizens residing abroad (*kaigai kōmin*). Precisely because we believe that our future lies here in Japan, we protest such legal forms of discrimination as the Alien Registration Act and at the same time wish to retain our ethnic culture in a symbolic manner (*shōchōteki ni*). We regard the Korean memorial relocation issue as an integral part of such issues."[33]

O concisely points to ideas of citizenship (*shiminken*) and civil rights (*kōminken*) that are divorced from the concept of nationality. That non-nationals should have the same rights as nationals in local and national communities because all residents equally share various obligations, including paying taxes and taking on responsibility for determining the community's future—this emerging awareness has generally guided protests, especially of the third generation of Korean resident aliens.[34] O has a leadership role in the Hiroshima branch of the Coalition for Combating Ethnic Discrimination (Minzoku Sabetsu to Tatakau Renraku Kyōgikai, or Mintōren). Mintōren is one of the nationwide civil rights groups established relatively recently that deals at the local community level with these issues. Local affiliates exist in many of the major cities in Japan; while fully utilizing the national network to exchange information, each branch sets strategy individually, according to the specific needs of the local community. The Hiroshima branch of Mintōren was established shortly after an incident in 1989 in which a local university student was found to have written anti-Korean slurs on the school wall. The branch consists of a core group of third-generation *zainichi* Korean (including both North and South Korean nationals), Japanese schoolteachers, and housewives. Most members belong to other organizations such as Mindan, the national association of teachers involved in Korean minority education, and the Christian Coalition against the Alien Registration Act. This loosely organized association unites individuals who differ in terms of nationality, gender, religious affiliation, occupation, or age but can collaborate on antidiscrimination issues.[35]

Mintōren's strategy of negotiating with the city administration has been assailed by others who have taken more confrontational measures, outside the established legal and political system. One important critique made by such radical groups is that negotiation simply allows the authorities to "manipulate"—and perhaps co-opt—ethnic minority issues. They argue that by negotiating and thus subscribing to the rules of the established game, Mintōren simply reinforces the dominant order. Indeed, this strategy sharply parts with that of earlier leftist politics in that it does not seek any radical transformation or an overthrow of the entire political and socioeconomic structure.

In younger *zainichi*'s perceptions of their relationship to the world, the sense of nationality tends to be less pronounced than their feelings of belonging to local and transnational communities. They engage politically and in the public sphere most often through their everyday interactions in the local community and at workplaces; at the same time, they envision themselves in the world transnationally. For example, Kim Yŏn-si, a high school graduate in his early twenties and a worker in an automobile subcontracting firm, expressed feelings of attachment to his particular community and network of interpersonal relations when he refused fingerprinting in 1985. His focus on *his* community of Hiroshima, not Japan, is typical of those in a similar socioeconomic position and underpinned his act of defiance.

> I hadn't really thought about these things seriously until I turned twenty, but it seemed like I had been living a life feeling shy about myself (*kata o chijime te ikite kita*). Refusal of fingerprinting was not about others. It had to do with myself, how I should live. . . . [The Hiroshima city administration] has no consideration for my situation at all, even when Hiroshima city boasts of itself as an International Peace City. . . . I wonder what's going to become of my life, really. I want to have my *ningensei* (humanness) admitted. I like Hiroshima and I don't intend to leave this place. Since I will continue to live here on this soil, I wish to be able to create a society in which I can have dialogues with my friends, including my Japanese friends.[36]

Likewise, O Sŏng-dŭk described to me his defiance of the fingerprinting practice as a form of "filial piety to parents" (*oya kōkō*), since he believes he has achieved something that his parents could not. He also said that to challenge the unreasonable legal measures imposed upon Koreans is similar "to protecting one's own neighbors' rights, to cherish one's own parents, siblings, spouse, and children."[37]

Asserting civil rights especially through the demand for enfranchisement at the prefectural level further differentiates these Korean youths from earlier generations, particularly with regard to their ideas about nationality and citizenship.[38] To be sure, an appreciation of their families' colonial memories, of the origins of their displacements and their present subaltern status, helps third-generation Koreans affirm their difference from the rest of Japanese society. Yet this avowal of difference paradoxically legitimates their belief that their future "lies here in Japan"; and it is precisely this sensibility that fuels their protests against institutional arrangements that treat them differently from Japanese nationals. These protests inform *sansei*'s political participation, centering not in the distant homeland but in their local communities and their everyday lives. "Their protests," writes Hong Tae-p'yo, "are not so much rebellions against Japanese society as excruciating love calls, in which [the *sansei*] probe their own self-being."[39]

The awareness that one can be a full citizen of a society while retaining a different nationality severs the memorial's signification from either a Korean or Japanese nationalist narrativization. Rather than providing witness to the collective experience of the national community, the memorial in their politics offers a heap of fragmented memories that need to be articulated and seized "at a moment of danger"— that is, at a moment when their participation in Japanese society and history *as* ethnic subjects is threatened by the erasure of the memories of their past and present struggles.

One element perceived to be in danger of such erasure was the Korean family name. For instance, in responding to the city administrators' official explanation that the central cenotaph in the Peace Park enshrines all souls lost to the bomb without discrimination, Chang pointed out that "Japanese are enshrined in the central cenotaph, but not Koreans. There are individuals whose names are recognizable as Koreans, such as Kimura or Kanemoto; but they are enshrined with their Japanese names. They are [in that sense] indistinguishable."[40] Most Korean resident aliens have at least two family names: an ethnically Korean name marking their paternal lineage, in the Japanese or Korean readings of the Chinese characters (or both), and a "Japanese-like" surname, often referred to as the "commonly used name" (*tsūmei*).[41] "Kimura" and "Kanemoto," the names Chang mentioned, are variations on the ethnically Korean name "Kim," onto which another syllable or a Chinese character has been added. At workplaces and administrative offices, Korean resident aliens are discouraged from using ethnic names; though informal, this guidance nonetheless constitutes forceful pressure. Most important, the imposition of Japanese-like surnames on Koreans is remembered as a legacy of Japanese colonial rule over Korea, when the Japanese government mandated such names.[42] The alteration of the memorial's inscription was therefore understood to epitomize the continuation of such assimilationist practices.

While the suggestion that the memorial's main inscription be altered received the most criticism, two other recommendations in the 1990 relocation proposal troubled those who feared that signs of difference and memories of Japanese colonialism were being suppressed and even eliminated. The first was to dispose of the informational plaque adjacent to the memorial; the second was to completely erase the already-edited historical description on the back of the memorial.

A three-sided plaque stands next to the memorial, slightly hidden in the shade of trees. Each of the post's faces bears an explanation of the memorial, in Korean, Japanese, and English, respectively. That the text appears in three languages indicates the urgent concern of those who donated the plaque to broadly disseminate knowledge about the memorial's historical conditions. It also betrays their anxiety about controlling the memorial's significatory processes—their desire that visitors not arbitrarily interpret the memorial. The English inscription explains:

> At the end of World War II, there were about 100,000 Koreans living in Hiroshima, as soldiers, civilian employees of army, mobilized students, and ordinary citizens. When the atomic bomb was dropped on August 6th, 1945, sacred lives of 20,000 Koreans were taken from our midst. Of the 200,000 Hiroshima citizens lost to the bomb, approximately 10 percent were Koreans. This tragic figure cannot be quietly left unnoticed.
>
> The Korean victims were given no funerals or memorial services, and their spirits hovered for years unable to pass onto heaven. Then, on April 10, 1970, this memorial was erected in this corner of Hiroshima, the City of Peace, by the Prefectural Branch of the Organization of Korean Residents in Japan. This memorial was erected in the hope that the souls of our compatriots, brought to misery through forces, will be able to rest in peace. It is also an expression of our demand that the A-bomb tragedy will never be repeated.
>
> We pray, of course, for the solace of these lost souls longing for their homelands, but killed on foreign soil. However, we also pray that the plight of the Korean survivors, poorly understood even today, will emerge into public awareness and that reasonable assistance for these survivors will be provided immediately. A memorial service for the Korean victims of the bomb is held here every year on August 5th.

What is remarkable about this narrative, signed by the Junior Federation of Commerce and Industry of Korean Residents in Japan and Concerned Volunteers, is its inscription of the material specificities that led to the memorial's construction. It opens with the historical conditions of Koreans in Hiroshima at the time of the bombing, identifies the name of the collectivity involved in the construction, and informs readers of the forgotten survivors. The high level of detail also demonstrates its authors' concern to emphasize that the memorial was constructed and continues to exist precisely because of its immediate relevance to their struggles against the unjust social practices that have circumscribed Koreans. The removal of this marker clearly would change the nature of the memorial dramatically.

The final problematic recommendation by the city and committee was to replace the present engraving on the memorial's back with an entirely new inscription written in both Japanese and Korean. The proposed inscription read: "This memorial was constructed in order to enshrine the souls of those from the Korean peninsula (*Chōsen hantō no katagata*) who fell victim to the atomic bomb dropped on Hiroshima on 6 August 1945, and also to pray for eternal world peace." The original, in contrast, describes Japanese colonial rule over Korea and its effects upon many people, including

> Prince Yi U, whose unknown sorrow and sufferings were probably even greater because of the fact that he was a member of the royal family that lost its country; as well as those comrade soldiers who had to die for no reason in the war fought for no just cause; those comrade mobilized workers who were made to work like cattle with hoes and sickles in their hands; and those comrade men and women who gathered together at the end of displacement and ruination.[43]

The proposed alteration would thus have blatantly denied colonial memories any place on the monument.

For some members of Mindan who agreed to the proposal, reminders of the colonial past were too shameful to have engraved on the triumphant icon of their nationalist pride.[44] For others, however, effacing these memories was tantamount to erasing their own presence in Japanese society and history. Ch'oe angrily contended that

> to retain [the present inscription together with the explanatory plaque] means to keep such words as "forced mobilization," "civilian war workers," "soldiers," and so on—namely, those things that are upsetting and unacceptable to high-ranking city officials. We simply wrote down what to us is obvious (*tōzen no koto*). The fact that we are Koreans will be erased. The fact of forced mobilization will be erased. How could we continue to live here in Japan? It truly makes me feel anxious about our future.[45]

This anxiety reflects a fundamental uneasiness that the very existence of Korean resident aliens is not and cannot be identified in the field of the signs and representations by which they see and live in the world. A *zainichi nisei* literary critic, Takeda Seiji, described it as a form of aphasia.[46] Adrienne Rich called such dismay at being unable to find oneself in the authoritative discourse a "psychic disequilibrium"; Kwak

Pok-sun, a middle-aged Korean *hibakusha* mother and storyteller, referred to her similar condition as "ghostly" (*yūrei mitai na mon*).[47]

Such desires to restore the materiality of difference in discourses on
the atomic devastation and a sense of urgency about recuperating certain cultural practices did not, however, presuppose an authentic and
essential cultural heritage that inherently unifies Koreans and differentiates them from others. Nor did *zainichi* and other protesters necessarily wish to establish another coherent and totalizing historical narrative about the nation's past. Though O, as we have seen, wished to
"retain [Korean] ethnic culture in a symbolic manner," that "culture"
is quite different from what has generally been regarded in social analysis as a stable, collectively shared, and coherent whole.[48] Some certainly
view the Korean language as an indispensable ingredient in their difference; others claim without hesitation, as one *sansei* did to me, "We
sansei do not necessarily have to be competent in our national language." The same individual, however, claims that an "inner drive," an
ethnic soul (*minzoku no kokoro*), constitutes their ethnicity. What actually constitutes their ethnic culture and what it means to live as an
ethnic subject are never perceived uniformly, even by those who belong
to the same generation.[49]

Thus while *chesa,* the household rites of ancestor worship, constitutes one powerful practice that can work to recruit and register individuals as members of the ethnic group through familial relations,[50] these
"traditional" Korean family relations do not signify ethnic essence for all.
As *sansei* sociologist Jung Yeong-hae observes in her interviews with
teenagers who refused to be fingerprinted, younger *zainichi* women are
beginning to question the conventional notion of ethnicity (*minzoku*)
that has in many ways subjugated women and others who have not con-
formed to the dominant Korean gender and family ideology. In other
words, they are beginning to challenge patrilineally constructed notions
of nationhood and ethnicity.[51] But even as some women seek elements
of ethnic difference that do not rely on what are considered authentic if
patriarchal Korean family relations, they are fully aware of the socioeconomic circumstances that have shaped negative stereotypes of *zainichi*
Korean men as frustrated fathers or failed husbands.

For some individuals, living with difference also means living through
the negative images of *zainichi* Koreans that currently prevail in society.[52] Yi Ki-shik, a man in his twenties who worked for a print shop
run by his father, would often exclaim as he became drunk, "When I
was younger, I used to accuse my parents, 'Why did you make me born

a Korean?' because when I was growing up, there were no good images of Koreans—*yakuza*, ragpickers, owners of pinball-game parlors, that's all." For those people like Yi who are self-consciously involved in the process of recuperating ethnicity, to "live as *zainichi*" means on the one hand to resist such stereotypes. Yet, on the other hand, since they are also keenly aware that they must live through the images that society imposes upon them, to be consciously ethnic also means to actively take up what has been ascribed to them. Thus Yi also turns around and asks what is wrong with being a worker at a pinball-game parlor or a *yakuza*, thereby challenging society's dominant bourgeois sensibilities. The same difference that was deemed to be a source of anguish and discrimination is transformed into something positive, a gain that is empowering and cannot be relinquished, once an individual realizes that the negativity attributed to signs of difference is not inherent but rather is a construction of dominant representations.

Given the extensive variety of regional, economic, political, and gender disparities, the Korean resident aliens' reality in Japan appears perhaps as fragmented as that of the "Asian American," a political category encompassing those who come from many different countries and class backgrounds. Each individual views his or her difference from other members of society and perceives the condition as oppressive and discriminatory in different ways. In this sense, the Korean resident aliens' indeterminate and self-perplexed conception of Koreanness confirms Michael M. J. Fischer's argument that the ethnic process is a dreamlike memory work—that is, in the making of ethnicity, fragments of images, stories, and cultural forms are "worked out through, and integrated with, [each individual's] ongoing experience."[53] Conventional sociological studies, unable to capture the fluidity and multifacetedness of individual ethnic subjectivity, have often dismissed such allegorical dimensions of ethnicity, instead conceptualizing ethnicity as a uniform entity with a coherent social agency that is grounded on stable and unproblematic linkages with the unified past.

At the same time, the construction of ethnic subjectivity, though often differing enormously according to each person's condition, is not entirely arbitrary. Regardless of what an individual deems appropriate in articulating difference, to live as an ethnic subject means living through the ways in which one has been interpellated, living with that which has been suppressed, with elements that have been consistently and forcibly rent from one's life. As I have shown, the relocation issue is critical specifically because the memorial crystallized for many people, though in different ways, the elements of difference that they believed had been wrested from them by other forms of remembering Hiroshima's atomic disaster.

The younger Korean resident aliens themselves are perhaps most acutely aware that their politics of remembering is selectively and strategically produced. As we have seen, Jung points out that Korean women are aware that aspirations for "authentic" Korean familial relations can in turn create totalizing and oppressive conditions of patriarchy and domination by elders. Many *zainichi* Koreans who have visited their supposed homeland return perplexed and dismayed by the nationalist imposition of Korean authenticity there observed. Jung, like many others, argues that nationality or "ethnicity" (*minzoku*) has no ultimate significance in life. "Though I may sound contradictory," she said to me, "I feel that in order to be able to say that *minzoku* is insignificant, we must first have it."[54] Names, language, ancestral rites, ways of life, and historical knowledge about war and Japanese colonialism—the materiality of such differences matter precisely to the extent that they are endangered and in need of discursive restitution.[55] This echoes the views of another *nisei* writer and critic, Sŏ Kyŏng-shik. Citing a passage from Franz Fanon, Sŏ underscores his point that the colonized have a pressing need for a dynamic and creative concept of ethnic tradition and culture:

> The native intellectual nevertheless sooner or later will realize that you do not show proof of your nation from its culture but that you substantiate its existence in the fight which the people wage against the forces of occupation. . . . The desire to attach oneself to tradition or bring abandoned traditions to life again does not only mean going against the current of history but also opposing one's own people. When a people undertakes an armed struggle or even a political struggle against a relentless colonialism the significance of tradition changes.[56]

• • •

The protests against the 1990 relocation plan ought to be understood within the context of a particular dialectics of memory, one in which assaults on memories about the past were translated into struggles over the present and future condition of remembering. Here, the conventional directionality of memory becomes reversed. The ethnic politics of remembering is not simply a task of making the past account for the present—of explaining, for example, the historical causes for the presence of a minority group in a given society. In this dialectics, current

battles wrest ethnic and national differences out of homogenizing social processes in order to recover critical, dissonant memories from the
nation's universalist and assimilationist historical representations.

The remembering of Japanese colonial violence against Korea is one
such memory that severs the formerly colonized from the colonizers
and their descendants. At the same time, we must recognize that the
protesters consisted not only of *zainichi* Koreans but also of Japanese
and other non-Japanese as well. The collaborative effort to save the inscription on the existing memorial should not be understood simply as
an attempt by ethnic Koreans to pledge loyalty to the splendor of their
nationality, or to secure their sense of belonging to a coherently stable
collectivity, whether unified by ethnic culture or a national narrative
about the past. Rather, for both Korean and non-Korean protesters, the
significance of transferring the memorial in its unaltered form onto the
official territory of memorialization lay in the possibility of recuperating the very suppression of "the suppressed," or "the excluded," into
society's present order of knowledge, without allowing that every pain
and injury be forgotten. For many *zainichi*, this site of memory, while
evoking a wealth of contradictory feelings, also provided an opportunity to reclaim the historical materiality of memories with which individuals might articulate their own being. For the Japanese protesters,
the memorial's presence no longer rendered them effectively invisible
(and therefore unaccountable) but instead identified them as Japanese;
it remembered and condemned them for their historical agency in the
violence and injustice committed by that named collectivity.

Perhaps we should also note here that involvement in the relocation
struggle often revealed that ethnicity and nationality are not the only
possible foundations for those attempting to foster change in their local community. Instead, many differentiating categories—gender, class,
age, religion, sexual and political orientation, status as *hibakusha* or non-
hibakusha, and so on—provide bases on which various constructive dialogues and alliances could be envisioned. For example, some began to
share an awareness and concern about the subordination of feminist issues in both the local liberation movement for the discriminated-against
communities and ethnic Koreans' organizational activities. And some
became aware of differences shaping their own identities that they had
not emphasized in the past. Still others wished to form broader, collaborative agenda for the municipal community and called for the establishment of a commission of concerned citizens. Such a group would
provide a forum where residents could openly discuss the condition of

the Peace Memorial Park and various other issues related to municipal planning, including the city's internationalization and multicultural policies. The commission was also to advise and negotiate with the city administration on these matters.

The protest against the relocation proposal interjected a discursive rupture, an opportunity for the memorial's historical "truths"—the irreducible whole of experiential self-evidence for *zainichi* Koreans, Ch'oe's "what to us is obvious"—to be allegorically inserted into society's broader coalitional memories. It generated, if only for a moment, new ties and alliances shaped by various differences. The next chapter examines a starkly contrasting memory practice, a mode of remembering that consolidates, rather than differentiates and diffuses, the subject of memory—in this case, Japanese womanhood.

CHAPTER 6

Postwar Peace and the Feminization of Memory

If "women" within political discourse can never fully
describe that which it names, that is neither because the
category simply refers without describing nor because
"women" are the lost referent, that which "does not exist,"
but because the term marks a dense intersection of social
relations that cannot be summarized through the terms
of identity.

> Judith Butler, *Bodies That Matter* (1993)

Acquitted of accusations regarding the [nation's] defeat in the
war, the maternal suavely altered its apparel to become the
postwar principle of "peace."

> Kano Mikiyo,
> "Kaisetsu: jiga no kanata e" (1990)

Reflecting on the intellectual genealogy of postwar Japan, political philosopher Maruyama Masao once identified the genesis of what he called a "community of contrition" (*kaikon kyōdōtai*) in the immediate aftermath of the war. Widely sharing experiences of the wartime regime, military defeat, and subsequent changes of the postwar years, the "community of contrition," as Maruyama observed, emerged out of a sense of urgency for a "new start based on some fundamental reflections upon the past."[1] In various ways, the intellectuals shared a compelling sense of guilt, remorse, and self-criticism; they were also keenly aware of the (ir)responsible positions they had taken in the face of expanding militarism and the institutionalization of increasingly repressive measures to contain critical practices in all sectors of society, including labor movements, anticolonial struggles, and attacks on the imperial system. Although Maruyama was primarily concerned with the activities of professional academics, writers, and critics, he found what he describes as an admixture of "joy in hopes for the future and

repentance for the past, or a sense of liberation and self-criticism," to
be pervasive throughout society.[2] Moreover, the sense of "repentance"
was gradually eroding. As war memories became less immediate, the
critical and self-reflexive thinking that had evolved out of experiential
knowledge of the past seemed to have become obsolete.[3]

Maruyama's community of contrition can best be interpreted as a
product of collective memory present at the war's end, a kind of remembering that was generated by, and in turn reinvigorated, a sense of
shared experience and unity among those who participated in the restructuring of postwar society and culture. The 1980s engagements in
the politics of memory and the discursive practices of countering the regime of forgetfulness, which I described in the introduction, can be understood as processes whereby disintegrating residues of what once constituted the immediate postwar mnemonic community began to take on
new significations as they became enmeshed in more current politics of
knowledge concerning the past and present. That original community,
however, consisted primarily of male political subjects.

I do not intend this observation to reflect on Maruyama's analysis.
My point is rather that "women" as political subjects, reconstituted under the postwar regime, could not have been included in this community of contrition in the same way as male intellectuals, precisely because masculine and feminine national/political subjects were differently
interpellated and recrafted at this historical juncture. In the prevailing
popular memory, "Japanese Women," unlike most men, are probably
remembered as "victims" who were liberated at the expense of the national defeat. To be sure, not all Japanese men experienced the end of
the war from the position of the defeated. Those who managed to with-
stand violent interrogations and attempts at thought control (some members of the Communist Party, for instance) emerged as "victors" in their
struggle against prewar militarism and the fascist polity. Yet "Japanese
Women"—the gendered and nationalized collectivity constructed through
the ruling historical narrative of postwar transformation—underwent a
wholesale enfranchisement. As postwar constitutional reforms produced
women as new national subjects, a feminine presence emerged in areas
from which women had previously been excluded. This increased visibility for the most part suggested Japanese women's liberation from the
patriarchal authority of the state, from militarism, and from the prewar
household system. Japanese women, as represented in narrations of the
nation's recent history, were to experience only half of what Maruyama's
"community of contrition" shared—namely, "joy in hopes for the fu-

ture" and a "sense of liberation," while being absolved from "repentance for the past" and "self-criticism."[4]

This critically gendered difference by which women were positioned vis-à-vis the past can perhaps best be captured by what one might call the feminization of memory. In the following discussion, I use the term "feminine memory" or "feminized memory" to characterize the dominant national and global representations in which past experiences, whether remembered by men or women, are marked and distinguished exclusively as those of "Japanese Women."

PEACE, NATION, AND THE MATERNAL

The late Moritaki Ichirō, a philosopher and longtime spiritual leader of *hibakusha* movements, once described to me a blueprint for a monument that he hoped would become Hiroshima's new shrine:

> The past will be expressed by a male image: it is the age of militarism, an era of force. His image will resemble the Deva king at Tōdaiji Temple—a stalwart, but somewhat prone and defeated figure. Next to him will stand a female icon, like a statue of Kannon, the goddess of mercy. And at her shoulder will be a figure of a newborn child, like that of a Shakyamuni (Buddha), who points with its finger far into the twenty-first century.[5]

The monument he envisioned, fashioned out of pure white marble, would be placed atop Hijiyama Hill. The three bodies would respectively represent the past, present, and future: the masculine image of prewar and wartime militarism would be contrasted to the merciful mother, an allegory for the postwar reborn nation; and the child would embody the future she nurtures.

Although Moritaki related his vision to me only in passing, it haunted me for some time. In its remarkable banality, this symbolism perfectly condensed clichés about the masculine nature of war and militarism and the inviolability of maternal nurturing and the procreative task. Like the image of the Christian Holy Family, the bodies of man, woman, and child sanctified the nuclear family, which was at the same time associated with postwar peace and orderliness. Moreover, the movement of the imaginary gaze from the defeated father figure, via the maternal Kannon, to the male child signified the linearity of the nation's history. Moritaki's fictive icon illustrates how gendered images underlie understandings of the transition from prewar to postwar Japan. The shaping of feminine memories took place as part of broader and interdependent recharacterizations affecting the image of the new nationhood, its foundational concept of peace, and the reconstitution of feminine political subjects. Still another significant element of his imagined monument was the location on which he proposed to erect it. Hijiyama, as we will see later in this chapter, has been a site of repeated physical inscriptions and reinscriptions of the nation's recent history.

As in many other cases of demilitarization and decolonization throughout the world, Japan's transition was seen by all as a gendered process.[6] Literary and other cultural representations contributed to the understanding of the nation's new position in the global order through the tropes of femininity, masculinity, and sexuality.[7] The racialized stories of Japanese women flirting with foreign soldiers or suffering metaphorical or actual rape, which suggested the inability of Japanese men to protect the chastity of "their women," underwrote images of Japanese men emasculated by the absolute power of the United States. Sexualized and gendered relations operated persuasively in popular memories of the period and helped figure the nation's (that is, the masculine subjects') inferior status in the postwar global order—more precisely, its political and economic subordination to the United States.

The transformations that were brought about by the end of the war and the U.S.-led military occupation were often perceived and expressed through changes that especially affected women. The postwar constitution certainly marked a radical shift, newly guaranteeing Japanese women nationals their full participation in the parliamentary process. Amendments to the civil code, though far from achieving perfect equity, enabled women to become heads of households and also stipulated equal inheritance for male and female siblings. Most important, the constitution mandated equal treatment of all national subjects regardless of their differences, including gender. "What became tough after the war," it was often remarked, "are women and panty hose." Such sayings derisively captured what appeared to many to be the abrupt elevation of women's institutional status.

Above all, the new status of Japanese women embodied and dramatically enacted the renewal of the national polity at large. In the 1946 House of Representatives election, which followed the extension of suffrage to women, 39 female Diet members were elected. In 1949, 794 women took local government offices, and 10 female candidates won their races in the 1947 House of Councilors election.[8] Moreover, this new status was to be performed and displayed for the eyes of the international community. The Occupation authorities encouraged Japanese women, now liberated, to actively participate in the national political process in order to displace the nation's male-dominated, militaristic image. Political scientist Susan Pharr notes that the Americans viewed their increasing presence as eloquently indicating the success of universal suffrage in "improving women's status" from that of the period before the Occupation.[9] For those authorities, and perhaps to some degree for Japanese politicians concerned about their nationalist interests, the visibility of women in the formal political sphere was understood as crucial in underscoring the dramatic renewal of Japan's postwar polity.

We should also keep in mind that even as Japanese women gained the vote and national visibility in politics, Japan's former colonial subjects, both men and women, were thoroughly disenfranchised. As chapter 5 discussed in detail, after the war Koreans, Taiwanese, and other former colonial subjects who had resided in Japan as "imperial subjects" were all categorized as non-Japanese aliens. Relying on archival research, the historian Mizuno Naoki has investigated why in 1945 an estimated two million Korean and Taiwanese men above age twenty-five, who were residing in what was then defined as Japan proper, were deprived of the rights that they had possessed until the war's end—namely, the right to vote and eligibility to serve in the Diet. He has concluded that the cause was the paranoiac fear that former colonial subjects, especially the communist and socialist Korean minority, might call for the abolition of the imperial system. According to a document he recently discovered, at least ten minority subjects were expected to be elected to the Diet immediately after the war.[10] This difference in treatment—appropriation into versus exclusion from the national political sphere—ensured that the construction of political desires and cultural concerns would occur quite differently for Japanese women and for resident alien women and men of other nationalities.

The accentuated feminine presence in formal politics, moreover, contributed to the demilitarization and emasculation of the nation's image, while consolidating the notion of peace as an icon of nationhood reborn. Among the elements signaling sharp changes in the polity—which in most discussions of the Occupation include such reforms as altering agricultural land policies, introducing universal adult suffrage, and lessening the emperor's status from that of a divine to a human "symbolic" monarch[11]—the newly announced state ideology of peace ideals, as opposed to military power, perhaps most powerfully helped redefine Japan's rebirth. The pronouncement that Japan would be a

"Nation of Peace" (*heiwa kokka*) was premised on Article Nine of the postwar constitution.[12] Though interpretations vary about the degree to which the constitution forbids military action, the article literally states that Japan will eternally renounce wars of aggression and the use of military force to resolve international conflicts. Despite the actual military rebuilding that took place during the latter half of the Occupation in accord with U.S. cold war strategy, the ideal of eternally renouncing wars stated in what later came to be known as the "Peace Constitution" (*heiwa kenpō*) underscored for many the transfiguration of nationhood: the militant empire had become a civil and peace-loving country.

This officialization of the concept of peace paralleled the increasing feminine prominence in peace-related domains. Postwar peace movements and antinuclear rallies provided theatrical sites at which feminine subjects enacted the link between the renewal of postwar nationhood and the concept of peace. The Gensuikin movements that swept the entire nation immediately after the Bikini incident, which I described in the introduction, were initiated by *shufu* (housewives, or, more strictly, female household heads) in Tokyo. In Hiroshima, a number of women's associations—including the Hiroshima Women's Coalition (Hiroshima Fujin Rengō Kai), a group that had been organizing the Women's Peace Conference (Heiwa Fujin Taikai) since 1949—proposed to hold an antinuclear forum in Hiroshima. This public forum later evolved into the annual Gensuikin World Conference.[13]

In tracing both the transformation of and continuity in the concept of "peace" in modern Japan, Ishida Takeshi highlights the opposing ways in which the notion has been appropriated in state slogans and used to characterize nationality since the beginning of the century: on the one hand, peace, defined as the state of nonviolence, is identified with the principle of pacifism; on the other hand, peace has been defined as the order of everyday life, which must be defended by force.[14] In the later postwar years the struggles over the apparently transparent meaning of the concept of "peace" have been even more diverse and complicated. For the former leaders of the conservative Liberal Democratic Party, postwar peace has stood for successful economic growth, affluence, and stability, all of which were achieved under their one-party rule (beginning in 1955). Similarly, defending peace could also mean maintaining order and harmony. In contrast, for ethnic minorities, new immigrants, members of the discriminated-against communities and other marginalized groups of people, peace has often been identified with democratic ideals, civil rights, and equality. In short, the concept of peace has constituted a hegemonic ideology in the public political arena. Because it has become endowed with moral authority, it must be claimed not only by the dominant forces that work to maintain the status quo but also by those who seek any form of transformation. With regard to feminized memory, "peace" has been inseparable from parliamentary democracy as articulated in the postwar constitution; moreover, as we will soon see, it has come to represent women's liberation from the male-dominated military regime.

Perhaps most crucial to feminized memory were the tropes of motherhood and assumptions about the maternal that came to prevail in peace and antinuclear discourses, producing memories of innocence, victimhood, and perseverance with regard to prewar and wartime women, Japanese and non-Japanese alike. The cultural significance of the Japan Mothers' Conference (*Nihon Hahaoya Taikai*)—which evolved out of the initiatives of *shufu* who were involved in launching the Gensuikin campaign—ought to be understood from this perspective. The Japan Mothers' Conference held its first meeting in Tokyo in June 1955. There Kuboyama Suzu appeared as a widow; her husband, Aikichi, a crewman of the Lucky Dragon Five tuna-fishing boat, had died from exposure to fallout from the nuclear test at Bikini atoll. Her speech was titled "The Hydrogen Bomb Took Away My Husband."

In the national discourse that grew out of the Mothers' Conference, the three primary goals—protecting children, women's lives and rights, and peace—were understood as being inseparable from maternal instincts, which were held to be universal and basic. The social critic Tanaka Sumiko wrote in no uncertain terms that "the objective of the political movements of these mothers is to defend peace 'for the sake of children's well-being.' . . . Peace is indeed the supreme aspiration of the entire nation in postwar Japan; but women react to peace with unconditional passion because of the maternal nature (*bosei*) that they inherently possess. . . . [Women's peace activities] are all related to the protection of children's lives."[15]

The immediate political issues in which individual women were involved at the local level—such as labor disputes, demands for better working conditions, opposition to the construction of military bases and arsenals and to the port calls of vessels suspected of carrying nuclear weapons, resistance to the U.S.-Japan Security Treaty, and so on—were not necessarily perceived as primarily maternal. Yet when represented in the national discourse, the cultural meanings of these activities were generalized such that all female participants were depicted as enacting natural maternal dispositions—creating and protecting lives, nurturing and caring for the weak. And it is through this narrativization that motherhood became a ubiquitous trope, shaping how many women understood their organized activities and alliances and enabling the further mobilization of women from a wide range of different sectors of society, both nationally and globally.

The memorial titled "Mother and Children in the Tempest," located at the main entrance to Hiroshima's Peace Memorial Park, both visually and discursively embodies the centrality of motherhood in peace and antinuclear discourse that typified the late 1950s and later years. The monument was constructed on the initiative of Hiroshima Fujin Rengō-kai (the Hiroshima Women's Coalition). After the first Gensuikin Conference held in Hiroshima, the coalition launched a fund-raising campaign, widely soliciting small donations from those in the community identified as mothers. Completed in 1960, it was transferred to its present location in 1980 when the city renovated the park's frontal space. Every year around 6 August, the members of local women's associations congregate at the monument's icon to hold a memorial ceremony, gathering with visitors from throughout the nation who have come to participate in the municipal Peace Memorial Ceremony and other related events. This site continues to offer a space where Hiroshima's atom bomb and military violence in general are remembered and narrated from women's, or more precisely mothers', point of view.

The centrality of its location as well as the massive size of the *Mother and Children* monument makes it especially conspicuous. Its aesthetic quality is also distinctive; unlike other memorial icons, it is overtly expressive, even melodramatic. The mother stands in a slouching posture. Her upper body is stooped over, almost horizontal to the ground, as she embraces a baby at her breast. Her head is bent down, buried in the baby's body, and her hand, hefty and thick, like those of robust workers often found in socialist realist sculptures, is grasping the baby. The mother's other bare, muscular arm stretches out to reach for another child, who is about to climb on her back from behind. Her long, skirted dress and hairstyle, as well as the children's clothing, do not display any specifically "Japanese" markings.

A widely circulated narrative that explains the monument's symbolism, though written some twenty years after the original Mothers' Conference, captures how the maternal was represented in that earlier discourse:

[The monument] captures the intense figure of a mother and her children as they try to endure the "tempest" of the ruthless era. It is different from figures of heroic warriors or robust youths: rather, it is an image [of a mother] who patiently perseveres "in the tempest." This statue, *Mother and Children in the Tempest*, in which the mother attempts to protect her children while the children follow, leaves the viewer with impressions of gentleness (*yasashisa*). But that is not all. This image further portrays a power that is unyielding to any raging storm. It is as if it says, Neither atom bomb nor hydrogen bomb can destroy the strong tie between this mother and her children. The monument must be impressive to people because it expresses such robustness and strength.[16]

The narrative further conjectures about what is imagined to be the typical experience on the day of the bombing, generalizing the mothers-and-children as a homogeneous historical subject:

Just before the atom bomb attack, it was a usual calm morning in Hiroshima. . . . Despite the tense wartime atmosphere, mothers and children greeted the morning just as the morning before. At 8:15 A.M., the moment when the atom bomb exploded, the town of Hiroshima turned into a hell. Mothers kept calling children's names; children did nothing but cry out, "mommy, mommy." What did mothers of Hiroshima do in the hellish fire and blasts? There were mothers who disappeared in flames, crying out their children's names; there were also mothers who were barely able to escape with their burned children in their arms. *Mother and Children in the Tempest* symbolically expresses human love—the love of mothers who protected their children and the love of children adoring their mothers in the hell.[17]

Like many other accounts of the nuclear devastation meant to represent the universal experiences of "Hiroshima's mothers," this portraiture links the signification of motherhood, civilian innocence, and victimhood. The relationship of mothers and children exchanging their usual greetings on a serene morning, juxtaposed to the "tense wartime atmosphere," accentuates their innocence and the everydayness of their lives. It immediately situates mothers and children in the demasculinized civilian domain. A mother's power is distinguished from that of "heroic warriors or robust youths." Her strength lies in patience and perseverance, resources of the dispossessed.

We should note that these victimized mothers are at the same time celebrated and revered as victorious heroines. Having overcome the adversities of the war and the bomb, Hiroshima's mothers, like all the others who participated in the Japan Mothers' Conference, have established themselves as the undaunted advocates of campaigns against war

and nuclear armament. The narrative thus concludes with an antinuclear cliché: "Hiroshima's mothers stood up in the postwar years in the
hope that the atom bomb will never again be used anywhere else in
the world."[18] It is no coincidence that this most visited of Hiroshima's
memorial icons, which crystallizes such heroic images of motherhood,
has a monumental quality. In this regard it resembles the memorial for
Korean atom bomb victims that I discussed in chapter 5. While the latter celebrates the reestablishment of (South) Korea's national sovereignty
and emancipation from Japanese colonial rule, the former glorifies mothers' triumphs. Thus Hiroshima's mothers are remembered as victims
oddly similar to those who suffered from Japanese colonial and military rule. But these feminized war memories, which equate the experiences of Japanese women as victims and their postwar liberation with
those of former colonial subjects, conveniently produce a forgetfulness
about how Japanese women's feminine subjectivities were, and have continued to be, interpellated as imperialist and militarist.

Furthermore, tropes of motherhood provided women with a gendered
yet universal position from which they might remember the atomic obliteration and talk about peace and the well-being of all of humanity. In
the above narrative, motherly love, which is understood as primordial
and given, emerges as an antithesis to modernity, science, and technology. It is hoped that maternal dispositions will provide an antidote to
the destructive course of human progress. "Hiroshima's mothers," and
their power to nurture their children, are assumed to be universal and
panhuman. If, as I argued in the introduction, the dominant way of remembering the war, the atom bombs, and other atrocities has been from
the anonymous position of humanity, then the ubiquity of mothers in
Hiroshima's exodus narratives—where they appear as self-sacrificial, devoted, persevering women who aid in their children's recovery and who
agonize over lost families—demonstrates how the maternal operates as
a gendered manifestation of universal humanism. Mothers, who by their
nature desire to create, protect, and nurture lives, are understood to oppose war and the use of nuclear bombs, anytime, anywhere. Motherhood thus supplements "ideological" and national particularities. However, such inclusion in the discourse of nuclear universalism is predicated
on assuming that the telos of women's subjectivity is reproductive and
on particular representations of their life experiences. As in Jean-Jacques
Rousseau's social contract theory, those marked by gender as women
are central to society, but only by virtue of being mothers.[19]

There is another critical dimension of the valorization of motherhood in remembering Hiroshima and in celebrating postwar peace, which might be thought of as sublimation. According to both Sigmund Freud and Jacques Lacan, though their accounts are somewhat different, that process often works to dislocate desires, passions, and yearnings that have been renounced or avoided, if not totally repressed. Thus it always intimates some lack or insufficiency that was replaced at the origin.[20] Here, that void is produced by the erasure of women's corporeality and their procreative acts. For there are stark contradictions between individual women's accounts of mothering and the dominant ideology and representation of the maternal. The *hibakusha* women who experienced the bombing at a relatively young age almost without exception refer to apprehensions, both their own and society's, about the still underinvestigated effects of radiation exposure. Women have witnessed numerous examples of abnormalities associated with childbirth, including infertility, miscarriage, deformity, stillbirth, and newborns developing leukemia and other health disorders, presumably resulting from prenatal exposure to the bomb. The reproductive telos that governs the narrativizing of women's experiences in peace and antinuclear discourses both produces and then intensifies anxieties concerning the physical abnormalities about which female *hibakusha* can testify. The sublimation of motherhood celebrates the majestic work of mothering as it erases disturbing knowledge about women's bodies. It obliterates nervousness about normalcy, corporeality, and the continuance of civilization—all of which one must necessarily confront while living in the postnuclear world.

The literary critic John Whittier Treat is thus insightful when he argues that Hayashi Kyōko, Gotō Minako, and Sata Ineko, female writers engaged with the Nagasaki atomic bombing, invariably deal with "the very issue of biology and culture, and thus our literal and symbolic survival."[21] Not because women are any closer to the biological and the corporeal than men but precisely because society has sublimated some aspects of motherhood, the literary works of these women attempt to recuperate that which the dominant discourse, through its monumentalization of motherly heroism, has turned into a void. These writers, as Treat puts it, point explicitly to "the insidious, permanent, and seemingly endless suffering of the bombing on the most private and intimate levels: mothers and sons, father and daughter, man and woman."[22] In astutely pointing out the disturbing quality of writings about Nagasaki, Treat is underscoring that Nagasaki was the second site of a nuclear bombing in human history and that whether it will be remembered as the second or the last is ineluctably tied to whether our civilization ends or continues.

In a way similar to their Nagasaki counterparts, those writing about Hiroshima's atom bombing have also dealt with female biology, gender, and sexuality, whether in literary or other representational forms. Nagoya Misao's writings, for instance, center on the death of her son, Fumiki. Born fifteen years after Nagoya survived the Hiroshima bombing, he developed leukemia as he was about to turn five years old. In one of her better-known prose poems, she laments:

If,
Away from these arms of mine
Fumiki must pass away
If Fumiki must pass away
Holding Fumiki,
I want to turn myself into a fossil.[23]

The name "Fumiki" is written with two Chinese characters that combine to mean the "tree of history." The irony is of course immediately obvious. The growth of this tree of history has been halted, and we suspect that the world's most scientifically advanced and historically unprecedented weapon is responsible. For most readers of the poem in Japanese, the characters for Fumiki's name will also resonate visually with the characters appearing in the closing line to form the word "fossil." The tree of history that cannot thrive is removed from the course of time, along with the author's body, which appears to have led the child into both life and death. Both bodies transform into a fossil, an object frozen in time immemorial. It allows no movement of memory, no genetic progression, no historical advance.

No direct connection between Fumiki's illness and Nagoya's past exposure to radiation was either proved or disproved by science. However, Nagoya's own knowledge about abnormalities among local children of survivors caused by prenatal exposures to the bomb, such as microcephaly (shōtōshō) and some similar cases of cancer and leukemia, made her suspicions of the linkage reasonable; she blamed his illness on her past. Nagoya's journal of her son's death, moreover, interweaves different writing styles. Her prose poems appear randomly amid factual accounts of her son's activities and conversations with him. The results of physical examinations—for example, figures documenting his body temperature, blood pressure, and blood cell counts—are also dispersed throughout. The treatments Fumiki underwent and his death are chronicled from multiple perspectives, as the journal occasionally in-

cludes diary entries from Nagoya's husband and her older son. Nagoya's
accounts contrast sharply with her husband's. Not only does she feel
responsible, because her exposed body might be the cause of her son's
fatal illness, but she is torn over what action to take. Nagoya agonizes
over whether to continue working at her job, which she felt largely
formed her subjecthood, or to devote herself entirely to caring for her son
as a mother; her husband shows no such indecision. In reality, reproductive anomalies are associated with *hibakusha* men as well as women,
as many accounts show.[24] Yet, when mediated through what is expected
culturally and socially of their sex, biological facts are understood by
women differently—the strains and uneasiness are felt more acutely.

One difference we might note is that when "biology and culture" are
treated in the literature on Hiroshima, the discussions demonstrate an
antipathy toward America that is somewhat more conspicuously pronounced than it is in writings on Nagasaki. I am by no means suggesting that the maternal discourse on the bombing of Nagasaki has
contained no such vocal condemnations of U.S. military dominance. Instead, my point is that the anti-American and anti-imperialist rhetoric
tended to be more salient in activities, such as this one, that were organized by self-identified mothers in Hiroshima. Nagoya expresses her
abhorrence of "America" without reservation as she beseeches the doctors of the world to save her son but insists,

> But
> Not America
> Do not touch
> Do not lay fingers
> With the filthy
> Hands
> Of peaceful disguise
> Do not touch
> My Son.[25]

The literary and political writings that appeared in the nineteen volumes
of *Rivers of Hiroshima* (*Hiroshima no kawa*) further demonstrate how
some women aligned their position as Japanese mothers and as Hiroshima *hibakusha* mothers with anti-Americanism and anti-imperialism.[26]
The journal was inaugurated by the members of the Gensuikin Mothers'
Association (Gensuibaku Kinshi Hiroshima Haha no Kai), a group con-
sisting of concerned local writers, poets, critics, and social activists, many
of whom were also *hibakusha* and mothers. The Gensuikin Mothers'
Association itself evolved out of a gathering held in 1959 during the

Fifth Gensuikin Conference. Although Gensuikin at the time was still a unified organization, conservative dissidents were already creating splits within it. The mothers' gathering was conceived of as a nonpartisan event: concerned women could participate as individuals, independent of their affiliation with other established organizations.[27] Reflecting the global tensions heightened by the Korean War, the escalating arms race between the Soviet Union and the United States, the continuing nuclear tests in the Pacific, and the U.S.-Japan Security Treaty, the journal's harshest condemnations were aimed at U.S. military and nuclear hegemony in the region. Articles often positioned "Hiroshima's mothers" as allies of mothers in other areas of the world who were seen both as victimized by and as confronting U.S. militarism and global nuclear policies.

One prominent target of maternal objections to U.S. dominance was the Atomic Bomb Casualty Commission (ABCC). Its presence, coupled with the strong reaction against the commission's earlier treatment of Hiroshima's mothers and their newborn babies, connected at a very deep level the ubiquitous effects of U.S. military policy and feminized memories of the city's postwar condition.

The Atomic Bomb Casualty Commission was established by the United States during the Occupation period. M. Susan Lindee's detailed study shows that it conducted medical research on the physical effects of the bomb but never intended to provide medical treatment for survivors. This notorious policy fed survivors' suspicions and resentment that they had been turned into "guinea pigs" for experimental use—that they were objects of scientific research and that the data drawn from their cooperation would be manipulated to justify the U.S. nuclear buildup.[28] Stimulated in part by the satanic image of ABCC portrayed in Agawa Hiroyuki's novel *Ma no Isan* (*Devil's Heritage*), some popular accounts even rumored that ABCC personnel were stealing the blood of survivors and that they would ship bottled mutilated body parts and deformed fetuses back to the United States. The ABCC therefore was a site at which the bomb's effects on human—and particularly Japanese—genetics were always at issue. Among those affiliated with *Rivers of Hiroshima*, novelist Yamaguchi Yūko and poet Shōda Shinoe were most vociferous in attacking the commission. Yamaguchi especially took up the question of genetic abnormalities and initiated a national campaign to promote awareness about the children of survivors, *hibaku nisei*. In a brief report on the inaugural gathering of the association for prenatal *hibakusha* and *hibaku nisei*, Yamaguchi condemned the ABCC's continuing presence. She wrote disapprovingly that its physical examinations of *hibaku nisei*—which included repetitive blood tests and possible over-exposure to X rays—did not yield adequate or even any productive information that could lead to institutional measures to lessen their psychological anxiety.[29]

Above all, the conspicuous presence of the ABCC in Hiroshima signified the quasi-colonial relationship between the United States and Japan. The commission's administration was criticized as being extraterritorial and colonial in nature; the practices singled out included its restriction of access in general and information in particular, its official policy of not treating survivors, its elitism, and its racialized and gendered hierarchies. Moreover, the position of the ABCC's complex on top of the Hijiyama Hill bore special significance. Prior to the construction of these facilities, the site was used as a cemetery for the Japanese Imperial Army. In order to prepare the location, the entire cemetery—together with its cherry trees, the popular symbol of Japaneseness as well as an aestheticized image of Japanese militarism—was removed and relocated, at a considerably reduced scale. The transfiguration of Hijiyama was part of a more general metamorphosis in the official representation of nationhood and of this prefectural city.[30] Another prominent example was the change of the name of the central downtown avenue from "Rijō Street"—meaning "Carp Castle Street," referring to the emblem of the Hiroshima Castle, the mnemonic site that testified to the glory of the imperial reign and the regime's military prowess—to "MacArthur Avenue."

It may be worthwhile contrasting this maternal antipathy to the ABCC with popular attitudes toward the "Atom Bomb Maidens" (*genbaku otome*). During the early 1950s, the national and international media sensationalized the project of sending to the United States young women survivors, who bore awful keloid scars on their bodies and faces from the nuclear weapon. In 1955, twenty-five women were selected and sent to New York for orthopedic surgery on their deformed limbs and other medical treatment.[31] A newspaper column observed that society's often sentimentalized and patronizing sympathies with the women led to the common perception that these "maidens are the only survivors of the atom bomb."[32] Such misgivings were certainly not directed against individual "Hiroshima maidens." Rather, critics questioned the ways in which media narratives and other representations of these women overshadowed the plight of thousands of other survivors who lacked even the means for daily sustenance or basic institutional support such as unemployment relief and medical benefits. The project also left many wondering why these youthful, single women were chosen as legitimate objects of salvation, exceptions to the ABCC's official stance that regarded offering remedies to survivors as tantamount to admitting U.S. fault in dropping the bombs.[33] Moreover, portrayals of these "maidens" as representing "friendship," "love," and "bridges" between the two nations contributed to obscuring ongoing Japanese opposition to the signing of the U.S.-Japan Security Treaty and antagonism to the increasingly close political, economic, and cultural ties to the United States. Finally, the same fraternal images at the national level concealed the fact that the Americans who had initially offered assistance to these women were critics of U.S. military policies and were thus themselves part of an oppositional movement.

We must take careful note here of the diametrically opposed ways in which women survivors came to be positioned in the feminized memories of the postwar years. On the one hand, the so-called Hiroshima maidens constituted a specular image of the oedipal relation between Japan and the United States. Though hinting at a possibility of miscegenation, the dominant images of these women—pure, virgin daughters—loyally figured the nation in its relation to the paternalized America, at least in popular discourse. On the other hand, the Hiroshima mothers, dominant in peace and antinuclear discourse, came to signify that which was antithetical to American militarism and imperialism. Their narratives spoke of the postwar relationship between United States and Japan through metaphors of anticolonial struggles. While the maidens suggested an official alliance and camaraderie between the United States and Japan, the maternal tropes helped consolidate the other narrative on nationhood—one in which Japan was remembered one-dimensionally as a victim of U.S. and Western imperialism and colonialism. I will return to the second narrative at the end of this chapter.

FEMININE DISSIDENTS

It is rarely noticed that when those who promoted peace and antinuclear campaigns during the 1950s were interpellated as feminine and national subjects, they were at the same time associated with a particular social class. In 1964, when Gensuikin split into three competing conferences as a result of conflicts over which political party should sponsor the organization, the members of the Gensuikin Mothers' Association, whose engagement in politics had previously been only literary, held a separate "unified" conference that was organized and attended exclusively by women. What needs to be problematized here are the ways in which these women's interventions were understood to be worthy, powerful, and effective. Womanly and motherly interventions were perceived by the women themselves, as well as by others, as the type of activities that could lead the peace movement, for it was believed that women and mothers, unlike men, were "ideologically" untainted. The Gensuikin movement was at an impasse, and women seemed to offer a "pure standpoint rooted within the residents of the local atom-bombed community."[34] Thus women in the peace campaigns did not speak—nor were they heard—as intellectuals, workers, teachers, authors, journalists, political leaders, or social activists. Rather, they were empowered and gained authority in public political spheres only insofar as they spoke as *shufu* and as mothers—in other words, as the everyday and de-ideologized constructs of patriarchal authority.

This habitual association of feminine political subjectivity with the ordinary and commonplace has continued to determine how female political actors are presented in the formal political arena. The 1990 House of Representatives election offers an exemplary text in this regard. During the election the womanly voice was understood as playing a major role in promoting the new values and styles of current political processes. Above all, the election was seen as an opportunity for Japanese women to become visible and vocal in formal parliamentary politics, for it was clear that despite postwar reforms and promises, women had continued to be grossly underrepresented in this area. Virtually every party expressed a concern about women, in part because of the Socialist Party's great success with female candidates and supporters in the previous year's House of Councilors election.[35] Headed by Doi Takako—the first woman ever to lead a major political party in Japan—the Socialist Party had won a landslide victory in that earlier election, gaining twenty-four seats. The 1989 contest was characterized by the media as the "women's election": a record-breaking 146 women ran for office, and 22 were in fact elected. The media repeatedly emphasized that the Socialist Party owed its astounding success to what they called the "madonna strategy": that is, the party's campaign tactic of aggressively recruiting female candidates.

More specifically, the women's role in the 1990 election centered on their opposition to the ruling Liberal Democratic Party's decision to raise the tax on consumer items. Believing that this sales tax would disproportionately affect those who were already disadvantaged, candidates from virtually every party felt obliged to present themselves as spokespersons for the common people (*shomin*), and especially for *shufu*. Women selected as candidates were expected to speak as *shufu* who had "charge over kitchens" (*daidokoro o azukaru*), and securing the female vote was thought crucial to winning the election. That vote, however, was understood to be cast mainly by mothers and *shufu*. At the opening of one of the campaign election offices, the wife of a city assembly member gave her reason for endorsing the local candidate: "As a mother, I want my family to be healthy. But unless the world is peaceful, one cannot hope for their health. . . . As a *shufu* and a mother, I would like to produce fortresses of peace."[36] Even as they endowed the feminine voice with certain authenticity and power in the formal political arena, such maternal tropes also confined it to a particular socioeconomic position. These mothers were coded as the common people, belonging to the local and everyday space of domesticity and consumption.

The madonna strategy needs to be placed within the context of a much broader reorganization of the Socialist Party as the party adjusted to the reality of its changing constituencies. The top level of the party believed that only women could compensate for the declining support of labor unions, whose memberships were steadily falling.[37] Women were perceived as the mainstay of other constituencies most likely to vote for the Socialist Party, for they appeared to be the most active members of grassroots organizations, ranging from consumer cooperatives and environmental and local civil rights movements to protest movements against nuclear power plants and military bases. More precisely, these were middle-aged women who often did not work full-time and who saw themselves as mothers and *shufu*. The process of transferring the party's base of support from the large-scale labor unions to broader coalitions of grassroots citizens' organizations thus entailed a conspicuous shift in gender configuration as well.

A brief examination of the Delta Women's Group (Delta Onna no Kai) illustrates how the change in the party's base constituency was understood in gendered terms, especially when organizational style and aesthetic preferences were at issue. The group is run exclusively and self-consciously by women. About twenty or more local residents of Hiroshima and its vicinity make up the membership.[38] The group was founded in 1982, immediately after the Hiroshima Action for Peace conference of 21 March, a gathering that, as I described in chapter 3, came at a critical historical juncture. Shortly after establishing the group, several members traveled to Greenham Common in England to visit a Japanese woman who was taking active part in an all-women camp protesting against a military base there.

A representative of the group described to me how at an early stage of their involvement in peace and antinuclear protests, she and others perceived distinct disparities between their style of activism and other groups that were primarily male. They first experienced this gender gap as conflicts and tension during the mass rallies that followed immediately after the Chernobyl incident. She explained, "We were in discordance with men (otoko). We were at odds with them about the styles of making political speeches. We wanted to make political appeals in the form of reading poems whereas men in the movement wouldn't accept them unless they were written in an authentic 'appeal style' (apīru chō). The men in the labor unions resisted especially strongly."[39] The "appeal style" refers to the type of language that has been conventionally deployed in leftist political rallies and meetings. It is usually heavily laden with noncolloquial idioms made up of Chinese character compounds such as kyōdō sensen (united front), tettei kyūmei (thorough scrutiny), danko hantai (resolute resistance), and rentai tōsō (united struggle). One member of the Women's Group caricatured such expressions as "the so-called four-character idioms." The preferred style for visual self-representation also emerged as a point of difference. The distinctive calligraphic form usually used for leftist campaign flyers, banners, or placards employs abbreviated Chinese characters that are written in a squarish and straight-line fashion, often conspicuously slanted upward to the right. In contrast, a rounded and cartoonlike calligraphy that first came into use during the 1970s among young girls, which is colloquially referred to as marumoji, has become increasingly common at demonstrations in recent years. Although the orthodox leftist style may contribute to creating a sense of noneverydayness, seriousness, and urgency, it is also considered to be "stiff" (katai) and antiquated in comparison to the new and popular handwriting, which is often accompanied by playful cartoons and imaginative slogans.

The "discordance" of this écriture féminine, which was expressed primarily as a matter of aesthetic preference, gave material form to the perceived gendered hierarchy. To my question of why the organization must be exclusively female, the representative responded in no uncertain terms that it is "because women face oppression (yokuatsu)." And it was clear that she meant oppression by the *ie*, the household institution. (Other members later ridiculed her for using the word "oppression," which seemed to them too pretentious.) Moreover, the choice of the word *onna* (woman) in naming the association suggests the group's genealogy within the 1970s women's liberation movement, or *ribu*.[40] *Onna* was used deliberately in opposition to other Japanese terms that mean "woman," including *shufu, fujin,* and *josei. Fujin* has the nuances of the word "lady," with its connotations of being escorted by chivalrous men; and the two parts of the first character making up the word signify "broom" and "woman." The more neutral *josei* is most commonly employed in administrative and bureaucratic language. By contrast, *onna* appears in such common phrases as "*onna kodomo,*" which literally means "woman and children" but has derogatory implications. The women who appropriated the term used it positively to imply not a space scorned by men but one in which men are irrelevant and unnecessary. To them, *onna* suggested the erotic and the sensual that existed outside of the male gaze: a linguistic category existing prior to masculinized, humanist, and domestic interpellation.

The difference of this *écriture féminine* was also perceived as sociological—that is, as involving social relations and the structuring of organizations and activities. As the representative told me, "We [women] also didn't appreciate the idea of speaking while on a high platform. Things that are decided on a platform are nothing more than rules and regulations. We cherish horizontal solidarities . . . not triangular ones. . . . Each individual is important. We had a hard time understanding when we were told about organizational logic (*soshiki no ronri*). As individuals we speak in our own words (*jibun no kotoba de*), free and unrestricted in our thinking (*jiyū na hassō de*)."[41] The self-portrait created by the Women's Group was saturated in male/female binarisms. The representative explained the incongruity between the male-led and female-led activities as a contrast between "the logic of organization" and individuals' "free and unrestricted thinking." Interactions were also understood in gendered terms, with authoritarian and hierarchical relations believed to be produced by men and egalitarian relations by women.

At the same time, feminine qualities are associated with patriarchally constructed class attributes. For instance, being "free and unrestricted" suggested that while male-dominated institutional settings are formal and artificial, individual women's gatherings are informal and natural extensions of daily life. Members of the Women's Group regarded this mundaneness to be of special significance. They often emphasized that the motivations of individual members emerged in the course of their daily routines. For example, one woman remembered that she decided to join the group when she noticed a two-line announcement about the group's first public meeting in the morning newspaper with which she was about to wrap some vegetables. That action suggests commonplace and earthy *shufu*, not the women of the urban or suburban middle class. The story can also be read as demonstrating that the members' political activities are an extension of natural and practical activities, like wrapping vegetables in the morning. Another member, a *shufu* with three children, recalled that when she heard about radioactive contamination of mothers' breast milk, the Chernobyl incident became something terribly immediate and urgent, for she was breast-feeding her youngest child at the time. Those who joined the group perceived themselves as having done so out of "simple and ingenuous" (*soboku na*) concerns for "women and for human lives" (*onna to inochi*).[42]

The autobiographical descriptions of these women's involvements in organized peace and antinuclear protests therefore resonate with representations of feminine dissidents in the 1990 campaign. In that election, irrespective of their intentions, women signified the "grass roots" and "common people" in contrast to men, who were usually associated with "union organizations" and conventional party politics. The local newspaper published a special postelection report that described how "ordinary citizens" and especially *shufu*, the latter described as "political amateurs" (*seiji no shirōto*), had become involved in the election campaign and had come to realize that "an election can be lots of fun."[43] Female candidates and activists were not simply constituted as political actors but were categorized as "ordinary citizens," "common people," or "amateurs." Thus they were distinguished not only by their gender but by their political naiveté. They were distinctively marked as lacking professionalism and as manifesting the ordinary, with special knowledge about the space and practices of the "everyday"—namely, the kitchen, mothering, and daily consumption.

The gendered articulations in both the self-definition of the Women's Group and the madonna strategy of the 1990 election are thus metonymically linked to signs of the ordinary. They also came to dissociate "women's" political concerns from those of production, work, and labor. Female dissidents gain authority as women only when they speak from the position of *shufu*, "mothers," and "common people" who manage the mundane domestic sphere. To be sure, this in part reflects women's strategic identification with such class and gendered positions.

Furthermore, we must recognize that in attempting to differentiate themselves from the existing male-dominated social and political processes,
some women have helped create a segregated, though perhaps not autonomous, space in which their voices could be raised and nurtured
without interruption by those who have conventionally been granted
authority. Yet that strategy has in turn confined women within a category provided by the dominant discourse, so that they unwittingly perpetuate the very arrangements that they have sought to overcome—
including the "oppression" felt by members of the Women's Group.[44]
The deployment of womanliness, a quality that was believed to introduce critical differences into the political process, in fact rearticulates
the communal and distinct space of women within the language of patriarchy and consumer capitalism. The discourse of gendered differentiation, through its very language of female distinctiveness, further subordinates women.

ON REWRITING "WOMEN'S" HISTORIES

We have thus far observed how feminization of memories of war, the
bombing of Hiroshima, and postwar transformations that can be linked
to the Occupation have produced the multifaceted representations of
Japanese Women through the tropes of peace, statehood, motherhood,
anti-imperialism, and the quotidian. In particular, the nationalization of
the maternal in the prevailing anti-American discourse on peace and
antinuclearism constituted and sustained the dominant perception that
Japanese women and mothers were and remain the innocent victims of
the prewar and wartime imperial system, of masculine militarism, and
of the postwar U.S. nuclear dominance in the region.

Among the various attempts to redress the ways in which Japanese
women's pasts have been conventionally known, the women's journal
Jūgoshi nōto (*Homefront Notes*) has perhaps made the most consistent
and systematic interventions.[45] Since its inception in 1977, the journal,
published by a women's circle called the Women's Group Questioning
Our Present (Onnatachi no Ima o Tou Kai), has uncovered and documented Japanese women's relations to Japan's war efforts since the
late nineteenth century. As its name suggests, the journal's central concern has been to interrogate Japanese women's complicitous relation
to the state, particularly their daily and active participation in the nation's imperialist and militarist expansion. The journal's particular slant,

and its cultural and historical significance, reflected the concerns of the founder, Kano Mikiyo, who is a feminist historian and critic. Kano survived the bomb in Hiroshima at the age of five and grew up hearing stories about how the bomb had destroyed women's lives. Her suspicions about the dominant image of Japanese women as innocent and passive victims of the war served as the impetus for the journal's focus. After almost two decades of activity, it ceased publication in the fall of 1996, a year after commemorating the fiftieth anniversary of Japan's surrender to the Allied Forces.

Following the pioneering works by Kano and others affiliated with the journal, a number of other historical writings from the 1980s on also focused on women's complicity with the Japanese state. The most extensive work to date has been done by feminist historian Suzuki Yūko, whose writings include studies of the collaboration of prewar and wartime feminists.[46] Suzuki has relentlessly exposed and condemned not only Japanese women's collusion with the state but also the ways in which they actively sought this avenue in order to fulfill their desires and become political subjects. Others have reevaluated the National Defense Women's Association (Kokubō Fujinkai), whose most dominant image is that of women in white aprons; they emphasize that under the slogan "discard the household and dedicate oneself to the public" (katei o sutete kōkyō no tame ni tsukuse), mothers and wives aggressively supported the military by offering care to soldiers and enthusiastically sending them off to the war of invasion.[47] In light of these recent reexaminations of the historical record, it is no longer difficult to detect the continuity of the prewar and wartime maternal ideology with the enthusiastic valorization of motherhood in the postwar years. This maternal sublimation, through which mothers' grassroots activities have been uncritically linked to the officialized discourse on peace, bears a striking resemblance to the discourse on maternal rights before and during the war.

The underlying problematic of this chapter certainly overlaps with some of the critical perspectives on Japanese women's history that have been offered and circulated by Jūgoshi nōto and those whom it has influenced.[48] I have attempted to explicate the process by which the condition of knowledge critiqued by Kano (and by others writing in a similar vein) was formed. As we have seen, the mystifying and pervasive amnesia about prewar Japanese women's nationalized and imperialized subjectivities was produced in conjunction with the multiple reconstitution of Japanese womanhood and motherhood as the state and the globe were also being reconfigured.[49] Yet while Kano's and others' counter-amnes(t)ic efforts are indispensable for problematizing the responsibility of those interpellated as "Japanese Women," reconstructing Japanese women as active agents mobilized by the Japanese Empire and total war is not sufficient. As in Benjamin's historical materialism, if knowledge about the past is to be relevant in a critical sense to our present concerns for social change and for a different future, we need to know not only what actually happened in the past. We must also explore the promises and alternative historical trajectories that were never realized. We certainly need more studies of how women became incorporated into nationalism and militarism. But we must also make visible how unrealized possibilities—for example, the formation of alliances between Japanese women and others in equally disenfranchised positions—came to be suppressed in order to enable such processes.

In closing we must also ask if a rewriting of women's pasts as the pasts belonging to women might break down what are believed to be essential differences between men and women. Might not accounts that begin to unsettle gender binaries, boundaries, and demarcations offer the greatest challenge to the existing order of historical knowledge, more threatening than any reinscriptions of the particularities of experiences distinguishable by the categories of gender and sex? Representations in which "women" act and think properly, in ways that are differentiated from "men," make conventional gender distinctions the "other" of the violent, cataclysmic, and extraordinary time of structural crisis and liminality.[50] It is thus hardly coincidental that the discourses that promote "peace" and everyday orderliness most ostentatiously articulate the differences—whatever they are taken to be—between masculinity and femininity.

Epilogue

When descriptions about a past incident have been expunged from official histories through formal or informal censorship, witnesses and their listeners tend to feel a painful—and, over time, growing—urgency about the task of contributing to positive knowledge through their recountings. As the recent lawsuits brought by women formerly subjected to sexual enslavement by the Japanese military demonstrate, the sense of crisis is heightened even more when the witnesses' firsthand accounts appear to provide the only means for verifying that an event took place.

Even in the case of Hiroshima, where those who used the atomic bomb have not so much denied as proclaimed worldwide its catastrophic effects, the degree of destruction, the number of human casualties, and the genetic and environmental effects of the bomb have been obscured. Under such conditions, the testimonies of *hibakusha*—which avow to tell the "actuality" (*jittai*) of the event, to tell it "as it really was" (*arinomama ni*), to be "loyal to the facts" (*jijitsu ni sokushite*), and to describe the past "with accuracy" (*seikaku ni*)—have rested upon realist and positivist assumptions about the possibilities of accurate historical reconstruction. In analyzing the fictional dimensions of Jewish Holocaust testimonies and documentaries, James E. Young has identified a similar "mimetic impulse" among survivors.[1] And in his monumental study of so-called atom bomb literature (*genbaku bungaku*), John Whittier Treat argues that especially in the case of *hibakusha* authors, their faithfulness to the idea of mimetic representation has led to a tendency to deny the presence of any elements that might indicate their works' affinities with literary fiction, including the use of tropes, similes, aestheticization, and other rhetorically sophisticated devices. Treat further notes that not only the survivor-writers but also the readers of their works have helped sustain this ideology of historical representation. One result has been a great deal of confusion in evaluations of the aesthetic and literary value of the body of writings from Hiroshima and Nagasaki.[2] We have seen in the preceding chapters what Hayden White has observed more generally of modern historiography: survivors' testimonies, too, are constituted by various rhetorical mediations such as figurality, tropes, and emplotments, despite the authors'/ narrators' desire to render factually accurate historical re-presentations of the event. In the course of testimonial practices, such textual and transtextual negotiations have produced different types of knowledge— didactic, moral, and aesthetic as well as cognitive.[3]

Insofar as *hibakusha* testimonial practices are predicated on an awareness of the presence of listeners, their narratives always display two contradictory impulses, to factualize and to allegorize. When testimonies about the disaster are transformed into tales of unfulfilled promises, anticipation, and potential, they cease to be simply stories about what happened in the past. The opposed yet inseparable dimensions of *hibakusha* testimonial practices therefore must be examined within a single analytical frame. On the one hand, we must seriously consider and appreciate survivors' insistence on telling the past as it really happened, despite their keen awareness of the limits of mimetic representation. On the other hand, we must also rethink, as *hibakusha* do themselves, the literalness of the testimonial accounts and evaluate their effects and meanings beyond the alleged objective of establishing positive historical knowledge. We have seen in earlier chapters how *hibakusha* testimonies engender skepticism about the self-evident world and indeed about "reality" itself. The testimonies can also lead listeners to imagine the alternative trajectories that history might have taken, urging them to question what appears inevitable.

Moreover, the moment the storyteller desires his or her testimony to be heard as a prophecy, or as a possible future event, the past event is relentlessly made allegorical, undermining faithfulness to the original occasion and the impulse toward mimetic representation. The remembered event is dislodged from the past and transfigured into a future happening in a fictive timespace. Hence, the survivors' testimonial practices traverse and confound the conventional course of time in standard historiography, which extends linearly from the past into the present and future.

The well-known slogan "No more Hiroshimas" is enabled by the same temporal intervention. Of course, the reasons why a particular event must be prevented from recurring cannot be properly understood unless we at least attempt to gain some realistic sense of the original devastation. Hence, the geohistorical particulars about what once occurred in Hiroshima become indispensable knowledge. But at the same time, without successfully casting memories of Hiroshima into the future, the aphorism alerting us to the possibility that a catastrophic nuclear disaster can recur at anytime, anywhere, beyond the spatial and temporal specificity of Hiroshima, 6 August 1945, is equally difficult to comprehend. Much like the narratives *of* and *for* the dead discussed in chapter 4, here again the criticalness of knowledge about Hiroshima emerges out of a dialectics between dis-identification and the possibility of reproducing the selfsame.

I hope that this book has shown some of the ways in which various mnemonic practices in Hiroshima have unsettled and transformed knowledge about the past and present. The importance of the survivors' testimonials and other social engagements, however, was not fully evident to me at the outset of my research. When I first visited Hiroshima in 1987 in search of a potential ethnographic "field site," I did not imagine that *hibakusha*'s testimonies would become central to my investigation. My proposed project tended to treat Japan as if it was an autonomously existing closed "text," and my original purpose was to critique the ideology of Hiroshima's symbolism within that coherent text. I had intended to examine the ways in which Hiroshima served as what Pierre Bourdieu might have called "symbolic capital" in Japan's political culture, how Hiroshima as a symbol of counterhegemonic discourse came to be appropriated by statist ideology in the postwar years, and how representations of the atom bombings have shaped the nation's self-representation and self-image. In this initial formulation of my study, "No more Hiroshimas" was but a cliché. Narratives about atomic victimization and Hiroshima's call for world peace seemed to me to have become so routinized and familiar that they had lost any relevance for critical discourse. This banality, moreover, appeared to have troubling effects. By masking the nation's history of military aggression and its dominating presence in the present global political economy, Hiroshima's and Nagasaki's representations of atomic victimization helped produce the image of postwar Japan as a peace-loving, harmless nation. By this account, survivors' recollections appeared to function in unison only to reinforce and naturalize the dominant ideology and national imagination.

To be sure, my "fieldwork" did confirm many of my initial assumptions. Memories of the city's destruction, especially when nationalized through discursive linkages with other instances of nuclear destruction such as Nagasaki and Bikini, have worked to construct a narrative of national innocence and victimhood. The Liberal Democratic Party–led government also successfully co-opted many of the survivors' demands for relief and reparations. Furthermore, the way in which the antinuclear discourse monumentalized nuclear destruction as the ultimate and foremost threat to humanity obscured other forms of violence, injustice, and environmental destruction that had occurred and have continued to take place in less visible yet immanent everyday contexts. It also became clear that the global political economy of urban redevelopment had turned the city into what might be called a theme park of peace and the atomic age. Yet, at the same time, as I listened closely to the survivors' testimonies and observed the various mnemonic practices that they and others are engaged in, I gradually began to wonder if, contrary to my prior assumptions, remembering the ghastly experience of atomic obliteration might have other effects besides uniformly generating a shared imaginary of collective victimization and identity.[4]

Especially in the years following my initial period of fieldwork, charges of Japanese amnesia about their nation's military and colonial atrocities were made with increasing frequency and were more widely acknowledged, both within and outside Japan. Yet these hotly contested debates concerning amnesia and insufficient remorse have usually been framed as a question of whether the Japanese people should remember themselves as victims (*higaisha*) or as military and colonial assailants (*kagaisha*). In such a dichotomizing discourse, in which the nation's historical identity is assumed to be coherent and monolithic, forgetfulness is usually simplistically blamed on the propensity of Japanese to recollect the war only through memories of having been victimized in the atom bombings of Hiroshima and Nagasaki. In the U.S. context, this short-circuited causal logic has served to legitimate the desire to avoid examining whether U.S. decision makers were morally justified in using weapons of unprecedented destructive force against the two populated cities.[5]

Memories of Hiroshima do not in and of themselves produce national self-intoxication on the myth of innocence and victimization, nor do they necessarily endorse the narrative of the national collectivity. Contrary to the assumption that remembering the devastation caused by the atomic bomb fosters only a collective national amnesia and thus obscures questions of responsibility for past atrocities and current social iniquities, we have seen that certain mnemonic practices in Hiroshima have helped produce critical attitudes and a fundamental skepticism toward the existing order of knowledge. With respect to the production of a national imaginary, I want to suggest that the dialectics of remembering Hiroshima's atomic devastation can serve to undo what Benedict Anderson has called "the magic of nationalism" that "turn[s] chance into destiny."[6] This "magic" conjures up the fantasy that the national community has always been and will eternally be bound together. Such a national collectivity is rendered real through imagining arbitrary events as part of a common and unalterable destiny; the survivors' testimonial practices, however, unsettle this construction by remembering the burden of sufferings that were and will continue to be unevenly distributed among the nation's members. The survivors' widespread disillusionment on learning of the late Showa emperor's remarks on his visit to Hiroshima in 1975—namely, that the atomic destruction "was inevitable" since the nation was in the midst of war—was one such moment in the unraveling of the national imaginary.

As the century's end nears, the continued excavation of abominable offenses committed in the name of imperial Japan, together with the partial officialization of such memories in the post-Hosokawa regime, has touched off a new wave of defensive and narcissistic reactions concerning the nation's history and has incited a new drive toward self-absolution. Particularly prominent in this recent revisionism is a study group made up of scholars, writers, and other prominent and not-so-prominent public figures who are busily propagating what they call the "Liberal View of History" (jiyūshugi shikan).[7] Through popular print media and legislative lobbying, members of this group have aggressively moved to eliminate descriptions about Japanese war atrocities and colonial brutality from history textbooks. Denouncing as "masochistic historiography" the historical research and writing that has publicized this heretofore suppressed information, they have consistently sought to downplay the disastrous consequences of Japanese imperialism and militarism for the people of the Asia Pacific region.

The resurgence of this familiar discourse, driven again by a renewed patriotic self-infatuation, has naturally met with fierce resistance. But since the progressive critics' counteramnes(t)ic efforts have been pursued most frequently within constitutional discourse and established institutional procedures, it might be argued that they are ultimately working within the boundaries of the national public sphere even while appearing to oppose the nationalist agenda. Just as Ian Buruma has observed that German self-flagellation might in fact be reaffirming German identity through a "neurotic narcissism,"[8] the debates over whether to apologize for Japanese atrocities could be interpreted as offering a new opportunity for making identification with the nation more complete, especially since they locate a clear and common point of origin for postwar national history and the national community. In these controversies Koreans and other former colonial subjects, Chinese, as well as new immigrants from "Asia" have once again been inscribed as the Other, the object in which Japanese apologies—that is, the desire to be forgiven— is invested. This supplementary other, unlike Emmanuel Levinas's existential alterity,[9] does not unsettle and rupture the self-fulfilled national self; instead, it serves to secure national containment and its boundaries.

Yet those involved in counteramnes(t)ic practices have not always envisioned the present and future in simply national terms. The demands to recognize the moral and legal responsibilities of redressing damages caused by Japan's colonial expansion and military aggression have been inextricably intertwined with the transnationalization of mnemonic communities. Those who remember the past as responsible members of the nation have often become unexpectedly aware of problems occurring in a number of other sites. As evidenced more recently in struggles concerning the Japanese military's sexual enslavement of women, feminist collaborations and coalitions of intellectuals and artists have transcended national and ideological borders, while demonstrating that the proliferating sites of contention need to be articulated in terms of gender, class, sexuality, ethnicity/race, and the other salient differentiations through which power is manifested locally. Thus the recent debates on the nation's historical amnesia do not simply revolve around the recovery and suppression of facts in national history. Rather, they are more than ever concerned with problematizing the very subject of remembering—that is, with analyzing from whose perspective and for whom remembering is urgently required.[10] For the advocates of the "Liberal View of History," the remembering and remembered subjects, as well as the listener to whom that remembered history should be told, are identical: they are "Japanese," members of the bounded national collectivity. Their critics, by contrast, are questioning precisely that self-referentiality, ensured by the assumed continuity and homogeneity of the nation. The current politics of memory may be understood as a battle between attempts to secure the stable contours of national history and the national community, on the one hand, and struggles to fashion a postnationalist cartography of memory, on the other.

Insofar as nation-states continue to exist as institutional entities, and their apparatuses of knowledge continue to interpellate their subjects, nationalization remains a powerful force in shaping our memories, knowledge, and representations. Residues of Hiroshima's catastrophe are constantly in danger of being recuperated for the establishment of coherent national narratives and identities. Nevertheless, these shards of memory, as traces, also carry the power to obstruct that same process. Countering and deferring the relentless processes through which nationalizing and renationalizing take place, tactful strategies of critical remembering, of piecing together the fragmented past, will take skill. As we listen to stories about both the past and present, we must be acutely attentive to the multiple and contradictory elements that refuse subsumption into the existing categories and boundaries of nation-states or other exclusionary collectivities. We all share this obligation regardless of our positions, for as listeners we too are already profoundly implicated in the production of the knowledges and memories that shape our world.

Notes

INTRODUCTION

1. Inoue Shōichi, *Ato, kicchu, japanesuku: daitōa no posuto modan* (Tokyo: Seidosha, 1987). The discussion of the similarities between Tange's two commemorative plans are found in chap. 6 (192–297). Although an architectural analysis is not central here, a brief summary of Inoue's work from the perspective of the politics of knowledge is worthwhile. Inoue characterizes Tange's commemorative plan as 1940s avant-garde or Japanese postmodernism. During this decade, the Japanese postmodern architectural style began displacing the modernist style used for buildings constructed in Japanese colonial cities throughout northeast Asia. According to Inoue, Tange's commemorative design, which subscribed to neither the earlier atavistic style (e.g., *teikan yōshiki*, or "imperial roofing style") nor the then-dominant modernism, was an attempt to overcome the modern (*kindai no chōkoku*) through architectural expression. Inoue was primarily interested in exposing the complicity between the Japanese fascist regime of the early twentieth century and the development of architectural modernism. Contrary to the conventional interpretation, he argues that the nature of modernist architecture was conducive to the instrumental rationality that the Japanese fascist project pursued. Other, competing architectural movements, such as the one Tange proposed here, in effect failed to support the Japanese fascist project aesthetically, chiefly because they, as genuine artistic movements, produced significatory excess and had an avant-garde quality. Inoue's optimism about these artists' inherent transcendence of mass politics allowed his otherwise ingenious analysis to absolve Tange of his participation in the war effort. Nevertheless, his perhaps most intriguing argument is convincing: the realization of Tange's prewar design indicates that the project to overcome the modern was fully effected in the postwar years—the period after the reign of fascism, at least according to conventional historical understanding. For an extensive discussion on the intellectual discourse on the

"overcoming of the modern," see H. D. Harootunian's "Visible Discourses/
Invisible Ideologies," in *Postmodernism and Japan*, ed. Masao Miyoshi and
H. D. Harootunian, a special issue of *South Atlantic Quarterly* 87, no. 3
(summer 1988): 445-74.

2. Inoue, *Ato, kicchu, japanesuku*, 288.

3. How one names the war is intimately linked to how one understands
and wishes to convey the nature of military and other related forms of violence. In this work, I use the term "the Asia Pacific War" (*Ajia taiheiyō sensō*),
an expression to which Japanese critics such as Utsumi Aiko and Murai Yoshinori called my attention in the early 1980s. Use of this label indicates an
awareness that "the Pacific War" (*Taiheiyō sensō*), the name that was common during most of the postwar years, signifies only the military confronta-
tion between the United States and Japan and fails to capture that Japanese
military violence and its invasions directly involved the peoples of China, Korea, Southeast Asia, the Pacific Islands, and other places in the Asia Pacific region. The "Asia Pacific War" also signifies that Japan not only surrendered to
the U.S.-led Allied Forces but was defeated by the anti-Japanese resistance in
Asia and the Pacific. To be sure, "Pacific War" was initially put into use by the
Occupation authorities as a progressive term to replace the official wartime
name, "the Greater East Asian War" (*Daitōa sensō*), which had been premised
on the idea that the war had the sacred mission of establishing the Co-prosperity Sphere. In 1956, long before the term "Asia Pacific War" was popularized,
cultural critic Tsurumi Shunsuke proposed a different name, "the Fifteen-Year
War" (*Jūgonen sensō*), in order to emphasize that the war was not only fought
between the Allied Forces and Japan from 1941 to 1945, but also had been a
conflict between the Chinese people and the Japanese in the years after Japan's
invasion of Manchuria in 1931. See Kisaka Junichirō, "Ajia/Taiheiyō sensō
no rekishiteki seikaku o megutte," *Nenpō Nihon gendaishi*, inaugural issue
(1995): 1-43.

4. According to Inoue, Tange later reminisced that the design for both structures had been inspired by *haniwa*, the clay figurines that have frequently been
excavated from ancient burial sites; see *Ato, kitchu, japanesuku*, 290-92.

5. Ibid., 286.

6. The quoted phrase appeared in the statement of the general theme of the
1942 design competition; see ibid., 192.

7. For important historical research on the Japanese Empire available in
English, see especially Peter Duus, *The Abacus and the Sword: The Japanese
Penetration of Korea, 1895-1910* (Berkeley: University of California Press,
1995), and *The Japanese Wartime Empire, 1931-1945*, ed. Peter Duus, Ramon H. Myers, and Mark R. Peattie (Princeton: Princeton University Press,
1996).

8. The concept of the "mainstream" deployed here is a relational one. The
mainstream is not taken to be a given, self-sufficient, and static category; rather,
it is constituted by the supplementary subjugation of what it excludes. In
chapter 5 I describe how the mainstream and the majority consciousness in
Japanese society are produced by the construction of particular knowledges
about the conditions of non-Japanese ethnic minorities.

9. Andreas Huyssen, *Twilight Memories: Marking Time in a Culture of Amnesia* (New York: Routledge, 1995), 5.

10. According to official records, despite the initial intention to eliminate "invasion," administrators stopped short of forcing the term's replacement. Instead, the ministry official in charge allegedly instructed Ienaga Saburō to deploy the term more widely, not only in portraying Japanese conduct but also in describing similar acts of Western nations. After the investigations, two national newspapers formally apologized for their false reports. See Tokinoya Shigeru, *Ienaga kyōkasho saiban to Nankin jiken: monbushō tantōsha wa shōgen suru* (Tokyo: Nihon Kyōbunsha, 1989), 126–33. That the incident was erroneously reported does not, however, undermine the national and international charges made against the ideological position of the LDP and the Ministry of Education. The textbook controversy was significant in bringing into public view the tendency of conservatives in Japan to deny or trivialize past atrocities committed by Japanese subjects and their military forces.

11. These include the Great Nanjing Massacre (*Nankin dai gyakusatsu*), in which somewhere between 50,000 and 300,000 people were massacred by Japanese soldiers; Unit 731's biological experiments on Chinese and other POWs, as well as military officials' destruction of evidence concerning this research; and the Japanese military's slaughter of residents during the ground battle of Okinawa. Ienaga's legal cases attest to the central government's consistent and active intervention in the writing and teaching of a national history that fosters a self-adulatory understanding of the past.

12. Alexander and Margarete Mitscherlich, *The Inability to Mourn: Principles of Collective Behavior*, trans. Beverley R. Placzek (New York: Grove Press, 1975). The Mitscherlichs argued that the Germans were unable to mourn, an act possible only when one can empathize with the lost object. Instead they suffered melancholic reactions to the loss of the Führer, an object in which they had deeply invested their narcissistic desires. T. Fujitani's study on the centrality of the Japanese monarchy as the transcendent Subject in the production of modern national subjects allows us to draw an intimate analogy between the German postwar psychology the Mitscherlichs observe and the Japanese loss of their emperor and the dream of the Co-prosperity Sphere; see *Splendid Monarchy: Power and Pageantry in Modern Japan* (Berkeley: University of California Press, 1996). See also note 21 below.

13. Yoshida, *Nihonjin no sensōkan: sengoshi no naka no henyō* (Tokyo: Iwanami Shoten, 1995), 127–28. This book offers a very comprehensive analysis of the fifty-year trajectory of historical understandings about the Asia Pacific War that have prevailed in Japanese society.

14. Although in some respects making concessions following subsequent backlash from conservative associations, including the Association of the War Bereaved, Hosokawa nonetheless did not retract his initial remarks. Kisaka Junichirō points out that Hosokawa was the first prime minister in office to have referred in detail to atrocities resulting from Japanese colonialism and militarism. These included the imposition of Japanese names and the Japanese language on Koreans, the forced mobilization (*kyōsei chōyō*) of Korean laborers, and the military's intimate involvement in the sexual enslavement of women

from occupied territories. See Kisaka, "Ajia/Taiheiyō sensō no rekishiteki sei-kaku," 17.

15. Two examples will suffice here. First, the Chinese who were forced to engage in hard labor for the Kashima-gumi construction company in Akita prefecture are demanding reparations. Under extreme conditions that included torture, harsh weather, and malnutrition, 418 of the 986 Chinese who were brought by Kashima-gumi died. Those who had survived the initial months organized a revolt on 30 June 1945 that has come to be known as the Hanaoka incident. For oral testimonies of those involved in the uprising, see Nozoe Kenji, *Hanaoka jiken no hitotachi: Chūgokujin kyōsei renkō no kiroku* (Tokyo: Hyō-ronsha, 1975). Second, Koreans who were engaged in forced labor have sued for retroactive payment of their full salaries from Mitsubishi Heavy Industry in Hiroshima. Immediately after the war, Mitsubishi formally entrusted its list of workers and their unpaid salaries to the Ministry of Justice, instead of paying the laborers themselves. Toyonaga Keisaburō has written on the relevant historical as well as legal processes; see especially "The Atomic Bomb, Forced Labor, and Other Problems of Koreans Living in Hiroshima during the Pacific War," paper presented at the conference "Politics of Remembering the Asia-Pacific War," East-West Center, Honolulu, September 1995.

16. Hirose Seigo succinctly summarizes the institutional factors that he believes led to contrasts in postwar compensation in Germany and Japan. Drawing on the works of Walter Swartz, Otake Hideo, and others, Hirose argues that the institutional differences between the two nations derive primarily from dissimilar treatments of Nazi crimes and Japanese military atrocities at the war tribunals in Nuremberg and Tokyo, the divergent effects of the occupations and U.S. cold war policies in the two geopolitical regions, and distinctions in asymmetries of power between assailants and the victimized in the two countries. See "Doitsu ni okeru sengo sekinin to sengo hoshō," in *Sensō sekinin/sengo sekinin: Nihon to Doitsu wa dō chigauka*, Awaya Kantarō et al. (Tokyo: Asahi Shinbunsha, 1994), 169–220.

17. Although I do not intend to frame my study only in national terms, Eric L. Santner's study of post-Holocaust identity in Germany was especially helpful in thinking about this difference between the two nationalized contexts; see *Stranded Objects: Mourning, Memory, and Film in Postwar Germany* (Ithaca: Cornell University Press, 1990). Following Jean-François Lyotard's accounts of Auschwitz, Saul Friedlander makes a similar observation in his introduction to *Probing the Limits of Representation: Nazism and the "Final Solution,"* ed. Saul Friedlander (Cambridge, Mass.: Harvard University Press, 1992), 1–21, esp. 5–6.

18. These intellectuals include liberal political scientists such as Otsuka Hisao and Maruyama Masao as well as Marxist intellectuals belonging to the so-called *Kōza-ha*, or the "lecture faction." For an extremely well-informed recent study of the debates over modernity and subjectivity in Japan, see J. Victor Koschmann, *Revolution and Subjectivity in Postwar Japan* (Chicago: University of Chicago Press, 1996). A detailed summary of the prewar development of *Kōza-ha* thought can be found in Germaine A. Hoston, *Marxism and the Crisis of Development in Prewar Japan* (Princeton: Princeton University Press, 1986). The seductive power of this argument—which explains away the

causes of social problems in contemporary Japan by attributing them to the lack of development of modernity and capitalism—can be evidenced even in the writings of the so-called new academics, such as Asada Akira, who have been considered as the intellectual vanguard of poststructuralism and postmodernism.

19. An equally important strain of progressive discourse—overlapping yet separate—argues for a recuperation and repoliticization of the folk and popular traditions that existed prior to the beginnings of the autocratic state's modernization project. For an important collection of essays written from this perspective, see Tsurumi Kazuko and Ichii Saburō, eds., *Shisō no bōken: shakai to henka no atarashii paradaimu* (Tokyo: Chikuma Shobō, 1974).

20. Yoshida, *Nihonjin no sensōkan*, 26–29. In "Sengo rekishigaku no senjiki kenkyū: kōchiku sareta sengo 'Nihon' to sono datsukōchiku e," forthcoming in English translation in *Positions*, Narita Ryūichi and Ouchi Hirokazu offer a succinct and intelligent mapping of the shifting perspectives that have shaped the postwar historiography of wartime Japan.

21. Yamaguchi Yasushi, "Futatsu no gendaishi: rekishi no aratana tenkanten ni tatte," in Awaya et al., *Sensō sekinin/sengo sekinin*, 221–65; see esp. 274, 258–59. In his similar observations on how the self-righteousness of postwar Marxist intellectuals "scapegoated" the military, capitalists, and the emperor system, thus obfuscating their collusion in prewar politics, Mishima Ken'ichi draws an analogy between Japan and East Germany; see "Doitsu chishikijin no hatashita yakuwari," in ibid., 123–68, esp. 144–45. The position of memory in Japanese society resembles that in postunification Germany, in that the former East German populations must also now confront the memories of Nazism that they believed they had overcome when their predecessors declared victory against fascism. In the sense that the general population and progressives must face charges of having being collaborators, the situation in Japan is also similar to that of European nations such as France, Switzerland, and Hungary, where ordinary people's involvements in Nazism have long been buried under the grand narrative of resistance and victory against fascism. To be sure, a number of personal memoirs and confessional accounts by ordinary individuals in Japan have been published. Yet historian Yoshimi Yoshiaki's *Kusa no ne no fashizumu*, published in 1987 (Tokyo: Tokyo Daigaku Shuppankai), was one of the first systematic analyses of people's participation in the war effort and in colonial expansion at the grassroots and everyday level.

22. This study is deeply indebted to recent attempts to radically rethink the ways in which "Japan" as a national entity has been historically represented, especially vis-à-vis modern temporalities and experiences. Particularly crucial critiques of the dominant discourse on the Enlightenment and modernity in postwar Japan are offered by those works that have sought to re-present Japan's prewar imperialist ideology by showing how it helped disseminate a discourse of subjectivity conducive to modern nationalism and the development of capitalism. I have already cited H. D. Harootunian's examination of the intellectual discourse of the so-called overcoming of the modern, or *kindai no chōkoku*, in "Visible Discourses/Invisible Ideologies." In his reexamination of Japanese modernity, T. Fujitani argues further that the Japanese emperor system, which has long been regarded in postwar historical studies as a paradigmatic vestige of feudalism, was in fact actively invented in the process of

modern nation building. On this account, Japan's modern monarch was deployed as a mechanism for disciplining and regulating subjects who could self-consciously and actively pursue their responsibilities as members of the new nation; see *Splendid Monarchy,* especially the sections on visual domination (24–28, 138–44, 241–45). Tomiyama Ichirō's *Kindai Nihon shakai to "Okina-wajin": "Nihonjin" ni naru to iu koto* (Tokyo: Nihon Keizai Hyōronsha, 1990) demonstrates how racialized assimilationist policies worked to interpellate Okinawans as Japanese imperial subjects, particularly through the modern management of their everyday practices. Miriam Silverberg writes extensively on the ambivalent yet alluring representations and practices of modernity, capitalism, and mass culture in the early twentieth century; see, for instance, "Constructing a New Cultural History of Prewar Japan," in *Japan in the World,* ed. Masao Miyoshi and H. D. Harootunian (Durham, N.C.: Duke University Press, 1993), 115–43. Likewise, Carol Gluck has also emphasized the importance of examining historiography as a terrain on which public memory and present politics intersect; see "The Past in the Present," in *Postwar Japan as History,* ed. Andrew Gordon (Berkeley: University of California Press, 1993), 64–95. How one grasps the temporality and nature of Japan's modern experiences— whether one sees them as lagging in comparison to the West, as never having happened, as distorted and perverted, or as overachievements—profoundly shapes how one understands the nation's current situation. For important ethnographies and cultural critiques of late-twentieth-century Japan that are based upon a similar rethinking of Japan's modernity, see above all Marilyn Ivy, *Discourses of the Vanishing: Modernity, Phantasm, Japan* (Chicago: University of Chicago Press, 1995); William W. Kelly, "Rationalization and Nostalgia: Cultural Dynamics of New Middle-Class Japan," *American Ethnologist* 13, no. 4 (November 1986): 603–18.

23. It is appropriate here to explain why I focus on Hiroshima and carefully distinguish the representations of Hiroshima's atomic destruction from Nagasaki's. That Hiroshima and Nagasaki are both Japanese cities does not automatically put the two cities in the same discourse. The naturalized and often normative idea that the atomic bombings of Hiroshima and Nagasaki ought to be treated as a pair is premised on a number of geohistorical assumptions. These assumptions include, for instance, an agreement that the disasters the two cities experienced were brought about by the same historical moment of the war, and that their destruction marked the inaugural moment of the nuclear age. More important, the coupling of Hiroshima and Nagasaki is predicated on and in turn naturalizes the assumption that the two cities belong to the same national community and have shared its history. As I will later discuss, adding the Bikini incident to the chain linking Hiroshima and Nagasaki further reinforced the sense of national victimhood. It is precisely these assumptions that have produced the conventional interpretations of Hiroshima's past and present that this study brackets and puts into question. Without the metanarratives that enable these significatory linkages, it would be equally "natural" to compare the historical experience of Hiroshima with other cities in the world—Baghdad, Dachau, Tel Aviv, Los Alamos, etc. As we will see in the discussion of Hiroshima's urban planning, the city's identity is not necessarily

linked to the historical narrative of atomic destruction. Rather, city planners hope that Hiroshima will be more frequently associated with other attractive tourist cities—for instance, Yokohama or Venice, cities renowned for their waterfront beauty.

By suspending what appears to be the essential historical identity of Hiroshima, this study aims to disentangle the various forces that produce representations of the city's past and present. Although references to Nagasaki's atomic bombing are not entirely neglected, an analysis of the politics of remembering Nagasaki's atomic bombing would in fact need to take into account its unique material specificities. A full investigation of this topic would require another entire study, but we might briefly note the particulars that any discussion of how Nagasaki's struggles over historical representation differ from Hiroshima's must consider: the city's historical identity prior to the bombing; the extent and nature of the atomic destruction; the peculiar local, national, and global forces within the political economy that have affected the city's postwar reconstruction; and the ways in which the city's disaster has been figured in national as well as global historical representations. For instance, the partial destruction of Nagasaki, as opposed to the near total annihilation of Hiroshima, produced a thoroughly different condition of remembering. In Nagasaki the social and cultural differences and inequities between those who were bombed (the minority) and those who were not came to be very acutely sensed. In contrast, the totality of Hiroshima's destruction produced a sense of uniformity and sharing as *hibakusha*. The difference in the degree of destruction also left the respective city planners with quite different starting points. In constructing municipal identities, Nagasaki could draw upon various cultural resources, such as its Christian icons and its historical identity as a port city, whereas the totality of Hiroshima's destruction did not leave much for postwar planners to work with, other than atomic ashes.

24. Awaya Kentarō, "Tokyo saiban ni miru sengo shori," in Awaya et al., *Sensō sekinin/sengo sekinin*, 73–122. See also his *Tokyo Saibanron* (Tokyo: Otsuki Shoten, 1989) and *Miketsu no sensō sekinin* (Tokyo: Kashiwa Shobō, 1994).

25. A similar kind of double erasure can be identified in the recent literature in colonial and postcolonial studies. Chungmoo Choi astutely interrogates current colonial and postcolonial discourses that privilege the historical experiences of the West and thereby once again render those formerly colonized by Japan invisible; see "The Discourse of Decolonization and Popular Memory: South Korea," *Positions* 1, no. 1 (spring 1993): 77–102, esp. 100. The Preparations Committee of the People's Court to Question Japan's War Responsibilities toward Asia (Ajia ni Taisuru Nihon no Sensō Sekinin o Tou Minshū Hōtei Junbikai), which was initiated by such scholars as Awaya Kentarō, Ienaga Saburō, and Utsumi Aiko, has specifically attempted to redress this shortcoming of the Tokyo War Crimes Tribunal.

26. See George Hicks, *The Comfort Women: Japan's Brutal Regime of Enforced Prostitution in the Second World War* (New York: W. W. Norton, 1994), esp. 168, 270, for the local trial's treatment of crimes committed against Dutch women. Hicks also discusses the relationship between the notion of

"crimes against humanity" and the international legal treatments of military enforced sexual labor (200). For the most comprehensive critiques to date on comfort women issues from a transnational perspective, see Chungmoo Choi, ed., *The Comfort Women: Colonialism, War and Sex*, a special issue of *Positions* 5, no. 1 (spring 1997).

27. This point, popularized through the work of U.S. historian Richard H. Minear, further legitimated the image of Japanese as primarily victims. Awaya, "Tokyo saiban ni miru sengo shori," 106. On both the significance and dangers of Richard H. Minear's work, see note 36 below on Rhadhabinod B. Pal's view of the Tokyo War Crimes Tribunal.

28. John Hersey's *Hiroshima* (1946; reprint, New York: Knopf, 1985) perhaps best exemplifies this view.

29. Henry L. Stimson, quoted by Richard Rhodes, *The Making of the Atomic Bomb* (New York: Simon and Schuster, 1988), 650.

30. Kurihara Sadiko, *The Songs of Hiroshima—When Hiroshima Is Spoken Of* (Hiroshima: Anthology Publishing Association, 1980), 8–9.

31. Ubuki Satoru points out that the characterization of Japan as the first and only "atom-bombed nation in the world" first appeared in a message from the prime minister in 1970, and became routinized thereafter. See "Heiwa kinen shikiten no hensen to heiwa sengen," in *Hiroshima shinshi: rekishi hen* (Hiroshima: Hiroshima-shi, 1984), 475–561; quotation, 482.

32. For one of the most engaged personal accounts and critical overviews of the Gensuikin movement's development, see Matsue Kiyoshi, *Hiroshima kara: gensuikin undo o ikite* (Tokyo: Seikyusha, 1984). Ubuki Satoru's "Gunshuku to shinmin undō: Nihon no gensuibaku kinshi undō o megutte," *Kokusai seiji*, no. 80 (October 1985): 112–26, provides a succinct summary of the Gensuikin movement's development.

33. Marxist and modernist Japanese intellectuals also split over the U.S.-Japan Security Treaty. Harry Harootunian writes: "The issue [of Ampo] was seen as a struggle over the choice between democratic politics or economic growth. In this breech, modernists retreated from positions they previously shared with Marxists devoted to barring the return of militarism and a powerful state." See "America's Japan/Japan's Japan," in Miyoshi and Harootunian, *Japan in the World*, 196–221; quotation, 213.

34. Oe Kenzaburo, *Hiroshima nōto*, 41st ed. (Tokyo: Iwanami Shoten, 1989), 147. The English translation of this book is likely to leave its readers with the erroneous impression that the nationalizing of Hiroshima's disaster was monolithic, because it obfuscates some of Oe's explicit references to the anti-statist, antiestablishment nature of activities in Hiroshima during the 1950s and 1960s. For instance, Oe's description of medical efforts in Hiroshima in the English version reads, "it will be clear that medical care for A-bomb victims has been sustained primarily by the strength of local and regional organizations, and that local leaders often had to cope with recalcitrant national agencies" (*Hiroshima Notes*, ed. David L. Swain, trans. Yonezawa Toshi [Tokyo: YMCA Press, 1981], 93). However, Oe's words more literally translate as "rather, the medical history of the atom bomb has been consistent in its determination to be antiestablishment" (*genbaku iryōshi wa mushiro hantaisei no kokorozashi ni yotte tsuranukarete kita; Hiroshima Nōto*, 93).

35. John W. Dower also describes the contradictory effects of the Hiroshima and Nagasaki atom bombings on national consciousness in Japan in "The Bombed: Hiroshimas and Nagasakis in Japanese Memory," *Diplomatic History* 19, no. 2 (spring 1995): 275–95. He makes the important observation that perceptions about the A-bombs have been enmeshed with postwar images of science and nationhood. A fine comparative analysis of how collective memories of the atomic bombings have been produced in the U.S. and Japanese national contexts can be found in Laura Hein and Mark Selden, "Commemoration and Silence: Fifty Years of Remembering the Bomb in America and Japan," in *Living with the Bomb: American and Japanese Cultural Conflict in the Nuclear Age*, ed. Laura Hein and Mark Selden (Armonk, N.Y.: M. E. Sharpe, 1997), 3–34.

36. In "The Other Within: Radhabinod Pal's Judgment of Culpability," in *The Savage Freud and Other Essays on Possible and Retrievable Selves* (Princeton: Princeton University Press, 1995), Ashis Nandy points out that Pal's judgment at the Tokyo War Crimes Tribunal was intended to "establish the continuity between the culpability of the accused and that of the plaintiffs" within the larger context of the twentieth-century global condition (79). Nandy also prefaces his discussion by describing the polarized appropriations of Pal's judgment: on the one hand by nationalists interested in absolving Japan of its war and colonial guilt, and on the other by pan-Asian pacifists (though the two groups were never entirely separate). A less sympathetic account of Pal's dissent can be found in Arnold C. Brackman, *The Other Nuremberg: The Untold Story of the Tokyo War Crimes Trials* (New York: William Morrow, 1987), 391–93. Richard Minear's *Victor's Justice* (Princeton: Princeton University Press, 1971) was one of the earliest works written by a professional historian that reexamined the significance of Pal's dissenting perspective. Unfortunately, Minear's important intervention into the dominant U.S. historiography on Japan has been appropriated, like Pal's judgment, by Japanese nationalists eager to find justifications for Japanese military and colonial aggression.

37. As might be expected, Pal's logic was enthusiastically welcomed by Japan's nationalists, pan-Asianists, and right-wingers, who had maintained that Japan's colonial project and its military expansion were acts to defend Asia against Western domination. For such an appropriation, see Tanaka Tadaaki, *Pāru hakase no Nihon muzairon* (1963; reprint, Sagamihara: Seibunsha, 1987).

38. Kosakai Yoshimitsu, *Hiroshima tokuhon* (Hiroshima: Hiroshima Heiwa Bunka Sentā, 1978), 42. In Japanese, the emphasized clause reads *tanni ikkoku ichiminzoku no giseisha dewa naku, jinrui zentai no ishizue to natte matsurarete iru koto.*

39. Ibid., 43.

40. Jichitai Mondai Kenkyūsho and Hiroshima Kenkyūkai, eds., *Hiroshima Hiroshima: daisanji Hiroshima shisei hakusho* (Hiroshima: Hiroshima-shi Shokuin Rōdō Kumiai, 1982), 249–54. Like a symptom of trauma, similar arguments continue to recur even in the 1990s, voiced especially by ultraconservative and nationalist politicians and critics. Kamei Shizuka, a LDP Diet member known for his vocal conservativism, recently condemned the cenotaph inscription.

41. Nearly thirty years ago Robert Jay Lifton observed the tendency to

conflate "the bomb" and "peace"; see *Death in Life: Survivors of Hiroshima* (New York: Basic Books, 1967). This astute remark still holds today. For instance, the park is named "Peace Memorial Park" (*Heiwa Kinen Kōen*), rather than "Atom Bomb Memorial Park." *Heiwa Kinenkan* means literally "Peace Memorial Hall," and the museum is named the "Peace Memorial Resource Museum" (*Heiwa Kinen Shiryōkan*), although people generally refer to it as the "Atom Bomb Resource Museum" (*Genbaku Shiryōkan*). Lifton's reading, however, was a psychological one; for him, "the general tendency to use 'Atomic Bomb' and 'Peace' almost interchangeably in naming these monuments suggests the psychological effort to equate the two in the sense of the latter springing from the ashes of the former" (271). Yet such a focus on "psychological efforts" results in only a limited explanation. I wish to bring into relief the intersecting works of power that tend to be ignored in that type of reading.

42. For example, the first clause of the law merely states, "This law aims to construct the city of Hiroshima as a Peace Memorial City, a symbol of the ideal to earnestly realize eternal peace." With respect to the mayor's role, the sixth clause reads: "Relying upon citizens' cooperation and the support of related institutions, the mayor of Hiroshima city must constantly exert efforts to complete the Hiroshima Peace Memorial City." When the bill for the "Hiroshima Peace Memorial City" was submitted to the Diet, lobbyists attached the following statement explaining their rationale: "To build Hiroshima city into a Peace Memorial City—which symbolizes at once the human ideal for the realization of eternal peace and our renunciation of war—is to respond to the world's hopes for the recovery of *Hiroshima* [written in *katakana*]. It also means to encourage its reconstruction. For this cause, a legal measure is necessary. We therefore propose this law." See Teramitsu Tadashi, *Hiroshima heiwa toshi hō: Hiroshima heiwa kinen toshi kensetu hō chūkai* (Hiroshima: Chūgoku Shinbunsha 1949), 12. Later in the same year Nagasaki proposed a similar bill.

43. After passing as a local referendum on 7 July 1949, the law officially went into effect. It gained the approval of 71,852 out of 78,962 voters. The voter turnout was unusually high (65 percent). See Chūgoku Shinbunsha, ed., *Nenpyō Hiroshima 40nen no kiroku* (Tokyo: Miraisha, 1986), 56. After the law's passage, discrepant recovery projects and city planning efforts all came to be subsumed under the rubric of the Peace Memorial City construction project. See Hiroshima-shi, ed., *Hiroshima shinshi: toshi bunka hen* (Hiroshima: Hiroshima-shi, 1983), 57–82. As many had anticipated, the city benefited in practical financial terms once the law was instituted. It facilitated, for instance, the transferal of government-owned property to the municipal government, enabled the receipt of special government subsidies, and allowed the city to use land formerly occupied by the military free of charge; see Hiroshima-shi, ed., *Hiroshima shinshi: shakai hen* (Hiroshima: Hiroshima-shi, 1984), 89–96. The law enabled the city to receive subsidies of over 900 million yen between 1950 and 1955; see Ishimaru Norioki et al., eds., *Toshi no fukkō: Hiroshima hibaku 40nenshi* (Hiroshima: Hiroshima-shi, 1986) 56–57.

44. Teramitsu, *Hiroshima heiwa toshi hō*, 16–17.

45. Monica Braw's *The Atomic Bomb Suppressed: American Censorship in Japan, 1945–1949* (Malmo, Sweden: Liber Forlag, 1986) discusses in detail

how the U.S.-led Occupation exercised the Press Code. Reflecting on the lack of awareness in the United States about the nuclear threat as we approach the end of the century, Robert Jay Lifton and Greg Mitchell quote Braw to argue that the Press Code had an extremely detrimental impact on the subsequent condition of knowledge about the nuclear age: "Censorship not only deleted certain facts, it hindered atomic bomb survivors from speaking out about their experiences, experiences that they alone had and that would have helped the rest of mankind understand what the world had come to. . . . One is hard put not to agree with the Japanese historian Seiji Imahori, who said that by silencing the voice of the atomic bomb survivors 'an important possibility to decisively influence the world situation was lost'" (quoted in Lifton and Mitchell, *Hiroshima in America: Fifty Years of Denial* [New York: G. P. Putnam's Sons, 1995], 57).

46. On the influence of the GHQ and the United States, see Hiroshima-shi, *Hiroshima shinshi: toshi bunkahen,* 19–57, esp. 39–40, 56. Japanese proponents of reconstruction also encouraged the idea of making Hiroshima into a site celebrating the new scientific discovery of atomic power. See *Nihon no genbaku kiroku,* ed. Ienaga Saburō et al. (Tokyo: Nihon Tosho Sentā 1991), 10:435, for the 1958 event in Hiroshima that celebrated the peaceful use of atomic energy. This memoir also discusses the debates and conflicts that occurred when American participants tried to donate portions of their exhibits to the Atom Bomb Museum.

47. In *The Decision to Use the Atomic Bomb and the Architecture of an American Myth* (New York: Alfred A. Knopf, 1995), Gar Alperovitz reasserts his earlier view that the mainstream U.S. understanding of the inevitability of the bomb's use was a myth that had been manufactured. Other seminal works that questioned official justification of the two atomic bombs' use include Gar Alperovitz, *Atomic Diplomacy: Hiroshima and Potsdam* (New York: Simon and Schuster, 1965); Martin J. Sherwin, *A World Destroyed: The Atomic Bomb and the Grand Alliance* (New York: Alfred A. Knopf, 1975); Barton Bernstein, "Atomic Diplomacy and the Cold War," in *The Atomic Bomb: The Critical Issues,* ed. Barton Bernstein (Boston: Little, Brown, 1976), 129–35 (see also other essays in the same volume). For the manipulation of estimates on American casualties and deaths, see Barton Bernstein, "Understanding the Atomic Bomb and the Japanese Surrender: Missed Opportunities, Little-Known Near Disasters, and Modern Memory," *Diplomatic History* 19, no. 2 (Spring 1995): 227–73. For a summary of the historians' new consensus, see J. Samuel Walker, "History, Collective Memory, and the Decision to Use the Bomb," included in the same special issue of *Diplomatic History* (319–28). The articles in this excellent special issue were republished in Michael J. Hogan, ed., *Hiroshima in History and Memory* (Cambridge: Cambridge University Press, 1996). For an insightful observation on the gendered and racialized dimensions concerning the use of the bombs, see Ronald Takaki, *Hiroshima: Why America Dropped the Bomb* (Boston: Little, Brown, 1995).

48. The Japanese government's decision to confer an imperial award on Major General Curtis E. LeMay in recognition of his contributions to building the Japanese Self-Defense Naval Force in the postwar years perhaps most emblematically demonstrates this relationship. LeMay, who was responsible for

directing the carpet bombing of major cities in Japan, was instrumental in the decision to use the atomic bomb against civilians. See Rhodes, *The Making of the Atomic Bomb,* esp. 596–600, for LeMay's understanding of the bombing of Tokyo.

49. For detailed accounts of the structural shifts and continuities between prewar and postwar Japan, as well as observations on the process whereby some prewar Japanese nationalist desires came to be realized in the postwar years through the military subordination of Japan to the United States, see J. W. Dower, *Empire and Aftermath: Yoshida Shigeru and the Japanese Experience, 1878–1954* (1979; reprint, Cambridge, Mass.: Harvard University Press, 1988). With regard to modernization theory, which has often been associated with the writings of W. W. Rostow and Edwin O. Reischauer, the historian Yasumaru Yoshio long ago pointed out the significance of Japanese intellectuals' collaboration in formulating the basic ideological components of the theory—namely, that economic growth under a capitalist economy would foster the democratic ideals of liberal civil society; see his 1962 article, "Nihon no kindaika ni tsuite no teikokushugiteki rekishikan," in *"Hōhō" toshite no shisōshi* (Tokyo: Azekura Shobō, 1996), 210–43. T. Fujitani assesses Yasumaru's work in relation to modernization theory, modernist social science, and Marxism in *"Minshushi* as Critique of Orientalist Knowledges," *Positions* 6, no. 6 (fall 1998).

50. The splits within the Gensuikin movement are summarized in detail in Hiroshima-shi, ed., *Hiroshima shinshi: rekishi hen* (Hiroshima: Hiroshima-shi, 1984), 275–88; quotation, 279.

51. Local reactions against the institutional split and the turmoil over the "any nation" issue are described in detail in Hiroshima-shi, ed., *Hiroshima shinshi: shimin seikatsu hen* (Hiroshima: Hiroshima-shi, 1984), 381–84.

52. Ibid., 383. Similar accounts are also collected in Matsue, *Hiroshima kara,* 178.

53. In Hiroshima, two local bodies of Gensuikyō were established: one affiliated with the former Gensuikyō's national body, the other with the newly established Gensuikin.

54. Especially in the early 1970s, the main concern of student and new left organizations was the Japanese government's involvement in escalating U.S. military operations in Vietnam. At roughly the same time, peace and antinuclear ideals were often linked to other antiestablishment movements, such as the protests against the airport construction at Sanrizuka-Narita. It was not until the late 1980s, when large labor unions gradually lost their mobilizing abilities, that Gensuikin began to explicitly acknowledge the need to rely on grassroots peace and antinuclear organizations. For observations on the broad-based new left peace politics of this period, see Thomas R. H. Havens, *Fire across the Sea: The Vietnam War and Japan, 1965–1975* (Princeton: Princeton University Press, 1987). David E. Apter and Nagayo Sawa's *Against the State: Politics and Social Protest in Japan* (Cambridge, Mass.: Harvard University Press, 1984) is a vivid account of the protests against the Narita Airport's construction. The Sanrizuka-Narita struggle became a central focus of antistatist, antiestablishment activities during the 1970s.

55. The complementary and mutually reinforcing relationship between uni-

versalism (e.g., of the historical subject of the West) and particularism (of the non-West) has been most clearly and extensively explicated in Naoki Sakai's "Modernity and Its Critique: The Problem of Universalism and Particularism," in *Postmodernism and Japan,* ed. Miyoshi and Harootunian, a special issue of *South Atlantic Quarterly* 87, no. 3 (summer 1988): 475–504. Sakai, for instance, succinctly argues that "the claim to universality frequently serves to promote the demands of nationalism" (480) and that universalism serves as a legitimating discourse for one society's domination over another.

56. Kanai Toshihiro's *Kaku kenryoku: Hiroshima no kokuhatsu* (Tokyo: Sanseidō, 1970) very forcefully discusses the structural relationships that have sustained the "nuclear umbrella."

57. *Asahi shinbun,* 28 June 1990.

58. Though complicated by the illegal nature of his entry, the seven-year lawsuit initiated by Son and his supporters ended in his victory. Above all, the trial clarified judicially that the legal relief measures were a form of governmental reparation. See Hiroshima-shi, *Hiroshima shinshi: shimin seikatsu hen,* 352–59. Haruko Taya Cook and Theodore F. Cook's *Japan at War: An Oral History* (New York: New Press, 1992) includes a rare account of a Korean survivor in Hiroshima; see 387–91.

59. Many Japanese who subscribe to right-wing ideology recall that Koreans fought "the war against Western imperialism" as members of the empire. Therefore, long before criticism of postwar national amnesia became a major item on the progressive agenda, a number of right-wing imperialists had been arguing that Korean victims should receive compensation equal to that for Japanese. It has been estimated that today there are some twenty thousand survivors living in South Korea alone.

60. We might also note that Sato followed the basic state policies that were laid out by his older brother, Kishi Nobusuke. Kishi was arrested as a Class-A war criminal soon after the war, but his indictment was suspended by the Occupation authorities, who saw the utility of his anticommunist stance. Kishi later played a key role in passing the U.S.-Japan Security Treaty.

61. Hiroshima-shi, *Hiroshima shinshi: shimin seikatsu hen,* 389. Hiroshima and Nagasaki acquired relative autonomy from the central government only after nongovernmental organizations in general gained visibility and legitimacy in the international arena. In October 1995 representatives of the two cities appeared at the International Court of Justice in Hague and testified that use of the bombs violated the Hague Convention on Land Warfare of 1899 and 1907, which had banned the use of inhumane weapons. At the hearing, however, the delegate from Japan's Ministry of Foreign Affairs contradicted the representatives from Hiroshima and Nagasaki. The Japanese national government has consistently suppressed attempts within Japan to disseminate information to the outside world about the extensiveness of nuclear destruction, especially to the United States and other Western nations. See *Asahi shinbun,* 8 November 1995. For a discussion on international law and the use of atomic bombs, see, for instance, Nicholas Grief, "The Legality of Nuclear Weapons," in *Nuclear Weapons and International Laws,* ed. Istvan Pogany (Brookfield, Vt.: Avebury, 1987), 22–52.

62. Santner, *Stranded Objects,* 52. It must be emphasized that the "posts"

in these contexts do not imply the conclusion or pastness of the conditions to which they are attached. Rather, they are used to indicate both the temporal location at which important breaks in the era, social structure, or episteme occurred and the continuities, modifications, repetitions, or even intensifications of former conditions. Thoughtful warnings that the term "postcolonial" might yet again lead to the endorsement of the singularity and unilinearity of global time, and that it serves to occlude continuing colonial and neocolonial realities, are offered by Masao Miyoshi, "A Borderless World?: From Colonialism to Transnationalism and the Decline of the Nation-State," *Critical Inquiry* 19, no. 4 (summer 1993): 726–51, and Anne McClintock, *Imperial Leather: Race, Gender and Sexuality in the Colonial Contest* (New York: Routledge, 1995), esp. 9–13. Indeed, the pastness of the cold war condition is not nearly as evident in Northeast Asia as in Europe. In this study, terms such as "postcolonial" are used not so much to address a particular strand of intellectual discourse within academia as to underscore the specific nature of the historical conditions in which the ethnographic observations have taken place.

63. The notion of "scattered hegemonies" as developed by Inderpal Grewal and Caren Kaplan captures discursive and material conditions similar to the ones I am describing here. See their "Introduction: Transnational Feminist Practices and Questions of Postmodernity," in *Scattered Hegemonies: Postmodernity and Transnational Feminist Practices,* ed. Inderpal Grewal and Caren Kaplan (Minneapolis: University of Minnesota Press, 1994), 1–33. The crucial point here is to pluralize and complicate rather than dismiss the concept of "hegemony."

64. In addition to works that have been or will be discussed in some detail in the main text, other important writings that have influenced my thinking on historical memory include Maurice Halbwachs, *On Collective Memory,* ed. and trans. Lewis Coser (Chicago: University of Chicago Press, 1992); articles that appeared in *Memory and Counter-Memory,* a special issue of *Representations,* no. 26 (spring 1989), esp. Pierre Nora's "Between Memory and History: Les Lieux de Mémoire" (7–25); and Richard Terdiman, *Present Past: Modernity and the Memory Crisis* (Ithaca: Cornell University Press, 1993). *Women and Memory,* a special issue of *Michigan Quarterly Review* 26, no. 1 (winter 1990), includes a number of articles dealing with the gendered dimensions of memory: see especially Elizabeth F. Loftus, Mahzarin R. Banaji, Jonathan W. Schooler, and Rachael A. Foster, "Who Remembers What?: Gender Differences in Memory" (64–85), and Jane Flax, "Re-Membering the Selves: Is the Repressed Gendered?" (92–110). Though the anthology is not centrally concerned with the politics of historical memory, Paul Antze and Michael Lambek, eds., *Tense Past: Cultural Essays in Trauma and Memory* (New York: Routledge, 1996) offers an interdisciplinary collection of essays that examine the ways in which past experiences are mediated by and interwoven through present recollection, narrativization, and cultural frameworks.

In addition to studies discussed later that consider the ways in which Nazi pasts shape the politics of knowledge in post-Nazi Europe, a number of important works treat the politics of memory and history in the United States. These include Michael Kammen, *Mystic Chords of Memory: The Transformation of Tradition in American Culture* (New York: Alfred A. Knopf, 1991);

Michael Schudson, *Watergate in American Memory: How We Remember, Forget, and Reconstruct the Past* (New York: Basic Books, 1992); John Bodnar, *Remaking America: Public Memory, Commemoration, and Patriotism in the Twentieth Century* (Princeton: Princeton University Press, 1992); and Edward Linenthal, *Sacred Ground: Americans and Their Battlefields* (Urbana: University of Illinois Press, 1991). For those studies that focus on the contestatory dimensions of war memorialization, see, for instance, Jay Winter, *Sites of Memory, Sites of Mourning* (Cambridge: Cambridge University Press, 1995), and Geoffrey M. White, "Remembering Guadalcanal: National Identity and Transnational Memory-Making," *Public Culture* 7, no. 3 (spring 1995): 529–55.

Some studies of popular culture have made intriguing observations on how memories have been pivotal in organizing everyday lives in modern societies and how they have served as repositories and battlegrounds for power and knowledge. See, for instance, Richard Johnson, Gregor McLennan, Bill Schwartz, and David Sutton, eds., *Making Histories: Studies in History-Writing and Politics* (London: Hutchinson, 1982). In *Time Passages: Collective Memory and American Popular Culture* (Minneapolis: University of Minnesota Press, 1990), George Lipsitz provides a unique and sophisticated account of the relationships among historical memory, modern aesthetics, and popular forms of cultural resistance. Similar observations on Latin America can be found, for instance, in Michael Taussig's *Shamanism, Colonialism, and the Wild Man: A Study in Terror and Healing* (Chicago: University of Chicago Press, 1987) and William Rowe and Vivian Shelling's *Memory and Modernity: Popular Culture in Latin America* (New York: Verso, 1991).

As exemplified in Taussig's work, the field of cultural anthropology has produced a number of important works on quotidian understandings of history and on the politics of memory waged over popular experiences of modernity, violence, and colonialism at specific geohistorical locations. See, for instance, Renato Rosaldo, *Ilongot Headhunting, 1883–1974: A Study in Society and History* (Stanford: Stanford University Press, 1980); Sylvia Junko Yanagisako, *Transforming the Past: Tradition and Kinship among Japanese Americans* (Stanford: Stanford University Press, 1985); Ana María Alonso, "The Effects of Truth: Re-Presentations of the Past and the Imaging of Community," *Journal of Historical Sociology* 1, no. 1 (March 1988): 33–57; Ted Swedenburg, *Memories of Revolt: The 1936–1939 Rebellion and the Palestinian National Past* (Minneapolis: University of Minnesota Press, 1995); Jun Jing, *The Temple of Memories: History, Power, and Morality in a Chinese Village* (Stanford: Stanford University Press, 1996); Veena Das, *Critical Events: Moments in the Life of a Nation* (Delhi: Oxford University Press, 1995); Kathleen Stewart, *A Space on the Side of the Road: Cultural Poetics in an "Other" America* (Princeton: Princeton University Press, 1996); and Jonathan Boyarin, ed., *Remapping Memory: The Politics of Timespace* (Minneapolis: University of Minnesota Press, 1994).

65. Elsewhere, I have discussed the problems that arise from such a simple dichotomizing of History and Memory. See my "Critical Warps: Facticity, Transformative Knowledge, and Postnationalist Criticism in the Smithsonian Controversy," *Positions* 5, no. 3 (winter 1997): 779–809.

66. In her thought-provoking analysis of cultural memory in the United

States, Marita Sturken eloquently reveals the intimate interplays between what have conventionally been distinguished as private memory and public history, as well as between personal and collective remembering. See *Tangled Memories: The Vietnam War, the AIDS Epidemic, and the Politics of Remembering* (Berkeley: University of California Press, 1997).

67. Joan W. Scott, "The Evidence of Experience," *Critical Inquiry* 17, no. 4 (summer 1991): 797.

68. Scott's critique of the term "experience" is especially illuminating when we try to understand the problematic implications of the often unreflexive popular use of the Japanese word *taiken*, which can be contrasted to that of another, *keiken*. *Taiken* and *keiken* are both translated "experience." The difference between the two may be likened to one between the German words *Erlebnis* and *Erfahrung*. The literal meaning of *taiken* would be the effects and outcomes of events undergone and evidenced by and through bodies. (The Chinese ideograph for *tai* indicates the body.) It implies organic, immediate, and sensory dimensions of the experience. In contrast, *keiken*—which has also been used to translate the Greek etymon *empeiria* in "empiricism" (*keiken shugi*)— consists of one ideograph that means "effects and evidence" and another that indicates "trajectory, constancy, and the act of passing." While the former underscores the spatial dimension of the traces of past in the present, the latter emphasizes the temporal dimension of experience, especially the pastness of the past event. In this study, the expressions translated into English as "the atom bomb experience" or "the war experience" originally appear in the discourse of survivors and others as "*hibaku taiken*" or "*senso taiken*," respectively.

69. Besides the works I discuss here, important writings on Benjamin's philosophy available in English include Fredric Jameson, "Walter Benjamin; or, Nostalgia," in *Marxism and Form: Twentieth-Century Dialectical Theories of Literature* (Princeton: Princeton University Press, 1971), 60–83; Terry Eagleton, *Walter Benjamin, or Towards a Revolutionary Criticism* (London: Verso, 1981); and articles compiled in the special issue on Benjamin in *New German Critique*, no. 39 (fall 1986). In the latter, Irving Wohlfarth, "Refusing Theology: Some First Responses of Walter Benjamin's Arcades Projects" (3–24), and H. D. Kittsteiner, "Walter Benjamin's Historicism," trans. Jonathan Monroe and Irving Wohlfarth (179–215), are especially illuminating. Also important are Richard Wolin, *Walter Benjamin: An Aesthetic Redemption* (New York: Columbia University Press, 1982), and Gary Smith, ed., *Benjamin: Philosophy, Aesthetics, History* (Chicago: University of Chicago Press, 1989); in the latter, see especially Rolf Tiedemann's discussion of the relationship between Benjamin's Marxist historical consciousness and motifs in Jewish theology, "Historical Materialism or Political Messianism? An Interpretation of the Theses 'On the Concept of History'" (175–209). With regard to Benjamin's understanding of temporality, Stanley Aronowitz's discussion on the contributions of Michel Foucault and Walter Benjamin to rethinking conventional historical writing is especially useful; see "History as Disruption: On Benjamin and Foucault," *Humanities in Society* 2, no. 2 (spring 1979): 125–47, esp. 134. In *The Politics of Time: Modernity and Avant-Garde* (New York: Verso, 1995), Peter Osborne offers a useful analysis of Benjamin's notion of history, tradition, and moder-

nity; see esp. 113–59. Jonathan Boyarin's *Storm from Paradise: The Politics of Jewish Memory* (Minneapolis: University of Minnesota Press, 1992) deploys a Benjaminian concept of temporality to observe the culture and history of the Jewish diaspora. See also Rebecca Comay, "Redeeming Revenge: Nietzsche, Benjamin, Heidegger, and the Politics of Memory," in *Nietzsche as Postmodernist: Essays Pro and Contra*, ed. Clayton Koelb (Albany: State University of New York Press, 1990), 21–38, for an intriguing discussion of when and how the nostalgia produced by the modern sense of history can become politicized in a critical way.

70. Walter Benjamin, "Theses on the Philosophy of History," in *Illuminations*, ed. Hannah Arendt, trans. Harry Zohn (New York: Schocken Books, 1969), 257, 262–63.

71. Walter Benjamin, "N [Re the Theory of Knowledge, Theory of Progress]," trans. Leigh Hafrey and Richard Sieburth, in *Benjamin: Philosophy, Aesthetics, History*, ed. Gary Smith (Chicago: University of Chicago Press, 1989), 43–83; quotation, 65.

72. I am grateful to Harry Harootunian for calling my attention to this link between the Benjaminian thesis on materialist history and survivors' storytellings. For Harootunian's reading of Benjamin within the context of discussing Japanese modernity, see "The Benjamin Effect: Modernism, Repetition, and the Path to Different Cultural Imaginaries," in *Walter Benjamin and the Demands of History*, ed. Michael P. Steinberg (Ithaca: Cornell University Press, 1996), 62–87.

73. Benjamin, "Theses," 255.

74. Susan Buck-Morss, *The Dialectics of Seeing: Walter Benjamin and the Arcades Project* (Cambridge, Mass.: MIT Press, 1989), 338.

75. Jürgen Habermas, *The Philosophical Discourse of Modernity: Twelve Lectures*, trans. Frederick G. Lawrence (Cambridge, Mass.: MIT Press, 1992), 14, 12.

76. Ibid., 15. For Habermas's critique of the conservative resurgence in German historiography on the Nazi period, see "Apologetic Tendencies," "On the Public Use of History," and "Historical Consciousness and Post-Traditional Identity," in *The New Conservatism: Cultural Criticism and the Historians' Debate*, ed. and trans. Shierry Weber Nicholsen (Cambridge, Mass.: MIT Press, 1992), 212–28, 229–40, 249–67. Habermas's notion of public sphere is deftly critiqued by Ping-hui Liao. Following the critiques of Nancy Fraser and others, Liao underscores the significance of modifying the Habermasian utopian presumption of a single, unitary public sphere with respect to the postcolonial condition in Taiwan, where multiple layers of modern experiences and historical identities coexist; "Rewriting Taiwanese National History: The February 28 Incident as Spectacle," *Public Culture* 5, no. 2 (winter 1993): 281–96. See also Nancy Fraser, "Rethinking the Public Sphere: A Contribution to the Critique of Actually Existing Democracy," in *Habermas and the Public Sphere*, ed. Craig Calhoun (Cambridge, Mass.: MIT Press, 1992), 109–42. For important criticisms of historical revisionism within the context of the European experience of Nazism, see the articles compiled in Geoffrey H. Hartman, ed., *Bitburg in Moral and Political Perspective* (Bloomington: Indiana

University Press, 1986), as well as Pierre Vidal-Naquet, *Assassins of Memory: Essays on the Denial of the Holocaust*, trans. and foreword Jeffrey Mehlman (New York: Columbia University Press, 1992).

77. Nandy, *The Intimate Enemy*, 57.

78. Adorno's essay on the politics of German memory was not translated into English until relatively recently. It appeared in a collection of essays that dealt with the memory crisis that had been incited by American president Ronald Reagan's 1985 visit to Bitburg, a military cemetery in the former West Germany that includes several Nazi S.S. soldiers' graves: "What Does Coming to Terms with the Past Mean?" in Hartman, *Bitburg in Moral and Political Perspective*, 114–29. The German expression may convey a variety of nuances; I borrow it here to indicate one of the senses to which Adorno draws attention—namely, that coming to terms with the past entails its domestication.

79. Ibid., 115. Dominick LaCapra observes that such crucial differences in coming to terms with the past are intimately related to relations of cathexis among rememberers and the remembered events; see "Representing the Holocaust: Reflections on the Historians' Debate," in *Probing the Limits of Representation: Nazism and the "Final Solution,"* ed. Saul Friedlander (Cambridge, Mass.: Harvard University Press, 1992), 108–27.

80. The double and simultaneous movement of remembering and forgetting (as well as forgiving) that I discuss here is different from what Homi K. Bhabha calls "forgetting to remember," a mechanism of producing temporal sychronicity that he believes is essential for both generating and disrupting the unity and identity of the nation; see *The Location of Culture* (New York: Routledge, 1994), esp. 160–61.

81. Michel Foucault, "Film and Popular Memory," in *Foucault Live (Interviews, 1966–84)*, ed. Sylvère Lotringer, trans. Martin Jordin (New York: Semiotext(e), 1989), 89–106, quotation, 102. The concept of memory also appears as an important tool when Foucault critiques the assumptions of continuity, linearity, and origin in conventional historical investigations; see "Nietzsche, Genealogy, History," trans. Donald F. Bouchard and Sherry Simon, in *Language, Counter-Memory, Practice: Selected Essays and Interviews*, ed. Donald F. Bouchard (Ithaca: Cornell University Press, 1977), 139–64.

82. Fredric Jameson, "Postmodernism and Consumer Society," in *The Anti-Aesthetic: Essays on Postmodern Culture*, ed. Hal Foster (Seattle: Bay Press, 1983), 111–25; quotation, 125.

83. Nancy Hartsock, "Rethinking Modernism," *Cultural Critique*, no. 7 (fall 1987): 196. For a further critique, particularly in the field of anthropology, see Frances E. Mascia-Lees, Patricia Sharpe, and Colleen Ballerino Cohen, who summarize Hartsock's admonition as follows: "the postmodern view that truth and knowledge are contingent and multiple may be seen to act as a truth claim itself, a claim that undermines the ontological status of the subject at the very time when women and non-Western peoples have begun to claim themselves as subjects"; "The Postmodernist Turn in Anthropology: Cautions from a Feminist Perspective," *Signs* 15, no 1 (autumn 1989): 7–33; quotation, 15.

84. In "On the Uses of Relativism: Fact, Conjecture, and Black and White Histories at Colonial Williamsburg" (*American Ethnologist* 19, no. 4 [Novem-

ber 1992]: 791–805), Eric Gable, Anna Lawson, and Richard Handler point out that the dominant museum discourse in Colonial Williamsburg, which tends to characterize historical representations of African Americans as constructionist and presentist, in effect serves to sustain the marginalization of African Americans as inauthentic and illegitimate historical actors.

85. Such a performative definition of identity and agency is well-articulated by Judith Butler in *Bodies That Matter: On the Discursive Limits of "Sex"* (New York: Routledge, 1993). For an important discussion of its potential to unsettle the existing categories and order of knowledge, see Dorinne Kondo, "*M. Butterfly*: Orientalism, Gender, and a Critique of Essentialist Identity," *Cultural Critique*, no. 16 (fall 1990): 5–29. Stuart Hall has also been endeavoring to capture the dialectical processes involving subjecthood and structure. See, for instance, his "Cultural Studies: Two Paradigms," in *Media, Culture, and Society: A Critical Reader*, ed. Richard Collins et al. (London: Sage, 1986), 33–48.

86. Sharon Zukin, for instance, has written an intriguing study of how the movement of capital has transformed American urban space; see *Landscape of Power: From Detroit to Disney World* (Berkeley: University of California Press, 1991).

87. David Harvey, *The Condition of Postmodernity* (Oxford: Blackwell, 1989), 213.

88. Edward W. Soja, *Postmodern Geographies: The Reassertion of Space in Critical Social Theory* (New York: Verso, 1989), 23.

89. Lifton's *Death in Life* and Ishida Tadashi's *Han genbaku: Nagasaki hibakusha no seikatsushi* (Tokyo: Miraisha, 1973) are the two most important works to have dealt extensively with the psychological effects of the atomic bombs on survivors.

90. One way of illustrating this point is to contrast my book with Lifton's work on *hibakusha*. Nearly thirty years ago, Lifton observed a conflict, similar to that discussed here, between the desire to move beyond the memory of atomic destruction and resistance to this tendency. He wrote, "Hiroshima has been particularly plagued with the problem of carving out a new city identity while trying to avoid becoming nothing but an A-bombed city" (*Death in Life*, 310). Arguing that for at least some survivors, "[t]he new attractiveness is associated with 'selling the bomb,' gaiety and sensuality with forbidden pleasure; and all such vitality becomes an insult to the dead," Lifton interpreted this resistance to pleasures and the affirmation of life as a manifestation of the survivors' "guilt-saturated antipathy to pleasure" (263, 313). Unlike Lifton, who sought to extract the universal aspects of individuals' deep psychology within the given sociohistorical context, I am interested in identifying the political and cultural effects of such ambivalence. Within the broader conditions of knowledge, what are the implications of conflicts between the desire to move beyond memories of death and destruction and the will to confront them?

91. These tours include the following destinations: Hiroshima Castle, which reminds visitors of imperial rule, and an obelisk found there that commemorates Japan's victory in its first modern imperialist war, the Sino-Japanese War; the hill at Hijiyama where the Atomic Bomb Casualty Commission complex

had been built, which recalls for visitors the semicolonial conditions under U.S. military occupation; and the graveyard for the Imperial Army's war dead, a site symbolizing prewar and wartime ultranationalism and militarism, which is ironically located on the same Hijiyama Hill. One tour also visited the Ujina port, a former military harbor from which soldiers departed for China and elsewhere; hundreds of residents would line up along the avenues to see them off. Ujina, as signified in this tour, was an iconic site of prewar militarism and of citizens' complicity in the war efforts.

92. For an important collection of testimonial accounts that have been translated into English, see *The Atomic Bomb: Voices from Hiroshima and Nagasaki*, ed. Kyoko and Mark Selden (Armonk, N.Y.: M. E. Sharpe, 1989).

93. In his introduction to an anthology of three *hibakusha* authors, Richard H. Minear points out that the survivors' sense of chronology is distinct from most others, for they remember the many nuclear tests and accidents as emblematic of the post-1945 era. See introduction to *Hiroshima: Three Witnesses*, ed. and trans. Richard H. Minear (Princeton: Princeton University Press, 1990), 3–11, esp. 9–11.

94. Yamazaki Kanji, interview with author, 9 November 1990.

95. Various works have considered the question of the domestication of death and the uncanny return of repressed images of death. Especially informative are Michael Taussig, *The Nervous System* (New York: Routledge, 1992), and Elisabeth Bronfen and Sarah Webster Goodwin, introduction to *Death and Representation*, ed. Elisabeth Bronfen and Sarah Webster Goodwin (Baltimore: John Hopkins University Press, 1993), 3–25.

96. In *The Texture of Memory: Holocaust Memorials and Meaning* (New Haven: Yale University Press, 1993), James E. Young offers a stimulating analysis of the performative dimension of memorial icons. Young's observations on the politics of remembering the Jewish Holocaust provide many important suggestions for analyzing narratives of recollection; quotations, 6–7. See also his *Writing and Rewriting the Holocaust: Narrative and the Consequences of Interpretation* (Bloomington: Indiana University Press, 1988).

97. The term "eccentric" is borrowed from Teresa de Lauretis, "Eccentric Subjects: Feminist Theory and Historical Consciousness," *Feminist Studies* 16, no. 1 (spring 1990): 115–50. The shifting and complex notion of subjecthood advocated by de Lauretis is analogous to what Eric Santner, modifying Habermas' observations in Europe, called "post-conventional identity" (*Stranded Objects*, esp. 53–54).

98. Trinh T. Minh-ha, *Woman, Native, Other: Writing Postcoloniality and Feminism* (Bloomington: Indiana University Press, 1989), 80.

CHAPTER 1. TAMING THE MEMORYSCAPE

1. During 1989 thirty-one Japanese cities celebrated the centennial of their municipal administrations. They commemorated the 1889 local government ordinance (*shichōson rei*) that had reorganized regional administrations under the centralized rule of the national government.

2. At that time, the prospects for building the "Peace Tower" appeared bleak

for reasons including a lack of financing and a suitable location, as well as weak support for the cause. Naturally, there were strong protests from survivors. Later, another newspaper article predicted difficulties; see *Chūgoku shinbun,* 29 December 1989.

3. *Asahi shinbun,* 12 March 1989.

4. The cultural politics of remaking regional communities in the early 1980s is discussed extensively in Jennifer Robertson's *Native and Newcomer: Making and Remaking a Japanese City* (Berkeley: University of California Press, 1991). See also Sug-in Kweon's illuminating case study of Aizu, which delineates how hegemonic administrative policies have generated ambivalent negotiations between statist and oppositional uses of localism and local identity: "*Furusato* Boom in Japan: Collusion and Collisions in Producing and Consuming the National Hometown" (Ph.D. diss., Stanford University, 1993). Marilyn Ivy's *Discourses of the Vanishing: Modernity, Phantasm, Japan* (Chicago: University of Chicago Press, 1995) deftly complicates the notion of *furusato* as an uncanny topos that centrally constitutes the Japanese discourse on modernity— as a discursive place or practice that was once lost, repressed, or endangered, yet returns and haunts as both the familiar and unfamiliar object of longing, nostalgia, and anxiety.

5. Harumi Befu has been questioning the production and the problematic effects of *Nihonjinron* since the early 1980s. See "Japan's Internationalization and *Bunkaron,*" in *The Challenge of Japan's Internationalization: Organization and Culture,* ed. Hiroshi Mannari and Harumi Befu (Tokyo: Kodansha International, 1983), 232–65, and "Nationalism and *Nihonjinron,*" in *Cultural Nationalism in East Asia: Representation and Identity,* ed. Harumi Befu, Research Papers and Policy Studies 39 (Berkeley: Institute of East Asian Studies, University of California, 1993), 107–35.

6. This discursive convergence is pointed out by H. D. Harootunian, "Posutomodan no anji," in *Sengo Nihon no Seishinshi,* ed. Tetsuo Najita, Maeda Ai, and Kamishima Jirō (Tokyo: Iwanami Shoten, 1989), 45–69; see also "Visible Discourses/Invisible Ideologies," in *Postmodernism and Japan,* ed. Masao Miyoshi and H. D. Harootunian, a special issue of *South Atlantic Quarterly* 87, no. 3 (summer 1988): 445–74.

7. Hiroshima was further named "the City of Water, Greenery, and Culture That Contributes to World Peace" (*kokusai heiwa bunka toshi—sekai heiwa ni kōken suru mizu to midori to bunka no machi*). A year later, detailed plans for realizing this official slogan were outlined for citizens in an easily accessible monthly newsletter published by the municipal Public Relations Department. See the summary of the Third Hiroshima Basic City Planning in Hiroshima-shi Shichōshitsu Kōhōka, *Shimin to shisei,* no. 893 (1 July 1989).

8. Ibid.

9. Administration official, interviews with author, 28 March and 20 April 1989.

10. Office of Tourism official, conversation of 9 March 1989, Hiroshima City Hall.

11. See Hiroshima-shi Kankō Kyōkai, "Tabi no uta ga kikoeru: Hiroshima" (n.d.).

12. The four-hundred-year history of the castle is sketched in Chūgoku Shinbunsha, *Hiroshimajō Yonhyakunen* (Tokyo: Daiichi Hōki Shuppan Kabushikigaisha, 1990).

13. The shrine memorializes the fallen soldiers from Hiroshima prefecture as Shintoist deities. It enshrines those who died in all battles fought between the 1868 Meiji Restoration and the Asia Pacific War. Hiroshima Gokoku Jinja, *Hiroshima Gokoku Jinja sengo fukkōshi* (Hiroshima: Hiroshima Gokoku Jinja, 1980) offers detailed descriptions of the rebuilding processes and imperial household members' visits to the shrine. Like the representations by right-wing critics, this publication portrays the war dead as those who sacrificed their lives to achieve "Peace in the Orient" and the liberation of all Asian races. I am grateful to head priest Murakami Yukihiko for providing me with literature concerning the shrine's status during our interview on 14 March 1989.

14. The maternal quality of *furusato*-making is pointed out by Robertson, *Native and Newcomer*, 19–22. One example of the use of *hiragana* can be found in a tourism campaign pamphlet issued by the prefectural government, *Sun Sun Hiroshima: Do yū Hiroshima.* "Sun" and "Do" are written with roman letters, as in English; "Hiroshima" is written with *hiragana* both times it appears. *Yū* is written using a Chinese character and is rendered into a translingual homonym, meaning both "play" and the English word "you." See Hiroshima-ken Kankō Kyanpēn Jikkō Iinkai Jimukyoku, *Sun Sun Hiroshima: do yū Hiroshima* (n.d.).

15. See Hara Tamiki, *Natsu no hana* (1949; reprint, Tokyo: Iwanami Shoten, 1988), 27. John W. Treat also notes that Hara's use of *katakana* was intended to visually convey a sense of "urgency and intensity"; *Writing Ground Zero: Japanese Literature and the Atomic Bomb* (Chicago: University of Chicago Press, 1995), 149.

16. All the quotations from the promotion office workers are from an interview I conducted on 6 December 1989.

17. For detailed historical and sociological research on the transformation of the Motomachi District, see Hiroshima-shi, ed., *Hiroshima shinshi: toshi bunka hen* (Hiroshima: Hiroshima-shi, 1983), 110–48, 180–216.

18. The project is described in this manner in the promotion pamphlet *Mirai e habataku machi o mezashite: miryokuteki na toshikūkan zukuri* (Hiroshima: NTT Motomachi Biru Kaihatsu Keikakuan, n.d.).

19. See Hiroshima-shi, *Hiroshima shinshi: toshi bunka hen*, 148.

20. See the campaign pamphlet issued by the city, Hiroshima-shi, *Hikari kankaku toshi Hiroshima keikaku* (Hiroshima: Hiroshima-shi, 1989).

21. Conversation with author, 10 March 1989, Hiroshima City Hall.

22. During her interview on 20 March 1989, Numata gave me a copy of this newspaper article, which was published in *Asahi shinbun*, 17 January 1989.

23. This and the following quotations from the city official are from our conversation of 7 August 1989 at the Hiroshima City Hall.

24. Some anthropologists have theorized the point made by this tourist section official, indicating structural analogies between tourism and pilgrimages. Victor and Ellis Turner and Nelson H. H. Graburn, for example, have argued that the noneveryday quality of tourist leisure and recreation can be structurally

associated with the ways in which the sacred can be experienced through rituals and religious pilgrimages. See Turner and Turner, *Images and Pilgrimage in Christian Culture: Anthropological Perspective* (Oxford: Blackwell, 1978), and Graburn, "Tourism: The Sacred Journey," in *Hosts and Guests: The Anthropology of Tourism,* ed. Valene L. Smith (Philadelphia: University of Pennsylvania Press, 1977), 17–31. In his extensive review of the emerging social scientific studies of the tourism phenomena, Malcolm Crick calls for studies of tourism that are attentive to issues of power and to contradictory local voices; see "Representations of International Tourism in the Social Sciences: Sun, Sex, Sights, Savings and Servility," *Annual Review of Anthropology* 18 (1989): 307–44. Similarly, my critique of the commodification of Hiroshima's past differs, for instance, from David Greenwood's insightful commentary on the selling of Spanish folk culture as a tourist attraction, "Culture by the Pound: An Anthropological Perspective on Tourism as Cultural Commoditization," in Smith, *Hosts and Guests,* 129–38. The problem I find in Hiroshima's tourism projects is not their assaults on a presumed integrated cultural whole or their threats to an assumed authentic history so much as their masking of ongoing battles over the cultural meanings and interpretations of historical experiences. Tourism promotion certainly plays a major role in the "brightening" of Hiroshima and the trivialization of history and culture that I delineate in this chapter. Yet such promotion is only one symptom of the much broader processes of late capitalism.

25. Interview, 7 August 1989.

26. *Chūgoku shinbun,* 7 May 1977.

27. *Chūgoku shinbun,* 26 April 1977; see also 17 July 1976.

28. *Chūgoku shinbun,* 25 March, 1977.

29. Quoted in ibid. It is not a coincidence that the term *akarui* (bright, lively, and jovial), as opposed to *kurai* (dark, dismal, and gloomy), a word that has become popular in the Japanese colloquial language in the last two decades, came to be used in the new local peace culture. The prominence of the linguistic dichotomy resonated with the ways in which the nation increasingly became aware of the shift from industrializing to postindustrial social conditions. Not unlike the notion of "cleanliness" that I discuss later, the pervading imagery of *akarusa* (brightness) is consonant with the growing perception of "the new age," the age of postmodernism. In their recent usage, these terms do not simply describe the qualities of things or events. They also create cultural forces that direct the various dimensions of social action, including local policies, work practices, popular culture, and interpersonal communication. To do something with gaiety and lightheartedness (*akaruku tanoshiku yaru*) means not only to participate joyously but also not to spoil the moment when everyone else is having fun together. Those who criticize or raise questions about any convivial occasion are often despised as "*nekura*": that is, as persons with a "fundamentally dark" personality. Whoever is tenaciously working while others are relaxing, or whoever tries to draw attention to critical issues when others are enjoying themselves, is condemned as *nekura,* as overly serious and refusing to conform to the collective joyous occasion.

30. *Chūgoku shinbun,* 3 May 1977; see also Hiroshima-shi, *Hiroshima shinshi: toshi bunka hen,* 263.

31. *Chūgoku shinbun,* 17 July 1976, 24 March 1977, 7 May 1977.

32. *Chūgoku shinbun,* 24 March 1977.

33. *Chūgoku shinbun,* 23 March 1977.

34. The interview was conducted on 24 July 1990 at the company office located in the Commerce and Industry Center complex.

35. See *Chūgoku shinbun,* 31 October 1976, for the quotations from the roundtable discussion.

36. Since the beginning of the festival, the newspaper has consistently emphasized two themes: citizens as the main actors of the festival and the symbolism of flowers. The 1989 Hiroshima Flower Festival used the slogan "Can you hear flowers singing?"; the 1990 festival used "Let's converse with flowers about our dreams and about our future." Robert Jay Lifton observed a similar aspiration for greenery among the people in Hiroshima in the 1960s, commenting, "[E]ven fourteen years after the bomb a commentator spoke of the city's 'nostalgia for greenery' and longing for the 'forest city' of the past (though when postwar allocations have been carried out, there will be a much higher percentage of land used for parks than there was in the prewar city). For . . . the hunger for it is a hunger for authentic symbolism of life"; *Death in Life: Survivors of Hiroshima* (New York: Basic Books, 1967), 264. It should be clear by now that the very symbolism of life itself has been manufactured, contested, and negotiated; rather than being natural, "authenticity" itself has been constantly questioned.

37. For writings in English language that discuss the centrality of the "citizen" in social practices, see, for instance, Matsushita Keiichi, "Citizen Participation in Historical Perspective," and Takabatake Michitoshi, "Citizen's Movements: Organizing the Spontaneous," both in *Authority and the Individual in Japan: Citizen Protest in Historical Perspective,* ed. J. Victor Koschmann (Tokyo: University of Tokyo Press, 1978), 171–87, 188–99. Takabatake has written extensively on the development of citizens' movements in postwar Japan. In a later essay, Takabatake describes the post-1960s transition from "citizens'" movements to "residents'" movements; see "6onen ikō no seiji ishiki to shimin undō," in *Gendai Nihon no seiji* 72–77 (Tokyo: Sanichi Shobō, 1978), 29–44. Political sociologist Kurihara Akira also emphasizes a similar transition in " 'Minshū risei' no sonzai shōmei: shimin undō, jūmin undō, nettowākingu no seishinshi," in Najita, Maeda, and Kamishima, *Sengo nihon no seishinshi,* 484–508. The "residents' movements" tend to naturalize and romanticize ideas about the indigenous community as well as its boundaries, history, and practices. But as we continue to observe the global restructuring of labor and the transnational trafficking of people that is making us redefine our notions of community, border, and citizens' rights and responsibilities, I find special significance in the concept of residency, as well as the need to attend to the cultural and social practices that are emerging around it. I discuss this point further in chapter 5.

38. *Chūgoku shinbun,* 7 May 1977.

39. *Chūgoku shinbun,* 17 July 1976. While the annual summer Shōkonsai (festival for welcoming dead souls) at the National Defense Shrine is often remembered as a festival celebrated by the entire community, it creates much conflict today because of its strong association with the nationalism and mili-

tarism of the prewar and wartime state. Similarly, several attempts to create festivals after the war, such as Hiroshima Matsuri or Minato Matsuri, all failed to involve the entire municipal community because they were not rooted in local history or because their themes did not capture people's interests (see *Chūgoku shinbun*, 30 March 1977).

40. *Chūgoku shinbun*, 15 September 1976. This contrast between the 6 August Peace Commemoration and the Flower Festival has been made in the press repeatedly since the event's initial conceptualization; see *Chūgoku shinbun*, 31 October 1976, 28 April 1977, 4 May 1977, and 6 May 1979.

41. Nagasaki has emerged as a locale of struggles against the national government since 1988, when its mayor, Motoshima Hitoshi, referred publicly to the war responsibilities of the late Showa emperor and was later attacked by right-wing terrorists for his statement. See especially Norma Field's *In the Realm of a Dying Emperor* (New York: Vintage Books, 1991) for further discussion of Nagasaki's mayor. His commemorative speeches have included references to the atom bomb victims in Korea and other countries; in contrast, Hiroshima's previous mayors long remained silent not only about Japan's colonial aggression and war of invasion but also about atom bomb survivors who are not Japanese nationals. The incumbent mayor, Hiraoka Takashi, a former corporate executive and journalist who had already written extensively on Korean atom bomb survivors before taking office, has been more aggressive in clarifying Japan's responsibilities for war and colonial rule over Asia. A major issue needing further examination is how to interpret such changes, given a milieu in which the discourse on Japan's history of aggression is becoming hegemonic in national politics, especially as debates develop on the status of the Self-Defense Forces and other constitutional issues. See also the introduction and chapter 5.

42. *Chūgoku shinbun*, 3 May 1989.

43. Interview with author, 1 November 1989.

44. The first extensive critical examination of the cultures of late modernity and postmodernity in Japan appeared in a special issue, *Postmodernism and Japan*, ed. Masao Miyoshi and H. D. Harootunian, of the *South Atlantic Quarterly* 67, no. 3 (summer 1988). Most of the articles were republished in an anthology: see Masao Miyoshi and H. D. Harootunian, eds., *Postmodernism and Japan* (Durham, N.C.: Duke University Press, 1989). For general observations on the cultural phenomena of late modernism in the West, see Fredric Jameson, "Postmodernism, or the Cultural Logic of Late Capitalism," *New Left Review*, no. 146 (September/October 1984): 53–92.

45. For example, in the 1960s, a television commercial for electronic appliances used the slogan "bright National, everyone's National" (*akarui nashonaru, minna no nashonaru*; "National" was the corporation's name). Around the same time, the Japan Broadcasting Corporation aired a weekly program on agriculture titled "bright agricultural village" (*akarui nōson*).

46. On image over substance, see Norma Field, "*Somehow*: The Postmodern as Atmosphere," in *Postmodernism and Japan*, ed. Miyoshi and Harootunian, a special issue of *South Atlantic Quarterly* 87, no 3 (summer 1988): 551–70; on commodifying knowledge, see in the same issue Marilyn Jeanette

Ivy, "Critical Texts, Mass Artifacts: The Consumption of Knowledge in Post-modern Japan," 419–44; and on trivializing history, see Takashi Fujitani, "Electronic Pageantry and Japan's Symbolic Emperor," *Journal of Asian Studies* 51, no. 4 (November 1992): 551–70.

47. See, for instance, Hal Foster, "Postmodernism: A Preface," in *The Anti-Aesthetic: Essays on Postmodern Culture,* ed. Hal Foster (Seattle: Bay Press, 1983), ix–xvi; Ivy, "Critical Texts, Mass Artifacts."

CHAPTER 2. MEMORIES IN RUINS

1. Out of the 142 major public buildings within five kilometers of the bomb's hypocenter, about 80 suffered only minimal damage. During the last fifty years, most of these surviving buildings were taken down; only 29 of them were still standing as of 1990 (*Asahi shinbun,* 8 December 1990). For a brief description in English of the current status of the atom-bombed buildings, see Naomi Shōno, "Mute Reminders of Hiroshima's Atomic Bombing," *Japan Quarterly* 40, no. 3 (July–September 1993): 267–76.

2. Interview with author, 26 November 1990.

3. Jean Baudrillard, *Simulations,* trans. Paul Foss, Paul Patton, and Philip Beitchman (New York: Semiotext(e), 1983), 12.

4. The idea of cult value and aura as a "unique phenomenon of a distance however close it may be" and its transformation in modern mass society, as well as aestheticizing reactions to such a shift, are discussed by Walter Benjamin in "The Work of Art in the Age of Mechanical Reproduction," in *Illuminations,* ed. Hannah Arendt, trans. Harry Zohn (New York: Schocken Books, 1969), 217–51; see esp. 223–43; quotation, 243.

5. Hibaku Kenzōbutsu o Kangaeru Kai, ed., *Hiroshima no hibaku kenzōbutsu: hibaku 45shūnen chōsa hōkokusho* (Hiroshima: Asahi Shinbun Hiroshima Shikyoku, 1990), 121–22.

6. *Asahi shinbun,* 7 December 1990.

7. Robert Jay Lifton, *Death in Life: Survivors of Hiroshima* (New York: Basic Books, 1967).

8. *Asahi shinbun,* 2 February 1989. The city decided to use 100 million out of the over 390 million yen donated as was initially planned, creating a fund with the remainder to cover the future cost of repairs.

9. The Dome is officially recognized by UNESCO as a part of the world's heritage.

10. Baudrillard, *Simulations,* 25.

11. *Chūgoku shinbun,* 26 December 1989.

12. *Chūgoku shinbun,* 6 August 1989; *Chūgoku shinbun,* 2 May 1989.

13. *Asahi shinbun,* 1 and 12 May 1989.

14. Some recalled that the tower stood like a goddess of mercy looking over the city that had been reduced to a charred plain. See "Shukishū" Hensan Iinkai, ed., *Inochi no tō: Hiroshima sekijūji/genbaku byōin e no shōgen* (Hiroshima: Chūgoku Shinbunsha, 1992). In the same anthology, architectural historian Ishimaru Norioki provides a detailed structural analysis of the building;

see "Hiroshima sekijūji/genbaku byōin no kenchiku ni tsuite: sono haran ni michita kenchiku no seimei" (134–56).

15. *Chūgoku shinbun,* 26 January 1990.

16. I conducted my first formal interviews with Kuboura on 10 April 1989. The quotations from Kuboura are from this interview, from our meetings on 26 April and 23 May, and also from his statements at various public meetings, including the 9 December 1989 symposium.

17. The testimony transcribed here was delivered at the 9 December 1989 meeting.

18. "Shukishū" Hensan Iinkai, ed., *Inochi no tō,* 118–33; quotation, 133.

19. Hibaku Kenzōbutus o Kangaeru Kai, *Hiroshima no hibaku kenzōbutsu,* too, included historical, scientific, and ethnographic accounts of a number of architectural structures that survived the atom bomb. The research was conducted by a group of citizen volunteers that formed in 1989; it consisted of prominent local scholars, poets, teachers, *hibakusha,* and others. Along with his photos, Kuboura also contributed observations on the conditions of wooden structures, mostly shrines and temples. Many of the essays appearing in the report attempted to reconstruct the ways in which people experienced the bombing at these architectural sites by piecing together citations and excerpts from various individuals' memoirs, testimonies, and literary accounts. This is yet another instance of the proliferation of mnemonic practices described here.

20. Benjamin saw the "angel of history" in Paul Klee's painting "Angelus Novus" and described it as follows:

> His face is turned toward the past. Where we perceive a chain of events, he sees one single catastrophe which keeps piling wreckage upon wreckage and hurls it in front of his feet. The angel would like to stay, awaken the dead, and make whole what has been smashed. But a storm is blowing from Paradise; it has got caught in his wings with such violence that the angel can no longer close them. This storm irresistibly propels him into the future to which his back is turned, while the pile of debris before him grows skyward. This storm is what we call progress.
> "Theses on the Philosophy of History," in *Illuminations,* 257–58

21. The official translation is "Let all the souls here rest in peace; for we shall not repeat the evil." See the introduction for the origin of, as well as the debates over, the interpretation of the epitaph.

22. This excerpt from Kurihara's poem is cited in *Asahi shinbun,* 10 August 1989.

CHAPTER 3. ON TESTIMONIAL PRACTICES

1. Derrida discusses the usefulness of the concept of "trace" in critiquing assumptions about origin, irreducibility, and fullness—all foundational to Continental writings on signification or what Derrida refers to as the metaphysics of presence. See, for example, *Of Grammatology,* trans. Gayatri Chakravorty Spivak (Baltimore: John Hopkins University Press, 1974), esp. 60–73.

2. Conversation with author, 3 August 1988.

3. Accounts of discrimination, hatred, ignorance, and prejudice appear repeatedly in survivors' recollections. For critical analyses of this situation, see,

for example, Oe Kenzaburo, *Hiroshima Notes,* ed. David L. Swain, trans. Toshi Yonezawa (Tokyo: YMCA Press, 1981), and Shiina Masae, *Genbaku hanzai: hibakusha wa naze hōchi saretaka* (Tokyo: Otsuki Shoten, 1985). Contrary to its intentions, Chūjo Kazuo's *Genbaku to sabetsu* (Tokyo: Asahi Shinbunsha, 1986), which criticizes the media for exaggerating the survivors' miseries, in fact gives further evidence of persistent prejudices against survivors.

4. From survey results in Hiroshima-ken, *Genbaku hibakusha taisaku jigyō gaiyō* (Hiroshima: Hiroshima-ken, 1988).

5. *Chūgoku shinbun,* 25 June 1990.

6. From the 23 June 1989 Rifuton Kenkyū Kai (Lifton Study Group) meeting.

7. Jacques Derrida, "No Apocalypse, Not Now (full speed ahead, seven missiles, seven missives)," *Diacritics* 14, no. 2 (summer 1984): 20–31; quotation, 23. Derrida further wrote that the nuclear war "has not taken place, it is a speculation, an invention in the sense of a fable or an invention to be invented in order to make a place for it or to prevent it from taking place" (28).

8. Michel Foucault, *The History of Sexuality,* vol. 1, *An Introduction,* trans. Robert Hurley (New York: Vintage Books, 1980), 62.

9. Information concerning the two laws can be found in Hiroshima-shi, ed., *Hiroshima shinshi: shakai hen* (Hiroshima: Hiroshima-shi, 1984), 193–203.

10. The original reads, "*sono hito ga genshibakudan ni yoru hibakusha de aru koto o shimesu isshu no shōmeisho dearu*"; Hiroshima-shi Eiseikyoku Genbakuhigai Taisakubu, *Genbaku hibakusha taisaku jigyō gaiyō* (Hiroshima: Hiroshima-shi Eiseikyoku, 1989), 47. This publication provides a detailed overview of the medical and social remedies currently provided to the survivors by the city. Similar information concerning the prefectural government's remedies for *hibakusha* can be found, for instance, in Hiroshima-ken, *Genbaku hibakusha taisaku jigyō gaiyō.*

11. A succinct summary of the biographic method used in Ishida's "life-history survey" project can be found in Ishida Tadashi, *Genbaku taiken no shisōka: han genbaku ronshū I* (Tokyo: Miraisha, 1986), 115–205. The survey's results have been published in several works that deal mainly with cases from Nagasaki. See, for example, Ishida, *Han genbaku: Nagasaki hibakusha no seikatsushi* (Tokyo: Miraisha, 1973). Ishida's understandings about *hibakusha* in general are guided by the works and life of a Nagasaki survivor, Fukuda Sumako, a poet and activist who died of cancer at age fifty-two. See Fukuda's autobiography, *Ware nao ikite ari* (1967; reprint, Tokyo: Chikuma Shobō, 1982), and Nagasaki no Shōgen no Kai, ed., *Genshiya ni ikiru: Fukuda Sumako shū* (Tokyo: Shōbunsha, 1989).

12. These shifts in the dynamic between the interviewer/authors and their interviewees are especially evident in Kanda Mikio, *Genbaku ni otto o ubawarete: Hiroshima no nōfutachi no shōgen* (Tokyo: Iwanami Shoten, 1982), and Kitabatake Hiroyasu, *Hitori hitori no sensō/Hiroshima* (Tokyo: Iwanami Shoten, 1984).

13. Ubuki Satoru makes the important observation that the link between *hibakusha*'s individual desires and the Gensuikin movements' formally articulated antinuclear discourse is not automatic or essential; see "Gunshuku to

shinmin undō: Nihon no gensuibaku kinshi undō o megutte," *Kokusai seiji,*
no. 80 (October 1985): 112–26.

14. *Mainichi shinbun,* 27 July 1982. "Hiroshima o Yomu" Kai, a group con-
sisting of journalists, scholars, city workers, and other citizens, also observed
the year 1982 as a turning point in which the print media paid unprecedented
attention to Hiroshima and Nagasaki. See its *Shiryō '82 Hankaku* (Hiroshima:
Tankeisha, 1983). The booklet—an exhaustive compilation of journal and mag-
azine special issues, newspaper articles, and books that were published during
1982—critiqued the way in which the publishing industry exploited the intensifying antinuclear concerns.

15. According to Ubuki Satoru and Uchida Emiko's detailed surveys, since
the late 1960s autobiographical memoirs authored by survivors of Hiroshima's
and Nagasaki's atom bombings have been published in Japan at somewhere
around four hundred volumes per year. However, these publications exceeded
one thousand in 1982 and continued to maintain this annual publication rate
throughout the late 1980s. See Ubuki and Uchida, "Kako 45nenkan no genbaku shuki no shuppan jōkyō," *Hiroshima igaku* 45, no. 3 (March 1992):
373–75.

16. The entire transcript of Pope John Paul II's appeal for peace can be
found in the Chugoku Shimbun and the Hiroshima International Cultural
Foundation, Inc., eds., *The Meaning of Survival: Hiroshima's Thirty-Six Year
Commitment to Peace* (Hiroshima: Chugoku Shimbun and the Hiroshima In-
ternational Cultural Foundation, 1983), 280–81. This is the only instance where
I romanize the newspaper company's name as *Chugoku Shimbun,* with an *m.*
Throughout the book I use the conventional romanization for both the com-
pany name, *Chūgoku Shinbunsha,* and the newspaper, *Chūgoku shinbun.*

17. "Hiroshima o Yomu" Kai's research argues that one reason why so
many books, journals, and magazines dealing with peace and antinuclear issues as well as the Hiroshima and Nagasaki bombings were published in 1982
was the publishing industry's anticipation that these topics would be market-
able due to the publicity generated by SSDII. See *Shiryō '82 Hankaku,* 21.

18. See the pamphlet issued by Hiroshima kara no Yobikake no Kai, *Hankaku: bungakusha no seimei* (Hiroshima: Hiroshima kara no Yobikake no Kai,
1982). Yoshimoto Takaaki's candid criticism of this manifesto drew fierce attacks from progressives. Yoshimoto faulted the consensual and nationalist nature of the writers' antinuclear manifesto, arguing that it was a reactionary
statement masquerading as oppositional. He also questioned the pro-Soviet,
anti-U.S. position that was cloaked under a universalist call against the nuclear arms race, asking if what was being celebrated as the new grassroots
antinuclear movement was nothing less than a reiteration of the established
left's 1960s anti-Ampo agenda. See his *"Hankaku" iron* (Tokyo: Shinya Sōshosha, 1989).

Yoshimoto's anti-antinuclear writing, which is filled with competitive rhetoric about who can legitimately claim to be a true progressive, does not necessarily lead to constructive dialogue or practical solutions. In it, I find a self-
righteousness similar to what Yoshimoto finds in his opponents. I also do not
agree with him that the consumerism enjoyed by those in their twenties can be

considered politically avant-garde (*"Hankaku" iron*, 90). However, he rightly observes that giving nuclear issues priority over other equally important social issues is problematic. He is also correct in pointing out that criticizing antinuclear discourse is not tantamount to promoting nuclear armament (see 105).

19. See *Chūgoku shinbun*, 20 June 1990.

20. It has not yet been scientifically demonstrated that radiation exposure does *not* have an effect on cancer rates in later years. For an unusual and intriguing account that interweaves the author's personal history with his lifelong scientific research on radiation's effect on children in Japan and the Marshall Islands, see James N. Yamazaki, *Children of the Atomic Bomb: An American Physician's Memoir of Nagasaki, Hiroshima, and the Marshall Islands* (Durham, N.C.: Duke University Press, 1995).

21. *Mainichi shinbun*, 30 August 1989.

22. Hiroshima o Kataru Kai, ed., *Hiroshima o kataru* (Hiroshima: Hiroshima o Kataru Kai, 1987).

23. Although John Beverley's definition of *testimonio* refers exclusively to first-person narratives of recollection in printed form, his observation that the narrators in *testimonio* represent historically and socially constituted collectivities is very relevant to the relationship between the witness survivor and his or her lost sociality, as I have described it here; see "The Margin at the Center: On *Testimonio* (Testimonial Narrative)," *Modern Fiction Studies* 35, no. 1 (spring 1989): 11–28.

24. It may also be worthwhile to note that the Japanese word *kataru*, like its English equivalent, "to narrate," does not necessarily require an object of narration, nor an assumed narratee. For example, in the sentence "*Kare wa katari hajimeta*," which means "He began to narrate," the act of narrating, not the object of narration, constitutes the subject. At the same time, the act of *kataru* can also entail an acute awareness about the presence of the narratee. When the association was named, the word was deployed with the clear idea that what is narrated needs to be communicated to the narratee. The term *kataru* thus evokes a double effect: while the act itself constitutes the narrating subject, the assumed presence of the audience also significantly shapes both the act and the narrator.

25. I am grateful to the medical and social workers, who were also members of the Rifuton Kenkyū Kai (Lifton Study Group), for sharing with me many of their reflections and long-term observations on the daily lives and psychological conditions of *hibakusha*.

26. See, for example, Oe Kenzaburo's *Hiroshima Notes* and Ishida Tadashi's *Han genbaku*. Yet a number of politically active *hibakusha* seriously question the representations of themselves in such writings as *Hiroshima Notes*. Lawrence L. Langer's critique of Charles Taylor may be useful in understanding why not a few *hibakusha* feel revulsion toward singular, integrated representations of their identity, morality, and desire. In his analysis of Holocaust testimonies Langer challenges Taylor's adherence to the ideas of unitary selfhood and integrated morality, arguing that such conceptualizations fail to grasp the post-Holocaust condition of selfhood. He stresses instead the need to imagine the possibility that survivors of extreme situations, such as the Holocaust, might live with multiple identities and inhabit multiple moral spheres simulta-

neously. See *Holocaust Testimonies: The Ruins of Memory* (New Haven: Yale University Press, 1991), 198–204.

27. Kawara Hirokazu, *Kizuna: kōkōsei to Hiroshima* (Tokyo: Komichi Shobō, 1987), 39.

28. Funahashi Yoshie, "Hibakusha no jibunshi ni torikunde," in *Ikiru: hibakusha no jibunshi,* ed. Hibakusha no Jibunshi Henshū Iinkai (Hiroshima: Hibakusha no Jibunshi Henshū Iinkai, 1989), 521–28. For an intriguing discussion on the implications of the recent popularity of writing practices of personal histories, see Gerald Figal, "How to *jinbunshi:* Making and Marketing Self-Histories of Showa among the Masses in Postwar Japan," *Journal of Asian Studies* 55, no. 4 (November 1996): 902–33.

29. The emphasized sentence is *sore ga sonogo no kakegae no nai jinsei no nakade, dono yōnā imi o mottaka;* Hibakusha no Jibunshi Henshū Iinkai, ed., *Ikiru* (n.p., n.d.).

30. Funahashi pointed out to me the historically specific implication of the word *ikizama* in a conversation we had, together with the social worker Murakami Sugako, on 1 April 1995.

31. Miyagawa's statement was made at a small gathering of several members of Kataru Kai and other associations held on 2 April 1995. At this function I was able to obtain valuable commentary and criticism on a piece I had contributed to their booklet, *Ikasarete* (Made to live), which was published in the previous year to commemorate the tenth anniversary of the association's establishment. In addition to Miyagawa, I would also like to thank Kwak Poksun, Katō Yōsuke, Chu Sŏk, Toyonaga Keisaburō, Yamazaki Kanji, and Yamada Tadafumi for candidly sharing their opinions with me.

32. See Julia Watson and Sidonie Smith, "De/Colonization and the Politics of Discourse in Women's Autobiographical Practices," in *De/Colonizing the Subject: The Politics of Gender in Women's Autobiography,* ed. Julia Watson and Sidonie Smith (Minneapolis: University of Minnesota Press, 1992), xxiii–xxxi. See also Sidonie Smith, *Subjectivity, Identity, and the Body: Women's Autobiographical Practices in the Twentieth Century* (Bloomington: Indiana University Press, 1993), esp. 1–23. A similar rethinking of the politics of autobiography can also be found in Françoise Lionnet, *Autobiographical Voices: Race, Gender, Self-Portraiture* (Ithaca: Cornell University Press, 1989).

CHAPTER 4. MNEMONIC DETOURS

1. I also learned much about Numata Fusako's life story from Nagai Hideaki's interview of her. See *Kakehashi,* no. 19 (January 1989): 4–5 (a monthly pamphlet published by the Hiroshima YMCA).

2. There are two important biographies of Numata: Hiroiwa Chikahiro, *Aogiri no shita de: "Hiroshima no kataribe" Numata Suzuko monogatari* (Tokyo: Akashi Shoten, 1993), and Kawara Hirokazu and Yamada Mariko, *Hiroshima hana ichirin monogatari: hibakusha/Numata Suzuko no owari naki seishun* (Tokyo: Komichi Shobō). On my visit to Hiroshima in March 1995, Numata gave me the two books as a gift.

3. A portion of the film was returned to the Japanese government in 1967, but the Japanese government, fearing infringement of individuals' privacy, made

only part of it public. The U.S. government's suppression of the films that were brought back to the United States is discussed by Abé Mark Nornes, "The Body at the Center—The Effects of the Atomic Bomb on Hiroshima and Nagasaki," in *Hibakusha Cinema: Hiroshima, Nagasaki, and the Nuclear Images in Japanese Film*, ed. Mick Broderick (London: Kegan Paul, 1996), 121–60; see esp. 152–55.

4. For a detailed account of the campaign, see Nagai Hideaki's *10 fīto eiga sekai o mawaru* (Tokyo: Asahi Shinbunsha, 1983).

5. See Hiroiwa, "*Hiroshima no kataribe*," 141–52; Kawara and Yamada, *Hiroshima hana ichirin mongatari*, 186–88.

6. Michael Mahon explores Foucault's notion of "subjugated knowledge" in detail in *Foucault's Nietzschean Genealogy: Truth, Power, and the Subject* (Albany: State University of New York Press, 1992), 120–21.

7. For detailed descriptions of atrocities committed on the Malaysian peninsula by the Japanese Imperial Army troops, see Takashima Nobuyoshi and Hayashi Hirofumi, eds., *Maraya no nihongun: Negurisenbiran-shū ni okeru kajin gyakusatsu* (Tokyo: Aoki Shoten, 1989). Takashima, a high school teacher, together with Hayashi, a college professor, have untiringly excavated archival documents regarding military operations in Malaysia and accumulated extensive interviews with survivors. They have also been instrumental in organizing conferences called "Ajia/Taiheiyō chiiki no sensō giseisha ni omoi o hase, kokoro ni kizamu shūkai," which began in 1986 after a series of nationalist statements and moves toward remilitarization by conservative political leader Nakasone Yasuhiro and his cabinet members. The conference is held at a number of major cities throughout Japan every summer and invites witnesses and survivors of Japanese colonial and military aggression from the Asia Pacific region. The meeting at which Numata met survivors of the Rape of Nanjing was one of the earliest of these conferences.

8. Numata Suzuko, lecture, 3 June 1989, at Heiwa Kaikan.

9. The concept of "narrative margin" is also deployed by Saul Friedlander to refer to the realm of the unspeakable within a given narrative—a gap, so to speak, that cautions us of the limits of realist representation. Friedlander, introduction to *Probing the Limits of Representation: Nazism and the "Final Solution,"* ed. Saul Friedlander (Cambridge, Mass.: Harvard University Press, 1992), 1–21; see esp. 17.

10. Numata's lecture is transcribed in Zenkoku Dōwa Kyōiku Kenkyū Kyōgikai Jimukyoku, *Heiwa/jinken/minshushugi o motomete—dōwa kyōiku e no teigen IV: dai 41 kai zenkoku dōwa kyōiku kenkyū taikai tokubetsu bukai kōenshū* (Osaka: Zenkoku Dōwa Kyōiku Kenkyū Kyōgikai, 1990), 5–36; quotation, 11.

11. Ibid., 29.

12. Broadcast on Hiroshima Terebi, *Weekday Evening News*, 14 July 1990.

13. Kawara Hirokazu, *Kizuna: kōkōsei to Hiroshima* (Tokyo: Komichi Shobō, 1987), 17.

14. Unless otherwise indicated, quotes from Matsuda are from our meeting of 23 July 1990.

15. First published by the Ministry of Education in 1947 and reprinted by Minshu Kyōiku o Mamoru Shimane Kenmin Kaigi, *Atarashii kenpō no hanashi* (Matsue: Minshu Kyōiku o Mamoru Shimane Kenmin Kaigi, n.d.).

16. Ishihara Masaie has compiled a number of oral testimonies in order to reconstruct long-suppressed knowledge about the Okinawan civilians' victimization by the Japanese military. See, for instance, *Gyakusatsu no shima: kōgun to shinmin no matsuro* (Tokyo: Banseisha, 1978) and *Shōgen, Okinawa-sen: senjō no kōkei* (Tokyo: Aoki Shoten, 1991). See also Norma Field's discussion of how remembering the community's trauma has led to protests against the subordination of Okinawa to Japan in current politics; *In the Realm of a Dying Emperor* (New York: Vintage Books, 1991), 33–104. Tomiyama Ichirō offers an insightful analysis of Okinawan residents' mass suicides during the Battle of Okinawa by placing them in the broader context of Japanese nationalization policies toward Okinawans during the first half of the twentieth century. See his anthology, *Senjō no kioku* (Tokyo: Nihon Keizai Hyōronsha, 1995).

17. From Matsuda's privately compiled pamphlet, "Konnichiwa—iwasete, iwasete." This testimony was also published in Shin-nihon Fujin no Kai Hiroshima-ken Honbu, ed., *Konoha no yō ni yakare te* (1966; reprint, Tokyo: Shin-nihon Shuppansha, 1985), 19.

18. The problematic effects of such universalist understanding of war victimization on the historical consciousness in postwar Japan has been discussed by journalist Honda Katsuichi. Some of his essays are translated in *The Impoverished Spirit in Contemporary Japan: Selected Essays of Honda Katsuichi*, ed. John Lie, trans. Eri Fujieda, Masayuki Hamazaki, and John Lie (New York: Monthly Review Press, 1993).

19. Excerpts from a collection of letters Matsuda received from his audiences and privately compiled: "Shūgaku ryokōsei wa kataru: migi ni katamuku Nihon—kako mitsume saguru mirai."

20. While I had a number of opportunities to learn of Yamazaki's ideas and attitudes toward storytellings, my most extensive interviews with him took place on 9 November 1990 at his house in Fuchū, and 4 August 1995 at the Peace Memorial Park.

21. This figure is accurate as of 6 August 1987. See Kosakai Yoshimitsu, *Hiroshima tokuhon* (1978; reprint, Hiroshima: Hiroshima Heiwa Bunka Sentā, 1988), 41. The destruction of the Tenjinmachi community and Yamazaki's relationship to its memorialization have been well publicized by the media; see, for instance, *Mainichi shinbun*, 5 August 1990; *Asahi shinbun*, 9 May 1994.

22. All the quotations from Saeki are taken from her storytelling on 7 August 1995 and a conversation I had with her thereafter.

23. For the origin of Tawara's pseudonym, see Hiroshima-shi, ed., *Hiroshima shinshi: shimin seikatsu hen* (Hiroshima: Hiroshima-shi, 1983), 418. The conversations with Tawara took place on 25 January, 29 January, 7 February, and 23 February 1990.

24. Though in a different context, James A. Fujii similarly points out that the twentieth-century notions of orality and storytelling cannot be dissociated from the modern experiences of fragmentation and alienation. Fujii, discussing the writings of an early-twentieth-century folklorist, Origuchi Shinobu, demonstrates how Origuchi's writing about performative communication, about the narrativity of the dead, and about storytellers attempted to produce "the intensity and reality of pure experience that has been lost of 'quotidian experience'—upon which the *kindai shōsetsu* [modern prose fiction] ostensibly rests."

See *Complicit Fictions: The Subject in the Modern Japanese Prose Narrative* (Berkeley: University of California Press, 1993), 222–56; quotation, 254.

25. Walter Benjamin, "N: [Re the Theory of Knowledge, Theory of Progress]," in *Benjamin: Philosophy, Aesthetics, History,* ed. Gary Smith, trans. Leigh Hafrey and Richard Sieburth (Chicago: University of Chicago Press, 1989), 43–83; quotation, 61.

26. Fredric Jameson, *The Political Unconscious: Narrative as a Socially Symbolic Act* (Ithaca: Cornell University Press, 1981), 296. Elsewhere, Jameson reiterates the doubleness of the task of critique: "[In aura] a mysterious wholeness of objects becomes visible. And where the broken fragments of allegory represented a thing-world of destructive forces in which human autonomy was drowned, the objects of aura represent perhaps the setting of a kind of utopia, a utopian present, . . . a kind of plenitude of existence in the world of things, if only for the briefest instant"; "Walter Benjamin; or, Nostalgia," in *Marxism and Form: Twentieth-Century Dialectical Theories of Literature* (Princeton: Princeton University Press, 1971), 64. Following Jameson, Christopher Norris described the ambivalence of Benjamin—in whose writings both the allegorical view of the world and a trust in the "aura" of messianic power coexist—as "the tension . . . between a 'negative hermeneutic' which deconstructs the forms of ideological mystification, and a positive or 'utopian' impulse which keeps alive the image of human fulfillment"; see "Image and Parable: Readings of Walter Benjamin," in *The Deconstructive Turn: Essays in the Rhetoric of Philosophy* (New York: Methuen, 1984), 107–27; quotation, 119.

27. Kawara, *Kizuna,* 82–83.

28. Naoki Sakai, "Kyōkan no kyōdōtai to hinin sareta teikokushugiteki kokuminshugi: 'yukiyukite shingun' josetsu," *Gendai shisō* 23, no. 1 (January 1995): 117–32; quotations, 131.

29. The effect of uncritical and nondialectical identification does more than homogenize social relations within a "community of sympathy": to claim that one understands the others' thoughts and experiences is to preempt their territory. The dangers of such an identification can be illustrated by the meaning of "empathy" itself. While of course focusing on a very different situation, Jonathan Boyarin's analysis is quite useful here. In his pioneering work on the politics of Jewish memory, he has noted that within the Western convention of hermeneutics, the notion of "empathy" has an affinity with the concept of "empire." "Empathy," which posits the idea that "I am you," has been one of the philosophical foundations for the nineteenth-century colonial expansion over non-Western others. The hegemony of empathy that enabled imagining that "I" feel and think like "you" made possible an identification with and command over the spatial other in ethnology and over the temporal others of historicism. See Boyarin, *Storm from Paradise: The Politics of Jewish Memory* (Minneapolis: University of Minnesota Press, 1992), 86–89.

CHAPTER 5. ETHNIC AND COLONIAL MEMORIES

1. The figure is taken from a leaflet published by Zaikan Hibakusha o Kyūen suru Shimin no Kai, *Zaikan hibakusha no jittai* (Osaka: Zaikan Hiba-

kusha o Kyūen suru Shimin no Kai, 1982), 18. Hiroshima-shi, ed., *Hiroshima shinshi: shimin seikatsu-hen* (Hiroshima: Hiroshima-shi, 1983), 284, indicates that among the approximately 20,000 Koreans who were victims of the Nagasaki bombing, 10,000 were killed. For testimonial accounts of the Korean survivors, see especially Pak Su-nam, *Chōsen/Hiroshima/panchoppari: watashi no tabi no kiroku* (Tokyo: Sanseido, 1973), and Hiroshima-ken Chōsenjin Hibakusha Kyōgikai, ed., *Shiroi chogori no hibakusha* (Tokyo: Rōdō Junpōsha, 1979). Among the journalists, Hiraoka Takashi, Hiroshima's current mayor, began to deal with the condition of survivors in Korea at a relatively early stage: see his *Henken to sabetsu: Hiroshima soshite Chōsenjin* (Tokyo: Miraisha, 1972) and *Muen no kaikyō: Hiroshima no koe, hibaku Chōsenjin no koe* (Tokyo: Kage Shobō, 1983). On the development of Japanese citizens' relief efforts for survivors in Korea, see Zaikan Hibakusha Mondai Shimin Kaigi, ed., *Zaikan hibakusha mondai o kangaeru* (Tokyo: Gaifūsha, 1988). Many of those who settled in Hiroshima were from Hyopch'ŏn, a village in southern Korea; they had immigrated to Japan and settled in Hiroshima at the turn of the century. Since most of those who left Hiroshima returned to their natal villages, the area has had the highest concentration of atomic bomb survivors in Korea; thus Hyopch'ŏn has become known as "the Hiroshima of Korea." See Kankoku no Genbaku Higaisha o Kyūen suru Shimin no Kai, ed., *Hiroshima e: Kankoku no hibakusha no shuki* (Hiroshima: Kankoku no Genbaku Higaisha o Kyūen suru Shimin no Kai, 1987). Also, for a critical assessment of how the governments of the United States, Japan, and South Korea have neglected Korean survivors both in Korea and Japan, see Michael Weiner, "The Representation of Absence and the Absence of Representation: Korean Victims of the Atomic Bomb," in *Japan's Minorities: The Illusion of Homogeneity*, ed. Michael Weiner (New York: Routledge, 1997), 79–107.

2. See, for instance, Hiroshima-ken Chōsenjin Hibakusha Kyōgikai, *Shiroi chogori no hibakusha*. For attempts to reconstruct the record concerning forced mobilization, see especially Pak Kyŏng-shik, *Chōsenjin kyōsei renkō no kiroku* (Tokyo: Miraisha, 1965), and Hayashi Eidai, *Kesareta Chōsenjin kyōsei renkō no kiroku* (Tokyo: Akashi Shoten, 1989). An example of local grassroots efforts in excavating historical evidence for forced Korean labor is Hyōgo Chōsen Kankei Kenkyūkai, ed., *Chika kōjō to Chōsenjin kyōsei renkō* (Tokyo: Akashi Shoten, 1990). Many of the victims and survivors were made to work at munitions industry factories, including Mitsubishi Shipbuilding Company and Tōyō Kōgyō. A *hibakusha* poet, Fukagawa Munetoshi, was one of the earliest to begin to focus on the relationship between Korean atom bomb victimization and forced labor mobilization. See his *Chinkon no kaikyō: kieta hibaku Chōsenjin chōyōkō nihyaku yonjū rokumei* (Tokyo: Gendaishi Shuppankai, 1973). For a personal memoir of an atom bomb survivor who was mobilized at Tōyō Kōgyō, see Chŏng Chun-he, *Chōsenjin chōyōkō no shuki*, trans. Inoshita Haruko (Tokyo: Kawai Shuppan, 1990).

3. See Kang Jae-ŏn and Kim Dong-hun, *Zainichi Kankoku/Chōsenjin: rekishi to tenbō* (Tokyo: Rōdō Keizaisha, 1989); Norma Field "Beyond Envy, Boredom, and Suffering: Toward an Emancipatory Politics for Resident Koreans and Other Japanese," *Positions* 1, no. 3 (winter 1993): 640–70; and

Changsoo Lee, "The Legal Status of Koreans in Japan," in *Koreans in Japan: Ethnic Conflict and Accommodation,* ed. Changsoo Lee and George De Vos (Berkeley: University of California Press, 1981), 133–58.

4. My critique of the totalizing concept of Korean ethnicity owes much to feminist writers who have interrogated the essentialist, determinist, and foundationalist notions of "community," "identity," and "subject." They have argued that these politically salient configurations should be conceptualized as, for instance, multifaceted locations for struggles, differentiations, and displacements. See especially Biddy Martin and Chandra Talpade Mohanty, "Feminist Politics: What's Home Got to Do with It?" in *Feminist Studies/Critical Studies,* ed. Teresa de Lauretis (Bloomington: Indiana University Press, 1986), 199–212; Gloria Anzaldúa, *Borderlands/La Frontera: The New Mestiza* (San Francisco: Aunt Lute, 1987); Teresa de Lauretis, "Feminist Studies/Critical Studies: Issues, Terms and Contexts," in *Feminist Studies/Critical Studies,* ed. Teresa de Lauretis (Bloomington: Indiana University Press, 1986), 1–19; and de Lauretis, "Eccentric Subjects: Feminist Theory and Historical Consciousness," *Feminist Studies* 16, no. 1 (spring 1990): 115–50.

5. Lisa Lowe makes a similar argument for the importance of capturing such a duality in ethnic processes in her analysis of Asian American women writers; see "Heterogeneity, Hybridity, Multiplicity: Marking Asian American Differences," *Diaspora* 1, no. 1 (spring 1991): 24–44. Arguing for the criticalness of the dialectical negotiation between an attempt "to organize, resist, and theorize *as* Asian Americans" and the task of warning against "the risks of a cultural politics that relies upon the construction of sameness and the exclusion of differences" (28), Lowe proposes, following Ernesto Laclau and Chantal Mouffe, a coalitional politics that can be organized along the multiple axes of oppositions based upon gender, sexuality, class, and other differences. See also her *Immigrant Acts: On Asian American Cultural Politics* (Durham, N.C.: Duke University Press, 1996).

6. There were heated exchanges among Korean survivors when the Council for the North Korean Atom Bomb Victims (Chōsenjin Genbaku Giseisha Kyōgikai) began to demand a memorial of their own in the Peace Park. Several articles appeared in *Tōitsu nippō,* a Japanese-language newspaper published by South Korean nationals, strongly criticizing the plan. Some argued, for example, that it is not necessary to build another memorial when over 90 percent of the Korean atomic bomb victims originated from what is now South Korea; some warned that constructing a separate memorial was yet another reinforcement of the homeland's division. See especially a booklet published by Tawara Genkichi and his voluntary research group composed of journalists and schoolteachers concerned with the issue of minority students' status; Pika Shiryō Kenkyūsho and Zenkoku Zanichi Chōsenjin Kyōiku Kenkyū Kyōgikai, eds., *Shiryō: Kankokujin genbaku giseisha irei hi* (Hiroshima: Hi no Kai, 1989), esp. 83–86. I am much indebted to this booklet, which is the first accessible and sizable resource collection concerning the memorial for the Korean atomic bomb victims.

7. George De Vos and Changsoo Lee offer a historical overview of the divisions among the Koreans in Japan and their implications for the status of

Korean resident aliens; see "Conclusions: The Maintenance of a Korean Ethnic Identity in Japan," in Lee and De Vos, *Koreans in Japan*, 354–83. In describing the formal political and institutional split that occurred within the Korean minority during U.S. Occupation, Edward W. Wagner's *Korean Minority in Japan, 1904–1950* (New York: International Secretariat, Institute of Pacific Relations, 1951) and Richard H. Mitchell's *Korean Minority in Japan* (Berkeley: University of California Press, 1967), esp. 100–118, take into account the larger context of U.S. anticommunist policies in East Asia; both works make clear the Supreme Commander of Allied Powers' inattention and outright reluctance to promote policies that would improve the status of minorities in Japan.

8. *Chūgoku shinbun*, 19 April 1990.

9. These contestatory interpretations of the erased portion, as well as the construction committee head's official announcement, are found in Pika, *Shiryō*, 80–82.

10. Pika, *Shiryō*, includes Japanese translations of the entire inscription that were provided by four different individuals. All are basically in agreement with one another: see 10–14; quotations, 14. For five different Japanese translations of the erased portion, see ibid., 78–79. *Shiryō* supports the interpretation that the erased portion referred to the thirteenth-century conquest of Korea by the Mongols during the Yuen dynasty and to the Chin dynasty's invasion of Korea in the seventeenth century.

11. Ibid., 55.

12. Tawara Genkichi, however, informed the public that the city had in fact allowed construction of at least seven memorials inside the park since the 1967 regulation's announcement. City representatives responded that some of the new memorials had been approved prior to 1967 and others, for one reason or another, fell outside the regulation's jurisdiction. *Chugoku shinbun*, 17 May 1988.

13. See Pika, *Shiryō*, 84–85, for a succinct summary of this reasoning.

14. Interview with author, 17 July 1990, coffee shop in Minami Kannon.

15. Ibid., 31.

16. In her analysis of the politics of the Vietnam Veterans Memorial, Marita Sturken draws attention to the difference between "memorials" and "monuments": the former tend to be associated with images of loss. Following other observers of the memorial, such as Arthur Danto and Charles Griswold, Sturken argues that "Monuments are not generally built to commemorate defeats"; instead, "the defeated dead are remembered in memorials. While a monument most often signifies victory, a memorial refers to the life or lives sacrificed for a particular set of values." See "The Wall, the Screen, and the Image: The Vietnam Veterans Memorial," *Representations*, no. 35 (summer 1991): 118–42; quotations, 118. Arguing against such a rigid distinction, James E. Young stresses the interchangeability of the two; see *The Texture of Memory: Holocaust Memorials and Meaning* (New Haven: Yale University Press, 1993), 3. I have found the differentiation useful as a heuristic tool in discussing the Korean Atom Bomb Memorial.

17. From Sō's lecture on 1 September 1990 at Nishikumin Bunka Sentā.

18. In contrast to the Showa emperor's vague expression of "regrets" for

the past, the Japanese government was now assigned concrete and urgent tasks through which it might demonstrate the meaningfulness of the emperor's public statement. These tasks included improving the legal status of Korean residents in Japan and adequately supporting and compensating Korean victims of the Asia Pacific War, including Koreans deserted in Sakhalin and atomic bomb survivors who had returned to Korea.

19. Theodor W. Adorno, "What Does Coming to Terms with the Past Mean?" in *Bitburg in Moral and Political Perspective*, ed. Geoffrey H. Hartman (Bloomington: Indiana University Press, 1986), 114–29.

20. In the initial proposal, the committee also announced that in order to unify the memorial for North and South Koreans, the present engraving would be deleted entirely and replaced with a new inscription that referred to the Korean peninsula (*Chōsen hantō*); the controversy is discussed later in this chapter. Although expressing some resistance to using the term *Chōsen*, which has some associations with the colonial period, Mindan reportedly welcomed the recommendation. Sōren also unconditionally accepted the new inscription and argued that *Chōsen hantō* is an internationally acknowledged geographical term. *Chūgoku shinbun*, 27 June 1990.

21. For a detailed summary of the 1990 relocation issue, see Hashimoto Manabu, "Hiroshima no heiwa shisei o tou: hibaku 45 shūnen o mukaeta Hiroshima no genjō." *Jōkyō to shutai*, no. 177 (September 1990): 42–59. I am thankful to Toyonaga Keisaburō for calling my attention to Hashimoto's essay.

22. *Asahi shinbun*, 28 June 1990.

23. All quotations from Ch'oe Sŏng-won are from a public symposium, 5 July 1990, at Katorikku Seibo Yōchien Hōru.

24. Gender is another crucial analytic category, especially as it affects the meanings and sentiments attached to the dead. This was brought out during my interview with a survivor in Taegu, Kim Im-sŏn. Kim, who was born and raised in Hiroshima and who returned to Korea with her husband after the war, expressed deep anguish over the loss of her younger brother, her parents' only son. In contrast to mainstream American and Japanese kinship rules, which allow either men or women as well as children who are not biologically related to carry on descent lines, Korean genealogy must be passed on through a biological son. Kim said,

> I should have died, and my younger brother should have survived; then the family genealogy could have continued. If I had died and my brother had lived, he could have succeeded the family. But [our family was] completely destroyed (*zenmetsu*)— no one survived. Once I die, no one will think about the family register. No one will care for it. It will remain [abandoned] for thousands and thousands of years. My son won't know about my family, would he? I am the only one who survived in my family. . . . [After the bomb] my father wandered about, with swollen legs, looking for my brother. . . . He died without having been able to find my brother. I wish I was the one who died.
>
> Hiroshima o Kataru Kai et al., *Kaikyō o koe te*
> (Hiroshima: Hiroshima o Kataru Kai, 1990), 40–41

25. The mistreatment of ethnic Koreans in the aftermath of the bombing is described in numerous personal accounts and memoirs. See, for instance,

Hiroshima-ken Chōsenjin Hibakusha Kyōgikai, *Shiroi chogori no hibakusha;* Hiraoka, *Muen no kaikyō;* and Chu Sŏk, *Hibaku Chōsenjin kyōshi no sengoshi: saigetsu yo! Ariran yo!* (Tokyo: Akashi Shoten, 1990).

26. From Nakajima's public lecture, "Zaikan hibakusha mondai no rekishi to genjō," 28 May 1989, Hiroshima YMCA. For further discussions of Korean atom bomb survivors by Nakajima and others, see Zaikan Hibakusha Mondai Shimin Kaigi, ed., *Zaikan hibakusha mondai o kangaeru* (Tokyo: Gaifūsha, 1988).

27. *Chūgoku shinbun,* 19 May 1990.

28. *Chūgoku shinbun,* 19 June 1990.

29. *Chūgoku shinbun,* 24 June 1990.

30. *Chūgoku shinbun,* 27 June 1990.

31. At 12 July 1990 meeting with city officials. The dominant idea that ethnic minorities are the root cause of social problems also affects interpretations of other societies. Former prime minister Nakasone's statement that Americans' average intelligence level has been lowered by minorities reappeared in somewhat different guise in a recent survey of Japanese views of the United States, in which 42 percent of those polled identified the presence of diverse ethnic minorities as the reason for the United States' economic breakdown. See *Business Week,* 18 December 1989, quoted in *Chūgoku shinbun,* 9 December 1989.

32. *Asahi shinbun,* 24 May 1990.

33. *Chūgoku shinbun,* 1 August 1990. On the Alien Registration Act, see Kang and Kim, *Zainichi Kankoku/Chōsenjin,* 162–234; Satō Akira and Yamada Teruyoshi, *Zainichi Chōsenjin: rekishi to genjō* (Tokyo: Akashi Shoten, 1986); and Lee, "The Legal Status of Koreans in Japan." The expression "legal forms of discrimination" against the Korean minority refers in particular to two legal documents that define the statutory position of Japan's 700,000 Koreans: the Alien Registration Act (ARA) and the Immigration Control Law (ICL). These two laws, which were put into effect immediately after the war, are regarded as the foundation for governmental control over the Koreans; they determine the administrative practices of "discrimination, assimilation, and expatriation." The ICL, revised as the Immigration Control and Refugee Recognition Act in 1982, went into effect in October 1951, a year before the San Francisco Peace Treaty. Under the guidance of the Allied Forces, the Japanese government unilaterally declared that Koreans should be restored to their former nationality. Those who resided in Japan would not be entitled to permanent residency. Instead, they were categorized as foreigners who were allowed long-term stays (those who fell under the category of Act 126) and became subject to the Immigration Control Law. The ARA, which was enacted in 1947, sought to control alien residents, 90 percent of whom at that time were Koreans. (In principle, Koreans were Japanese imperial subjects when the law was enacted.) It obliges foreigners who stay in the country more than 90 days to be registered. It also required, until recently, fingerprinting and the carrying of an Alien Registration Card at all times, even for permanent residents.

While the ARA supervises the activities of Koreans, the ICL deprives them of stable legal status. The ARA assigns the Korean minority a vulnerable position as foreigners, particularly because the ICL's regulation concerning deportation applies also to Koreans who were granted permanent residency under the ROK-Japan Treaty in 1965. Moreover, each individual's status is determined and permission for the period of stay granted entirely at the discretion of the Ministry of Justice. At the same time, the ICL's strict selection process makes it difficult for Koreans to acquire permanent residency or to naturalize. For example, the applicant for permanent residency or naturalization must submit proof that she or he is a person of good conduct and possesses skills or property to maintain an independent livelihood. Criminal records, violations of traffic rules, tax payment records, and various aspects of personal conduct are also checked. Critics have also noted that at the time of naturalization, registration officers informally coerce applicants to take up "Japanese" surnames.

34. O, for instance, argues that in order to create "an environment in which we can live as ethnic selves" (*minzoku toshite ikite yukeru kankyō*), it is necessary to generate conditions in which "the municipal community will approve our membership as community residents" (*chiiki jūmin toshite ukeire rareru*). He is pressing the municipal administration to work toward granting all ethnic members unconditional permanent residency, community services including social welfare and opportunities for ethnic education, and eligibility to vote as resident aliens, at least at the prefectural level. Eliminating the so-called nationality requirement (*kokuseki jōkō*) in municipal hiring practices is also considered crucial to ensuring socioeconomic stability for resident aliens. See also Nakai Kiyomi, *Teijū gaikokujin to kōmu shūninken: 70mannin o shimedasu ronri* (Tokyo: Takushoku Shobō, 1989), for a comprehensive critique of the official logic concerning the nationality requirement.

35. At the time of my fieldwork, the members of Mintōren's Hiroshima branch were holding bimonthly public meetings in which they discussed such issues as the legal environment, the history and culture of *zainichi*, and educating the general public as well as younger *zainichi* on the condition of the Korean minority. The group also met monthly with city officials and attempted to persuade the city administration to take the initiative in eliminating the nationality requirement in the city's hiring codes entirely. Members also encouraged the public relations department to enlighten citizens about the minority situation. They also regularly sent delegates to Mintōren's national gatherings and informed the public about the Korean minority in Hiroshima—for example, providing information on the relocation of the Korean Atom Bomb Memorial.

36. Kim Yŏn-si, at the Mintōren public symposium on 4 February 1990.

37. Conversation with author, after negotiation meeting with the city on 30 August 1990.

38. In her recent study of Korean resident alien women writers, Norma Field has noted the younger generation of *zainichi* similarly questioning the conventional notion of citizenship. See "Beyond Envy, Boredom, and Suffering."

39. Hong Tae-p'yo, "Joshō: zainichi no atarashii rekishi o kizamu wakamonotachi no shimon ōnatsu kyohi," in *Ore shimon oshitehennen: shimon*

kyohi to jūdai no hatsugen, ed. Jung Yeong-hae (Tokyo: Akashi Shoten, 1986), 1–8; quotation, 4–5.

40. Interview with author, 17 July 1990.

41. According to a 1984 survey in Kanagawa prefecture, about two-thirds of the Korean residents there usually or exclusively use their *tsūmei,* while about 20 percent use both names, depending on the occasion. The survey also shows that while more than 90 percent of Korean residents hold two names, over 80 percent of Chinese residents in Kanagawa use only their Chinese surname. See Rekishigaku Kenkyūkai and Nihonshi Kenkyūkai, eds., *Kōza Nihon rekishi* (Tokyo: Tokyo Daigaku Shuppankai, 1985), 13:41; and Kinbara Samon et al., eds., *Nihon no naka no Kankoku/Chōsenjin, Chūgokujin: Kanagawa kennai zaijū gaikokujin jittai chōsa yori* (Tokyo: Akashi Shoten, 1986), 180. A series of recent lawsuits, in which ethnic Koreans who had been forced to adopt Japanese family names at the time of their naturalization have demanded that the government accept their ethnic names, has introduced the new category of "Korean Japanese"—that is, Japanese nationals who are unassimilated Koreans. See Minzokumei o Torimodosu Kai, ed., *Minzokumei o torimodoshita Nihonseki Chōsenjin: watashitachi no namae/uri irŭm* (Tokyo: Akashi Shoten, 1990).

42. Many argue that the use of Japanese-like names is desirable because of Japanese narrow-mindedness. This practice, they point out, helps prevent the complications that might arise from dealing with prejudiced Japanese clients at work or ignorant children at school; it is thus seen as promoting an economy of communication. Nevertheless, the conscious and consistent use of Korean family names is one of the most effective and important ethnic political practices *zainichi* can exercise. Like the refusal of fingerprinting in the past, it is a political act that can be practiced on an individual basis, irrespective of organizational affiliation (e.g., Mindan or Sōren), occupation, sex, age, or locality.

Progressive schoolteachers in Japan also encourage students to consistently use their Korean names. This practice is often called *honmyō sengen* (lit., "declaration of autonym"). While such efforts by Japanese teachers are certainly understood to be significant, some criticize the teachers for perceiving minority issues too narrowly and seemingly presuming that the use of Korean names can resolve discrimination. To concentrate pedagogical efforts on the use of Korean names also risks making the minority solely responsible for emancipation, rather than urging the active involvement of Japanese students. However, there is evidence that as part of a larger practice well integrated into the students' everyday lives, *honmyō sengen* can foster political alliances between *zainichi* and socially marginalized Japanese students. See Fujiwara Shirō, "Shimon ōnatsu kyohi no kora o sasaen ga tame ni," in *Ore shimon oshitehennen,* 177–203, esp. 189–94.

43. Pika, *Shiryō,* 14.

44. For newspaper coverage of the meeting at which Mindan members attempted to reach a consensus about whether to agree to the city's proposal to eliminate the existing inscription, see *Chugoku shinbun,* 1 August 1990.

45. Public symposium on 15 July 1990.

46. Takeda Seiji, "Kurushimi no yurai," in *Yume no gaibu* (Tokyo: Kawade Shobō Shinsha, 1989), 13–15.

47. While on a trip to visit survivors in South Korea, on 3 May 1990, Kwak used this expression to speak specifically about the ways in which *zainichi* Koreans have been relegated to an obscure and precarious status in both Japanese and Korean legal discourse. Adrienne Rich is quoted in Renato Rosaldo, *Culture and Truth: The Remaking of Social Analysis* (Boston: Beacon Press, 1989), ix.

48. During the past decade, a number of scholars have begun to criticize the anthropological notion of culture as a bounded and timeless entity that prescribes actions and emotions. For example, see James Clifford, *The Predicament of Culture: Twentieth-Century Ethnography, Literature, and Art* (Cambridge, Mass.: Harvard University Press, 1988); Richard Handler, *Nationalism and the Politics of Culture in Quebec* (Madison: University of Wisconsin Press, 1988); George E. Marcus and Michael M. J. Fischer, *Anthropology as Cultural Critique: An Experimental Moment in the Human Sciences* (Chicago: University of Chicago Press, 1986); and Rosaldo, *Culture and Truth*. See also Nicholas B. Dirks, ed., *Colonialism and Culture* (Ann Arbor: University of Michigan Press, 1992), for an important discussion of how such an idea of culture was produced and functioned within the contexts of colonial rule.

49. It is important to note that I am observing the narratives produced by those Korean resident aliens who are living in an environment in which it is not possible to organize their lives around a sizable and institutionally distinguishable community, such as an ethnic language school or a "Koreatown." The naturalness of being Korean and the sense of belonging to the Korean collectivity are quite different in such areas as Ikaino (Ikuno district in Osaka), where there is a high concentration of Korean resident aliens and greater exposure to new immigrants from Korea. Likewise, the "identity" of being a Korean national is quite different among those individuals who have received extensive education in Korean ethnic schools and other organizations. For a sophisticated ethnographic account of ethnic identity formations among those affiliated with North Korean organizations, see Sonia Ryang, *North Koreans in Japan: Language, Ideology, and Identity* (Boulder, Colo.: Westview Press, 1997). Maruyama Kōichi offers sociohistorical observations on the development of the Korean community in Hiroshima city; see "Toshi no naka no mainoritī: zainichi Chōsenjin no sengo seikatsu to bunka," in Hiroshima-shi, ed., *Hiroshima shinshi: toshi bunka hen*, 302–90.

50. Harajiri Hideki notes the pervasiveness of the *chesa* practice among all generations of Korean resident aliens he interviewed in a community in northern Kyūshū. They "are not aware of the detailed meanings of *chesa*, but emphasize its significance in paying respects to ancestors" (*Zainichi Chosenjin no seikatsu sekai* [Tokyo: Kōbundō, 1989], 154). Harajiri observes that the *zainichi*'s rites differ from those performed in Korea but argues that the use of Japanese words and practices does not indicate that Koreans in this community are assimilated to Japanese culture. Instead, it shows that these *zainichi* constitute their own ethnic culture that is integral to the regional community.

See especially the ethnographic portrayals in his section on religion (147–57). For a unique ethnographic observation of the Korean minority's Buddhist/shamanistic religious practices as being distinct from those of either Japan or Korea, see Helen Hardacre, *The Religion of Japan's Korean Minority: The Preservation of Ethnic Identity*, Korea Research Monograph 9 (Berkeley: Institute of East Asian Studies, University of California, Berkeley, and Center for Korean Studies, 1984).

51. Jung Yeong-hae, "Atogaki," in *Ore shimon oshitehennen: shimonkyohi to jūdai no hatsugen*, ed. Jung Yeong-hae (Tokyo: Akashi Shoten, 1986), 217–22; esp. 219.

52. Among a number of works available in English that portray the extent to which Korean minorities have been negatively stereotyped in Japan, see especially Michael Weiner, *The Origins of the Korean Community in Japan, 1910–1923* (Atlantic Highlands, N.J.: Humanities Press International, 1989), and *Race and Migration in Imperial Japan* (London: Routledge, 1994); and De Vos and Lee, "The Maintenance of a Korean Ethnic Identity in Japan."

53. Michael M. J. Fischer, "Ethnicity and the Post-Modern Arts of Memory," in *Writing Culture: The Poetics and Politics of Ethnography*, ed. James Clifford and George E. Marcus (Berkeley: University of California Press), 194–233; quotation, 208.

54. Personal communication.

55. The *zainichi* Koreans' notion of provisional ethnic culture that I describe here is not identical to what Gayatri Chakravorty Spivak once called, in referring to feminists' deployment of the category of woman, "strategic essentialism." Spivak has also referred to the writing practices of Indian subaltern historiography as "a strategic use of positivistic essentialism in a scrupulously visible political interest"; "Subaltern Studies: Deconstructing Historiography," in *Selected Subaltern Studies,* ed. Ranajit Guha and Gayatri Chakravorty Spivak (Oxford: Oxford University Press, 1988), 13. Mobilizing political alliances around a shared narrative about how one has been interpellated historically is not the same as claiming a solidarity based on ahistorical categories of difference that are assumed to be naturally and prediscursively given. Nor is it the same as subscribing to the idea that certain historical knowledges can exist prior to discursive mediations and that past events can reveal their significance in and of themselves. Rather, what is strategically sought in the attempts to restitute "the suppressed" and the "excluded" are the discursive effects that unsettle the given order of signification and knowledge. The disruptive effects, moreover, are understood to derive not from some quality of knowledge inherent in "the recuperated" but from a change in the complementary *relation* between the established (that is, the center) and the suppressed and the marginalized. For a further discussion of the antiessentialist, strategic use of negative political identification, see Judith Butler's *Bodies That Matter: On the Discursive Limits of "Sex"* (New York: Routledge, 1993). I am also grateful to Sylvia Yanagisako for providing me with useful suggestions.

56. Franz Fanon, *The Wretched of the Earth*, trans. Constance Farrington (New York: Grove Weidenfeld, 1963), 223–24, quoted in Sŏ Kyŏn-shik, "Kim

Ji-ha e no tegami," in *Bundan o ikiru: "zainichi" o koete* (Tokyo: Kage Shobō, 1997), 242–43.

CHAPTER 6. POSTWAR PEACE
AND THE FEMINIZATION OF MEMORY

1. Maruyama Masao, "Kindai Nihon no chishikijin," in *Kōei no ichi kara: "gendai seiji no shisō to kōdō" tsuiho* (Tokyo: Miraisha, 1982), 71–133; quotation, 115.

2. Ibid., 114. Similar observations can be found in, for instance, Kuno Osamu and Tsurumi Shunsuke, *Gendai Nihon no shisō: sono itsutsu no uzu* (Tokyo: Iwanami Shoten, 1978). Tsurumi especially places the postwar intellectual transformation in the broader terms of a "postwar apostasy" (*sengo tenkō*). See Tsurumi, *Tenkō kenkyū* (Tokyo: Chikuma Shobō, 1976). The Japan Teachers' Association's slogan, "never send our students to the battlefield," can also be read as another manifestation of "repentance" and a consciousness in the immediate postwar period of responsibility.

3. Maruyama, "Kindai Nihon no chishikijin," 124. Yoshida Yutaka notes that Maruyama was quick to point out that although many did indeed feel a deep sense of repentance for not having been able to effectively resist militarism and the state's encroachment on prodemocracy activities, they did not necessarily feel individual responsibility for committing atrocities in the war. Rather they were filled with joy at having been liberated from the oppressive regime. See Maruyama's 1968 statement in Kuno Osamu et al., " 'Heiwa mondai danwakai' ni tsui te," *Sekai*, July 1985; quoted in Yoshida Yutaka, *Nihonjin no sensōkan: sengoshi no nakano henyō* (Tokyo: Iwanami Shoten, 1995), 81. Intellectual historian Yonehara Ken also makes a similar observation in *Nihonteki "kindai" e no toi: shisōshi to shite no sengo seiji* (Tokyo: Shinhyōron, 1995), 24.

4. I do not mean to imply that individual women did not feel repentant or to argue that women never reflected about their participation in wartime national policy. Ichikawa Fusae and other prominent prewar thinkers did express regrets when realizing that they had deferred the pursuit of gender equity and universal suffrage in the interests of promoting nationalist policies and war efforts. What I discuss here are "Women" as discursive constructs, as well as the historical and cultural positions of those who have been identified by nationality and gender as "Japanese Women."

5. Interview with author, 19 April 1989. This statement was made in response to my question regarding the city's then-current urban renewal projects. Like many other survivors I interviewed, Moritaki doubted that ongoing renewal policies could adequately "express the authentic Hiroshima." As an alternative plan, he described an image of the new monument, which he deemed to be the truthful representation of Hiroshima's pacifist spirit.

6. Cynthia Enloe has been one of the most insistent proponents of the urgent need to bring perspectives on gender and sexualities to studies of those domains that are usually not considered in these terms. Gendered analysis, En-

loe argues, reveals that the arenas of international politics and diplomacy, militarization, colonialism, and war do not just involve relations among formal institutions but are inseparably enmeshed in the everyday and immanent workings of power. Another notable feature of Enloe's work is her attentiveness to the multiplicity of forms of masculinities and femininities. Although militarism and peace are conventionally understood to be masculine and feminine, respectively, the particular ways in which they have become gendered vary according to specific processes of militarism and demilitarization, nationalism, capital formation, and colonial relations. See Enloe, *Bananas, Beaches, and Bases: Making Feminist Sense of International Politics* (Berkeley: University of California Press, 1990) and *The Morning After: Sexual Politics at the End of the Cold War* (Berkeley: University of California Press, 1993). Another important contribution to the gendered analysis of war is Susan Jeffords, *The Remasculinization of America: Gender and the Vietnam War* (Bloomington: Indiana University Press, 1989). For a unique study of the gendered use of military language and its effects on knowledge about the world, see Carol Cohn, "Sex and Death in the Rational World of Defense Intellectuals" *Signs* 12, no. 4 (summer 1987): 687–718. My discussion of the postwar peace campaign and antinuclearism, as well as the production of knowledge about prewar and wartime Japanese women's experiences, aims precisely at illuminating the historically and socially specific processes whereby the concepts of peace, nationhood, and civilian victimhood were (re)constructed in association with the production of postwar femininity and maternity.

7. See, for example, Nosaka Akiyuki's "American *Hijiki*," trans. Jay Rubin, in *Contemporary Japanese Literature: An Anthology of Fiction, Film, and Other Writing Since 1945,* ed. Howard Hibbett (New York: Alfred A. Knopf, 1977), 436–68. Ueno Chizuko astutely portrays Japanese male writers' paranoiac and sexualized obsessions with America. America, she argues, has been a dominant and ubiquitous presence in the postwar years and has been associated with the (hetero)sexual liberation of women, which allows them to "choose" (American) men, in contrast to the lack of such power on the part of defeated and frustrated Japanese men. Ueno, *Kindai kazoku no seiritsu to shūen* (Tokyo: Iwanami Shoten, 1994), 213.

8. Nishi Kiyoko, *Senryōka no Nihon fujin seisaku: sono rekishi to shōgen* (Tokyo: Domesu Shuppan, 1985), 25.

9. Susan J. Pharr, *Political Women in Japan: The Search for a Place in Political Life* (Berkeley: University of California Press, 1981), 30–31. See the interviews in Nishi, *Senryōka no,* for descriptions of how Japanese women self-consciously manipulated the Occupation authorities to pursue women's rights.

10. *Asahi shinbun,* 5 February 1996, introduced Mizuno's research and at the same time announced that his results would be used in the lawsuit of Korean resident aliens who sought to regain their electoral rights at the prefectural level. See also Mizuno Naoki, "Zainichi Chōsenjin/Taiwanjin sanseiken 'teishi' jōkō no seiritsu: zainichi Chōsenjin sanseiken mondai no rekishiteki kentō (1)," *Sekai jinken mondai kenkyū sentā kenkyū kiyō,* no. 1 (March 1996): 43–65.

11. For the detail of Occupation reforms, see Robert E. Ward and Sakamoto Yoshikazu, eds., *Democratizing Japan: The Allied Occupation* (Honolulu:
University of Hawaii Press, 1987).

12. Many have noted the officialization of "peace" in Japan's statehood
and ideology. With respect to the international image of Japan's nationhood,
Igarashi Takeshi cites a statement by Prime Minister Yoshida Shigeru arguing
that it was necessary to eliminate all suspicions among the international community that Japan continued to be a nation prone to war. Igarashi further shows
that the idea that Japan ought to become "the nation of peace" appeared in
the press as early as 1946. See Igarashi Takeshi, "'Heiwa kokka' to Nihongata
gaikō," in *Sengo Nihon: senryō to sengo kaikaku*, ed. Nakamura Masanori
et al., vol. 6 of *Sengo kaikaku to sono isan* (Tokyo: Iwanami Shoten, 1995),
253–89, esp. 257–58. In *Japan in War and Peace: Selected Essays* (New York:
New Press, 1993), John W. Dower demonstrates how the concepts of peace
and war, as well as the lived experiences of the two, have profoundly shaped
postwar Japanese culture, politics, and society.

13. The conference held in May 1954 was a small citizens' forum. The plan
for a larger international conference developed as the nationwide signature collection campaign grew. The first Gensuikin Sekai Taikai was held on 6 August
of the following year. For detailed descriptions of the history of women's social
and political activities in Hiroshima, see Suzuki Yūko, *Hiroshima ken josei undōshi* (Tokyo: Domesu Shuppan, 1985).

14. Ishida Takeshi, *Nihon no seiji to kotoba: heiwa to kokka*, vol. 2 (Tokyo:
Tokyo Daigaku Shuppan Kai, 1989). He begins with the usage of "peace" in
the late-nineteenth-century period of nation building, and then considers its
meaning in the ideology of "Peace in the Orient" (*tōyō heiwa*), the "Peaceful
Order" of the East Asia Co-prosperity Sphere, the postwar "Peace Constitution," and in the 1960s idea of "peaceful home" and peace protests against the
Vietnam War.

15. Tanaka Sumiko, "Nihon ni okeru hahaoya undō no rekishi to yakuwari," *Shisō*, no. 439 (1961): 97–107; quotation, 98. See also Yamabe Emiko,
"Dai ikkai hahaoya taikai o megutte: jūgoshi nōto sengohen," in *55nen taisei
seiritsu to onnatachi*, ed. Onnatachi no Ima o Tou Kai, vol. 3 of *Jūgoshi nōto
sengohen* (Tokyo: Impakuto Shuppankai, 1987), 53–67.

16. Hiroshima-ken Rekishisha Kyōikusha Kyōgikai, "Ano hi, Hiroshima no
hahatachi wa: arashi no naka no boshizō," in *Genbaku monumento monogatari* (Tokyo: Sekibunsha, 1984), 19.

17. Ibid., 22–23.

18. Ibid., 24.

19. Jean Bethke Elshtain, *Women and War* (New York: Basic Books, 1987),
69. In reviewing essays compiled in Esashi Akiko et al., eds., *Onna ga Hiroshima o kataru* (Tokyo: Inpakuto Shuppankai, 1996), Mizugaki Natsuko criticizes the problematic persistence of the "maternal myth" in the writings and
research about women's Hiroshima experience. See "Bosei o koeru koto no kon-
nansa," *Gekkan fōramu*, no. 8 (November 1996): 99–100.

20. See, for instance, Sigmund Freud, *Civilization and Its Discontents*, ed.
and trans. James Strachey (New York: W. W. Norton, 1961), esp. 21–32. Jacques

Lacan, who saw even greater significance in the lack of fulfillment, pointed out that the process of sublimation produces and works through the void that it simultaneously creates. See Roland Chemama, *Dictionnaire de la psychanalyse* (Paris: Larousse, 1993), translated by Koide Hiroyuki et al. as *Seishin bunseki jiten* (Tokyo: Kōbundō, 1995), 142–43.

21. John Whittier Treat, *Writing Ground Zero: Japanese Literature and the Atomic Bomb* (Chicago: University of Chicago Press, 1995), 347.

22. Ibid.

23. Nagoya Misao, *Hiroshima haha no ki: Fumiki no "shi" o ikite* (1985; reprint, Tokyo: Heiwa Bunka/Chōbun Sha, 1990), 120–21.

24. See, for example, the anxieties of the survivor in his sixties (Yamazaki Kanji) described in the introduction.

25. Nagoya, *Hiroshima haha no ki*, 54.

26. The journal involved nationally renowned poets such as Shōda Shinoe; Kurihara Sadako; Hizume Shinobu, who organized one of the first relief associations for the survivors; Konishi Nobuko, the founder of the Hiroshima office of the Women's Democratic Society (Fujin Minshu Kurabu); and many other important writers, critics, and social activists. The Women's Democratic Society is a national organization that was founded in 1956 by writers, including Sata Ineko and Miyamoto Yuriko. Because its central promoters were primarily poets and writers, the journal came to offer a space where the experience of the Hiroshima bombing could be represented through literary and other creative means; nevertheless, it retained a degree of nonprofessional casualness. The articles published in the journal included mostly poetry, short stories, autobiographical accounts, personal memoirs, and transcriptions of oral interviews with other survivors. The editors also occasionally included reports on international and national political gatherings and nuclear protest conferences. The journal ceased publication in 1975.

27. From a report on the group's history and activities: Maeda Tomiko, "Gensuibaku kinshi Hiroshima haha no kai no katsudō ni tsuite," *Hiroshima no kawa*, no. 2 (August 1961): 15. See also "Gensuikin haha no kai: sekai heiwa e onna no kokoro kesshū," in *Hiroshima no onnatachi*, ed. Hiroshima Joseishi Kenkyūkai (Tokyo: Domesu Shuppan, 1987), 79–85.

28. During the early 1970s, various sorts of data concerning the atom bomb's effects collected earlier—including surveys conducted by the city and film taken by both Japanese and Occupation personnel immediately after the bombing— gradually began to be restored to the Japanese government and to Hiroshima. In 1973, Japan and the United States agreed to jointly run and finance the ABCC on an equal basis. In March 1975, responsibility for the building and for some of the staffing of the ABCC were handed over to the newly founded Radiation Effect Research Foundation. See M. Susan Lindee, *Suffering Made Real: American Science and the Survivors at Hiroshima* (Chicago: University of Chicago Press, 1994).

29. Yamaguchi Yūko, "Tainai hibakusha/hibaku nisei o mamoru to iu koto," in Shin-Nihon Fujin no Kai Hiroshima-ken Honbu, ed., *Konoha no yōni yakarete* (1966; reprint, Tokyo: Shin-Nihon Shuppansha, 1985), 62–66.

30. Lindee summarizes the Japanese and non-Japanese reactions to the

Hiroshima ABCC at the time that a complex to house the group was constructed and in subsequent years. The words of one American are especially suggestive, describing the expensive, unattractive, yet prominent white structures on the hill as "the most conspicuous symbol in the city of Japan's defeat." The Nagasaki ABCC, in contrast, was built in a far less controversial location. See Lindee, *Suffering Made Real*, 144.

31. The women received treatment at Mt. Sinai Hospital. The project was promoted by Tanimoto Kiyoshi, a Christian minister who appears in John Hersey's *Hiroshima*, and Norman Cousins, who had earlier become known through the "Spiritual Adoption Project" (*seishin yōshi undō*). This project advocated a kind of foster parenting whereby Americans might donate money to children in Hiroshima who were orphaned by the bombing. See the Chugoku Shimbun and the Hiroshima International Cultural Foundation, Inc., *The Meaning of Survival: Hiroshima's Thirty-Six Year Commitment to Peace* (Hiroshima: Chugoku Shimbun and the Hiroshima International Cultural Foundation, 1983), 94. Rodney Barker has traced the personal life trajectories of twenty-five women who visited the United States to receive medical treatment in *The Hiroshima Maidens: A Story of Courage, Compassion, and Survival* (New York: Penguin, 1985). A similar treatment project was spearheaded within Japan in 1952 by writers such as Masugi Shizue. Hiroshima Joseishi Kenkyūkai, ed., *Hiroshima no onnatachi* (Tokyo: Domesu Shuppan, 1987), also includes brief personal histories of Yamaoka Michiko and Matsubara Miyoko, who identify themselves as having been labeled "Atom Bomb Maidens." For another account on the representation of women *hibakusha*, see Maya Todeschini, "Death and the Maiden: Female *Hibakusha* as Cultural Heroines, and the Politics of A-bomb Memory," in *Hibakusha Cinema: Hiroshima, Nagasaki, and the Nuclear Images in Japanese Film*, ed. Mick Broderick (London: Kegan Paul, 1996), 223-53.

32. Chūgoku Shinbunsha, "Honoo no keifu," in *Nihon no genbaku kiroku*, ed. Ienaga Saburō et al. (Tokyo: Nihon Tosho Sentā, 1991), 10:265.

33. See Lindee's *Suffering Made Real* for detailed discussion of the consequences of the non-treatment policy, esp. chap. 7 (117-42).

34. Chūgoku Shinbunsha, ed., *Nenpyō Hiroshima 40nen no kiroku* (Tokyo: Miraisha, 1986), 167.

35. As was noted in the media and elsewhere, the several sexual scandals involving male leaders of the LDP played a crucial role in shaping women's voting behavior. Another issue seen as of special concern to women was the newly introduced 3 percent consumption tax (*shōhi zei*). The opposition parties denounced the "LDP's tyranny" in forcibly introducing a tax generally thought to disproportionately affect low- and middle-income households on a daily basis. The LDP suffered great losses in the July 1989 election for the Tokyo Metropolitan District Assembly. Uno, the prime minister in office at the time, echoed male reporters and analysts in attributing the cause of the defeat to women's "instinctive and emotional" (*kankakuteki*) judgment on this issue. See *Asahi shinbun*, 4 July 1989.

36. She spoke at the opening ceremony in the city of Hiroshima on 4 December 1989.

37. See, for instance, *Asahi shinbun*, 24 January 1990. Of course, the pres-

ence of women was believed to be important even in ways that were totally irrelevant to substantive political issues. At one local campaign scene I happened to observe, a young male campaign organizer claimed that "women alone [could] make up" for the predicted weakness of his candidate. In their efforts to turn the election into a festive event, he and another male campaign organizer stressed the strategic importance of recruiting women into crowds of supporters for their exchange value, for "men are also attracted to events where women gather."

38. Most of the founding members had been involved in the nationwide campaign to raise to eighteen the age limit to qualify for governmental child-rearing support. They also were active in fighting the institutional discrimination against divorced women. They demanded, for instance, an increase in state relief for divorced single-mother families so that it would match the amount given to bereaved single-mother families. Their decade-long involvement in the campaign and their engagement with governments at all levels are summarized and recalled in Jidō Fuyō Teate o 18sai ni Hikiageru Kai, ed., *Semete kodomo o kōkō ni: rikon shita onna no negai, 1onen no tatakai, soshite ima* (Hiroshima: Jidō Fuyō Teate o 18sai ni Hikiageru Kai, 1985).

39. Interview with author, 1 June 1989.

40. For instance, "*onna*" appeared in the title of a women's liberation journal of the 1970s, *Onna—erosu* (Women—eros), which was influential in opening a public space where women talked about their work, bodies, experiences of discrimination, homes, and sexuality.

41. Interview, 1 June 1989.

42. Conversation at the group's meeting, 22 July 1989.

43. *Chūgoku shinbun*, 19 February 1992.

44. A similar process, whereby working women's strategic appropriation of assigned attributes to empower themselves unwittingly perpetuates the given power structure, is described by Dorinne K. Kondo, *Crafting Selves: Power, Gender, and Discourses of Identity in a Japanese Workplace* (Chicago: University of Chicago Press, 1990), 258–99.

45. While maintaining general reservations about the journal's amateurism, because its members were "women activists and *shufu* who were not so-called professional researchers," sociologist Takahashi Saburō nevertheless acknowledges its pioneering significance for the study of Japanese women's active participation in the war effort. Takahashi, "Sensō to josei," in *Senjika no Nihon: shōwa zenki no rekishi shakaigaku*, ed. Senjika Nihon Shakai Kenkyūkai (Kyoto: Kōrosha, 1990), 247–75; quotation, 266.

46. See, for instance, Suzuki Yūko, *Feminizumu to sensō: fujin undōka no sensō kyōryoku* (Tokyo: Marujusha, 1986).

47. Fujii Tadatoshi's *Kokubō fujinkai: hinomaru to kappōgi* (Tokyo: Iwanami Shoten, 1985) offers a comprehensive history of the association's development under this slogan. For a local history of the association's activities, see Maritani Mikiko, *Sensō o ikita onna tachi: shōgen—kokubō funjin kai* (Kyoto: Mineruva Shoten, 1985).

48. Important historical accounts that have similarly disrupted our conventional knowledge about "Japanese women" can be found especially in Robert

J. Smith and Ella Lury Wiswell, *The Women of Suye Mura* (Chicago: University of Chicago Press, 1982), and in a number of innovative essays compiled in Gail Lee Bernstein, ed., *Recreating Japanese Women, 1600–1945* (Berkeley: University of California Press, 1991).

49. The prewar deployment of the concept of the maternal to recruit and mobilize women into state ideology and the nationalist agenda is discussed most extensively by Kano Masanao, *Senzen/"ie" no shisō* (Tokyo: Sōbunsha, 1973). Kano Mikiyo's *Jiga no kanata e: kindai o koeru feminizumu* (Tokyo: Shakai Hyōronsha, 1990) is a compilation of foundational writings by prewar women writers, critics, activists, and suffragists and traces the transfigurations of the concept of the maternal in early-twentieth-century feminist thought and practices. Kano Mikiyo especially identifies Takamure Itsue, Mizoue Yasuko, and Koura Tomi as the key thinkers in monumentalizing motherhood in nationalist and imperialist discourses. Historian Narita Ryūichi, who has examined the writings and activities of Oku Mumeo, the early-twentieth-century suffragist and the founder of Shufu Rengōkai (the Shufu League), has eloquently shown a similar continuity in the deployment of the *shufu* identity—constructed as women of a particular class—across the prewar and postwar divide. See Narita, "Haha no kuni no onna tachi: Oku Mumeo no 'senji' to 'sengo,'" in *Sōryokusen to gendaika,* ed. Yamanouchi Yasushi, Victor Koschmann, and Narita Ryūichi (Tokyo: Kashiwa Shobō, 1995), 163–84. Like Narita's article, Ueno Chizuko's essay "'Kokumin kokka' to 'jendā': 'josei no kokuminka' o megutte," *Gendai shisō* 24, no. 12 (October 1996): 8–45, examines the politics of knowledge within various historical studies that analyze the interrelations among nationalization, militarism, and gender.

50. This emphasis on gender difference in peace discourse might well be contrasted to *hibakusha*'s testimonial accounts. A striking convention in these testimonies is the frequent reference to the inability to distinguish between men and women during the turmoil of nuclear destruction. That it was difficult to discern gender and sexual identity and that such distinctions were grossly violated establish these narratives as portraying the extraordinary chaos and turmoil of the city under the atomic attack. Many of the survivor storytellers disrupt naturalized sensibilities regarding the everyday, peace, and the orderliness of knowledge by testifying to such gender ambiguities. There are countless examples of such testimonies; for example, see Hara Tamiki, *Natsu no hana* (1949; reprint, Tokyo: Iwanami Shoten, 1988), and Shin-Nihon Fujin no Kai Hiroshima-ken Honbu, *Konoha no yō ni,* esp. 43, 95. The questions regarding the problematic use of essentialized categories of gender are explored in Denise Riley, *"Am I That Name?": Feminism and the Category of "Women" in History* (Minneapolis: University of Minnesota Press, 1988), and Joan Wallach Scott, *Gender and the Politics of History* (New York: Columbia University Press, 1988).

EPILOGUE

1. James E. Young, *Writing and Rewriting the Holocaust: Narrative and the Consequences of Interpretation* (Bloomington: Indiana University Press, 1988), 17.

2. See John Whittier Treat, *Writing Ground Zero: Japanese Literature and the Atomic Bomb* (Chicago: University of Chicago Press, 1995).

3. See especially Hayden White, *Tropics of Discourse: Essays in Cultural Criticism* (Baltimore: Johns Hopkins University Press, 1978), and *The Content of the Form: Narrative Discourse and Historical Representation* (Baltimore: John Hopkins University Press, 1987).

4. The results of much of my field research conducted between 1987 and 1990 were published as "Hiroshima Narratives and the Politics of Memory: A Study of Power, Knowledge, and Identities" (Ph.D. diss., Stanford University, 1992).

5. I discuss the transnational appropriation of critical discourse in greater detail in "Critical Warps: Facticity, Transformative Knowledge, and Postnationalist Criticism in the Smithsonian Controversy," *Positions* 5 (winter 1997): 779–809.

6. Benedict Anderson, *Imagined Communities,* rev. ed. (New York: Verso, 1991), 12.

7. The study group's members have published a great many works: for example, Fujioka Nobukatsu, *Ojoku no kingendaishi: ima kokufuku no toki* (Tokyo: Tokuma Shoten, 1996). Fujioka Nobukatsu and Jiyūshugi Shikan Ken-kyūkai continue to publish the multivolume anthology *Kyōkasho ga oshienai rekishi* (Tokyo: Sankei Shinbunsha, 1996–).

8. Ian Buruma, *The Wages of Guilt: Memories of War in Germany and Japan* (New York: Farrar, Straus, Giroux, 1994), 91. In his very astute critique, Masao Miyoshi points out that Buruma's writings on Japan generally operate according to the principle of "temporalizing of the essence," whereby cultural differences are treated as frozen, self-contained, and exceptional; see *Off Center: Power and Culture Relations between Japan and the United States* (Cambridge, Mass.: Harvard University Press, 1991), 80–88; quotation, 80. Moreover, Buruma's otherwise illuminating comparisons in *The Wages of Guilt* tend to pathologize and infantalize counteramnes(t)ic efforts in Japan. In reviewing his book, Michiko Kakutani quotes from Buruma's earlier writing on Japan to remind readers that he views Japan as "a nation of people longing to be 12-year-olds, or even younger"; *New York Times,* 1 July 1994. As a casual piece of travel writing, Buruma's chapter on Hiroshima may perhaps be excused for its factual errors and omissions. Yet, more serious flaws derive from his culturalist assumptions. In analyzing the intellectually legitimate question of "why the collective German memory should appear to be so different from the Japanese," Buruma undercuts his investigations by drawing on assumptions about Japanese cultural patterns that were offered by Ruth Benedict during the 1940s. Elsewhere, I discuss how Benedict's simplistic paradigm makes her readers believe that their knowledge of Japanese society is complete and enables them to feel a possessive power and authority over Japan; see "Bunka to iu tsumi," in *Bunka no kadai,* ed. Kajiwara Kageaki et al., vol. 13 of *Iwanami kōza bunka jinruigaku* (Tokyo: Iwanami Shoten, 1998), 41–66.

9. Philosopher Takahashi Tetsuya carefully distinguishes the two. "'Aitō' o meguru kaiwa: 'haisengo ron' hihan saisetsu," *Gendai shisō* 23, no. 12 (November 1995): 238–54, esp. 244–48. Takahashi has been one of the central

critics who made an important intervention by politicizing Levinas's notion of alterity to counter the renewed desire for self-absolution that I have described.

10. Among the many analyses developed from this critical perspective, a noteworthy example may be found in Okoshi Aiko and Takahashi Tetsuya, "Jendā to sensō sekinin," *Gendai shisō* 24, no. 10 (September 1997): 132–54. Certainly, not all attempts to retaliate against revisionists' arguments subscribe to postnationalist perspectives. For examples of writings that also criticize Fujioka and his collaborators, but continue to posit Japan and the Japanese nation as the primary discursive sphere within which the correct historical consciousness must be established, see Fujiwara Akira and Morita Toshio, eds., *Kingendaishi no shinjitsu wa nani ka: Fujioka Nobukatsu-shi no "rekishi kyōiku/heiwa kyōiku"-ron hihan* (Tokyo: Otsuki Shoten, 1996).

Bibliography

Adorno, Theodor W. "What Does Coming to Terms with the Past Mean?" In *Bitburg in Moral and Political Perspective*, edited by Geoffrey H. Hartman. Bloomington: Indiana University Press, 1986.

Alonso, Ana María. "The Effects of Truth: Re-Presentations of the Past and the Imaging of Community." *Journal of Historical Sociology* 1, no. 1 (March 1988): 33–57.

Alperovitz, Gar. *Atomic Diplomacy: Hiroshima and Potsdam*. New York: Simon and Schuster, 1965.

———. *The Decision to Use the Atomic Bomb and the Architecture of an American Myth*. New York: Alfred A. Knopf, 1995.

Antze, Paul, and Michael Lambek, eds. *Tense Past: Cultural Essays in Trauma and Memory*. New York: Routledge, 1996.

Anzaldúa, Gloria. *Borderlands/La Frontera: The New Mestiza*. San Francisco: Aunt Lute, 1987.

Apter, David E., and Nagayo Sawa. *Against the State: Politics and Social Protest in Japan*. Cambridge, Mass.: Harvard University Press, 1984.

Aronowitz, Stanley. "History as Disruption: On Benjamin and Foucault." *Humanities in Society* 2, no. 2 (spring 1979): 125–47.

Awaya Kentarō. *Miketsu no sensō sekinin*. Tokyo: Kashiwa Shobō, 1994.

———. "Tokyo saiban ni miru sengo shori." In *Sensō sekinin/sengo sekinin: Nihon to Doitsu wa dō chigau ka*, Awaya Kentarō et al. Tokyo: Asahi Shinbunsha, 1994.

———. *Tokyo Saibanron*. Tokyo: Otsuki Shoten, 1989.

Barker, Rodney. *The Hiroshima Maidens: A Story of Courage, Compassion, and Survival*. New York: Penguin, 1985.

Baudrillard, Jean. *Simulations*. Translated by Paul Foss, Paul Patton, and Philip Beitchman. New York: Semiotext(e), 1983.

Befu, Harumi. "Japan's Internationalization and *Bunkaron*." In *The Challenge of Japan's Internationalization: Organization and Culture,* edited by Hiroshi Mannari and Harumi Befu. Tokyo: Kodansha International, 1983.

———. "Nationalism and *Nihonjinron.*" In *Cultural Nationalism in East Asia: Representation and Identity,* edited by Harumi Befu. Research Papers and Policy Studies 39. Berkeley: Institute of East Asian Studies, University of California, 1993.

Benjamin, Walter. "N: [Re the Theory of Knowledge, Theory of Progress]," translated by Leigh Hafrey and Richard Sieburth. In *Benjamin: Philosophy, Aesthetics, History,* edited by Gary Smith. Chicago: University of Chicago Press, 1989.

———. "Theses on the Philosophy of History." In *Illuminations.* Edited by Hannah Arendt, translated by Harry Zohn. New York: Schocken Books, 1969.

———. "The Work of Art in the Age of Mechanical Reproduction." In *Illuminations.* Edited by Hannah Arendt, translated by Harry Zohn. New York: Schocken Books, 1969.

Bernstein, Barton. "Atomic Diplomacy and the Cold War." In *The Atomic Bomb: The Critical Issues,* edited by Barton Bernstein. Boston: Little, Brown, 1976.

———. "Understanding the Atomic Bomb and the Japanese Surrender: Missed Opportunities, Little-Known Near Disasters, and Modern Memory." *Diplomatic History* 19, no. 2 (spring 1995): 227–73.

Bernstein, Gail Lee, ed. *Recreating Japanese Women, 1600–1945.* Berkeley: University of California Press, 1991.

Beverley, John. "The Margin at the Center: On *Testimonio* (Testimonial Narrative)." *Modern Fiction Studies* 35, no. 1 (spring 1989): 11–28.

Bhabha, Homi K. *The Location of Culture.* New York: Routledge, 1994.

Bodnar, John. *Remaking America: Public Memory, Commemoration, and Patriotism in the Twentieth Century.* Princeton: Princeton University Press, 1992.

Boyarin, Jonathan. *Storm from Paradise: The Politics of Jewish Memory.* Minneapolis: University of Minnesota Press, 1992.

———, ed. *Remapping Memory: The Politics of Timespace.* Minneapolis: University of Minnesota Press, 1994.

Brackman, Arnold C. *The Other Nuremberg: The Untold Story of the Tokyo War Crimes Trials.* New York: William Morrow, 1987.

Braw, Monica. *The Atomic Bomb Suppressed: American Censorship in Japan, 1945–1949.* Malmo, Sweden: Liber Forlag, 1986.

Bronfen, Elisabeth, and Sarah Webster Goodwin. Introduction to *Death and Representation,* edited by Elisabeth Bronfen and Sarah Webster Goodwin. Baltimore: John Hopkins University Press, 1993.

Buck-Morss, Susan. *The Dialectics of Seeing: Walter Benjamin and the Arcades Project.* Cambridge, Mass.: MIT Press, 1989.

Buruma, Ian. *The Wages of Guilt: Memories of War in Germany and Japan.* New York: Farrar, Straus, Giroux, 1994.

Butler, Judith. *Bodies That Matter: On the Discursive Limits of "Sex."* New York: Routledge, 1993.

Certeau, Michel de. *Heterologies: Discourse on the Other.* Translated by Brian Massumi, foreword by Wlad Godzich. Theory and History of Literature 17. Minneapolis: University of Minnesota Press, 1986.

———. *The Practice of Everyday Life.* Translated by Steven F. Rendall. Berkeley: University of California Press, 1984.

Chemama, Roland. *Seishin bunseki jiten.* Translated by Koide Hiroyuki et al. Tokyo: Kōbundō, 1995.

Choi, Chungmoo. "The Discourse of Decolonization and Popular Memory: South Korea." *Positions* 1, no. 1 (spring 1993): 77–102.

———. Introduction to *The Comfort Women: Colonialism, War, and Sex,* edited by Chungmoo Choi. A special issue of *Positions* 5, no. 1 (spring 1997): v–xiv.

Chŏng Chun-he. *Chōsenjin chōyōkō no shuki.* Translated by Inoshita Haruko. Tokyo: Kawai Shuppan, 1990.

Chu Sŏk. *Hibaku Chōsenjin kyōshi no sengoshi: saigetsu yo! Ariran yo!* Tokyo: Akashi Shoten, 1990.

Chugoku Shimbun and the Hiroshima International Cultural Foundation, Inc., eds. *The Meaning of Survival: Hiroshima's Thirty-Six Year Commitment to Peace.* Hiroshima: Chugoku Shimbun and the Hiroshima International Cultural Foundation, 1983.

Chūgoku Shinbunsha. *Hiroshimajō Yonhyakunen.* Tokyo: Daiichi Hōki Shuppan Kabushikigaisha, 1990.

———. "Honoo no keifu." In *Nihon no genbaku kiroku,* edited by Ienaga Saburō et al. Vol. 10. Tokyo: Nihon Tosho Sentā, 1991.

———, ed. *Nenpyō Hiroshima 40nen no kiroku.* Tokyo: Miraisha, 1986.

Chūjo, Kazuo. *Genbaku to sabetsu.* Tokyo: Asahi Shinbunsha, 1986.

Clifford, James. *The Predicament of Culture: Twentieth-Century Ethnography, Literature, and Art.* Cambridge, Mass.: Harvard University Press, 1988.

Cohn, Carol. "Sex and Death in the Rational World of Defense Intellectuals" *Signs* 12, no. 4 (summer 1987): 687–718.

Comay, Rebecca. "Redeeming Revenge: Nietzsche, Benjamin, Heidegger, and the Politics of Memory." In *Nietzsche as Postmodernist: Essays Pro and Contra,* edited by Clayton Koelb. Albany: State University of New York Press, 1990.

Cook, Haruko Taya, and Theodore F. Cook. *Japan at War: An Oral History.* New York: New Press, 1992.

Crick, Malcolm. "Representations of International Tourism in the Social Sciences: Sun, Sex, Sights, Savings, and Servility." *Annual Review of Anthropology* 18 (1989): 307–44.

Das, Veena. *Critical Events: Moments in the Life of a Nation.* Delhi: Oxford University Press, 1995.

de Lauretis, Teresa. "Eccentric Subjects: Feminist Theory and Historical Consciousness." *Feminist Studies* 16, no. 1 (spring 1990): 115–50.

———. "Feminist Studies/Critical Studies: Issues, Terms and Contexts." In *Feminist Studies/Critical Studies,* edited by Teresa de Lauretis. Bloomington: Indiana University Press, 1986.

De Vos, George, and Changsoo Lee. "Conclusions: The Maintenance of a Korean Ethnic Identity in Japan." In *Koreans in Japan: Ethnic Conflict and Accommodation,* edited by Changsoo Lee and George De Vos. Berkeley: University of California Press, 1981.

Derrida, Jacques. "No Apocalypse, Not Now (full speed ahead, seven missiles, seven missives)." *Diacritics* 14, no. 2 (summer 1984): 20–31.

———. *Of Grammatology.* Translated by Gayatri Chakravorty Spivak. Baltimore: John Hopkins University Press, 1974.

Dirks, Nicholas B., ed. *Colonialism and Culture.* Ann Arbor: University of Michigan Press, 1992.

Dower, J. W. "The Bombed: Hiroshimas and Nagasakis in Japanese Memory." *Diplomatic History* 19, no. 2 (spring 1995): 275–95.

———. *Empire and Aftermath: Yoshida Shigeru and the Japanese Experience, 1878–1954.* 1979. Reprint, Cambridge, Mass.: Harvard University Press, 1988.

———. *Japan in War and Peace: Selected Essays.* New York: New Press, 1993.

Duras, Marguerite, and Alain Resnais. *Hiroshima Mon Amour.* Translated by Richard Seaver. New York: Grove Press, 1961.

Duus, Peter. *The Abacus and the Sword: The Japanese Penetration of Korea, 1895–1910.* Berkeley: University of California Press, 1995.

Duus, Peter, Ramon H. Myers, and Mark R. Peattie, eds. *The Japanese Wartime Empire, 1931–1945.* Princeton: Princeton University Press, 1996.

Eagleton, Terry. *Walter Benjamin, or Towards a Revolutionary Criticism.* London: Verso, 1981.

Ejima Shūsaku, Kasuga Kōfu, and Aoki Hideo. "Hiroshima-shi ni okeru 'hibaku taiken' no shakai tōgō kinō o meguru ichi kenkyū." *Shōgyō keizai kenkyūsho hō,* no. 15 (June 1977): 1–90.

Elshtain, Jean Bethke. *Women and War.* New York: Basic Books, 1987.

Enloe, Cynthia. *Bananas, Beaches, and Bases: Making Feminist Sense of International Politics.* Berkeley: University of California Press, 1990.

———. *The Morning After: Sexual Politics at the End of the Cold War.* Berkeley: University of California Press, 1993.

Esashi Akiko et al., eds. *Onna ga Hiroshima o kataru.* Tokyo: Inpakuto Shuppankai, 1996.

Fanon, Franz. *The Wretched of the Earth.* Translated by Constance Farrington. New York: Grove Weidenfeld, 1963.

Field, Norma. "Beyond Envy, Boredom, and Suffering: Toward an Emancipatory Politics for Resident Koreans and Other Japanese." *Positions* 1, no. 3 (winter 1993): 640–70.

———. *In the Realm of a Dying Emperor.* New York: Vintage Books, 1991.

———. "*Somehow:* The Postmodern as Atmosphere." In *Postmodernism and Japan,* edited by Masao Miyoshi and H. D. Harootunian. A special issue of the *South Atlantic Quarterly* 87, no. 3 (summer 1988): 551–70.

———. "War and Apology: Japan, Asia, the Fiftieth, and After." *Positions* 5, no. 1 (spring 1997): 1–49.

Figal, Gerald. "How to *jinbunshi:* Making and Marketing Self-Histories of

Showa among the Masses in Postwar Japan." *Journal of Asian Studies* 55, no. 4 (November 1996): 902–33.

Fischer, Michael M. J. "Ethnicity and the Post-Modern Arts of Memory." In *Writing Culture: The Poetics and Politics of Ethnography*, edited by James Clifford and George E. Marcus. Berkeley: University of California Press, 1986.

Flax, Jane. "Re-Membering the Selves: Is the Repressed Gendered?" *Michigan Quarterly Review* 26, no. 1 (winter 1990): 92–110.

Foster, Hal. "Postmodernism: A Preface." In *The Anti-Aesthetic: Essays on Postmodern Culture*, edited by Hal Foster. Seattle: Bay Press, 1983.

Foucault, Michel. "Film and Popular Memory," translated by Martin Jordin. In *Foucault Live (Interviews, 1966–84)*. Edited by Sylvère Lotringer. New York: Semiotext(e), 1989.

———. *The History of Sexuality.* Vol. 1, *An Introduction.* Translated by Robert Hurley. New York: Vintage Books, 1980.

———. "Nietzsche, Genealogy, History," translated by Donald F. Bouchard and Sherry Simon. In *Language, Counter-Memory, Practice: Selected Essays and Interviews*, edited by Donald F. Bouchard. Ithaca: Cornell University Press, 1977.

Fraser, Nancy. "Rethinking the Public Sphere: A Contribution to the Critique of Actually Existing Democracy." In *Habermas and the Public Sphere*, edited by Craig Calhoun. Cambridge, Mass.: MIT Press, 1992.

Freud, Sigmund. *Civilization and Its Discontents.* Edited and translated by James Strachey. New York: W. W. Norton, 1961.

Friedlander, Saul. Introduction to *Probing the Limits of Representation: Nazism and the "Final Solution,"* edited by Saul Friedlander. Cambridge, Mass.: Harvard University Press, 1992.

———, ed. *Probing the Limits of Representation: Nazism and the "Final Solution."* Cambridge, Mass.: Harvard University Press, 1992.

Frow, John. "Tourism and the Semiotics of Nostalgia." *October*, no. 57 (summer 1991): 123–51.

Fujii, James A. *Complicit Fictions: The Subject in the Modern Japanese Prose Narrative.* Berkeley: University of California Press, 1993.

Fujii Tadatoshi. *Kokubō fujinkai: hinomaru to kappōgi.* Tokyo: Iwanami Shoten, 1985.

Fujioka Nobukatsu. *Ojoku no kingendaishi: ima kokufuku no toki.* Tokyo: Tokuma Shoten, 1996.

Fujioka Nobukatsu/Jiyūshugi Shikan Kenkyūkai. *Kyōkasho ga oshienai rekishi.* Tokyo: Sankei Shinbunsha, 1996–.

Fujitani, T. "Electronic Pageantry and Japan's Symbolic Emperor." *Journal of Asian Studies* 51, no. 4 (November 1992): 551–70.

———. "*Minshūshi* as Critique of Orientalist Knowledges." *Positions* (forthcoming in fall 1998).

———. *Splendid Monarchy: Power and Pageantry in Modern Japan.* Berkeley: University of California Press, 1996.

Fujiwara Akira and Morita Toshio, eds. *Kingendaishi no shinjitsu wa nani ka: Fujioka Nobukatsu-shi no "rekishi kyōiku/heiwa kyōiku"-ron hihan.* Tokyo: Otsuki Shoten, 1996.

Fujiwara Shirō. "Shimon ōnatsu kyohi no kora o sasaen ga tameni." In *Ore shimon oshitehennen: shimonkyohi to jūdai no hatsugen,* edited by Jung Yeong-hae. Tokyo: Akashi Shoten, 1986.

Fukagawa Munetoshi. *Chinkon no kaikyō: kieta hibaku Chōsenjin chōyōkō nihyaku yonjū rokumei.* Tokyo: Gendaishi Shuppankai, 1973.

Fukuda Sumako. *Ware nao ikite ari.* 1967. Reprint, Tokyo: Chikuma Shobō, 1982.

Funahashi Yoshie. "Hibakusha no jibunshi ni torikunde." In *Ikiru: hibakusha no jibunshi,* edited by Hibakusha no Jibunshi Henshū Iinkai. Hiroshima: Hibakusha no Jibunshi Henshū Iinkai, 1989.

Gable, Eric, Anna Lawson, and Richard Handler. "On the Uses of Relativism: Fact, Conjecture, and Black and White Histories at Colonial Williamsburg." *American Ethnologist* 19, no. 4 (November 1992): 791–805.

Gluck, Carol. "The Past in the Present." In *Postwar Japan as History,* edited by Andrew Gordon. Berkeley: University of California Press, 1993.

Graburn, Nelson H. H. "Tourism: The Sacred Journey." In *Hosts and Guests: The Anthropology of Tourism,* edited by Valene L. Smith. Philadelphia: University of Pennsylvania Press, 1977.

Greenwood, David. "Culture by the Pound: An Anthropological Perspective on Tourism as Cultural Commoditization." In *Hosts and Guests: The Anthropology of Tourism,* edited by Valene L. Smith. Philadelphia: University of Pennsylvania Press, 1977.

Grewal, Inderpal, and Caren Kaplan. "Introduction: Transnational Feminist Practices and Questions of Postmodernity." In *Scattered Hegemonies: Postmodernity and Transnational Feminist Practices,* edited by Inderpal Grewal and Caren Kaplan. Minneapolis: University of Minnesota Press, 1994.

Grief, Nicholas. "The Legality of Nuclear Weapons." In *Nuclear Weapons and International Laws,* edited by Istvan Pogany. Brookfield, Vt.: Avebury, 1987.

Habermas, Jürgen. *The New Conservatism: Cultural Criticism and the Historians' Debate.* Edited and translated by Shierry Weber Nicholsen. Cambridge, Mass.: MIT Press, 1992.

———. *The Philosophical Discourse of Modernity: Twelve Lectures.* Translated by Frederick G. Lawrence. Cambridge, Mass.: MIT Press, 1992.

Halbwachs, Maurice. *On Collective Memory.* Edited and translated by Lewis Coser. Chicago: University of Chicago Press, 1992.

Hall, Stuart. "Cultural Studies: Two Paradigms." In *Media, Culture, and Society: A Critical Reader,* edited by Richard Collins et al. London: Sage, 1986.

Handler, Richard. *Nationalism and the Politics of Culture in Quebec.* Madison: University of Wisconsin Press, 1988.

Hara Tamiki. *Natsu no hana.* 1949. Reprint, Tokyo: Iwanami Shoten, 1988.

Harajiri, Hideki. *Zainichi Chōsenjin no seikatsu sekai.* Tokyo: Kōbundō, 1989.

Hardacre, Helen. *The Religion of Japan's Korean Minority: The Preservation of Ethnic Identity.* Korea Research Monograph 9. Berkeley: Institute of East Asian Studies, University of California, Berkeley, and Center for Korean Studies, 1984.

Harootunian, H. D. "America's Japan/Japan's Japan." In *Japan in the World,* edited by Masao Miyoshi and H. D. Harootunian. Durham, N.C.: Duke University Press, 1993.

———. "The Benjamin Effect: Modernism, Repetition, and the Path to Different Cultural Imaginaries." In *Walter Benjamin and the Demands of History,* edited by Michael P. Steinberg. Ithaca: Cornell University Press, 1996.

———. "Posutomodan no anji." In *Sengo Nihon no Seishinshi,* edited by Tetsuo Najita, Maeda Ai, and Kamishima Jirō. Tokyo: Iwanami Shoten, 1988.

———. "Visible Discourses/Invisible Ideologies." In *Postmodernism and Japan,* edited by Masao Miyoshi and H. D. Harootunian. A special issue of the *South Atlantic Quarterly* 87, no. 3 (summer 1988): 445–74.

Hartman, Geoffrey H., ed. *Bitburg in Moral and Political Perspective.* Bloomington: Indiana University Press, 1986.

Hartsock, Nancy. "Rethinking Modernism." *Cultural Critique,* no. 7 (fall 1987): 187–206.

Harvey, David. *The Condition of Postmodernity.* Oxford: Blackwell, 1989.

Hashimoto Manabu. "Hiroshima no heiwa shisei o tou: hibaku 45 shūnen o mukaeta Hiroshima no genjō." *Jōkyō to shutai,* no. 177 (September 1990): 42–59.

Havens, Thomas R. H. *Fire across the Sea: The Vietnam War and Japan, 1965–1975.* Princeton: Princeton University Press, 1987.

Hayashi Eidai. *Kesareta chōsenjin kyōseirenkō no kiroku.* Tokyo: Akashi Shoten, 1989.

Hein, Laura, and Mark Selden. "Commemoration and Silence: Fifty Years of Remembering the Bomb in America and Japan." In *Living with the Bomb: American and Japanese Cultural Conflict in the Nuclear Age,* edited by Laura Hein and Mark Selden. Armonk, N.Y.: M. E. Sharpe, 1997.

Hersey, John. *Hiroshima.* 1946. Reprint, New York: Alfred A. Knopf, 1985.

Hibaku Kenzōbutsu o Kangaeru Kai, ed. *Hiroshima no hibaku kenzōbutsu: hibaku 45shūnen chōsa hōkokusho.* Hiroshima: Asahi Shinbun Hiroshima Shikyoku, 1990.

Hibakusha no Jibunshi Henshū Iinkai, ed. *Ikiru: hibakusha no jibunshi.* Hiroshima: Hibakusha no Jibunshi Henshū Iinkai, 1989.

Hicks, George. *The Comfort Women: Japan's Brutal Regime of Enforced Prostitution in the Second World War.* New York: W. W. Norton, 1994.

Hiraoka Takashi. *Henken to sabetsu: Hiroshima soshite Chōsenjin.* Tokyo: Miraisha, 1972.

———. *Muen no kaikyō: Hiroshima no koe, hibaku Chōsenjin no koe.* Tokyo: Kage Shobō, 1983.

Hiroiwa Chikahiro. *Aogiri no shita de: 'Hiroshima no kataribe' Numata Suzuko monogatari.* Tokyo: Akashi Shoten, 1993.

Hirose Seigo. "Doitsu ni okeru sengo sekinin to sengo hoshō." In *Sensō sekinin/sengo sekinin: Nihon to Doitsu wa dō chigau ka,* Awaya Kentarō et al. Tokyo: Asahi Shinbunsha, 1995.

Hiroshima Gokoku Jinja. *Hiroshima Gokoku Jinja sengo fukkōshi.* Hiroshima: Hiroshima Gokoku Jinja, 1980.

Hiroshima Joseishi Kenkyūkai, ed. *Hiroshima no onnatachi.* Tokyo: Domesu Shuppan, 1987.

Hiroshima kara no Yobikake no Kai. *Hankaku: bungakusha no seimei*. Hiroshima: Hiroshima kara no Yobikake no Kai, 1982.

Hiroshima o Kataru Kai, ed. *Hiroshima o kataru*. Hiroshima: Hiroshima o Kataru Kai, 1987.

———. *Kaikyō o koete*. Hiroshima: Hiroshima o Kataru Kai, 1990.

Hiroshima o Yumu Kai. *Shiryo '82 Hankaku*. Hiroshima: Tankeisha, 1983.

Hiroshima YMCA. *Kakehashi*, no. 19 (January 1989).

Hiroshima-ken. *Genbaku hibakusha taisaku jigyō gaiyō*. Hiroshima: Hiroshima-ken, 1988.

Hiroshima-ken Chōsenjin Hibakusha Kyōgikai, ed. *Shiroi chogori no hibakusha*. Tokyo: Rōdō Junpōsha, 1979.

Hiroshima-ken Kankō Kyanpēn Jikkō Iinkai Jimukyoku. *Sun Sun Hiroshima: do yū Hiroshima*. N.p., n.d.

Hiroshima-ken Rekishisha Kyōikusha Kyōgikai. *Genbaku monyumento monogatari*. Tokyo: Sekibunsha, 1984.

Hiroshima-shi. *Hikari kankaku toshi Hiroshima keikaku*. Hiroshima: Hiroshima-shi, 1989.

Hiroshima-shi, ed. *Hiroshima shinshi: rekishi hen*. Hiroshima: Hiroshima-shi, 1984.

———. *Hiroshima shinshi: shakai hen*. Hiroshima: Hiroshima-shi, 1984.

———. *Hiroshima shinshi: shimin seikatsu hen*. Hiroshima: Hiroshima-shi, 1983.

———. *Hiroshima shinshi: toshi bunka hen*. Hiroshima: Hiroshima-shi, 1983.

Hiroshima-shi Eiseikyoku Genbakuhigai Taisakubu. *Genbaku hibakusha taisaku jigyō gaiyō*. Hiroshima: Hiroshima-shi Eiseikyoku, 1989.

Hiroshima-shi Kankō Kyōkai. *Tabi no uta ga kikoeru: Hiroshima*. Hiroshima: Hiroshima-shi Kankō Kyōkai, n.d.

Hiroshima-shi Shichōshitsu Kōhōka. *Shimin to shisei*, no. 893 (1 July 1989).

Hogan, Michael J., ed. *Hiroshima in History and Memory*. Cambridge: Cambridge University Press, 1996.

Honda Katsuichi. *The Impoverished Spirit in Contemporary Japan: Selected Essays of Honda Katsuichi*. Edited by John Lie and translated by Eri Fujieda, Masayuki Hamazaki, and John Lie. New York: Monthly Review Press, 1993.

Hong Tae-p'yo. "Joshō: zainichi no atarashii rekishi o kizamu wakamonotachi no shimon ōnatsu kyohi." In *Ore shimon oshitehennen: shimon kyohi to jūdai no hatsugen*, edited by Jung Yeong-hae. Tokyo: Akashi Shoten, 1986.

Hoston, Germaine A. *Marxism and the Crisis of Development in Prewar Japan*. Princeton: Princeton University Press, 1986.

Huyssen, Andreas. *Twilight Memories: Marking Time in a Culture of Amnesia*. New York: Routledge, 1995.

Hyōgo Chōsen Kankei Kenkyūkai, ed. *Chika kōjō to Chōsenjin kyōsei renkō*. Tokyo: Akashi Shoten, 1990.

Igarashi Takeshi. "'Heiwa kokka' to Nihongata gaikō." In *Sengo Nihon: senryō to sengo kaikaku*, ed. Nakamura Masanori et al. Vol. 6 of *Sengo kaikaku to sono isan*. Tokyo: Iwanami Shoten, 1995.

Inoue Shōichi. *Ato, kicchu, japanesuku: daitōa no posuto modan*. Tokyo: Seidosha, 1987.

Ishida Tadashi. *Genbaku taiken no shisōka: han genbaku ronshū I.* Tokyo: Miraisha, 1986.

———. *Han genbaku: Nagasaki hibakusha no seikatsushi.* Tokyo: Miraisha, 1973.

Ishida Takeshi. *Nihon no seiji to kotoba: heiwa to kokka.* Vol. 2. Tokyo: Tokyo Daigaku Shuppan Kai, 1989.

Ishihara Masaie. *Gyakusatsu no shima: kōgun to shinmin no matsuro.* Tokyo: Banseisha, 1978.

———. *Shōgen, Okinawa-sen: senjō no kōkei.* Tokyo: Aoki Shoten, 1991.

Ishimaru Norioki. "Hiroshima sekijūji/genbaku byōin no kenchiku ni tsuite: sono haran ni michita kenchiku no seimei." In *Inochi no tō: Hiroshima sekijūji/genbaku byōin eno shōgen,* ed. "Shukishū" Hensan Iinkai. Hiroshima: Chūgoku Shinbunsha, 1992.

Ishimaru Norioki et al., eds. *Toshi no fukkō: Hiroshima hibaku 40nenshi.* Hiroshima: Hiroshima-shi, 1986.

Ivy, Marilyn Jeanette. "Critical Texts, Mass Artifacts: The Consumption of Knowledge in Postmodern Japan." In *Postmodernism and Japan,* edited by Masao Miyoshi and H. D. Harootunian. A special issue of the *South Atlantic Quarterly* 87, no. 3 (summer 1988): 419–44.

———. *Discourses of the Vanishing: Modernity, Phantasm, Japan.* Chicago: University of Chicago Press, 1995.

Jameson, Fredric. *The Political Unconscious: Narrative as a Socially Symbolic Act.* Ithaca: Cornell University Press, 1981.

———. "Postmodernism and Consumer Society." In *The Anti-Aesthetic: Essays on Postmodern Culture,* edited by Hal Foster. Seattle: Bay Press, 1983.

———. "Postmodernism, or the Cultural Logic of Late Capitalism." *New Left Review,* no. 146 (September/October 1984): 53–92.

———. "Walter Benjamin; or, Nostalgia." In *Marxism and Form: Twentieth-Century Dialectical Theories of Literature.* Princeton: Princeton University Press, 1971.

Japan, Ministry of Education. *Atarashii kenpō no hanashi.* Tokyo: Jitugyō Kyōkasho Kabushikigaisha. 1947. Reprinted by Minshu Kyōiku o Mamoru Shimane Kenmin Kaigi (Matsue: Minshu Kyōiku o Mamoru Shimane Kenmin Kaigi, n.d).

Jeffords, Susan. *The Remasculinization of America: Gender and the Vietnam War.* Bloomington: Indiana University Press, 1989.

Jichitai Mondai Kenkyūsho and Hiroshima Kenkyūkai, eds. *Hiroshima Hiroshima: Daisanji Hiroshima shisei hakusho.* Hiroshima: Hiroshima-shi Shokuin Rōdō Kumiai, 1982.

Jidō Fuyō Teate o 18sai ni Hikiageru Kai, ed. *Semete kodomo o kōkō ni: Rikon shita onna no negai, 10nen no tatakai, soshite ima.* Hiroshima: Jidō Fuyō Teate o 18sai ni Hikiageru Kai, 1985.

Jing, Jun. *The Temple of Memories: History, Power, and Morality in a Chinese Village.* Stanford: Stanford University Press, 1996.

Johnson, Richard, Gregor McLennan, Bill Schwartz, and David Sutton, eds. *Making Histories: Studies in History-Writing and Politics.* London: Hutchinson in association with the Centre for Contemporary Cultural Studies, University of Birmingham, 1982.

Jung Yeong-hae. "Atogaki." In *Ore shimon oshitehennen: shimonkyohi to jū-dai no hatsugen*, edited by Jung Yeong-hae. Tokyo: Akashi Shoten, 1986.

Kammen, Michael. *Mystic Chords of Memory: The Transformation of Tradition in American Culture*. New York: Alfred A. Knopf, 1991.

Kanai Toshihiro. *Kaku kenryoku: Hiroshima no kokuhatsu*. Tokyo: Sanseidō, 1970.

Kanda Mikio. *Genbaku ni otto o ubawarete: Hiroshima no nōfutachi no shōgen*. Tokyo: Iwanami Shoten, 1982.

Kang Jae-ŏn and Kim Dong-hun. *Zainichi kankoku/Chōsenjin: rekishi to tenbō*. Tokyo: Rōdō Keizaisha, 1989.

Kankoku no Genbaku Higaisha o Kyūen suru Shimin no Kai, ed. *Hiroshima e: Kankoku no hibakusha no shuki*. Hiroshima: Kankoku no Genbaku Higaisha o Kyūen suru Shimin no Kai, 1987.

Kano Masanao. *Senzen/"ie" no shisō*. Tokyo: Sōbunsha, 1973.

Kano Mikiyo. "Kaisetsu: jiga no kanata e." In *Jiga no kanata e: kindai o koeru feminizumu*, edited by Kano Mikiyo. Tokyo: Shakai Hyōronsha, 1990.

Kawara Hirokazu. *Kizuna: kōkōsei to Hiroshima*. Tokyo: Komichi Shobō, 1987.

Kawara Hirokazu and Yamada Mariko. *Hiroshima hana ichirin monogatari: hibakusha/Numata Suzuko no owari naki seishun*. Tokyo: Komichi Shobō.

Kelly, William W. "Rationalization and Nostalgia: Cultural Dynamics of New Middle-Class Japan." *American Ethnologist* 13, no. 4 (November 1986): 603-18.

Kinbara Samon et al., eds. *Nihon no naka no Kankoku/Chōsenjin, Chūgokujin: Kanagawa kennai zaijū gaikokujin jittai chōsa yori*. Tokyo: Akashi Shoten, 1986.

Kisaka Junichirō. "Ajia/Taiheiyō sensō no rekishiteki seikaku o megutte." *Nenpō Nihon gendaishi*. Inaugural issue (1995): 1-43.

Kitabatake Hiroyasu. *Hitori hitori no sensō/Hiroshima*. Tokyo: Iwanami Shoten, 1984.

Kittsteiner, H. D. "Walter Benjamin's Historicism," translated by Jonathan Monroe and Irving Wohlfarth. *New German Critique*, no. 39 (fall 1986): 179-215.

Kondo, Dorinne K. *Crafting Selves: Power, Gender, and Discourses of Identity in a Japanese Workplace*. Chicago: University of Chicago Press, 1990.

———. "*M. Butterfly*: Orientalism, Gender, and a Critique of Essentialist Identity." *Cultural Critique*, no. 16 (fall 1990): 5-29.

Kosakai Yoshimitsu. *Hiroshima tokuhon*. 1978. Reprint, Hiroshima: Hiroshima Heiwa Bunka Sentā, 1988.

Koschmann, J. Victor. *Revolution and Subjectivity in Postwar Japan*. Chicago: University of Chicago Press, 1996.

———, ed. *Authority and the Individual in Japan: Citizen Protest in Historical Perspective*. Tokyo: University of Tokyo Press, 1978.

Kuno Osamu and Tsurumi Shunsuke. *Gendai nihon no shisō: sono itsutsu no uzu*. Tokyo: Iwanami Shoten, 1978.

Kurihara Akira. "'Minshū risei' no sonzai shōmei: shimin undō, jūmin undō, nettowākingu no seisehinshi." In *Sengo nihon no seisehinshi*, edited by Tetsuo Najita, Maeda Ai, and Kamishima Jirō. Tokyo: Iwanami Shoten, 1988.

Kurihara Sadako. *The Songs of Hiroshima—When Hiroshima Is Spoken Of.* Hiroshima: Anthology Publishing Association, 1980.

Kweon, Sug-in. *"Furusato* Boom in Japan: Collusion and Collisions in Producing and Consuming the National Hometown." Ph.D. diss., Stanford University, 1993.

LaCapra, Dominick. "Representing the Holocaust: Reflections on the Historians' Debate." In *Probing the Limits of Representation: Nazism and the "Final Solution,"* edited by Saul Friedlander. Cambridge, Mass.: Harvard University Press, 1992.

Lawrence L. Langer. *Holocaust Testimonies: The Ruins of Memory.* New Haven: Yale University Press, 1991.

Lee, Changsoo. "The Legal Status of Koreans in Japan." In *Koreans in Japan: Ethnic Conflict and Accommodation,* edited by Changsoo Lee and George De Vos. Berkeley: University of California Press, 1981.

Lee, Changsoo, and George De Vos, eds. *Koreans in Japan: Ethnic Conflict and Accommodation.* Berkeley: University of California Press, 1981.

Liao, Ping-hui. "Rewriting Taiwanese National History: The February 28 Incident as Spectacle." *Public Culture* 5, no. 2 (winter 1993): 281–96.

Lifton, Robert Jay. *Death in Life: Survivors of Hiroshima.* New York: Basic Books, 1967.

Lifton, Robert Jay, and Greg Mitchell. *Hiroshima in America: Fifty Years of Denial.* New York: G. P. Putnam's Sons, 1995.

Lindee, M. Susan. *Suffering Made Real: American Science and the Survivors at Hiroshima.* Chicago: University of Chicago Press, 1994.

Linenthal, Edward. *Sacred Ground: Americans and Their Battlefields.* Urbana: University of Illinois Press, 1991.

Lionnet, Françoise. *Autobiographical Voices: Race, Gender, Self-Portraiture.* Ithaca: Cornell University Press, 1989.

Lipsitz, George. *Time Passages: Collective Memory and American Popular Culture.* Minneapolis: University of Minnesota Press, 1990.

Loftus, Elizabeth F., Mahzarin R. Banaji, Jonathan W. Schooler, and Rachael A. Foster. "Who Remembers What?: Gender Differences in Memory." *Michigan Quarterly Review* 26, no. 1 (winter 1990): 64–85.

Lowe, Lisa. "Heterogeneity, Hybridity, Multiplicity: Marking Asian American Differences." *Diaspora* 1, no. 1 (spring 1991): 24–44.

———. *Immigrant Acts: On Asian American Cultural Politics.* Durham, N.C.: Duke University Press, 1996.

Maeda Tomiko. "Gensuibaku kinshi Hiroshima haha no kai no katsudō ni tsuite." *Hiroshima no kawa,* no. 2 (August 1961): 15.

Mahon, Michael. *Foucault's Nietzschean Genealogy: Truth, Power, and the Subject.* Albany: State University of New York Press, 1992.

Marcus, George E., and Michael M. J. Fischer. *Anthropology as Cultural Critique: An Experimental Moment in the Human Sciences.* Chicago: University of Chicago Press, 1986.

Maritani Mikiko. *Sensō o ikita onna tachi: shōgen—kokubō funjin kai.* Kyoto: Mineruva Shoten, 1985.

Martin, Biddy, and Chandra Talpade Mohanty. "Feminist Politics: What's Home

Got to Do with It?" In *Feminist Studies/Critical Studies,* edited by Teresa de Lauretis. Bloomington: Indiana University Press, 1986.

Maruyama Kōichi. "Toshi no naka no mainoritī: zainichi Chōsenjin no sengo seikatsu to bunka." In *Hiroshima shinshi: toshi bunka hen,* edited by Hiroshima-shi. Hiroshima: Hiroshima-shi, 1983.

Maruyama Masao. "Kindai Nihon no chishikijin." In *Kōei no ichi kara: "gendai seiji no shisō to kōdō" tsuiho.* Tokyo: Miraisha, 1982.

Mascia-Lees, Frances E., Patricia Sharpe, and Colleen Ballerino Cohen. "The Postmodernist Turn in Anthropology: Cautions from a Feminist Perspective." *Signs* 15, no. 1 (autumn 1989): 7–33.

Matsuda Gō, ed. "Kon'nichiwa—iwasete, iwasete." N.p., n.d.

———. "Shūgaku ryokōsei wa kataru: migi ni katamuku Nihon—kako mitsume saguru mirai." N.p., n.d.

Matsue Kiyoshi. *Hiroshima kara: Gensuikin undō o ikite.* Tokyo: Seikyusha 1984.

Matsumoto Hiroshi. *Hiroshima to iu shisō: "shinanai tame ni" dewa naku "ikiru tame ni."* Tokyo: Tokyo Sōgensha, 1995.

Matsushita Keiichi. "Citizen Participation in Historical Perspective." In *Authority and the Individual in Japan: Citizen Protest in Historical Perspective,* edited by J. Victor Koschmann. Tokyo: University of Tokyo Press, 1978.

McClintock, Anne. *Imperial Leather: Race, Gender, and Sexuality in the Colonial Contest.* New York: Routledge, 1995.

Minear, Richard H. Introduction to *Hiroshima: Three Witnesses.* Translated and edited by Richard H. Minear. Princeton: Princeton University Press, 1990.

———. *Victor's Justice.* Princeton: Princeton University Press, 1971.

Minzoku sabetsu to tatakau renraku kyōgikai. *Zenkoku mintōren nyūsu,* no. 56 (June 1991).

Minzokumei o Torimodosu Kai, ed. *Minzokumei o torimodoshita nihonseki chōsenjin: Watashitachi no namae/uri irŭm.* Tokyo: Akashi Shoten, 1990.

Mirai e habataku machi o mezashite: miryokutekina toshikūkan zukuri. Hiroshima: NTT Motomachi Biru Kaihatsu Keikakuan, n.d.

Mishima Ken'ichi. "Doitsu chishikijin no hatashita yakuwari." In *Sensō sekinin/sengo sekinin: Nihon to Doitsu wa dō chigauka,* Awaya Kentarō et al. Tokyo: Asahi Shinbunsha, 1995.

Mitchell, Richard H. *The Korean Minority in Japan.* Berkeley: University of California Press, 1967.

Mitscherlich, Alexander, and Margarete Mitscherlich. *The Inability to Mourn: Principles of Collective Behavior.* Translated by Beverley R. Placzek. New York: Grove Press, 1975.

Miyoshi, Masao. "A Borderless World?: From Colonialism to Transnationalism and the Decline of the Nation-State." *Critical Inquiry* 19, no. 4 (summer 1993): 726–51.

———. *Off Center: Power and Culture Relations between Japan and the United States.* Cambridge, Mass.: Harvard University Press, 1991.

Miyoshi, Masao, and H. D. Harootunian, eds. *Postmodernism and Japan.* A special issue of the *South Atlantic Quarterly* 87, no. 3 (summer 1988).

———. *Postmodernism and Japan.* Durham, N.C.: Duke University Press, 1989.

Mizugaki Natsuko. "Bosei o koeru koto no konnnansa." *Gekkan fōramu*, no. 8 (November 1996): 99–100.

Mizuno Naoki. "Zainichi Chōsenjin/Taiwanjin sanseiken 'teishi' jōkō no seiritsu: zainichi Chōsenjin sanseiken mondai no rekishiteki kentō (1)." *Sekai jinken mondai kenkyū sentā kenkyū kiyō*, no. 1 (March 1996): 43–65.

Moeller, Robert G. "War Stories: The Search for a Usable Past in the Federal Republic of Germany." *American Historical Review* 101, no. 4 (October 1996): 1008–48.

Nagai Hideaki. *10 fīto eiga sekai o mawaru*. Tokyo: Asahi Shinbunsha, 1983.

Nagasaki no Shōgen no Kai, ed. *Genshiya ni ikiru: Fukuda Sumako shū*. Tokyo: Shōbunsha, 1989.

Nagoya Misao. *Hiroshima haha no ki: Fumiki no "shi" o ikite*. 1985. Reprint, Tokyo: Heiwa Bunka/Chōbun Sha, 1990.

Najita Tetsuo, Maeda Ai, and Kamishima Jirō, eds. *Sengo Nihon no seishinshi*. Tokyo: Iwanami Shoten, 1989.

Nakai Kiyomi. *Teijyū gaikokujin to kōmu shūninken: 70mannin o shimedasu ronri*. Tokyo: Takushoku Shobō, 1989.

Nandy, Ashis. *The Intimate Enemy: Loss and Recovery of Self under Colonialism*. Delhi: Oxford University Press, 1983.

———. "The Other Within: Radhabinod Pal's Judgment of Culpability." In *The Savage Freud and Other Essays on Possible and Retrievable Selves*. Princeton: Princeton University Press, 1995.

Narita Ryūichi. "Haha no kuni no onna tachi: Oku Mumeo no 'senji' to 'sengo.'" In *Sōryokusen to gendaika*, edited by Yamanouchi Yasushi, Victor Koschmann, and Narita Ryūichi. Tokyo: Kashiwa Shobō, 1995.

Narita Ryūichi and Ouchi Hirokazu. "Sengo rekishigaku no senjiki kenkyū: kōchiku sareta sengo 'Nihon' to sono datsukouchiku e." Translated in *Positions* (forthcoming).

Nishi Kiyoko. *Senryōka no Nihon fujin seisaku: sono rekishi to shōgen*. Tokyo: Domesu Shuppan, 1985.

Nora, Pierre. "Between Memory and History: Les Lieux de Mémoire." *Representations*, no. 26 (spring 1989): 7–25.

Nornes, Abé Mark. "The Body at the Center—The Effects of the Atomic Bomb on Hiroshima and Nagasaki." In *Hibakusha Cinema: Hiroshima, Nagasaki, and the Nuclear Images in Japanese Film*, edited by Mick Broderick. London: Kegan Paul, 1996.

Norris, Christopher. "Image and Parable: Readings of Walter Benjamin." In *The Deconstructive Turn: Essays in the Rhetoric of Philosophy*. New York: Methuen, 1984.

Nosaka Akiyuki. "American *Hijiki*," translated by Jay Rubin. In *Contemporary Japanese Literature: An Anthology of Fiction, Film, and Other Writing Since 1945*, edited by Howard Hibbett. New York: Alfred A. Knopf, 1977.

Nozoe Kenji. *Hanaoka jiken no hitotachi: Chūgokujin kyōsei renkō no kiroku*. Tokyo: Hyōronsha, 1975.

Oe Kenzaburo. *Hiroshima Notes*. Edited by David L. Swain, translated by Toshi Yonezawa. Tokyo: YMCA Press, 1981.

———. *Hiroshima Nōto*. 41st ed. Tokyo: Iwanami Shoten, 1989.

Okoshi Aiko and Takahashi Tetsuya. "Jendā to sensō sekinin." *Gendai shisō* 24, no. 10 (September 1997): 132–54.

Osborne, Peter. *The Politics of Time: Modernity and Avant-Garde.* New York: Verso, 1995.

Pak Kyŏng-shik. *Chōsenjin kyōsei renkō no kiroku.* Tokyo: Miraisha, 1965.

Pak Su-nam. *Chōsen/Hiroshima/panchoppari: watashi no tabi no kiroku.* Tokyo: Sanseido, 1973.

Perlman, Michael. *Imaginal Memory and the Place of Hiroshima.* Albany: State University of New York Press, 1988.

Pharr, Susan J. *Political Women in Japan: The Search for a Place in Political Life.* Berkeley: University of California Press, 1981.

Pika Shiryō Kenkyūsho and Zenkoku Zanichi Chōsenjin Kyōiku Kenkyū Kyōgikai, eds. *Shiryō: Kankokujin genbaku giseisha irei hi.* Hiroshima: Hi no Kai, 1989.

Rekishigaku Kenkyūkai and Nihonshi Kenkyūkai, eds. *Kōza nihon rekishi.* Vol. 13. Tokyo: Tokyo Daigaku Shuppankai, 1985.

Rhodes, Richard. *The Making of the Atomic Bomb.* New York: Simon and Schuster, 1988.

Riley, Denise. *"Am I That Name?": Feminism and the Category of "Women" in History.* Minneapolis: University of Minnesota Press, 1988.

Robertson, Jennifer. *Native and Newcomer: Making and Remaking a Japanese City.* Berkeley: University of California Press, 1991.

Rosaldo, Renato. *Culture and Truth: The Remaking of Social Analysis.* Boston: Beacon Press, 1989.

———. *Ilongot Headhunting, 1883–1974: A Study in Society and History.* Stanford: Stanford University Press, 1980.

Rowe, William, and Vivian Shelling. *Memory and Modernity: Popular Culture in Latin America.* New York: Verso, 1991.

Ryang, Sonia. *North Koreans in Japan: Language, Ideology, and Identity.* Boulder, Colo.: Westview Press, 1997.

Sakai, Naoki. "Kyōkan no kyōdōtai to hinin sareta teikokushugiteki kokuminshugi: 'yukiyukite shingun' josetsu." *Gendai shisō* 23, no. 1 (January 1995): 117–32.

———. "Modernity and Its Critique: The Problem of Universalism and Particularism." In *Postmodernism and Japan*, edited by Masao Miyoshi and H. D. Harootunian. A special issue of the *South Atlantic Quarterly* 87, no. 3 (summer 1988): 475–504.

Saldívar, Ramón. *Chicano Narrative: The Dialectics of Difference.* Madison: University of Wisconsin Press, 1990.

Santner, Eric L. *Stranded Objects: Mourning, Memory, and Film in Postwar Germany.* Ithaca: Cornell University Press, 1990.

Satō Akira and Yamada Teruyoshi. *Zainichi Chōsenjin: rekishi to genjō.* Tokyo: Akashi Shoten, 1986.

Schudson, Michael. *Watergate in American Memory: How We Remember, Forget, and Reconstruct the Past.* New York: Basic Books, 1992.

Scott, Joan W. "The Evidence of Experience." *Critical Inquiry* 17, no. 4 (summer 1991): 773–97.

————. *Gender and the Politics of History*. New York: Columbia University Press, 1988.

Selden, Kyoko, and Mark Selden, eds. *The Atomic Bomb: Voices from Hiroshima and Nagasaki*. Armonk, N.Y.: M. E. Sharpe, 1989.

Sensō Giseisha o Kokoro ni Kizamu Kai, ed. *Nihon gun no Mareishia jyūmin gyakusatsu: Ajia no koe daisanshū*. Osaka: Tōhō Shuppan, 1989.

Sherwin, Martin J. *A World Destroyed: The Atomic Bomb and the Grand Alliance*. New York: Alfred A. Knopf, 1975.

Shiina Masae. *Genbaku hanzai: hibakusha wa naze hōchi saretaka*. Tokyo: Otsuki Shoten, 1985.

Shimizu Kiyoshi. *Genbaku bakushinchi*. Tokyo: Nihon Hōsō Shuppan Kyōkai, 1969.

Shin-Nihon Fujin no Kai Hiroshima-ken Honbu, ed. *Konoha no yōni yakarete*. 1966. Reprint, Tokyo: Shin-Nihon Shuppansha, 1985.

Shōno, Naomi. "Mute Reminders of Hiroshima's Atomic Bombing." *Japan Quarterly* 40, no. 3 (July/September 1993): 267–76.

"Shukishū" Hensan Iinkai, ed. *Inochi no tō: Hiroshima sekijūji/genbaku byōin e no shōgen*. Hiroshima: Chūgoku Shinbunsha, 1992.

Silverberg, Miriam. "Constructing a New Cultural History of Prewar Japan." In *Japan in the World*, edited by Masao Miyoshi and H. D. Harootunian. Durham, N.C.: Duke University Press, 1993.

————. "Remembering Pearl Harbor, Forgetting Charlie Chaplin, and the Case of the Disappearing Western Woman: A Picture Story." *Positions* 1, no. 1 (spring 1993): 24–76.

Smith, Gary, ed. *Benjamin: Philosophy, Aesthetics, History*. Chicago: University of Chicago Press, 1989.

Smith, Robert J., and Ella Lury Wiswell. *The Women of Suye Mura*. Chicago: University of Chicago Press, 1982.

Smith, Sidonie. *Subjectivity, Identity, and the Body: Women's Autobiographical Practices in the Twentieth Century*. Bloomington: Indiana University Press, 1993.

Sŏ Kyŏn-shik. "Kim Ji-ha e no tegami." In *Bundan o ikiru: "zainichi" o koete*. Tokyo: Kage Shobō, 1997.

Soja, Edward W. *Postmodern Geographies: The Reassertion of Space in Critical Social Theory*. New York: Verso, 1989.

Spivak, Gayatri Chakravorty. "Subaltern Studies: Deconstructing Historiography." In *Selected Subaltern Studies*, edited by Ranajit Guha and Gayatri Chakravorty Spivak. Oxford: Oxford University Press, 1988.

Stewart, Kathleen. *A Space on the Side of the Road: Cultural Poetics in an "Other" America*. Princeton: Princeton University Press, 1996.

Sturken, Matrita. *Tangled Memories: The Vietnam War, the AIDS Epidemic, and the Politics of Remembering*. Berkeley: University of California Press, 1997.

————. "The Wall, the Screen, and the Image: The Vietnam Veterans Memorial." *Representations*, no. 35 (summer 1991): 118–42.

Suzuki Yūko. *Feminizumu to sensō: fujin undōka no sensō kyōryoku*. Tokyo: Marujusha, 1986.

————. *Hiroshima ken josei undōshi.* Tokyo: Domesu Shuppan, 1985.

Swedenburg, Ted. *Memories of Revolt: The 1936–1939 Rebellion and the Palestinian National Past.* Minneapolis: University of Minnesota Press, 1995.

Takabatake Michitoshi. "Citizen's Movements: Organizing the Spontaneous." In *Authority and the Individual in Japan: Citizen Protest in Historical Perspective,* edited by J. Victor Koschmann. Tokyo: University of Tokyo Press, 1978.

————. "6onen ikō no seiji ishiki to shimin undō." In *Gendai Nihon no seiji* 72–77. Tokyo: Sanichi shobō, 1978.

Takahashi Saburō. "Sensō to josei." In *Senjika no Nihon: Shōwa zenki no rekishi shakaigaku,* edited by Senjika Nihon Shakai Kenkyūkai. Kyoto: Kōrosha, 1990.

Takahashi Tetsuya. "'Aitō' o meguru kaiwa: 'haisengo ron' hihan saisetsu." *Gendai shisō* 23, no. 12 (November 1995): 238–54.

Takaki, Ronald. *Hiroshima: Why America Dropped the Bomb.* Boston: Little, Brown, 1995.

Takashima Nobuyoshi and Hayashi Hirofumi, eds. *Maraya no nihongun: Negurisenbiran-shū ni okeru kajin gyakusatsu.* Tokyo: Aoki Shoten, 1989.

Takeda Seiji. "Kurushimi no yurai." In *Yume no gaibu.* Tokyo: Kawade Shobō Shinsha, 1989.

Takita, Sachiko. "'Tan'itsu minzoku kokka' shinwa no datsushinwaka: Nihon no baai." In *Kokusai shakaigaku: kokka o koeru genshō o dō toraeru ka,* edited by Kajita Takamichi. Nagoya: Nagoya Daigaku Shuppankai, 1992.

Tanaka, Stefan. *Japan's Orient: Rendering Pasts into History.* Berkeley: University of California Press, 1993.

Tanaka Sumiko. "Nihon ni okeru hahaoya undō no rekishi to yakuwari." *Shisō,* no. 439 (1961): 97–107.

Tanaka Tadaaki. *Pāru hakase no Nihon muzairon.* 1963. Reprint, Sagamihara: Seibunsha, 1987.

Taussig, Michael. *The Nervous System.* New York: Routledge, 1992.

————. *Shamanism, Colonialism, and the Wild Man: A Study in Terror and Healing.* Chicago: University of Chicago Press, 1987.

Teramitsu Tadashi. *Hiroshima heiwa toshi hō: Hiroshima heiwa kinen toshi kensetu hō chūkai.* Hiroshima: Chūgoku Shinbunsha, 1949.

Terdiman, Richard. *Present Past: Modernity and the Memory Crisis.* Ithaca: Cornell University Press, 1993.

Tiedemann, Rolf. "Historical Materialism or Political Messianism? An Interpretation of the Theses 'On the Concept of History'" (1983). In *Benjamin: Philosophy, Aesthetics, History,* edited by Gary Smith. Chicago: University of Chicago Press, 1989.

Todeschini, Maya. "Death and the Maiden: Female *Hibakusha* as Cultural Heroines, and the Politics of A-bomb Memory." In *Hibakusha Cinema: Hiroshima, Nagasaki, and the Nuclear Images in Japanese Film,* edited by Mick Broderick. London: Kegan Paul, 1996.

Tokinoya Shigeru. *Ienaga kyōkasho saiban to Nankin jiken: monbushō tantōsha wa shōgen suru.* Tokyo: Nihon Kyōbunsha, 1989.

Tomiyama Ichirō. *Kindai Nihon shakai to "Okinawajin": "Nihonjin" ni naru to iu koto.* Tokyo: Nihon Keizai Hyōronsha, 1990.

———. *Senjō no kioku*. Tokyo: Nihon Keizai Hyōronsha, 1995.

Toyonaga, Keisaburō. "The Atomic Bomb, Forced Labor, and Other Problems of Koreans Living in Hiroshima during the Pacific War," translated by Eric Cazdyn. In *Perilous Memories: Asia-Pacific Wars*, edited by T. Fujitani, Geoffrey M. White, and Lisa Yoneyama. Durham, N.C.: Duke University Press, forthcoming.

Treat, John Whittier. *Writing Ground Zero: Japanese Literature and the Atomic Bomb*. Chicago: University of Chicago Press, 1995.

Trinh, T. Minh-ha. *Woman, Native, Other: Writing Postcoloniality and Feminism*. Bloomington: Indiana University Press, 1989.

Tsurumi Kazuko and Ichii Saburō, eds. *Shisō no bōken: shakai to henka no atarashii paradaimu*. Tokyo: Chikuma Shobō, 1974.

Tsurumi Shunsuke. *Tenkō kenkyū*. Tokyo: Chikuma Shobō, 1976.

Turner, Victor, and Ellis Turner. *Images and Pilgrimage in Christian Culture: Anthropological Perspective*. Oxford: Blackwell, 1978.

Ubuki Satoru. "Gunshuku to shimin undō: Nihon no gensuibaku kinshi undō o megutte." *Kokusai seiji*, no. 80 (October 1985): 112–26.

———. "Heiwa kinen shikiten no hensen to heiwa sengen." In *Hiroshima shinshi: rekishi hen* (Hiroshima: Hiroshima-shi, 1984).

Ubuki Satoru and Uchida Emiko. "Kako 45nenkan no genbaku shuki no shuppan jōkyō." *Hiroshima igaku* 45, no. 3 (March 1992): 373–75.

Ueno Chizuko. *Kindai kazoku no seiritsu to shūen*. Tokyo: Iwanami Shoten, 1994.

———. "'Kokumin kokka' to 'jendā': 'josei no kokuminka' o megutte." *Gendai shisō* 24, no. 12 (October 1996): 8–45.

Vidal-Naquet, Pierre. *Assassins of Memory: Essays on the Denial of the Holocaust*. Translated and foreword by Jeffrey Mehlman. New York: Columbia University Press, 1992.

Wagner, Edward W. *The Korean Minority in Japan, 1904–1950*. New York: International Secretariat, Institute of Pacific Relations, 1951.

Walker, J. Samuel. "History, Collective Memory, and the Decision to Use the Bomb." *Diplomatic History* 19, no. 2 (spring 1995): 319–28.

Ward, Robert E., and Sakamoto Yoshikazu, eds. *Democratizing Japan: The Allied Occupation*. Honolulu: University of Hawaii Press, 1987.

Watson, Julia, and Sidonie Smith. "De/Colonization and the Politics of Discourse in Women's Autobiographical Practices." In *De/Colonizing the Subject: The Politics of Gender in Women's Autobiography*, edited by Julia Watson and Sidonie Smith. Minneapolis: University of Minnesota Press, 1992.

Weiner, Michael. *The Origins of the Korean Community in Japan, 1910–1923*. Atlantic Highlands, N.J.: Humanities Press International, 1989.

———. *Race and Migration in Imperial Japan*. New York: Routledge, 1994.

———. "The Representation of Absence and the Absence of Representation: Korean Victims of the Atomic Bomb." In *Japan's Minorities: The Illusion of Homogeneity*, edited by Michael Weiner. New York: Routledge, 1997.

White, Geoffrey M. "Remembering Guadalcanal: National Identity and Transnational Memory-Making." *Public Culture* 7, no. 3 (spring 1995): 529–55.

White, Hayden. *The Content of the Form: Narrative Discourse and Historical Representation*. Baltimore: Johns Hopkins University Press, 1987.

———. *Tropics of Discourse: Essays in Cultural Criticism*. Baltimore: Johns Hopkins University Press, 1978.

———. "The Value of Narrativity in the Representation of Reality." In *On Narrative*, edited by W. J. T. Mitchell. Chicago: University of Chicago Press, 1981.

Winter, Jay. *Sites of Memory, Sites of Mourning*. Cambridge: Cambridge University Press, 1995.

Wohlfarth, Irving. "Refusing Theology: Some First Responses of Walter Benjamin's Arcades Projects." *New German Critique*, no. 39 (fall 1986): 3–24.

Wolin, Richard. *Walter Benjamin: An Aesthetic Redemption*. New York: Columbia University Press, 1982.

Yamabe Emiko. "Dai ikkai hahaoya taikai o megutte." In *55nen taisei seiritsu to onnatachi: jūgoshi nōto sengohen*, edited by Onnatachi no Ima o Tou Kai. Vol. 3 of *Jūgoshi nōto*. Tokyo: Impakuto Shuppankai, 1987.

Yamaguchi Yasushi. "Futatsu no gendaishi: rekishi no aratana tenkanten ni tatte." In *Sensō sekinin/sengo sekinin: Nihon to Doitsu wa dō chigauka*, Awaya Kentarō et al. Tokyo: Asahi Shinbunsha, 1994.

Yamaguchi Yūko. "Tainai hibakusha/hibaku nisei o mamoru to iu koto." In *Konoha no yōni yakarete*, ed. Shin-nihon Fujin no Kai Hiroshima-ken Honbu. 1966. Reprint, Tokyo: Shin-nihon Shuppansha, 1985.

Yamazaki, James N. *Children of the Atomic Bomb: An American Physician's Memoir of Nagasaki, Hiroshima, and the Marshall Islands*. Durham, N.C.: Duke University Press, 1995.

Yanagisako, Sylvia Junko. *Transforming the Past: Tradition and Kinship among Japanese Americans*. Stanford: Stanford University Press, 1985.

Yasumaru, Yoshio. "Nihon no kindaika ni tsuite no teikokushugiteki rekishikan" (1962). In *"Hōhō" toshite no shisōshi*. Tokyo: Azekura Shobō, 1996.

Yonehara, Ken. *Nihonteki "kindai" e no toi: shisōshi to shite no sengo seiji*. Tokyo: Shinhyōron, 1995.

Yoneyama, Lisa. "Bunka to iu tsumi." In *Bunka to iu kadai*, edited by Kajiwara Kageaki et al. Vol. 13 of *Iwanami kōza bunka jinruigaku*. Tokyo: Iwanami Shoten, 1998.

———. "Critical Warps: Facticity, Transformative Knowledge, and Postnationalist Criticism in the Smithsonian Controversy." *Positions* 5, no. 3 (winter 1997): 779–809.

———. "Ekkyōsuru sensō no kioku: sumisonian genbakuten ronsō wo yomu." *Sekai*, no. 614 (October 1995): 173–83.

———. "Hiroshima Narratives and the Politics of Memory: A Study of Power, Knowledge, and Identities." Ph.D. diss., Stanford University, 1992.

———. "Kioku no benshōhō—Hiroshima." *Shisō*, no. 866 (August 1996): 5–29.

———. "Memory Matters: Hiroshima's Korean Atom Bomb Memorial and the Politics of Ethnicity." In *Living with the Bomb: American and Japanese Cultural Conflicts in the Nuclear Age*, edited by Laura Hein and Mark Selden. New York: M. E. Sharpe, 1997.

———. "Taming the Memoryscape: Hiroshima's Urban Renewal." In *Remap-*

ping Memory: The Politics of Timespace, edited by Jonathan Boyarin. Minneapolis: University of Minnesota Press, 1994.

Yoshida Yutaka. *Nihonjin no sensōkan: sengoshi no nakano henyō.* Tokyo: Iwanami Shoten, 1995.

Yoshimi Yoshiaki. *Kusa no ne no fashizumu.* Tokyo: Tokyo Daigaku Shuppankai, 1987.

Yoshimoto Takaaki. *"Hankaku" iron.* Tokyo: Shinya Sōshosha, 1989.

Young, James E. *The Texture of Memory: Holocaust Memorials and Meaning.* New Haven: Yale University Press, 1993.

————. *Writing and Rewriting the Holocaust: Narrative and the Consequences of Interpretation.* Bloomington: Indiana University Press, 1988.

Zaikan Hibakusha Mondai Shimin Kaigi. *Zaikan hibakusha mondai o kangaeru.* Tokyo: Gaifūsha, 1988.

Zaikan Hibakusha o Kyūen suru Shimin no Kai. *Zaikan hibakusha no jittai.* Osaka: Zaikan Hibakusha o Kyūen suru Shimin no Kai, 1982.

Zenkoku Dōwa Kyōiku Kenkyū Kyōgikai Jimukyoku. *Heiwa/jinken/minshushugi o motomete—dōwa kyōiku e no teigen IV: dai 41 kai zenkoku dōwa kyōiku kenkyū taikai tokubetsu bukai kōenshū.* Osaka: Zenkoku Dōwa Kyōiku Kenkyū Kyōgikai Jimukyoku, 1990.

Zukin, Sharon. *Landscape of Power: From Detroit to Disney World.* Berkeley: University of California Press, 1991.

Index

Compositor: Prestige Typography
Text: 10/13 Sabon
Display: Sabon